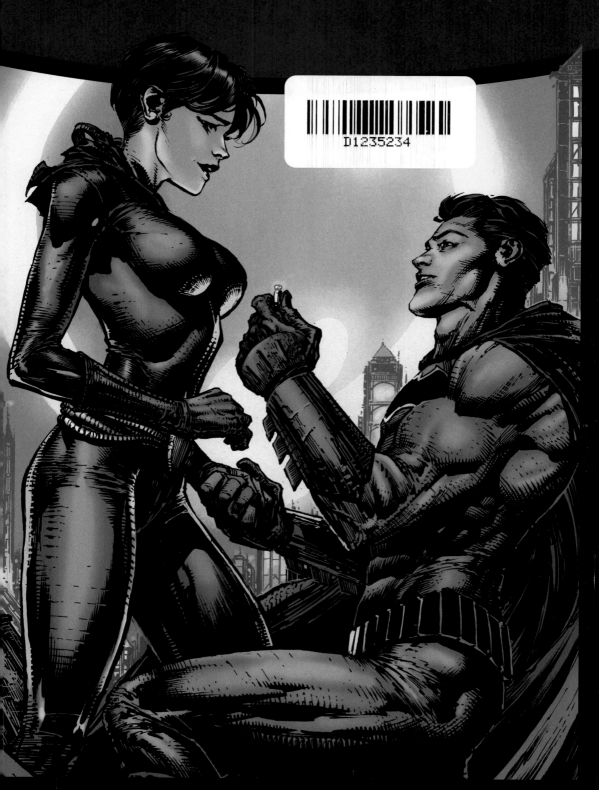

BATMAN
VOL.7 THE WEDDING

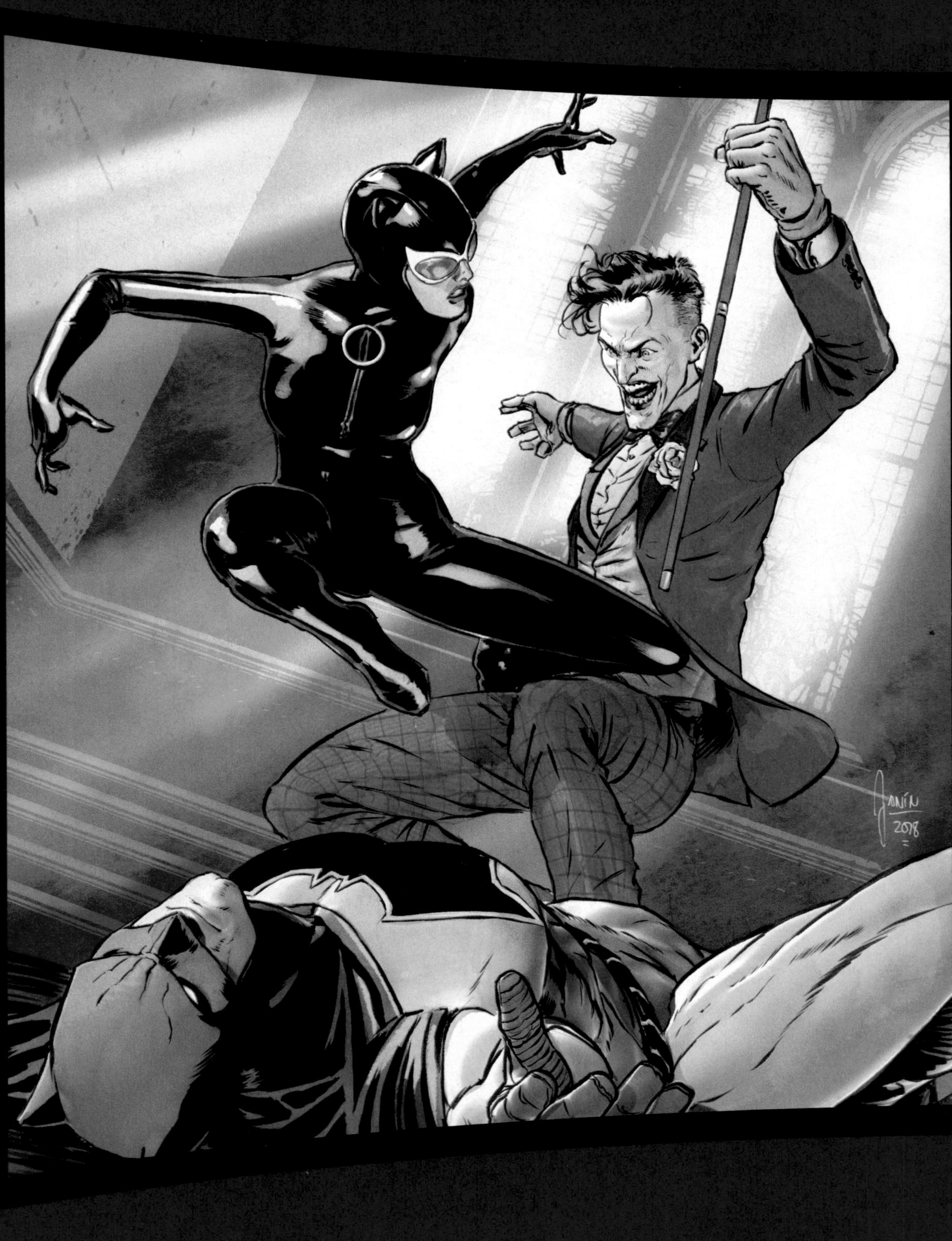

BATMAN
VOL.7 THE WEDDING

TOM KING
writer

MIKEL JANÍN ✷ TONY S. DANIEL ✷ CLAY MANN
SANDU FLOREA ✷ JOHN LIVESAY ✷ DANNY MIKI
artists

JUNE CHUNG ✷ TOMEU MOREY ✷ JORDIE BELLAIRE
colorists

CLAYTON COWLES
letterer

MIKEL JANÍN
collection cover artist

JOSÉ LUIS GARCÍA-LÓPEZ ✷ BECKY CLOONAN ✷ JASON FABOK ✷ FRANK MILLER
LEE BERMEJO ✷ NEAL ADAMS ✷ AMANDA CONNER ✷ RAFAEL ALBUQUERQUE
ANDY KUBERT ✷ TIM SALE ✷ PAUL POPE ✷ MITCH GERADS ✷ TY TEMPLETON
JOËLLE JONES ✷ DAVID FINCH ✷ JIM LEE ✷ SCOTT WILLIAMS ✷ GREG CAPULLO ✷ LEE WEEKS
TRISH MULVIHILL ✷ BRAD ANDERSON ✷ ALEX SINCLAIR ✷ HI-FI ✷ PAUL MOUNTS ✷ JOSÉ VILLARRUBIA
KEIREN SMITH ✷ FCO PLASCENCIA
special guests

BATMAN created by BOB KANE with BILL FINGER
BOOSTER GOLD created by DAN JURGENS

JAMIE S. RICH Editor - Original Series * **BRITTANY HOLZHERR** Associate Editor - Original Series
JEB WOODARD Group Editor - Collected Editions * **ROBIN WILDMAN** Editor - Collected Edition
STEVE COOK Design Director - Books * **MONIQUE NARBONETA** Publication Design

BOB HARRAS Senior VP - Editor-in-Chief, DC Comics
PAT McCALLUM Executive Editor, DC Comics

DAN DiDIO Publisher * **JIM LEE** Publisher & Chief Creative Officer
AMIT DESAI Executive VP - Business & Marketing Strategy, Direct to Consumer & Global Franchise Management
BOBBIE CHASE VP & Executive Editor, Young Reader & Talent Development * **MARK CHIARELLO** Senior VP - Art, Design & Collected Editions
JOHN CUNNINGHAM Senior VP - Sales & Trade Marketing * **BRIAR DARDEN** VP - Business Affairs
ANNE DePIES Senior VP - Business Strategy, Finance & Administration * **DON FALLETTI** VP - Manufacturing Operations
LAWRENCE GANEM VP - Editorial Administration & Talent Relations * **ALISON GILL** Senior VP - Manufacturing & Operations
JASON GREENBERG VP - Business Strategy & Finance * **HANK KANALZ** Senior VP - Editorial Strategy & Administration
JAY KOGAN Senior VP - Legal Affairs * **NICK J. NAPOLITANO** VP - Manufacturing Administration
LISETTE OSTERLOH VP - Digital Marketing & Events * **EDDIE SCANNELL** VP - Consumer Marketing
COURTNEY SIMMONS Senior VP - Publicity & Communications * **JIM (SKI) SOKOLOWSKI** VP - Comic Book Specialty Sales & Trade Marketing
NANCY SPEARS VP - Mass, Book, Digital Sales & Trade Marketing * **MICHELE R. WELLS** VP - Content Strategy

BATMAN VOL. 7: THE WEDDING

DC Comics, 2900 West Alameda Ave., Burbank, CA 91505
Printed by LSC Communications, Kendallville, IN, USA. 9/21/18. First Printing.
ISBN: 978-1-4012-8338-4

Library of Congress Cataloging-in-Publication Data is available.

PEFC Certified
Printed on paper from sustainably managed forests, controlled sources
PEFC
PEFC/29-31-337
www.pefc.org

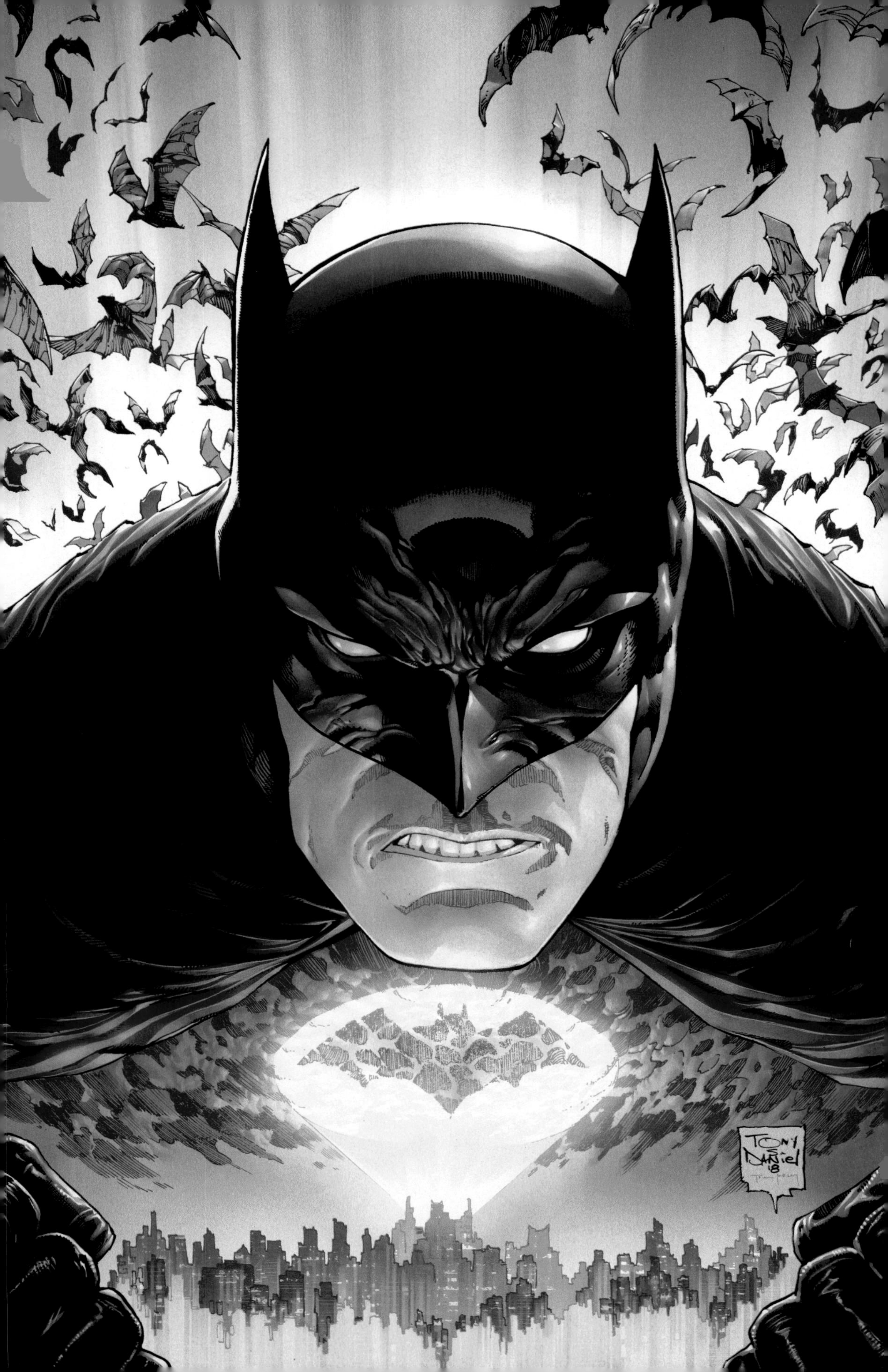

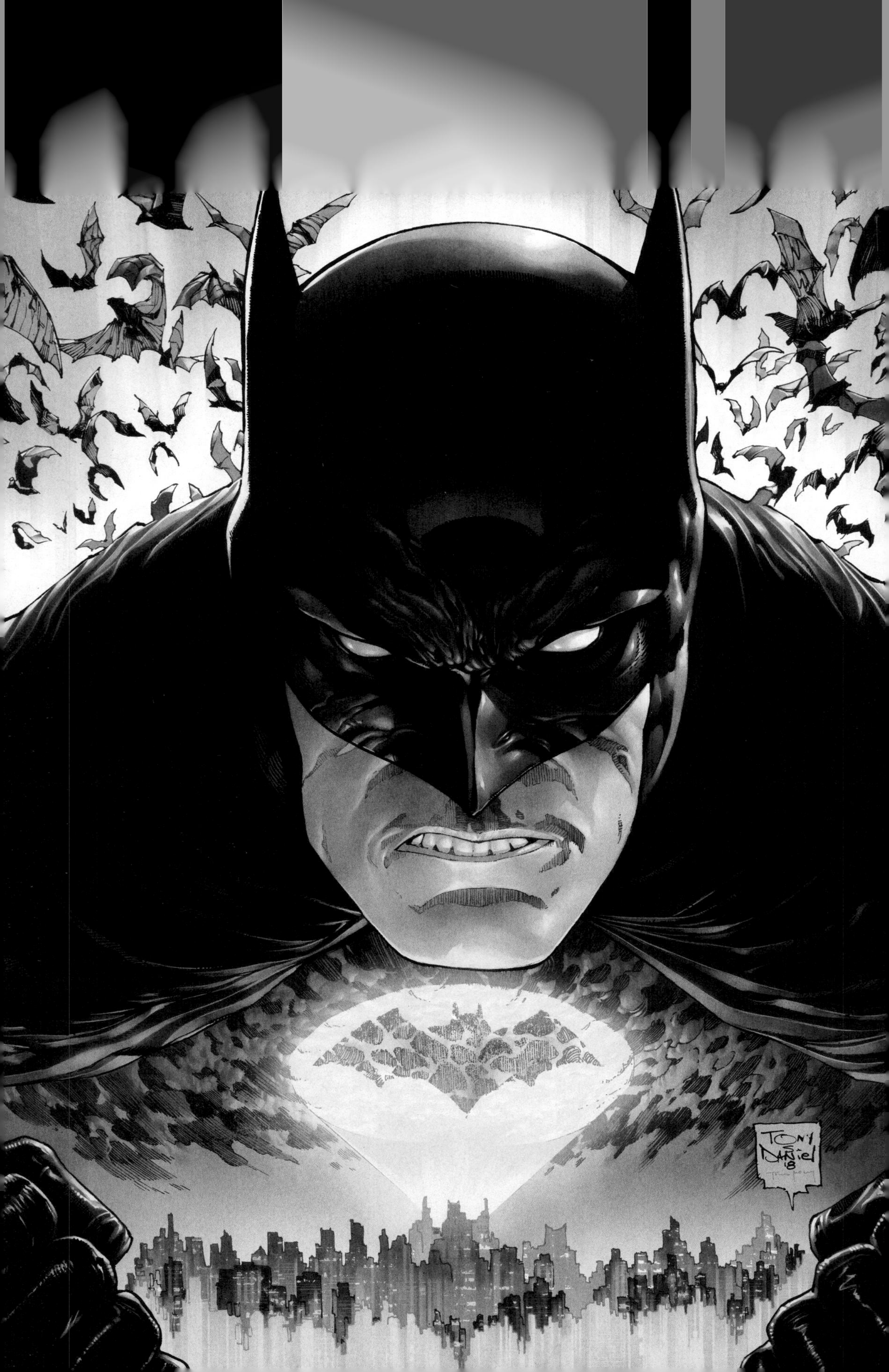
TONY S DANIEL '18

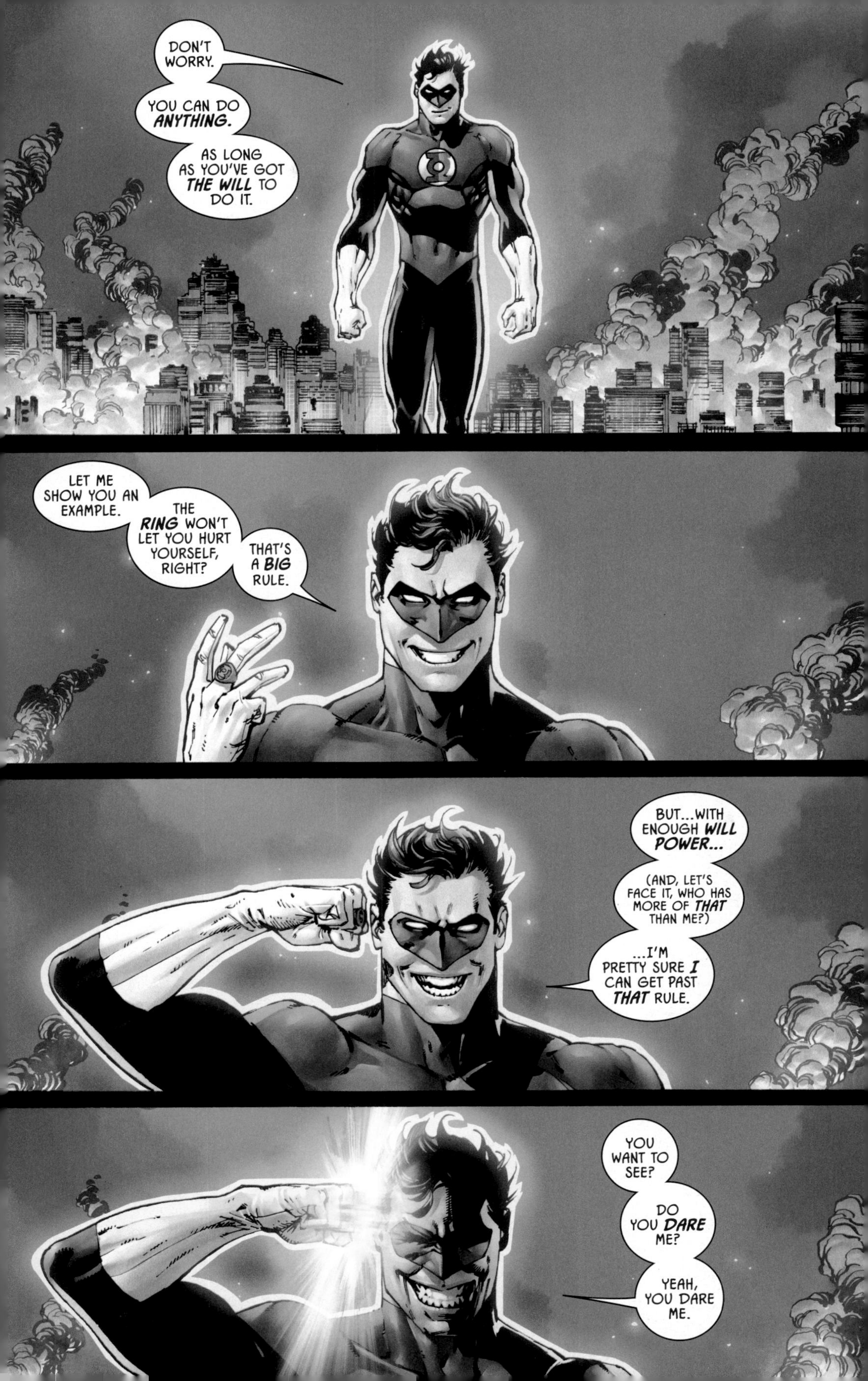
DON'T WORRY.
YOU CAN DO ANYTHING.
AS LONG AS YOU'VE GOT THE WILL TO DO IT.
LET ME SHOW YOU AN EXAMPLE.
THE RING WON'T LET YOU HURT YOURSELF, RIGHT?
THAT'S A BIG RULE.
BUT...WITH ENOUGH WILL POWER...
(AND, LET'S FACE IT, WHO HAS MORE OF THAT THAN ME?)
...I'M PRETTY SURE I CAN GET PAST THAT RULE.
YOU WANT TO SEE?
DO YOU DARE ME?
YEAH, YOU DARE ME.

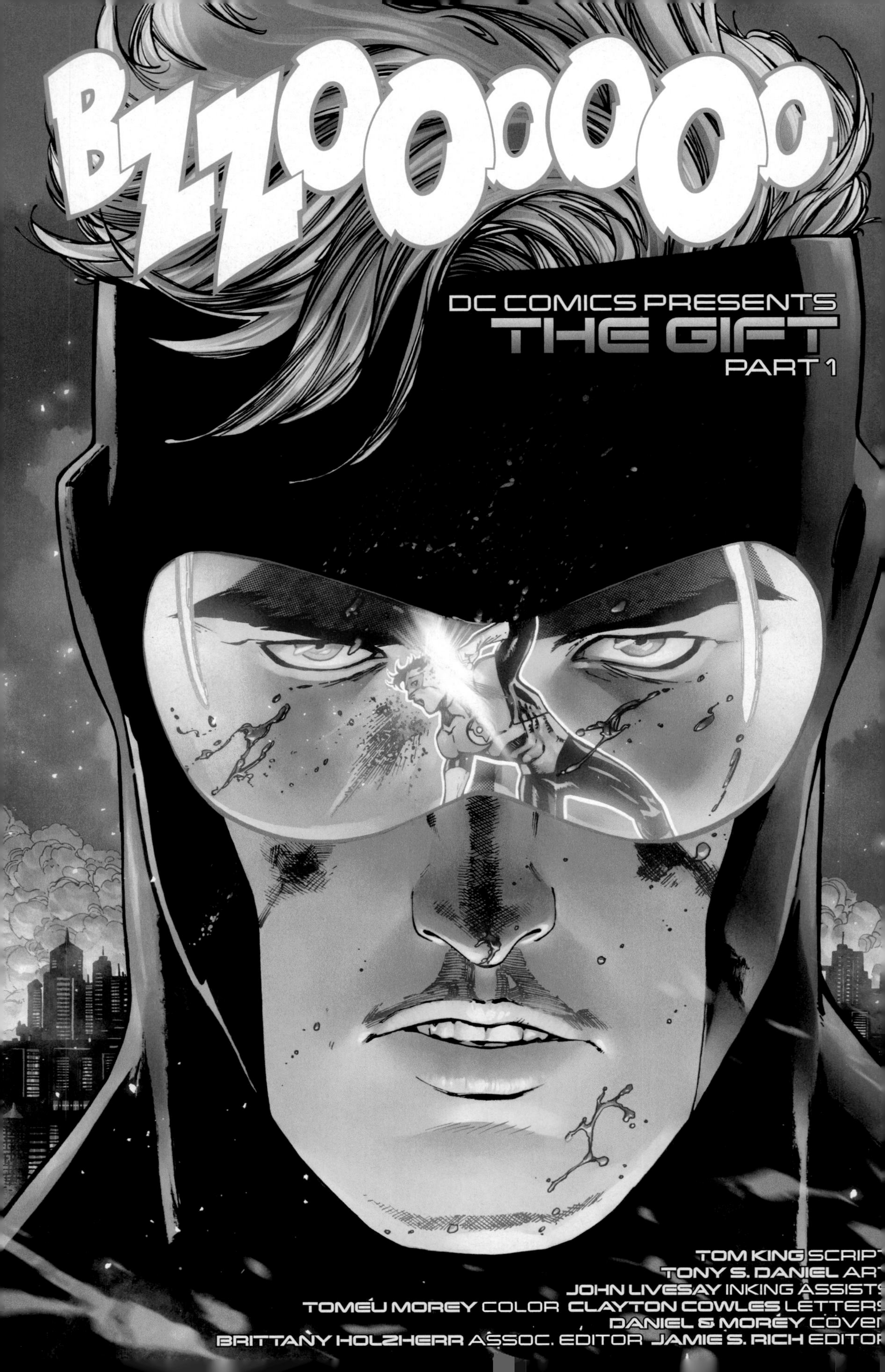
BZZOOOOOO
DC COMICS PRESENTS
THE GIFT
PART 1
TOM KING SCRIPT
TONY S. DANIEL ART
JOHN LIVESAY INKING ASSISTS
TOMEU MOREY COLOR CLAYTON COWLES LETTERS
DANIEL & MOREY COVER
BRITTANY HOLZHERR ASSOC. EDITOR JAMIE S. RICH EDITOR

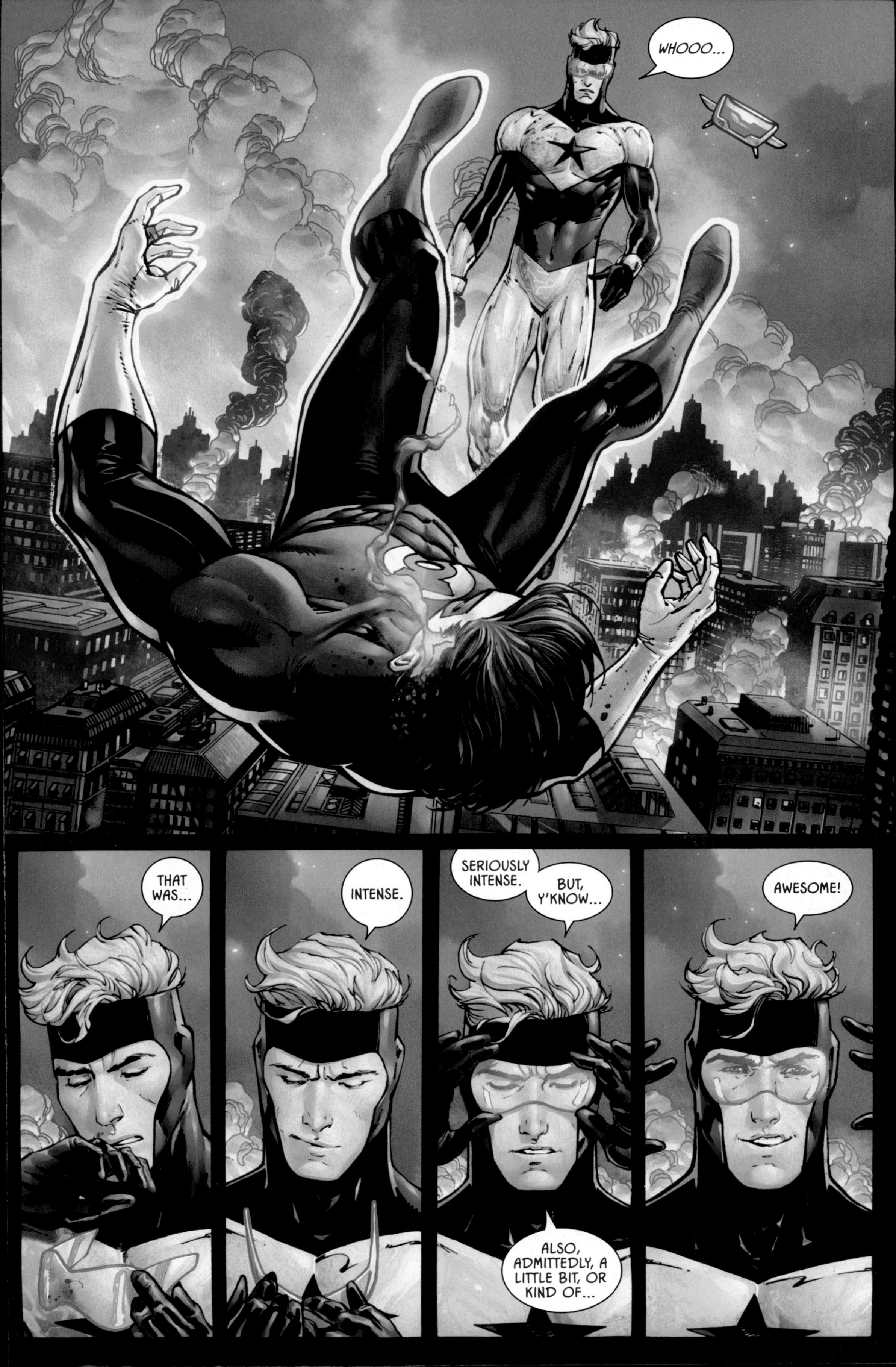
WHOOO...
THAT WAS...
INTENSE.
SERIOUSLY INTENSE.
BUT, Y'KNOW...
ALSO, ADMITTEDLY, A LITTLE BIT, OR KIND OF...
AWESOME!

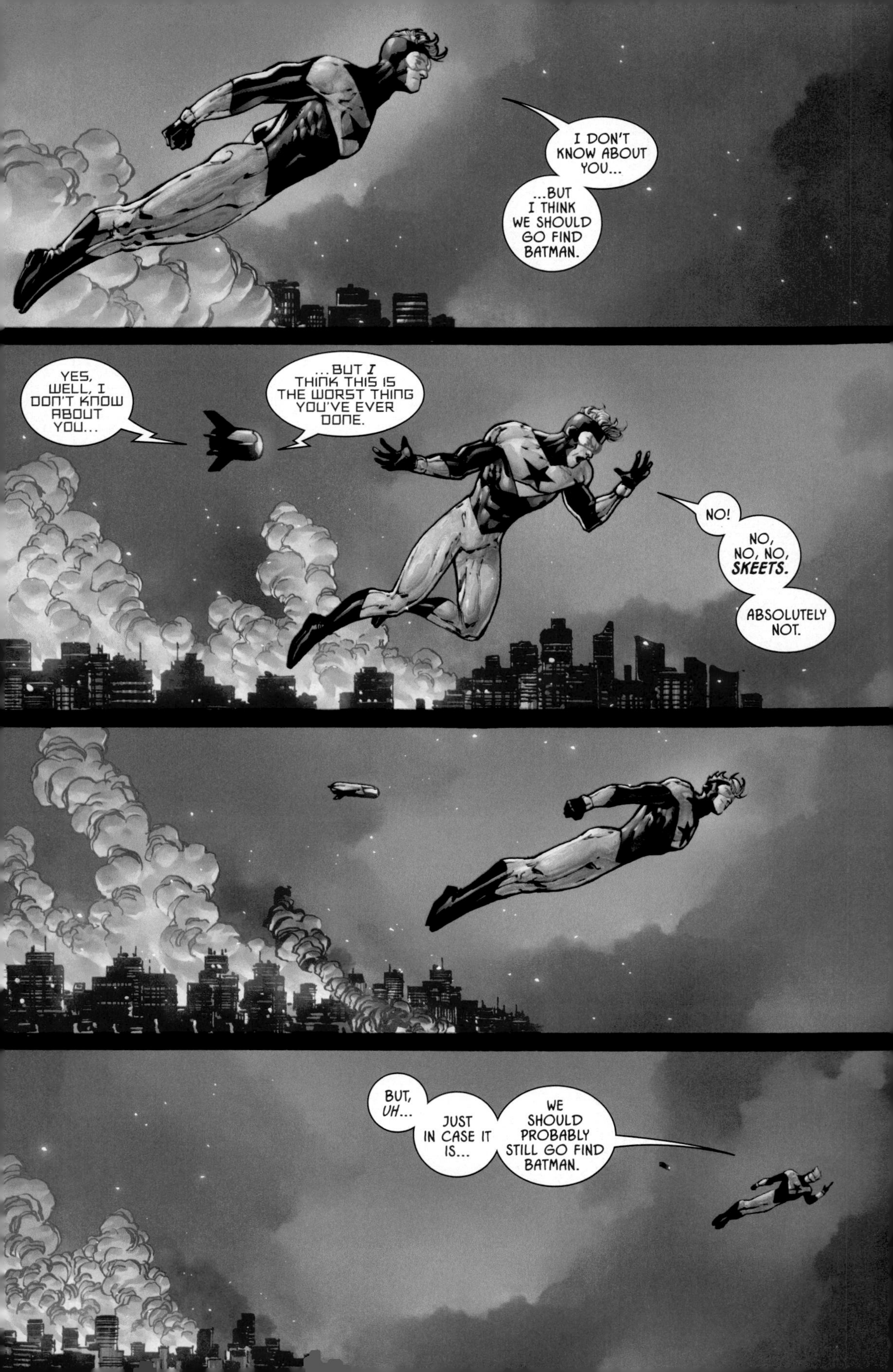
I DON'T KNOW ABOUT YOU...
...BUT I THINK WE SHOULD GO FIND BATMAN.
YES, WELL, I DON'T KNOW ABOUT YOU...
...BUT I THINK THIS IS THE WORST THING YOU'VE EVER DONE.
NO!
NO, NO, NO, SKEETS.
ABSOLUTELY NOT.
BUT, UH...
JUST IN CASE IT IS...
WE SHOULD PROBABLY STILL GO FIND BATMAN.

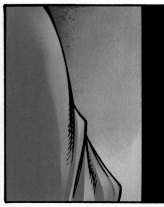

WAYNE ENGINEERING
USERNAME: TIMDRAKE7337
PASSWORD: _

A JOKER WAS ON MY BUS THIS MORNING.

HE STABBED THIS LADY.

IN HER FACE. IT WAS GROSS.

SHE WAS SCREAMING.

I WAS GOING TO USE MY GUN, BUT ANOTHER GUY HAD HIS OUT FIRST.

THEN HE SHOT THE JOKER. A BUNCH OF TIMES.

HE ALSO SHOT THIS OTHER LADY. I THINK IT WAS BY ACCIDENT.

IT'S, LIKE, THE THIRD TIME THIS MONTH. IT'S STUPID.

I DON'T *WANT* TO SAY IT, BUT PRESIDENT COBBLEPOT IS RIGHT.

EVERYTHING'D BE BETTER IF WE LET HIM RUN THIS PLACE LIKE GHUL DOES IN EURASIA.

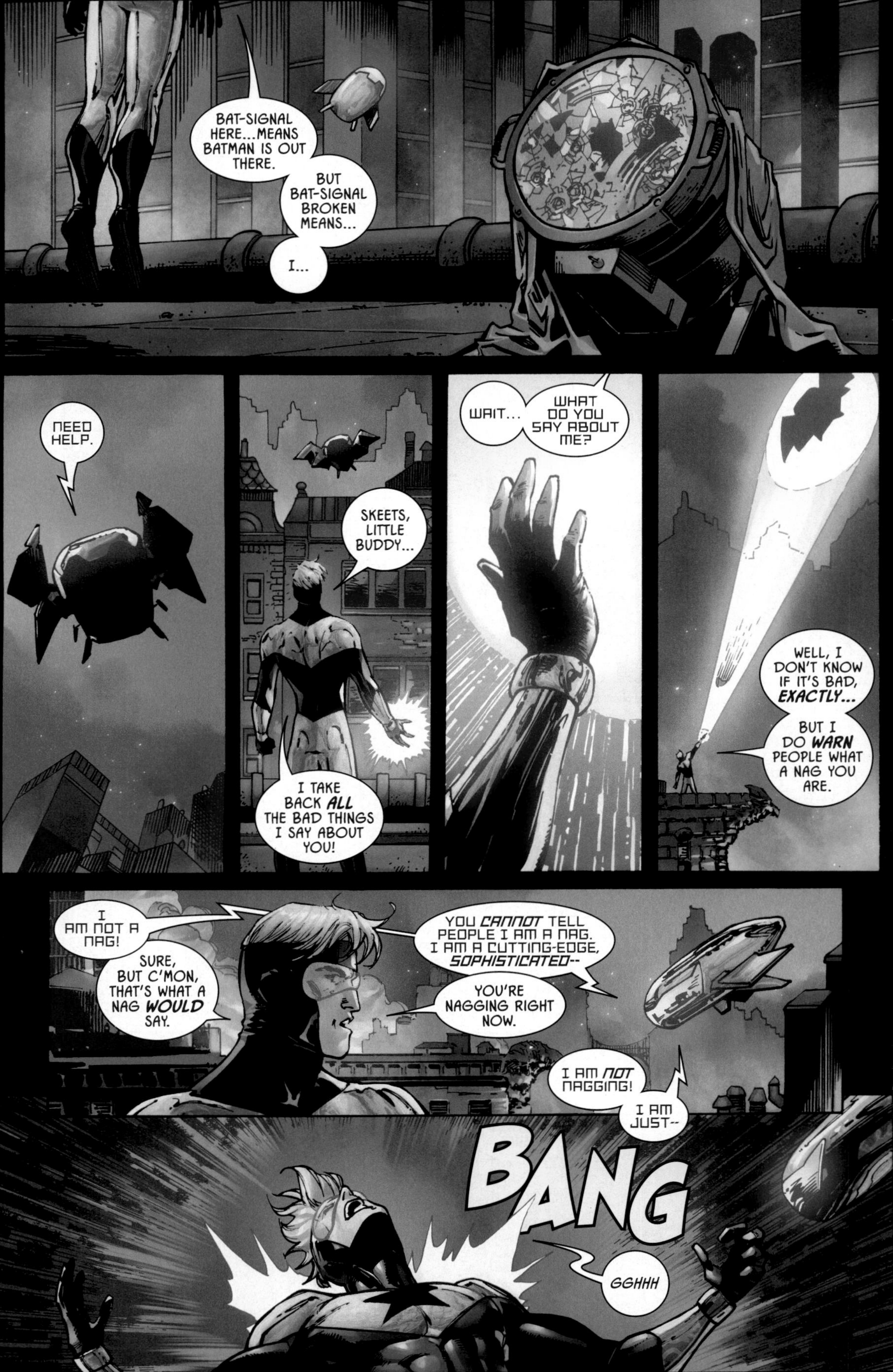
BAT-SIGNAL HERE...MEANS BATMAN IS OUT THERE.
BUT BAT-SIGNAL BROKEN MEANS...
I...
NEED HELP.
SKEETS, LITTLE BUDDY...
I TAKE BACK ALL THE BAD THINGS I SAY ABOUT YOU!
WAIT...
WHAT DO YOU SAY ABOUT ME?
WELL, I DON'T KNOW IF IT'S BAD, EXACTLY...
BUT I DO WARN PEOPLE WHAT A NAG YOU ARE.
I AM NOT A NAG!
SURE, BUT C'MON, THAT'S WHAT A NAG WOULD SAY.
YOU CANNOT TELL PEOPLE I AM A NAG. I AM A CUTTING-EDGE, SOPHISTICATED--
YOU'RE NAGGING RIGHT NOW.
I AM NOT NAGGING!
I AM JUST--
BANG
GGHHH

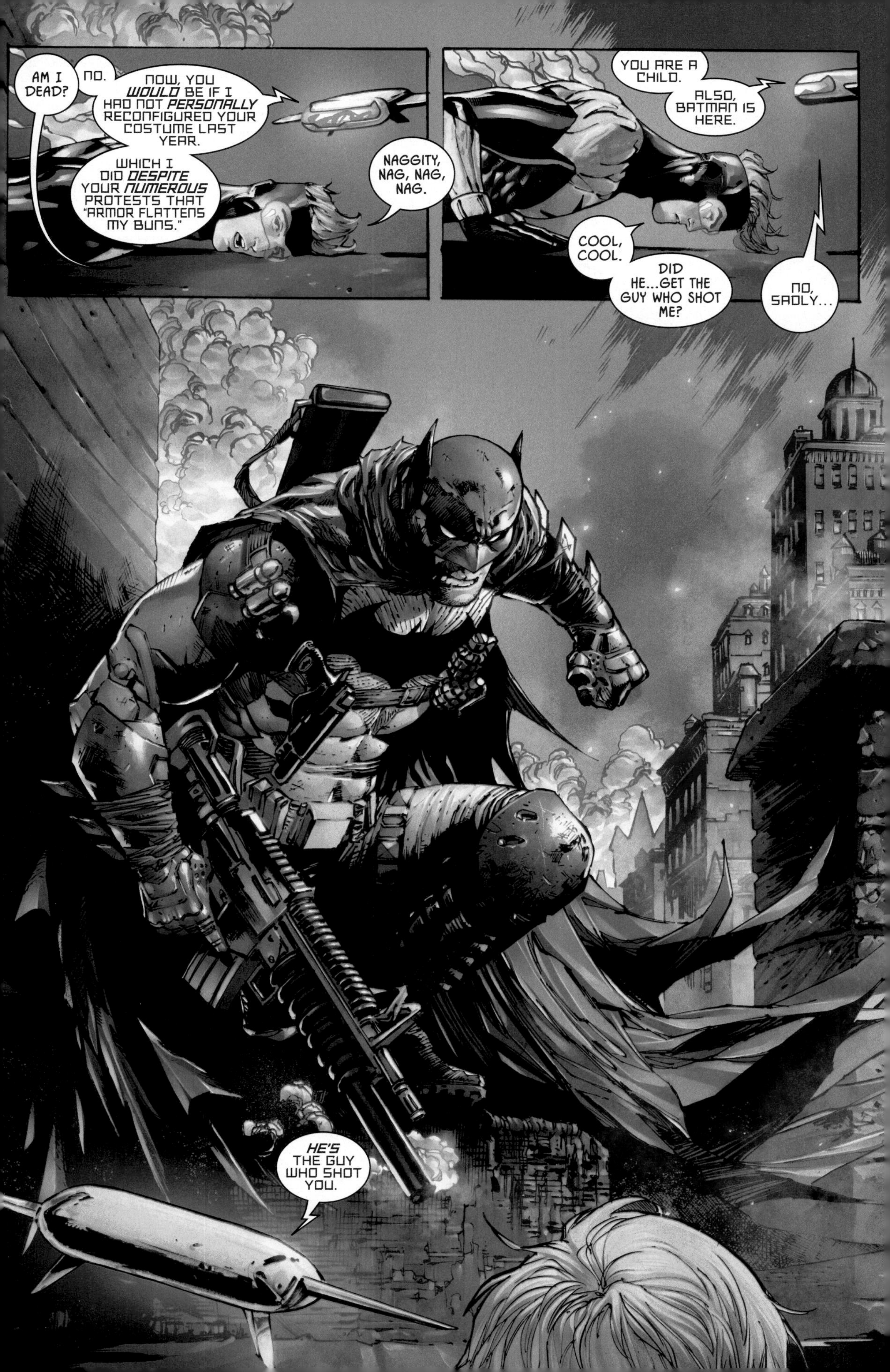

AM I DEAD?
NO.
NOW, YOU WOULD BE IF I HAD NOT PERSONALLY RECONFIGURED YOUR COSTUME LAST YEAR.
WHICH I DID DESPITE YOUR NUMEROUS PROTESTS THAT "ARMOR FLATTENS MY BUNS."
NAGGITY, NAG, NAG, NAG.
YOU ARE A CHILD.
ALSO, BATMAN IS HERE.
COOL, COOL.
DID HE...GET THE GUY WHO SHOT ME?
NO, SADLY...
HE'S THE GUY WHO SHOT YOU.

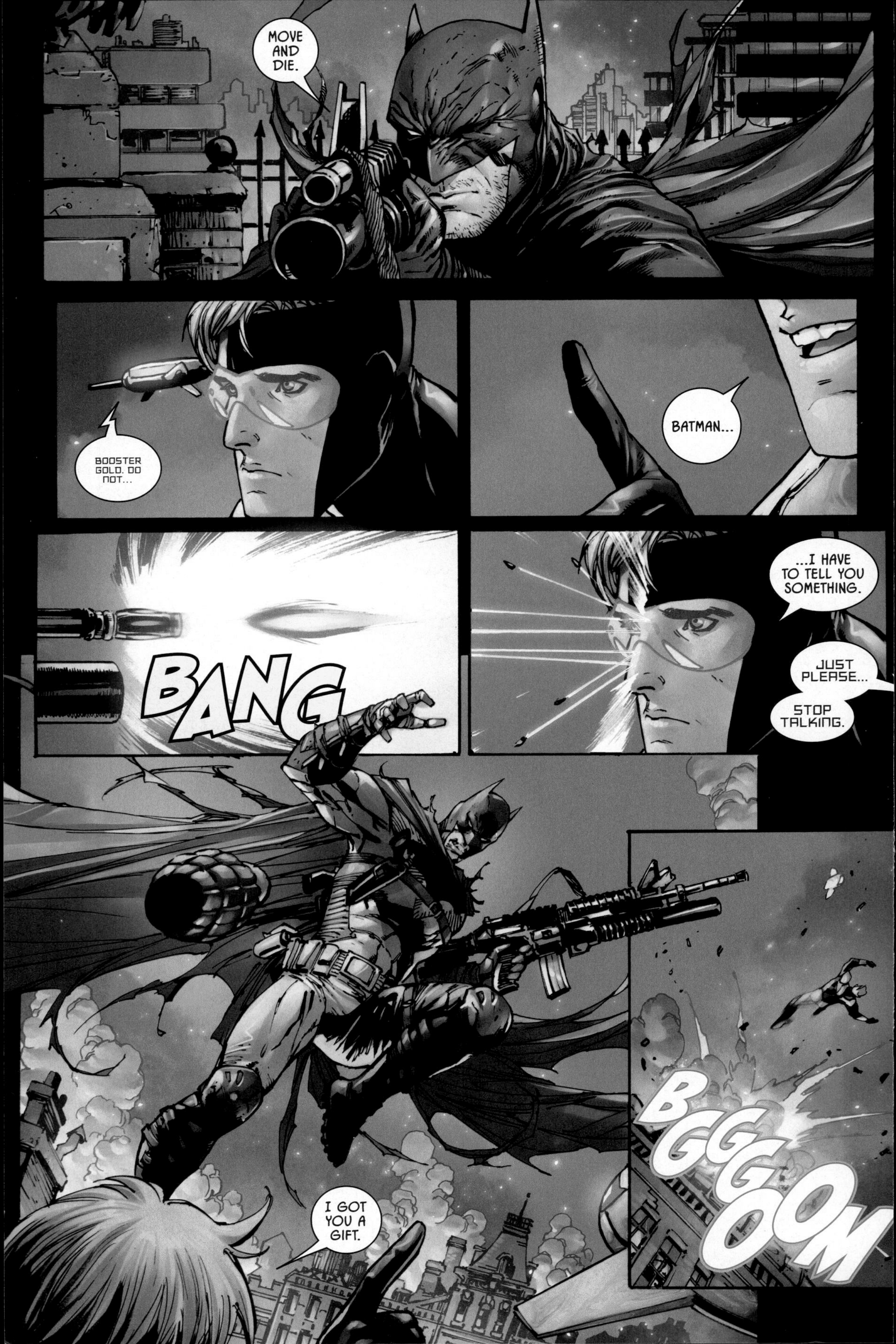
MOVE AND DIE.
BOOSTER GOLD. DO NOT...
BATMAN...
BANG
...I HAVE TO TELL YOU SOMETHING.
JUST PLEASE...
STOP TALKING.
I GOT YOU A GIFT.
BGGGOOM

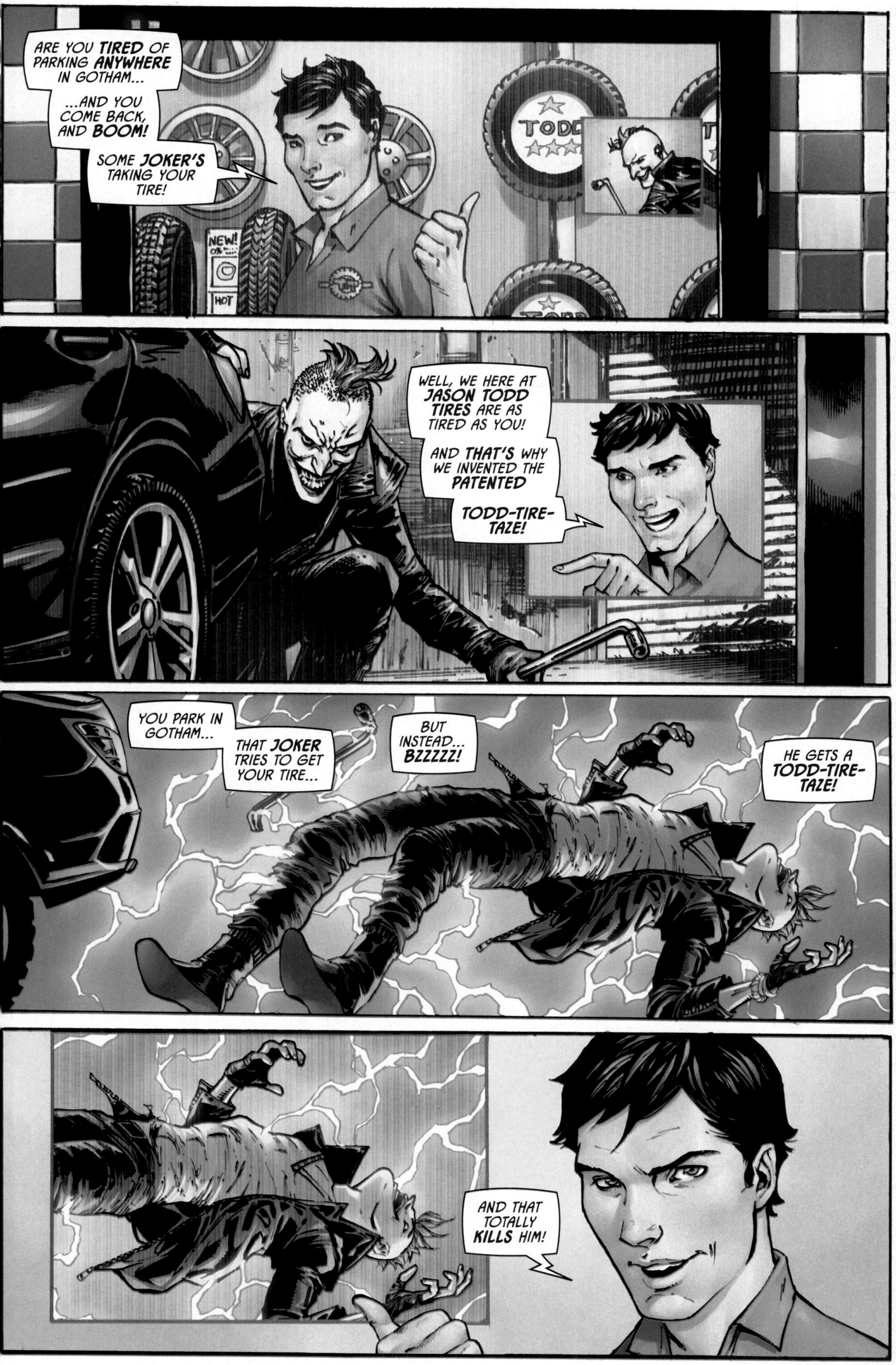
ARE YOU TIRED OF PARKING ANYWHERE IN GOTHAM...
...AND YOU COME BACK, AND BOOM!
SOME JOKER'S TAKING YOUR TIRE!
TODD
NEW!
HOT
WELL, WE HERE AT JASON TODD TIRES ARE AS TIRED AS YOU!
AND THAT'S WHY WE INVENTED THE PATENTED
TODD-TIRE-TAZE!
YOU PARK IN GOTHAM...
THAT JOKER TRIES TO GET YOUR TIRE...
BUT INSTEAD... BZZZZZ!
HE GETS A TODD-TIRE-TAZE!
AND THAT TOTALLY KILLS HIM!

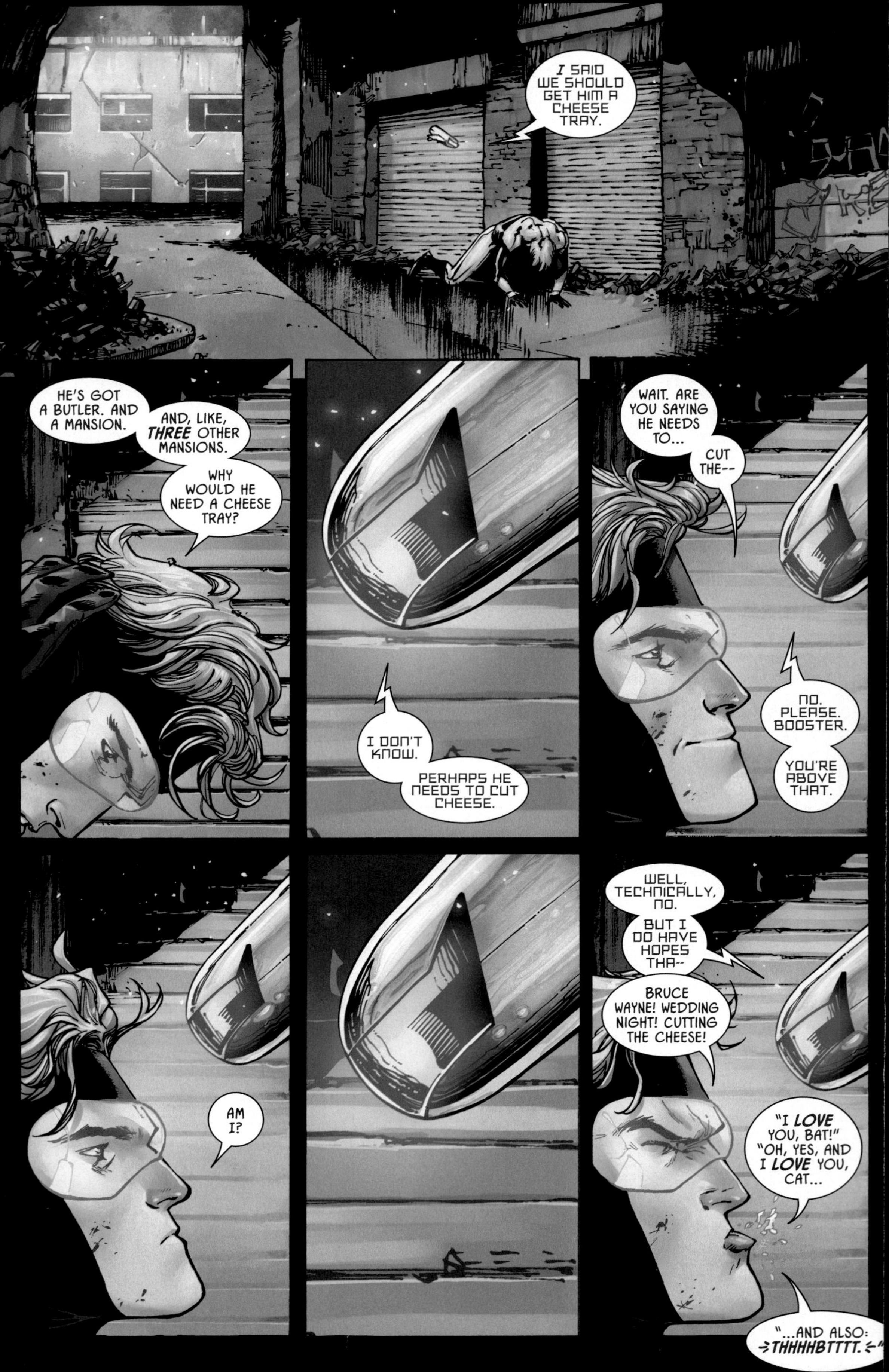

I SAID WE SHOULD GET HIM A CHEESE TRAY.
HE'S GOT A BUTLER. AND A MANSION.
AND, LIKE, ***THREE*** OTHER MANSIONS.
WHY WOULD HE NEED A CHEESE TRAY?
I DON'T KNOW.
PERHAPS HE NEEDS TO CUT CHEESE.
WAIT. ARE YOU SAYING HE NEEDS TO...
CUT THE--
NO. PLEASE. BOOSTER.
YOU'RE ABOVE THAT.
AM I?
WELL, TECHNICALLY, NO.
BUT I DO HAVE HOPES THA--
BRUCE WAYNE! WEDDING NIGHT! CUTTING THE CHEESE!
"I ***LOVE*** YOU, BAT!" "OH, YES, AND I ***LOVE*** YOU, CAT...
"...AND ALSO: ***THHHHBTTTT.***"

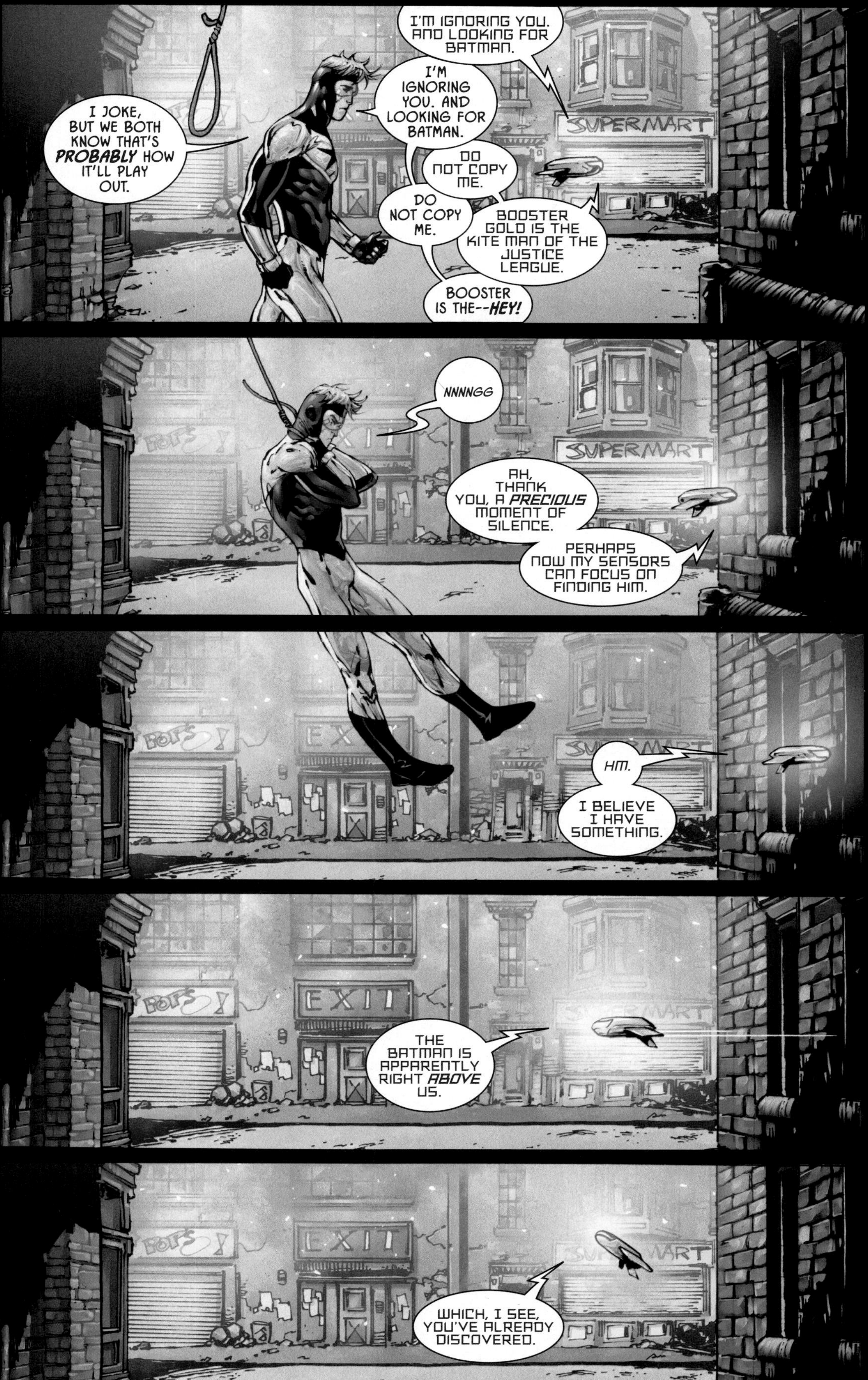

I JOKE, BUT WE BOTH KNOW THAT'S *PROBABLY* HOW IT'LL PLAY OUT.
I'M IGNORING YOU. AND LOOKING FOR BATMAN.
I'M IGNORING YOU. AND LOOKING FOR BATMAN.
SUPERMART
DO NOT COPY ME.
DO NOT COPY ME.
BOOSTER GOLD IS THE KITE MAN OF THE JUSTICE LEAGUE.
BOOSTER IS THE--*HEY!*
NNNNGG
EXIT
AH, THANK YOU, A *PRECIOUS* MOMENT OF SILENCE.
PERHAPS NOW MY SENSORS CAN FOCUS ON FINDING HIM.
HM.
I BELIEVE I HAVE SOMETHING.
EXIT
THE BATMAN IS APPARENTLY RIGHT *ABOVE* US.
EXIT
WHICH, I SEE, YOU'VE ALREADY DISCOVERED.

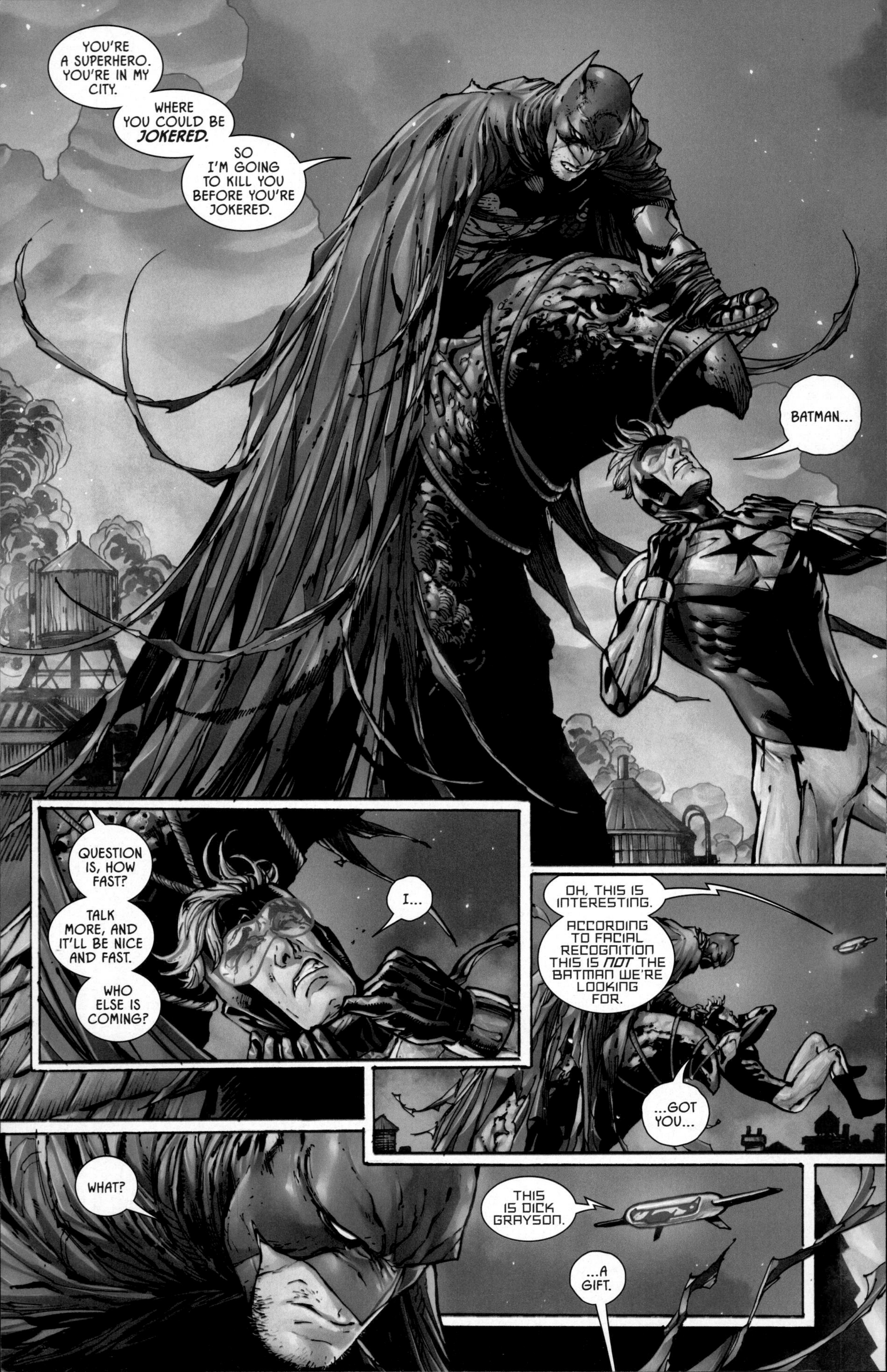
YOU'RE A SUPERHERO. YOU'RE IN MY CITY.
WHERE YOU COULD BE *JOKERED.*
SO I'M GOING TO KILL YOU BEFORE YOU'RE JOKERED.
BATMAN...
QUESTION IS, HOW FAST?
TALK MORE, AND IT'LL BE NICE AND FAST.
WHO ELSE IS COMING?
I...
OH, THIS IS INTERESTING.
ACCORDING TO FACIAL RECOGNITION THIS IS *NOT* THE BATMAN WE'RE LOOKING FOR.
...GOT YOU...
WHAT?
THIS IS DICK GRAYSON.
...A GIFT.

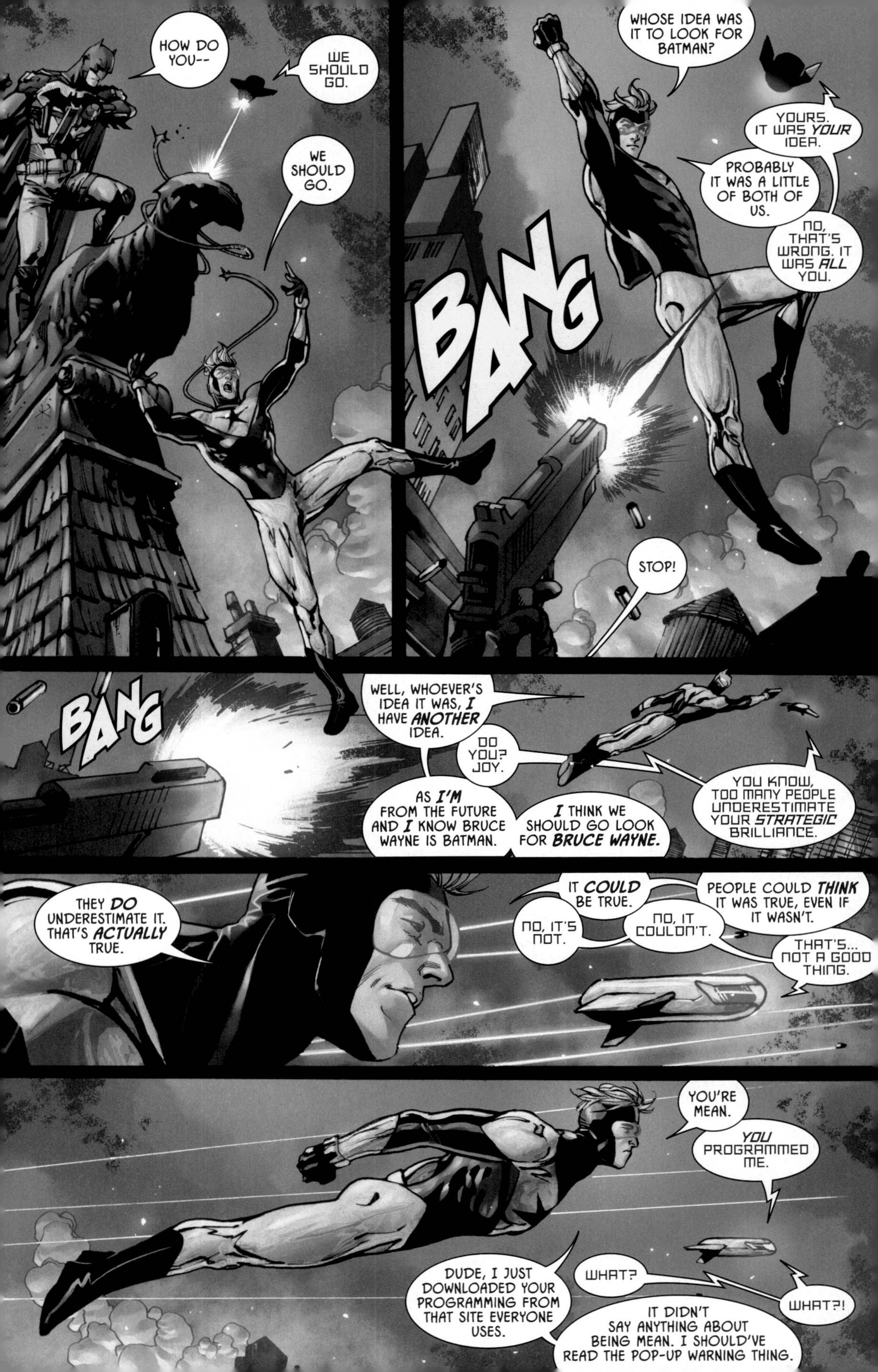
HOW DO YOU--
WE SHOULD GO.
WE SHOULD GO.
WHOSE IDEA WAS IT TO LOOK FOR BATMAN?
YOURS. IT WAS YOUR IDEA.
PROBABLY IT WAS A LITTLE OF BOTH OF US.
NO, THAT'S WRONG. IT WAS ALL YOU.
BANG
STOP!
BANG
WELL, WHOEVER'S IDEA IT WAS, I HAVE ANOTHER IDEA.
DO YOU? JOY.
AS I'M FROM THE FUTURE AND I KNOW BRUCE WAYNE IS BATMAN.
I THINK WE SHOULD GO LOOK FOR BRUCE WAYNE.
YOU KNOW, TOO MANY PEOPLE UNDERESTIMATE YOUR STRATEGIC BRILLIANCE.
THEY DO UNDERESTIMATE IT. THAT'S ACTUALLY TRUE.
NO, IT'S NOT.
IT COULD BE TRUE.
NO, IT COULDN'T.
PEOPLE COULD THINK IT WAS TRUE, EVEN IF IT WASN'T.
THAT'S... NOT A GOOD THING.
YOU'RE MEAN.
YOU PROGRAMMED ME.
DUDE, I JUST DOWNLOADED YOUR PROGRAMMING FROM THAT SITE EVERYONE USES.
WHAT?
WHAT?!
IT DIDN'T SAY ANYTHING ABOUT BEING MEAN. I SHOULD'VE READ THE POP-UP WARNING THING.

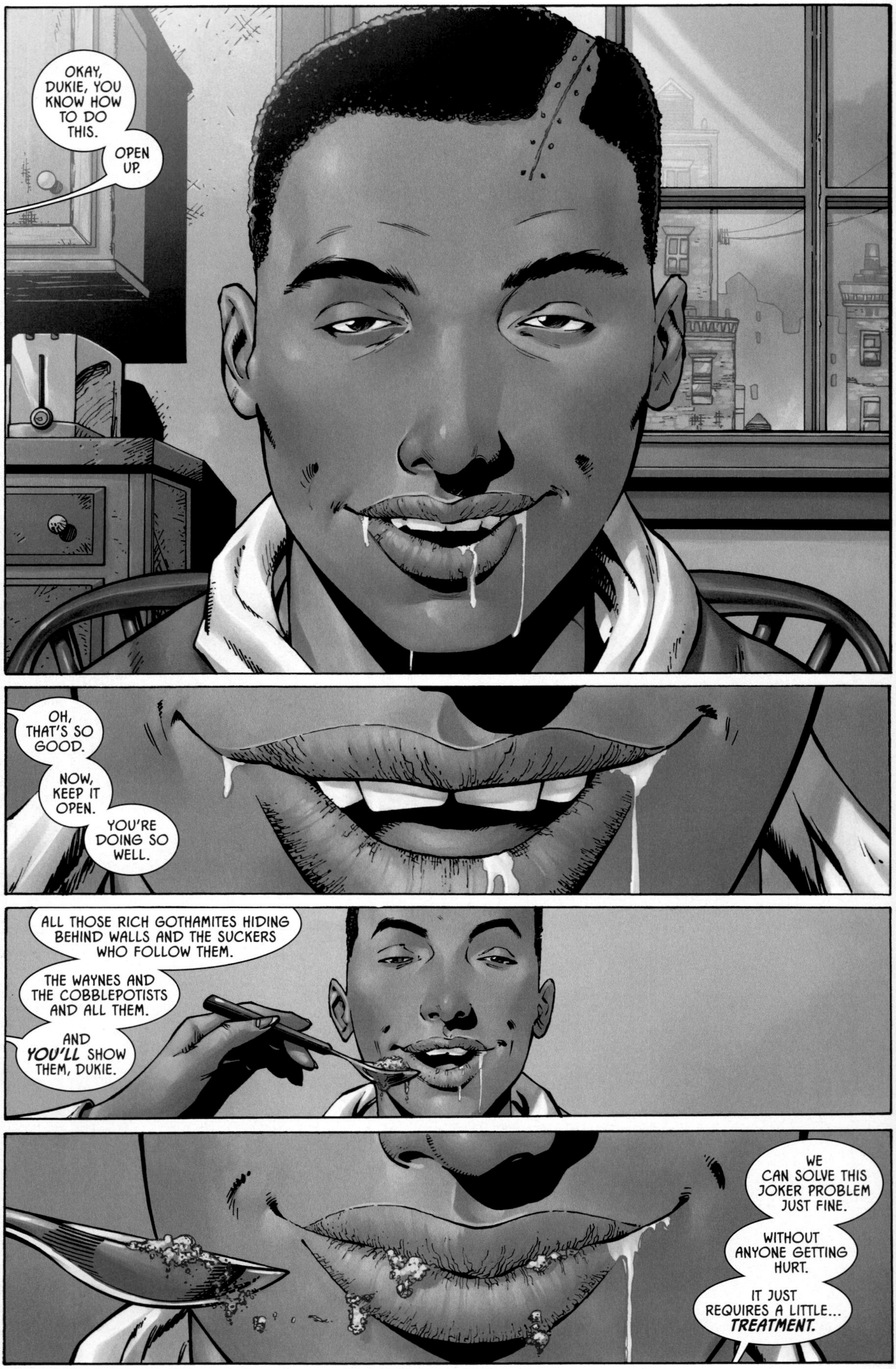
OKAY, DUKIE, YOU KNOW HOW TO DO THIS.
OPEN UP.
OH, THAT'S SO GOOD.
NOW, KEEP IT OPEN.
YOU'RE DOING SO WELL.
ALL THOSE RICH GOTHAMITES HIDING BEHIND WALLS AND THE SUCKERS WHO FOLLOW THEM.
THE WAYNES AND THE COBBLEPOTISTS AND ALL THEM.
AND ***YOU'LL*** SHOW THEM, DUKIE.
WE CAN SOLVE THIS JOKER PROBLEM JUST FINE.
WITHOUT ANYONE GETTING HURT.
IT JUST REQUIRES A LITTLE... ***TREATMENT.***

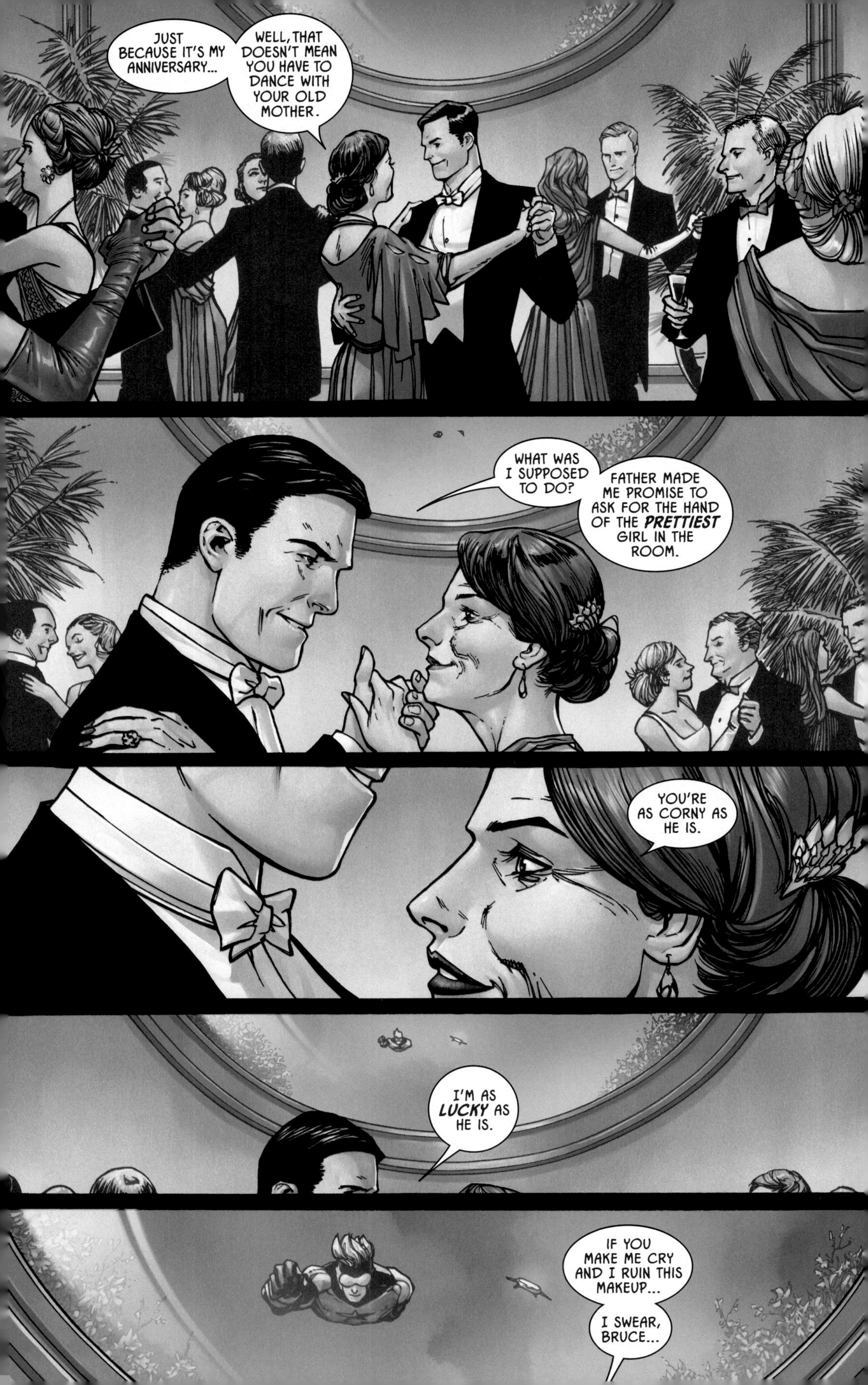
JUST BECAUSE IT'S MY ANNIVERSARY...
WELL, THAT DOESN'T MEAN YOU HAVE TO DANCE WITH YOUR OLD MOTHER.
WHAT WAS I SUPPOSED TO DO?
FATHER MADE ME PROMISE TO ASK FOR THE HAND OF THE PRETTIEST GIRL IN THE ROOM.
YOU'RE AS CORNY AS HE IS.
I'M AS LUCKY AS HE IS.
IF YOU MAKE ME CRY AND I RUIN THIS MAKEUP...
I SWEAR, BRUCE...

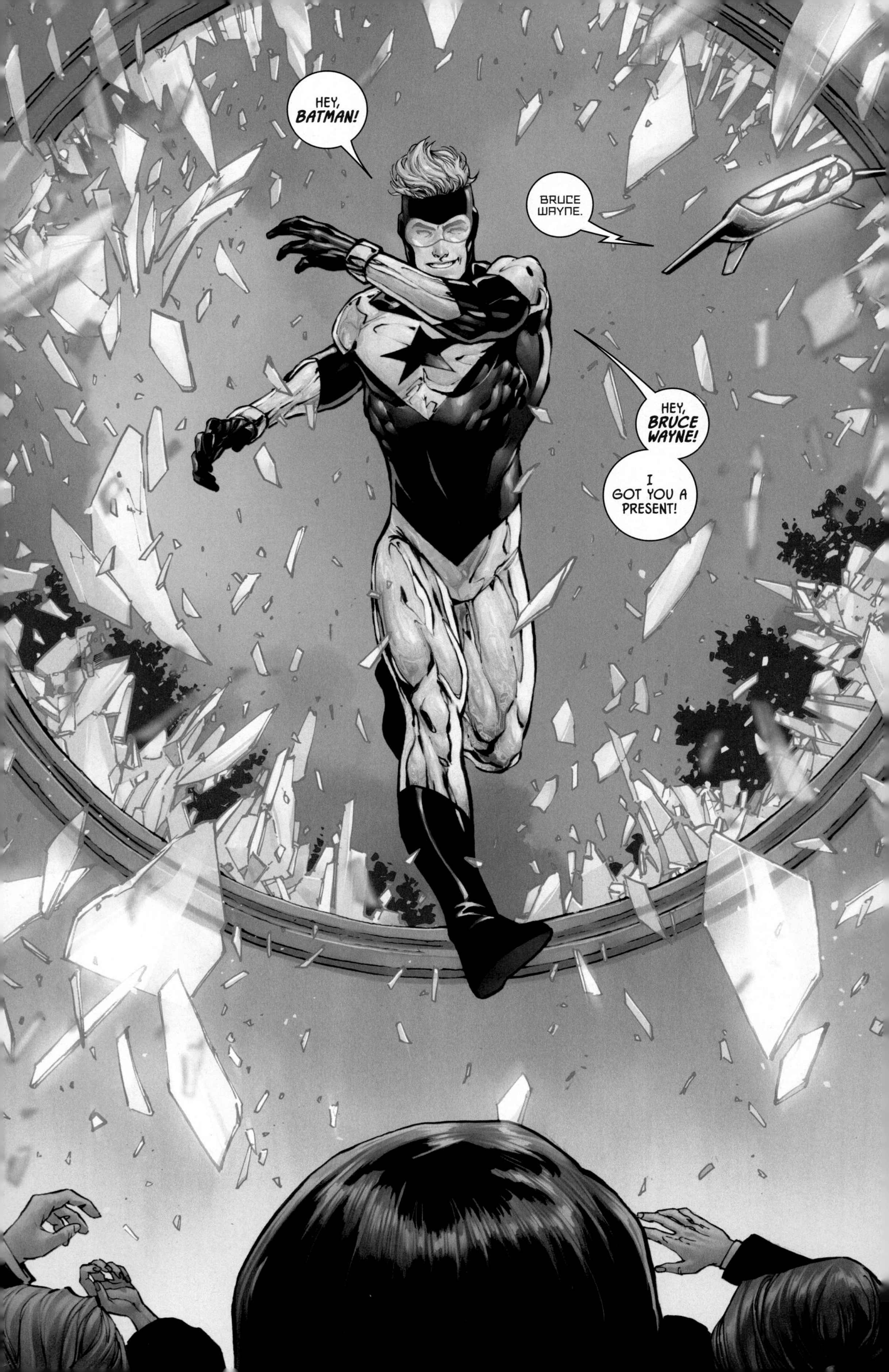
HEY, BATMAN!
BRUCE WAYNE.
HEY, BRUCE WAYNE!
I GOT YOU A PRESENT!

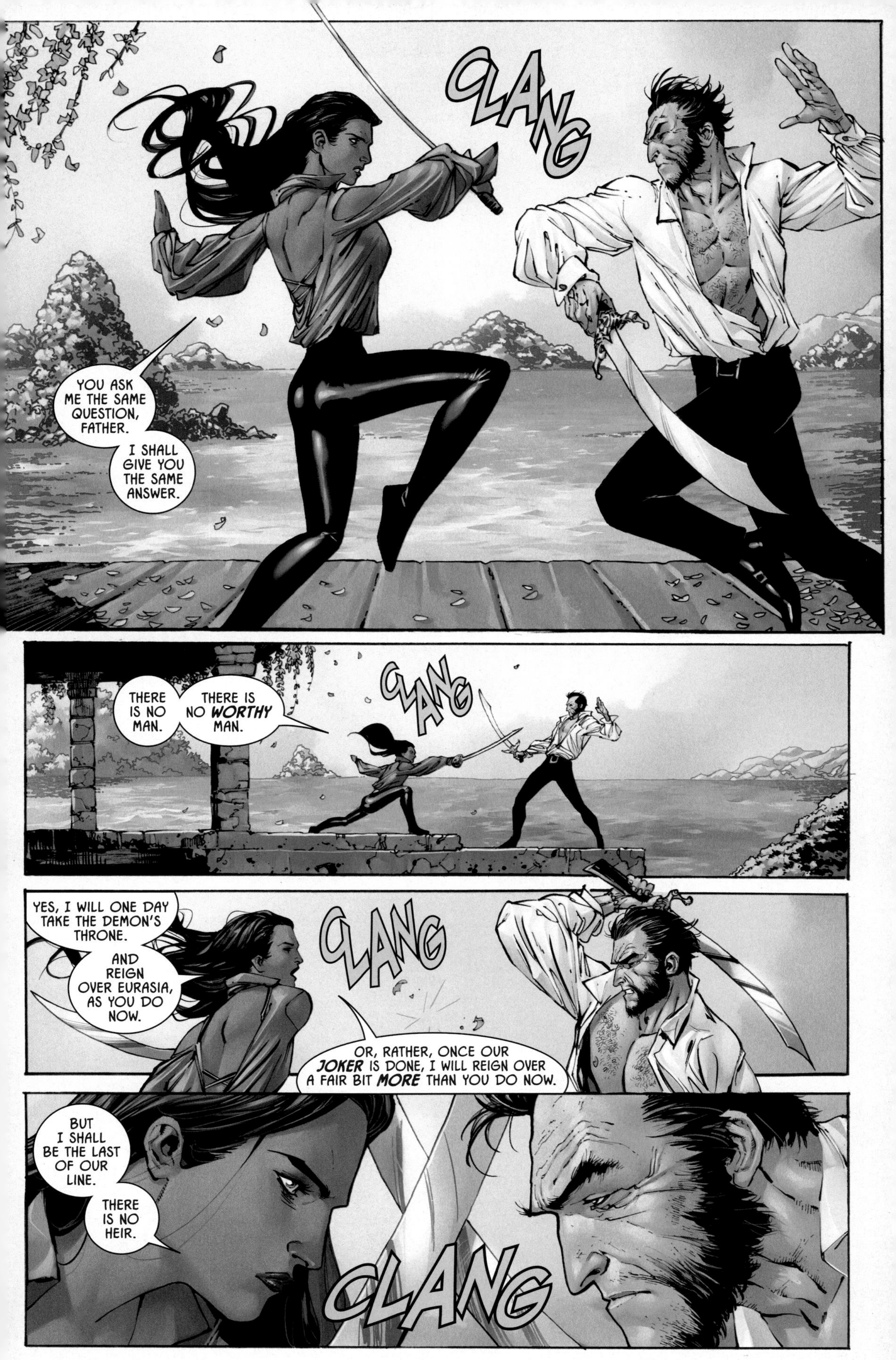CLANG
YOU ASK ME THE SAME QUESTION, FATHER.
I SHALL GIVE YOU THE SAME ANSWER.
CLANG
THERE IS NO MAN.
THERE IS NO WORTHY MAN.
YES, I WILL ONE DAY TAKE THE DEMON'S THRONE.
CLANG
AND REIGN OVER EURASIA, AS YOU DO NOW.
OR, RATHER, ONCE OUR JOKER IS DONE, I WILL REIGN OVER A FAIR BIT MORE THAN YOU DO NOW.
BUT I SHALL BE THE LAST OF OUR LINE.
THERE IS NO HEIR.
CLANG

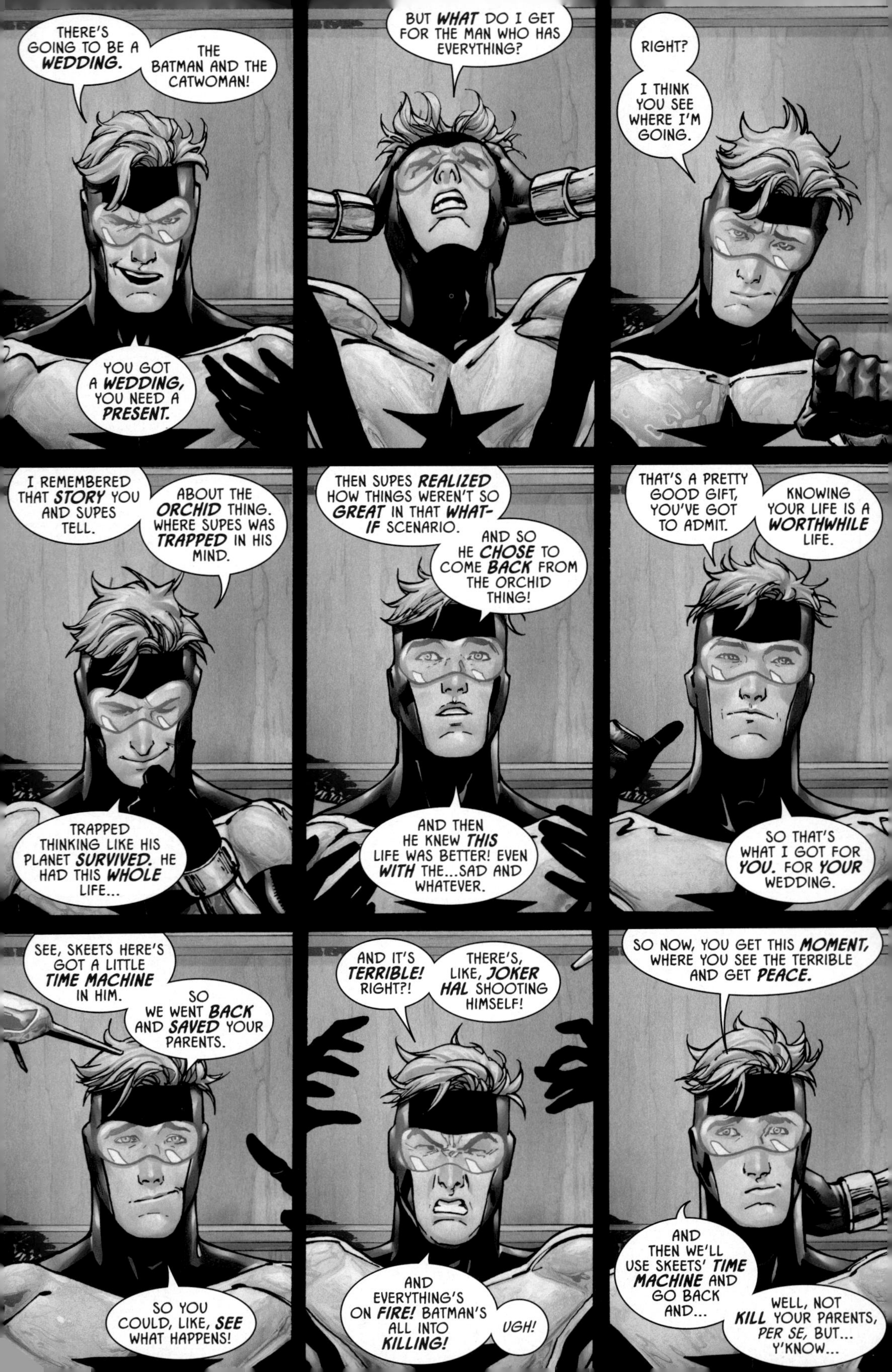

THERE'S GOING TO BE A WEDDING.
THE BATMAN AND THE CATWOMAN!
YOU GOT A WEDDING, YOU NEED A PRESENT.
BUT WHAT DO I GET FOR THE MAN WHO HAS EVERYTHING?
RIGHT?
I THINK YOU SEE WHERE I'M GOING.
I REMEMBERED THAT STORY YOU AND SUPES TELL.
ABOUT THE ORCHID THING. WHERE SUPES WAS TRAPPED IN HIS MIND.
TRAPPED THINKING LIKE HIS PLANET SURVIVED. HE HAD THIS WHOLE LIFE...
THEN SUPES REALIZED HOW THINGS WEREN'T SO GREAT IN THAT WHAT-IF SCENARIO.
AND SO HE CHOSE TO COME BACK FROM THE ORCHID THING!
AND THEN HE KNEW THIS LIFE WAS BETTER! EVEN WITH THE...SAD AND WHATEVER.
THAT'S A PRETTY GOOD GIFT, YOU'VE GOT TO ADMIT.
KNOWING YOUR LIFE IS A WORTHWHILE LIFE.
SO THAT'S WHAT I GOT FOR YOU. FOR YOUR WEDDING.
SEE, SKEETS HERE'S GOT A LITTLE TIME MACHINE IN HIM.
SO WE WENT BACK AND SAVED YOUR PARENTS.
SO YOU COULD, LIKE, SEE WHAT HAPPENS!
AND IT'S TERRIBLE! RIGHT?!
THERE'S, LIKE, JOKER HAL SHOOTING HIMSELF!
AND EVERYTHING'S ON FIRE! BATMAN'S ALL INTO KILLING!
UGH!
SO NOW, YOU GET THIS MOMENT, WHERE YOU SEE THE TERRIBLE AND GET PEACE.
AND THEN WE'LL USE SKEETS' TIME MACHINE AND GO BACK AND...
WELL, NOT KILL YOUR PARENTS, PER SE, BUT... Y'KNOW...

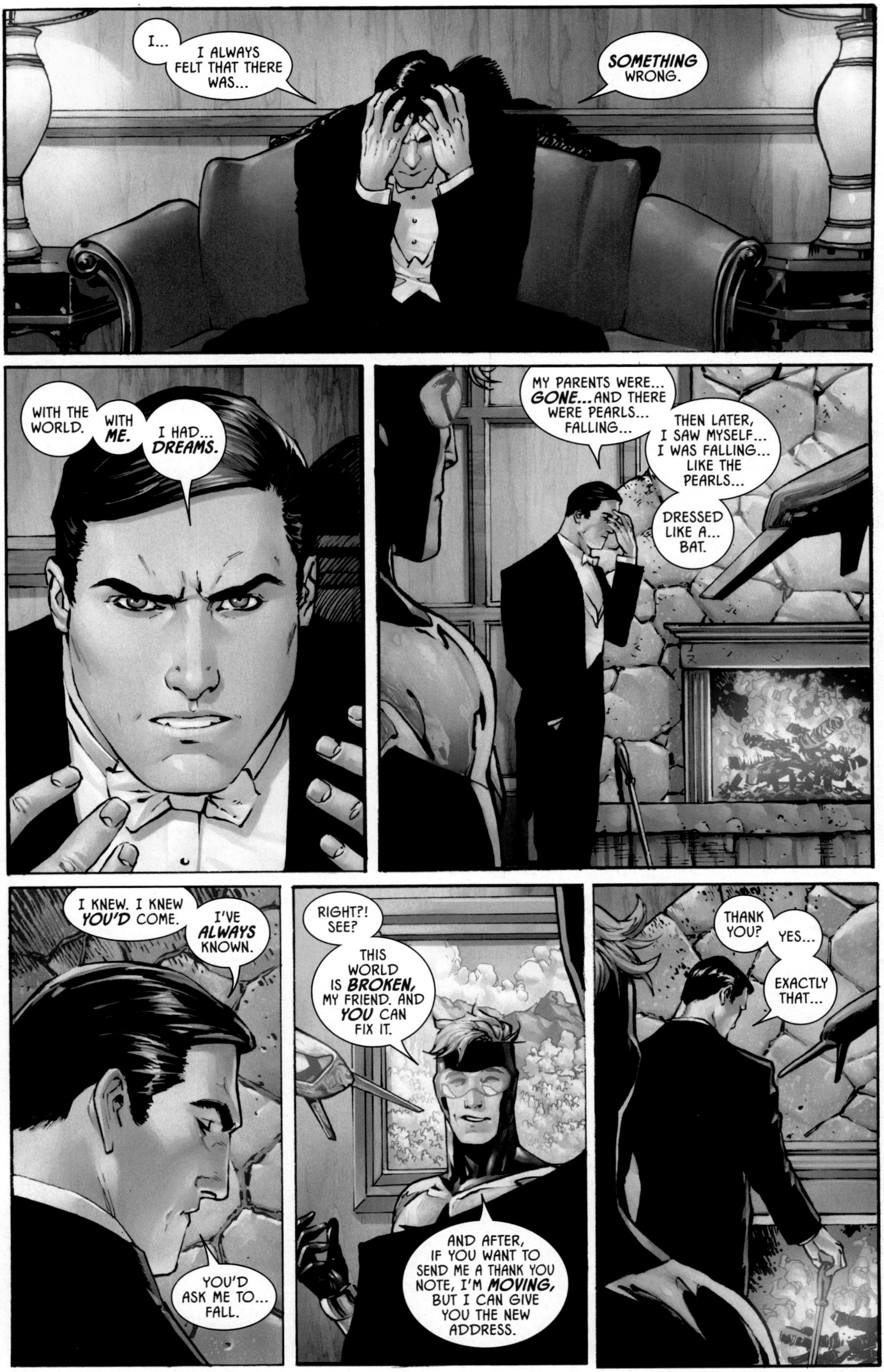
I...
I ALWAYS FELT THAT THERE WAS...
SOMETHING WRONG.
WITH THE WORLD.
WITH ME.
I HAD... DREAMS.
MY PARENTS WERE... GONE... AND THERE WERE PEARLS... FALLING...
THEN LATER, I SAW MYSELF... I WAS FALLING... LIKE THE PEARLS...
DRESSED LIKE A... BAT.
I KNEW. I KNEW YOU'D COME.
I'VE ALWAYS KNOWN.
YOU'D ASK ME TO... FALL.
RIGHT?! SEE?
THIS WORLD IS BROKEN, MY FRIEND. AND YOU CAN FIX IT.
AND AFTER, IF YOU WANT TO SEND ME A THANK YOU NOTE, I'M MOVING, BUT I CAN GIVE YOU THE NEW ADDRESS.
THANK YOU?
YES...
EXACTLY THAT...

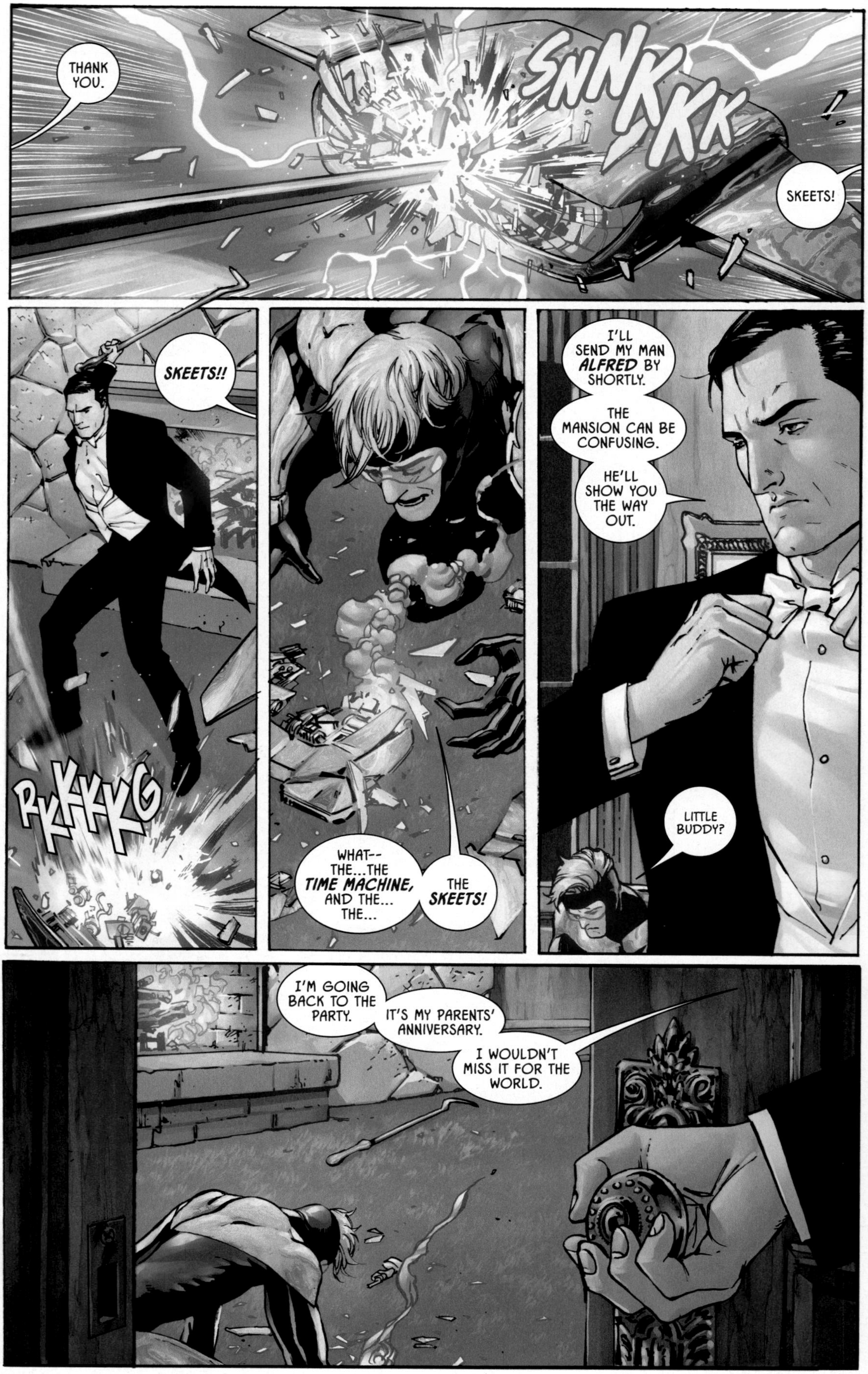
THANK YOU.
SNNKKK
SKEETS!
SKEETS!!
RKKKKG
WHAT-- THE...THE TIME MACHINE, AND THE... THE...
THE SKEETS!
I'LL SEND MY MAN ALFRED BY SHORTLY.
THE MANSION CAN BE CONFUSING.
HE'LL SHOW YOU THE WAY OUT.
LITTLE BUDDY?
I'M GOING BACK TO THE PARTY.
IT'S MY PARENTS' ANNIVERSARY.
I WOULDN'T MISS IT FOR THE WORLD.

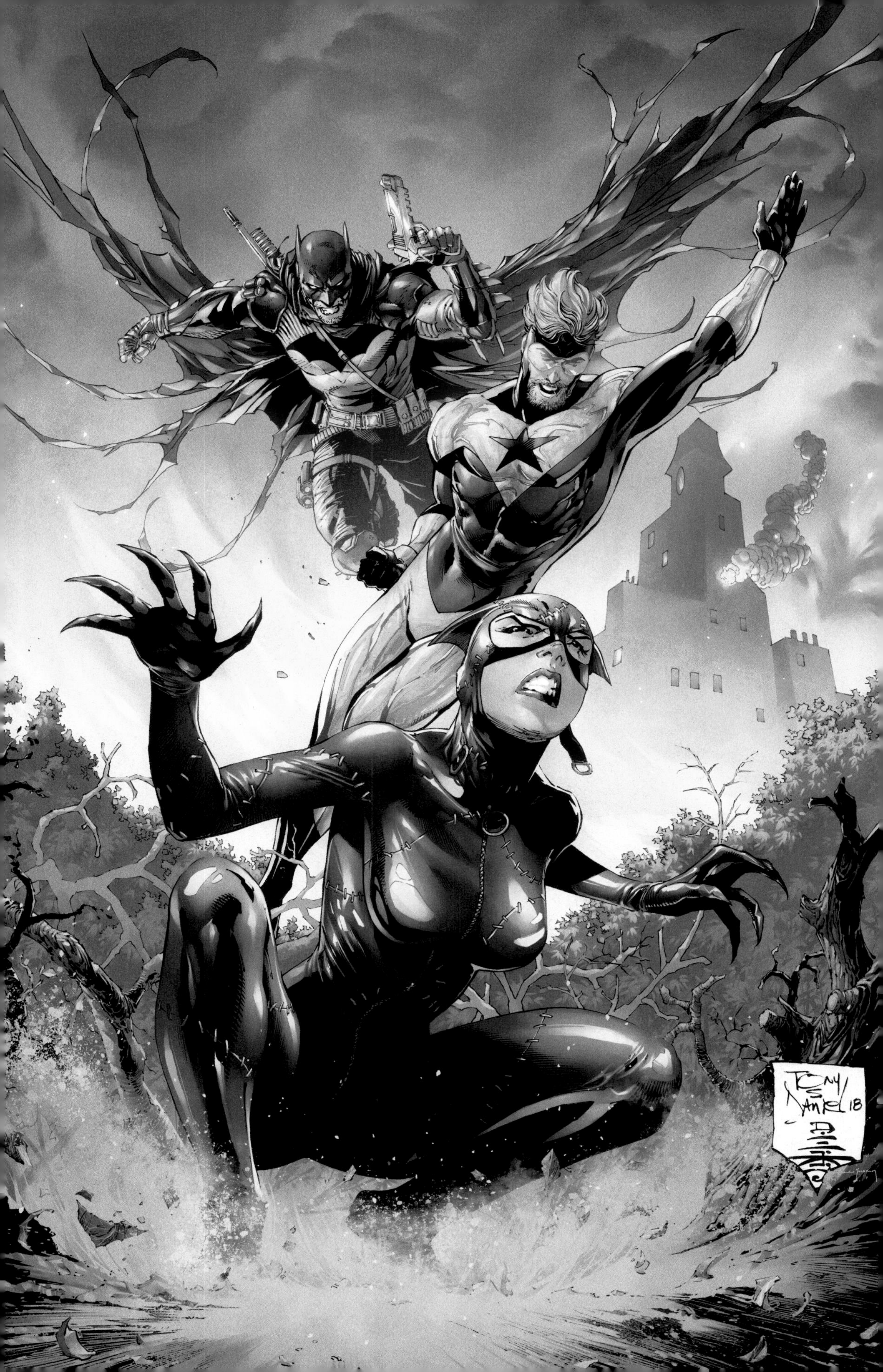

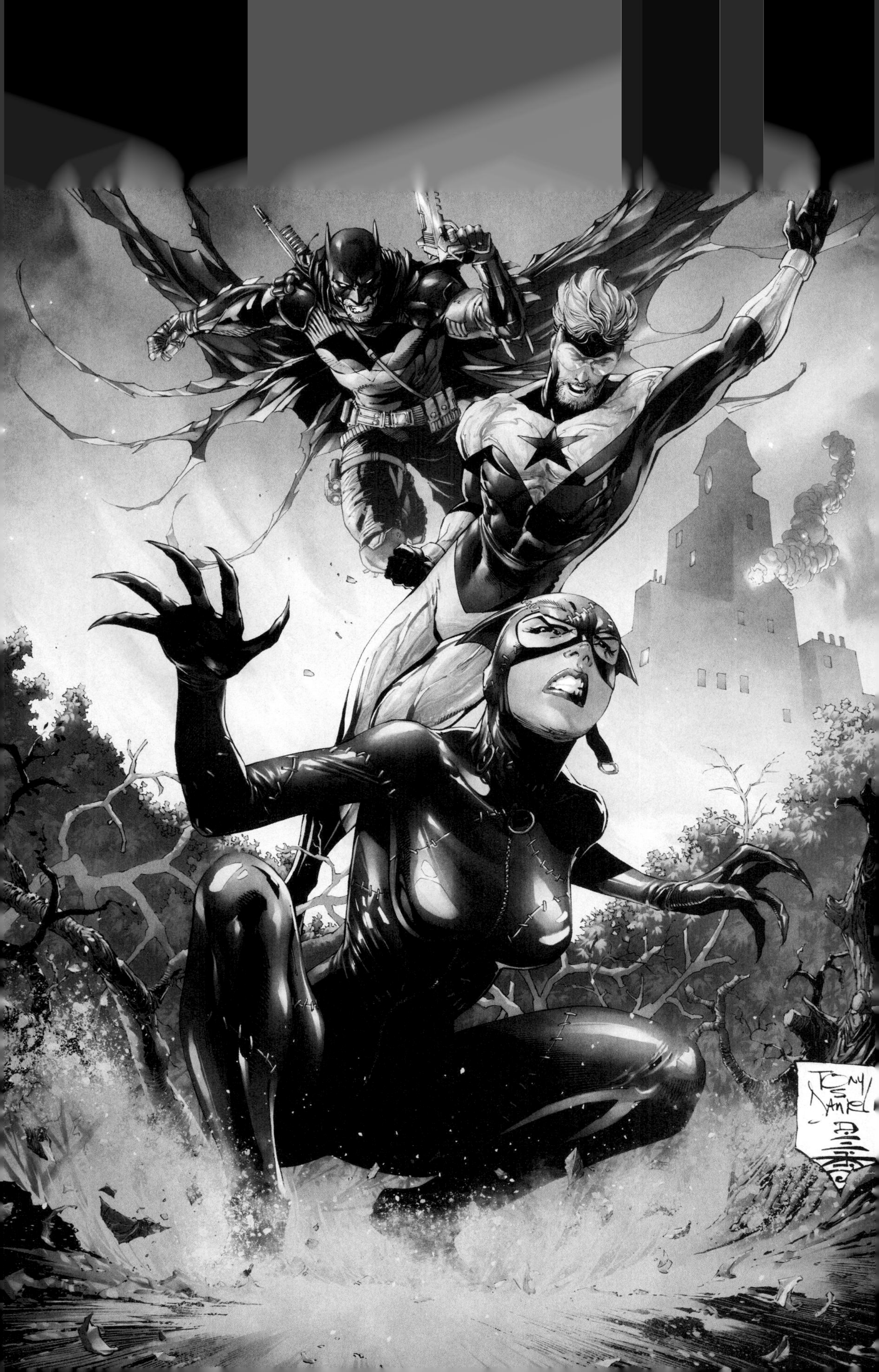

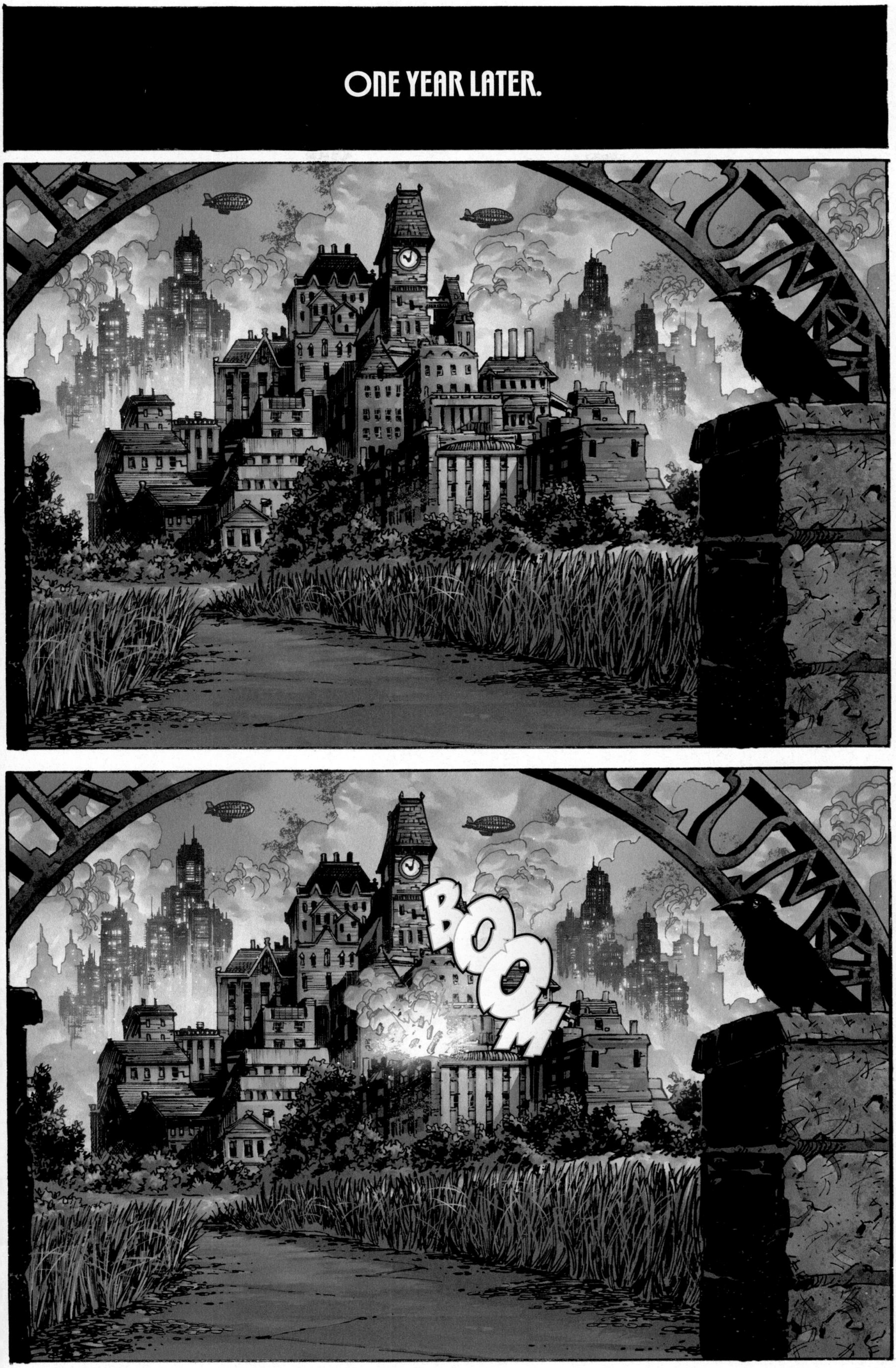
ONE YEAR LATER.
BOOM

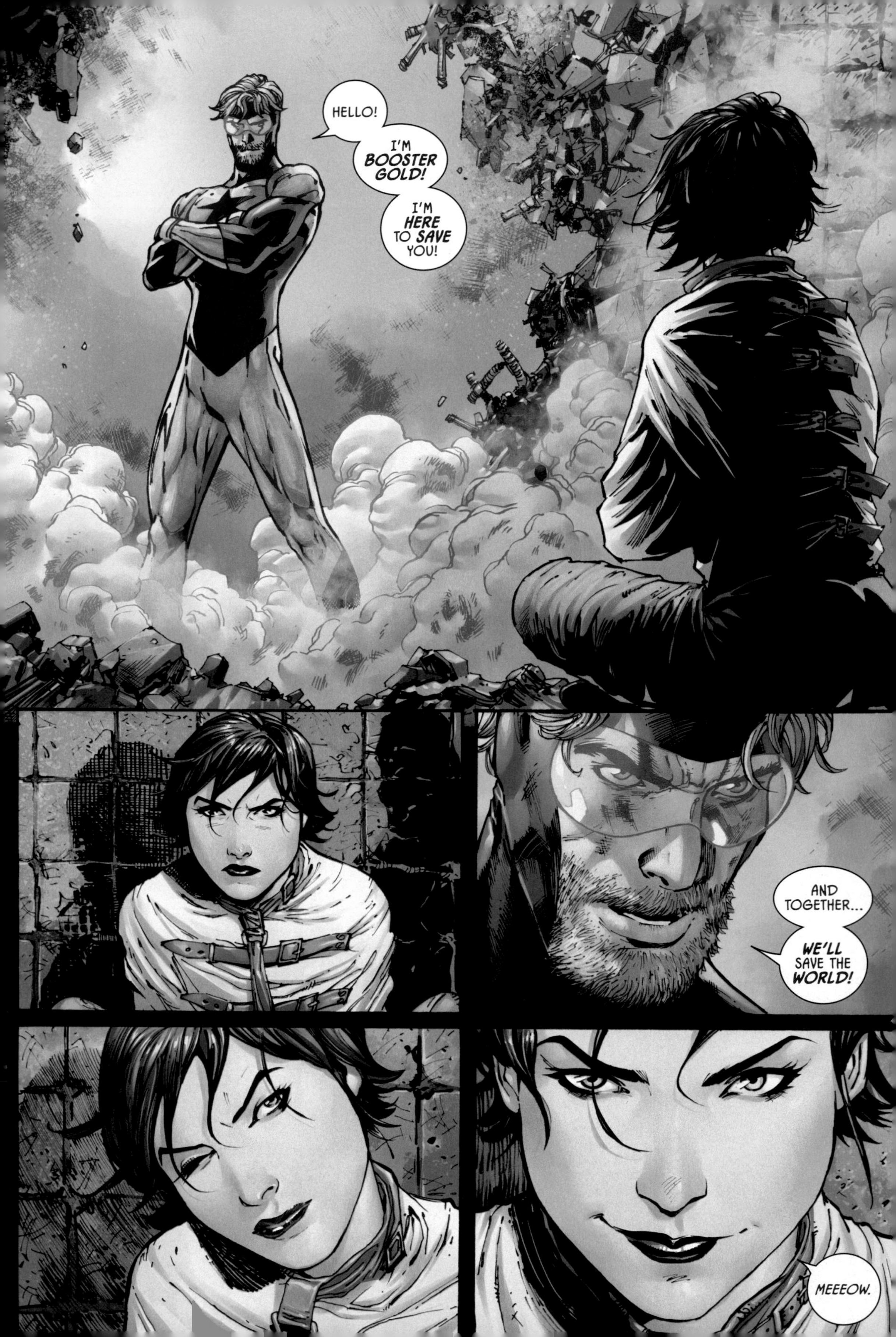
HELLO!
I'M BOOSTER GOLD!
I'M HERE TO SAVE YOU!
AND TOGETHER...
WE'LL SAVE THE WORLD!
MEEEOW.

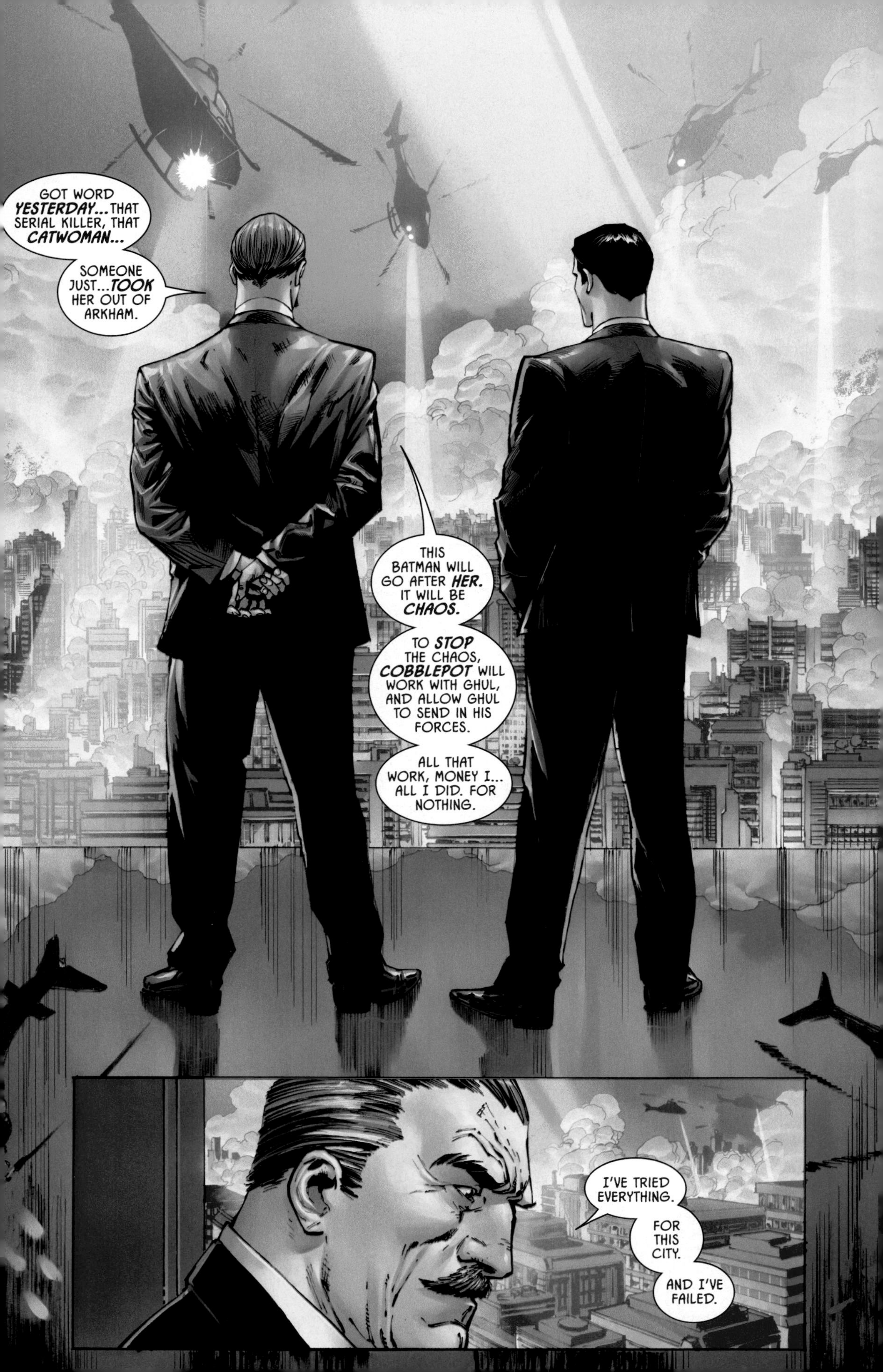
GOT WORD YESTERDAY...THAT SERIAL KILLER, THAT CATWOMAN...
SOMEONE JUST...TOOK HER OUT OF ARKHAM.
THIS BATMAN WILL GO AFTER HER. IT WILL BE CHAOS.
TO STOP THE CHAOS, COBBLEPOT WILL WORK WITH GHUL, AND ALLOW GHUL TO SEND IN HIS FORCES.
ALL THAT WORK, MONEY I... ALL I DID. FOR NOTHING.
I'VE TRIED EVERYTHING.
FOR THIS CITY.
AND I'VE FAILED.

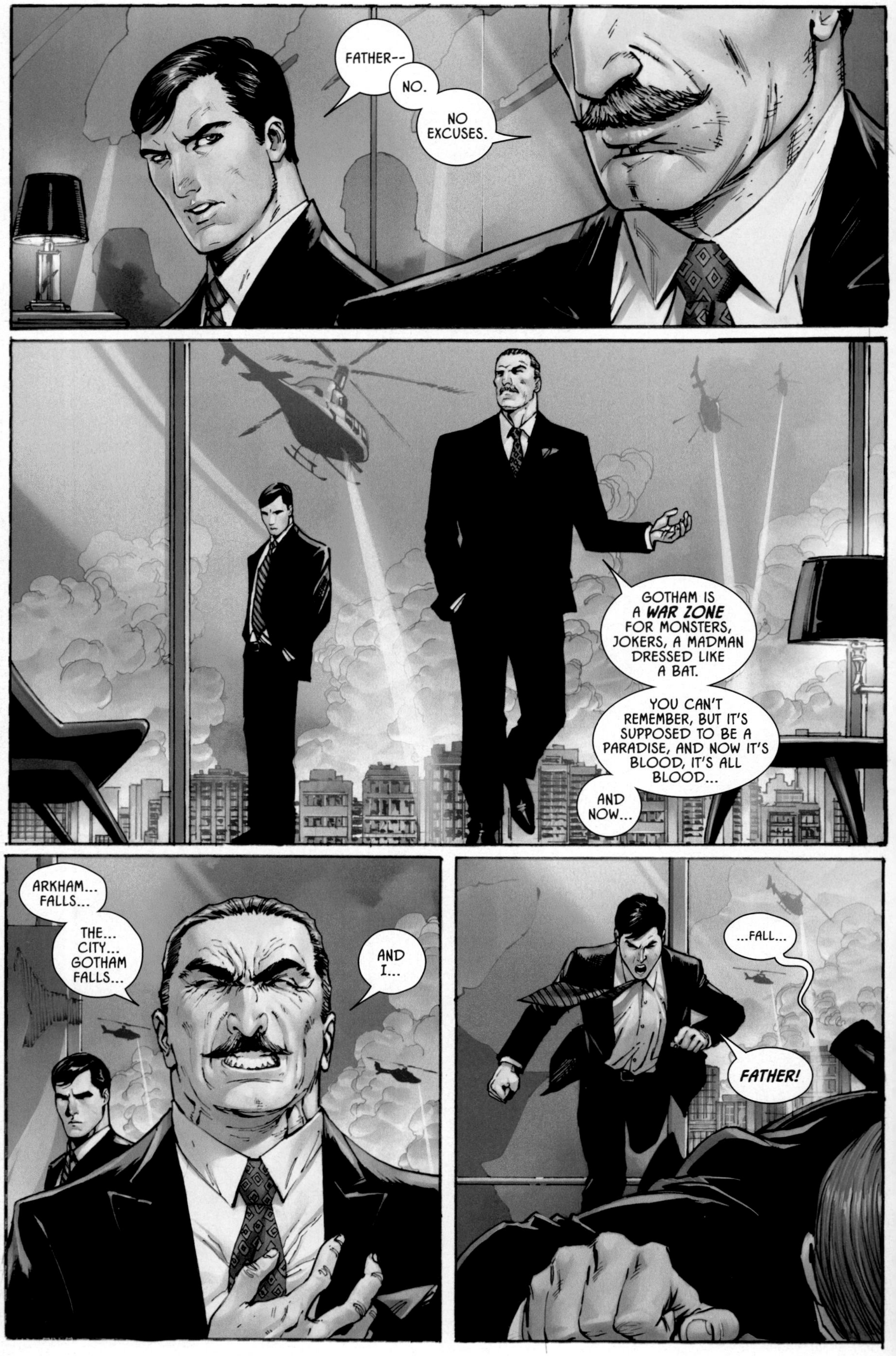
FATHER--
NO.
NO EXCUSES.
GOTHAM IS A ***WAR ZONE*** FOR MONSTERS, JOKERS, A MADMAN DRESSED LIKE A BAT.
YOU CAN'T REMEMBER, BUT IT'S SUPPOSED TO BE A PARADISE, AND NOW IT'S BLOOD, IT'S ALL BLOOD...
AND NOW...
ARKHAM... FALLS...
THE... CITY... GOTHAM FALLS...
AND I...
...FALL...
FATHER!

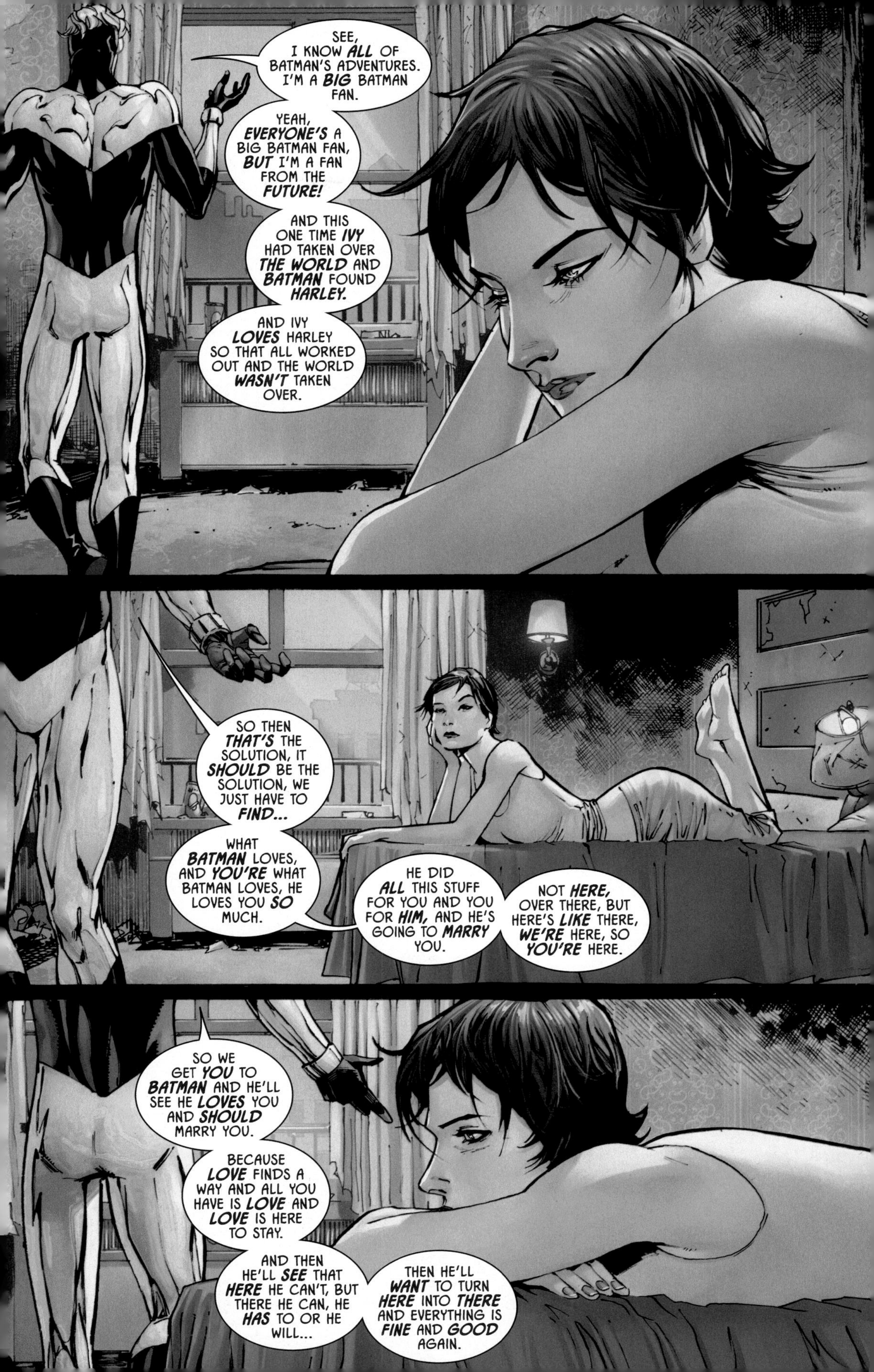
SEE, I KNOW ALL OF BATMAN'S ADVENTURES. I'M A BIG BATMAN FAN.
YEAH, EVERYONE'S A BIG BATMAN FAN, BUT I'M A FAN FROM THE FUTURE!
AND THIS ONE TIME IVY HAD TAKEN OVER THE WORLD AND BATMAN FOUND HARLEY.
AND IVY LOVES HARLEY SO THAT ALL WORKED OUT AND THE WORLD WASN'T TAKEN OVER.
SO THEN THAT'S THE SOLUTION, IT SHOULD BE THE SOLUTION, WE JUST HAVE TO FIND...
WHAT BATMAN LOVES, AND YOU'RE WHAT BATMAN LOVES, HE LOVES YOU SO MUCH.
HE DID ALL THIS STUFF FOR YOU AND YOU FOR HIM, AND HE'S GOING TO MARRY YOU.
NOT HERE, OVER THERE, BUT HERE'S LIKE THERE, WE'RE HERE, SO YOU'RE HERE.
SO WE GET YOU TO BATMAN AND HE'LL SEE HE LOVES YOU AND SHOULD MARRY YOU.
BECAUSE LOVE FINDS A WAY AND ALL YOU HAVE IS LOVE AND LOVE IS HERE TO STAY.
AND THEN HE'LL SEE THAT HERE HE CAN'T, BUT THERE HE CAN, HE HAS TO OR HE WILL...
THEN HE'LL WANT TO TURN HERE INTO THERE AND EVERYTHING IS FINE AND GOOD AGAIN.

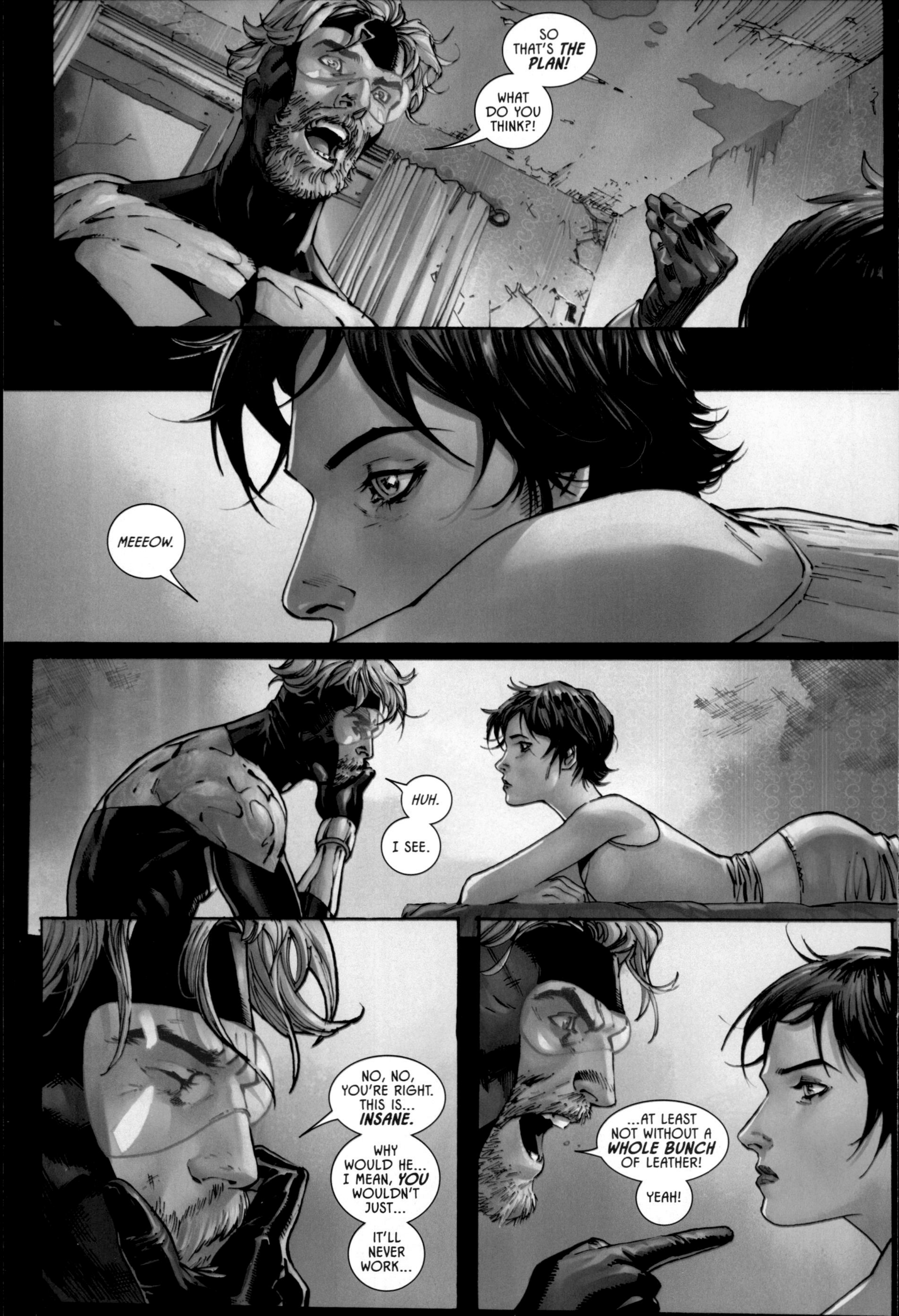
SO THAT'S THE PLAN!
WHAT DO YOU THINK?!
MEEEOW.
HUH.
I SEE.
NO, NO, YOU'RE RIGHT. THIS IS... INSANE.
WHY WOULD HE... I MEAN, YOU WOULDN'T JUST...
IT'LL NEVER WORK...
...AT LEAST NOT WITHOUT A WHOLE BUNCH OF LEATHER!
YEAH!

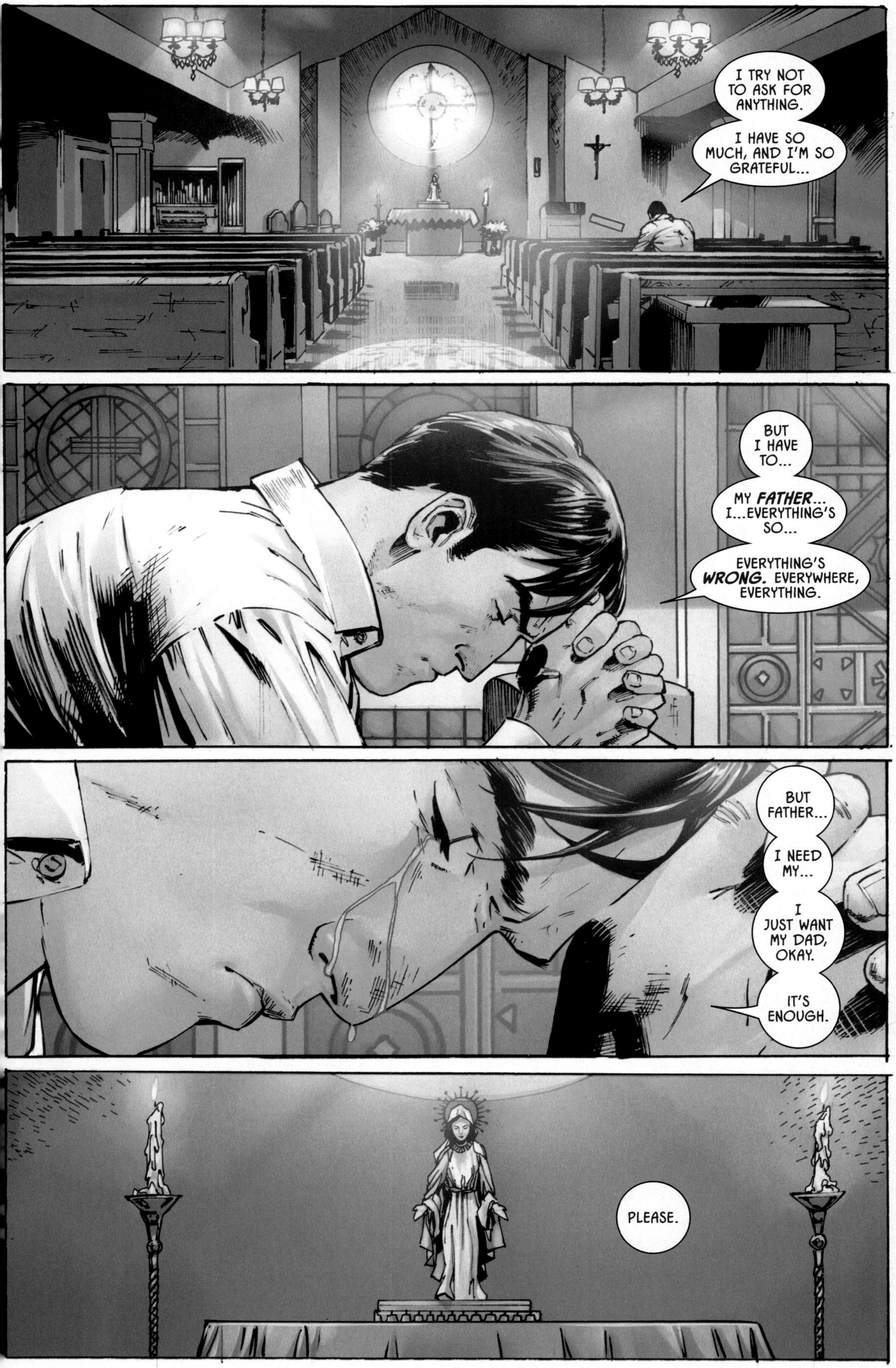

I TRY NOT TO ASK FOR ANYTHING.
I HAVE SO MUCH, AND I'M SO GRATEFUL...
BUT I HAVE TO...
MY *FATHER*... I...EVERYTHING'S SO...
EVERYTHING'S ***WRONG.*** EVERYWHERE, EVERYTHING.
BUT FATHER...
I NEED MY...
I JUST WANT MY DAD, OKAY.
IT'S ENOUGH.
PLEASE.

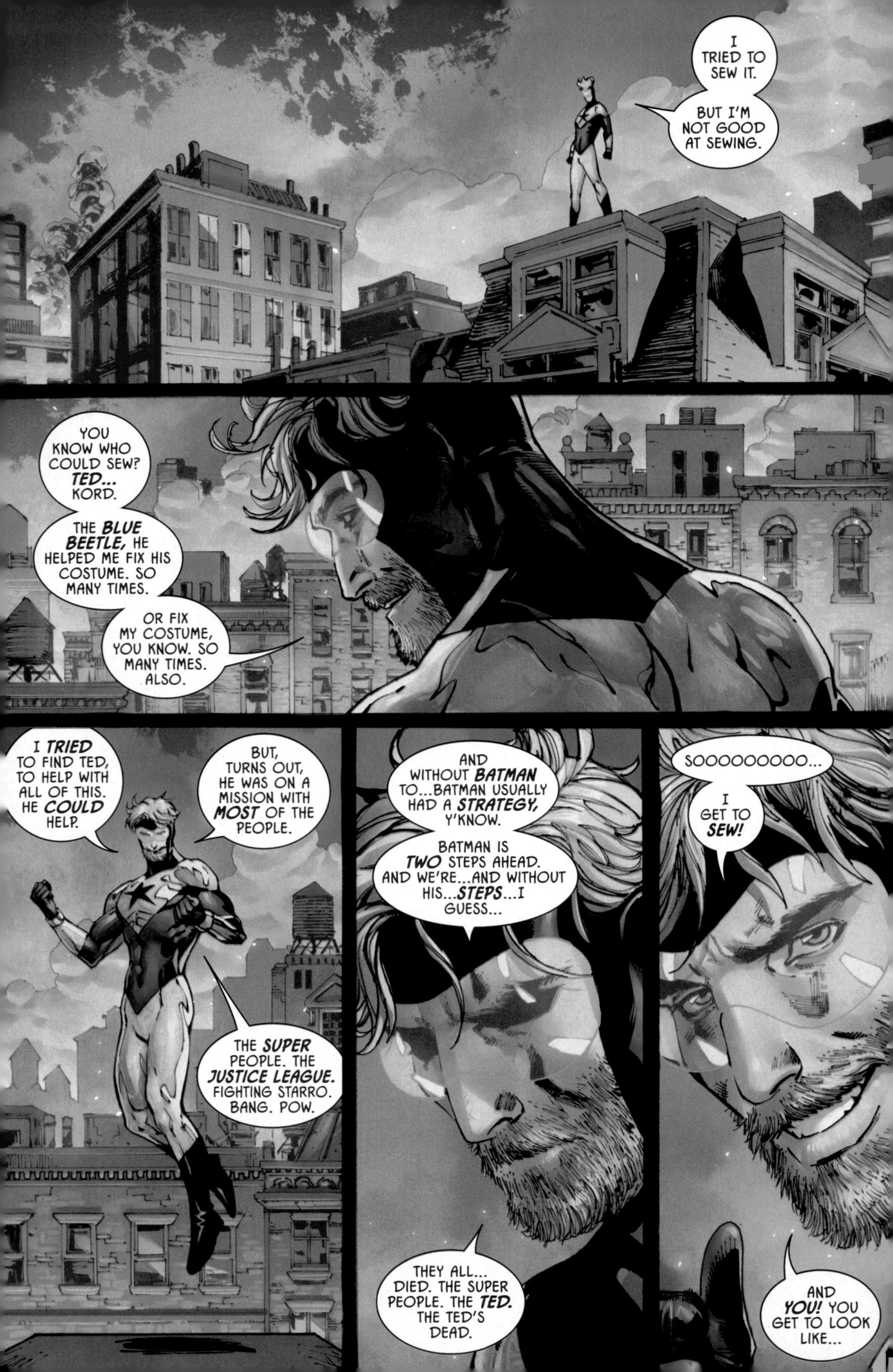
I TRIED TO SEW IT.
BUT I'M NOT GOOD AT SEWING.
YOU KNOW WHO COULD SEW? TED... KORD.
THE BLUE BEETLE, HE HELPED ME FIX HIS COSTUME. SO MANY TIMES.
OR FIX MY COSTUME, YOU KNOW. SO MANY TIMES. ALSO.
I TRIED TO FIND TED, TO HELP WITH ALL OF THIS. HE COULD HELP.
BUT, TURNS OUT, HE WAS ON A MISSION WITH MOST OF THE PEOPLE.
THE SUPER PEOPLE. THE JUSTICE LEAGUE. FIGHTING STARRO. BANG. POW.
AND WITHOUT BATMAN TO...BATMAN USUALLY HAD A STRATEGY, Y'KNOW.
BATMAN IS TWO STEPS AHEAD. AND WE'RE...AND WITHOUT HIS...STEPS...I GUESS...
THEY ALL... DIED. THE SUPER PEOPLE. THE TED. THE TED'S DEAD.
SOOOOOOOOOO...
I GET TO SEW!
AND YOU! YOU GET TO LOOK LIKE...

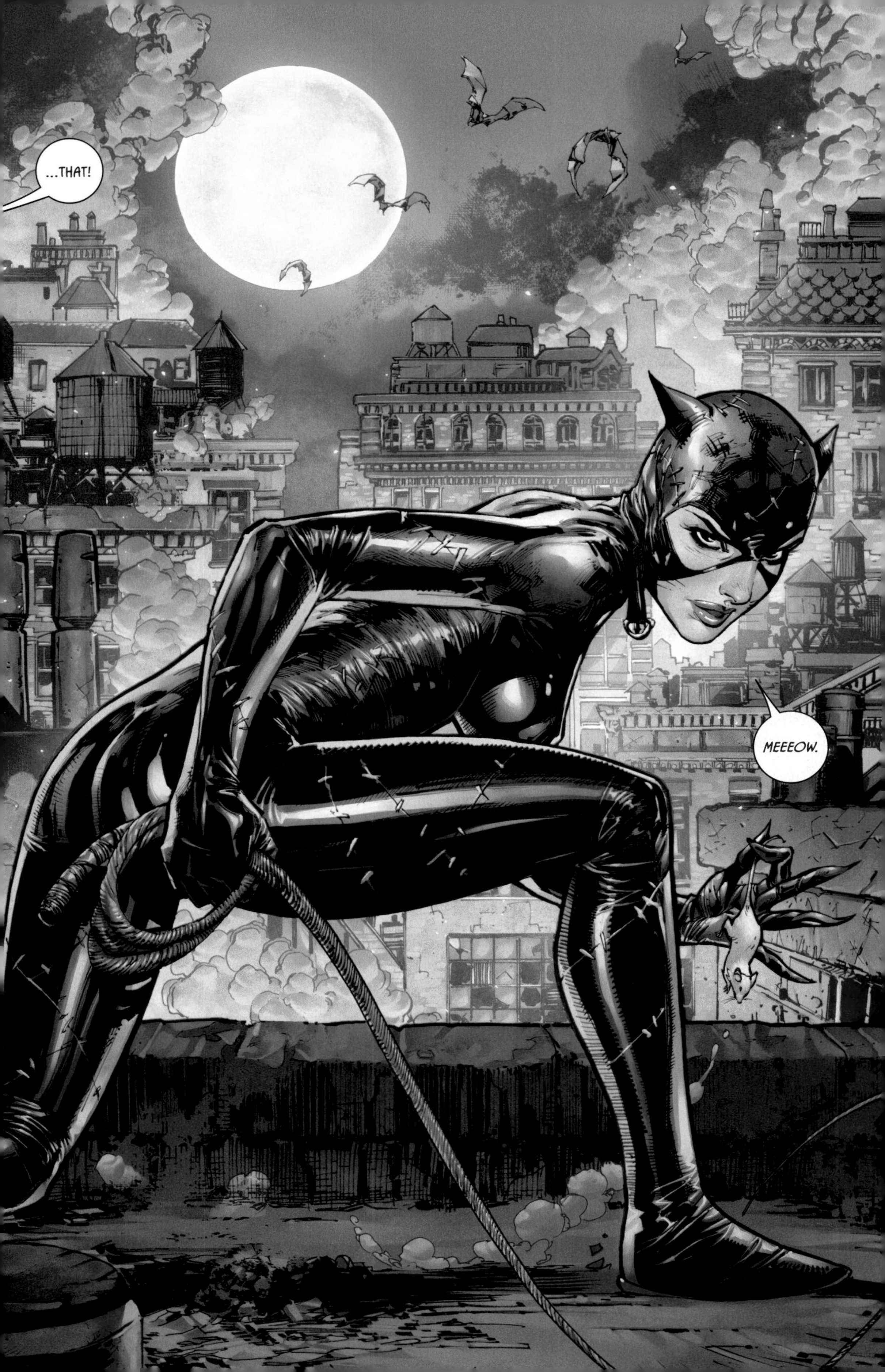
...THAT!
MEEEOW.

LOCAL CHARACTER **JASON TODD** WAS RELEASED ON BAIL TODAY.

MR. TODD IS THE CEO OF **"TODD-TIRE-TAZE,"** A CAR SECURITY DEVICE.

THE DEVICE SHOCKS **JOKERS** WHO **ATTEMPT** TO STEAL YOUR TIRES.

COURT DOCUMENTS REVEAL THAT **ACCIDENTS** INVOLVING TOUCHING THE TIRES HAVE RESULTED IN THE UNINTENDED **DEATHS** OF SIXTEEN CHILDREN.

I'M SORRY, THAT'S **SEVENTEEN** CHILDREN.

OVER THE LAST YEAR.

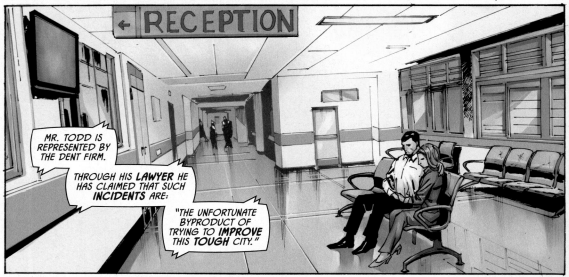

MR. TODD IS REPRESENTED BY THE DENT FIRM.

THROUGH HIS **LAWYER** HE HAS CLAIMED THAT SUCH **INCIDENTS** ARE:

"THE UNFORTUNATE BYPRODUCT OF TRYING TO **IMPROVE** THIS **TOUGH** CITY."

MOTHER, IT'S...GOING TO BE FINE.

OH, **BRUCIE,** YOU NEVER WERE THE WORLD'S GREATEST DETECTIVE.

IN SPORTS, AFTER ANOTHER STELLAR OUTING, KNIGHTS QUARTERBACK CHRIS CAMPBELL WHO REMAINS THE FAVORITE FOR MVP...

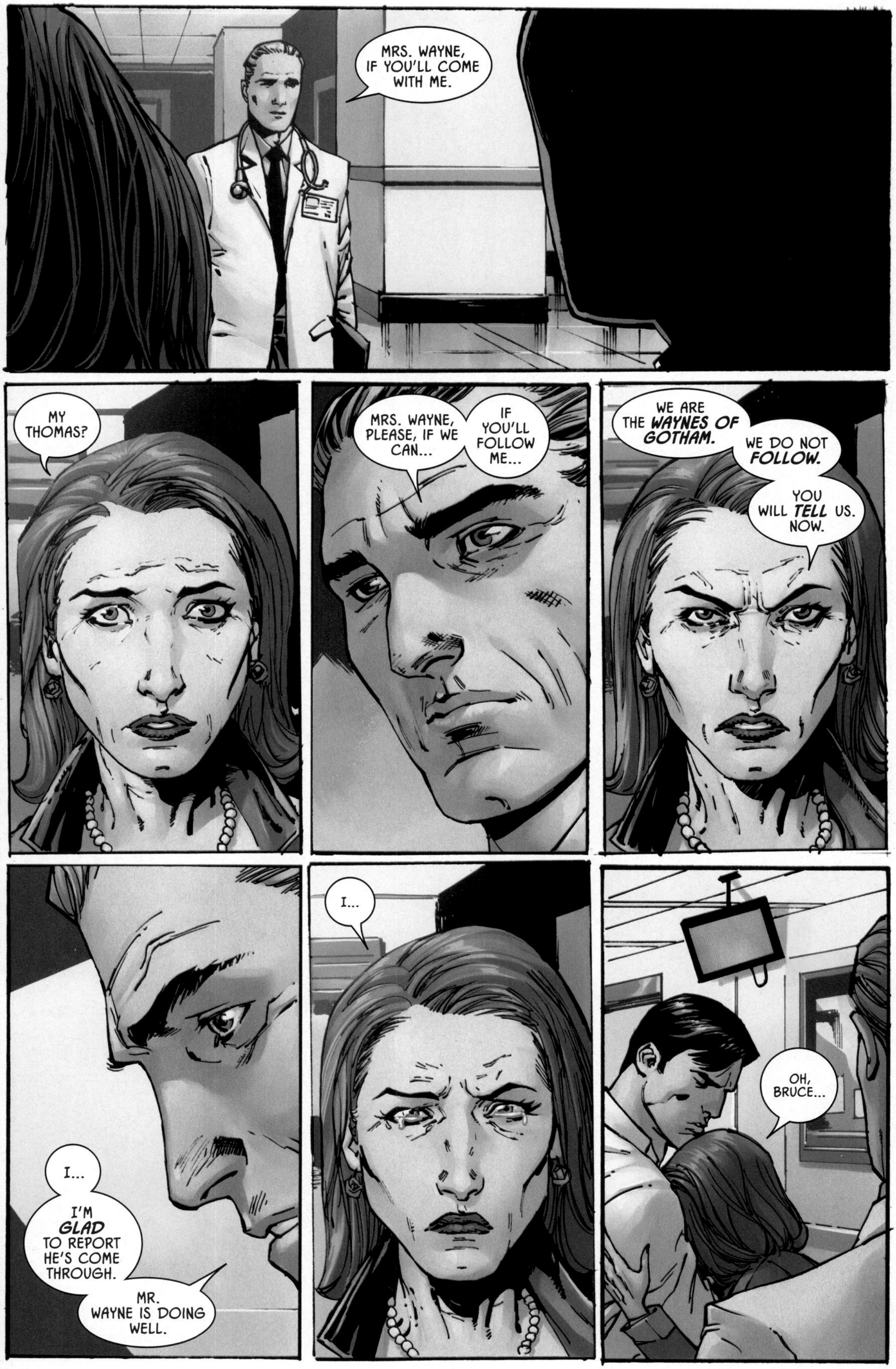
MRS. WAYNE, IF YOU'LL COME WITH ME.
MY THOMAS?
MRS. WAYNE, PLEASE, IF WE CAN...
IF YOU'LL FOLLOW ME...
WE ARE THE WAYNES OF GOTHAM.
WE DO NOT FOLLOW.
YOU WILL TELL US. NOW.
I...
I'M GLAD TO REPORT HE'S COME THROUGH.
MR. WAYNE IS DOING WELL.
I...
OH, BRUCE...

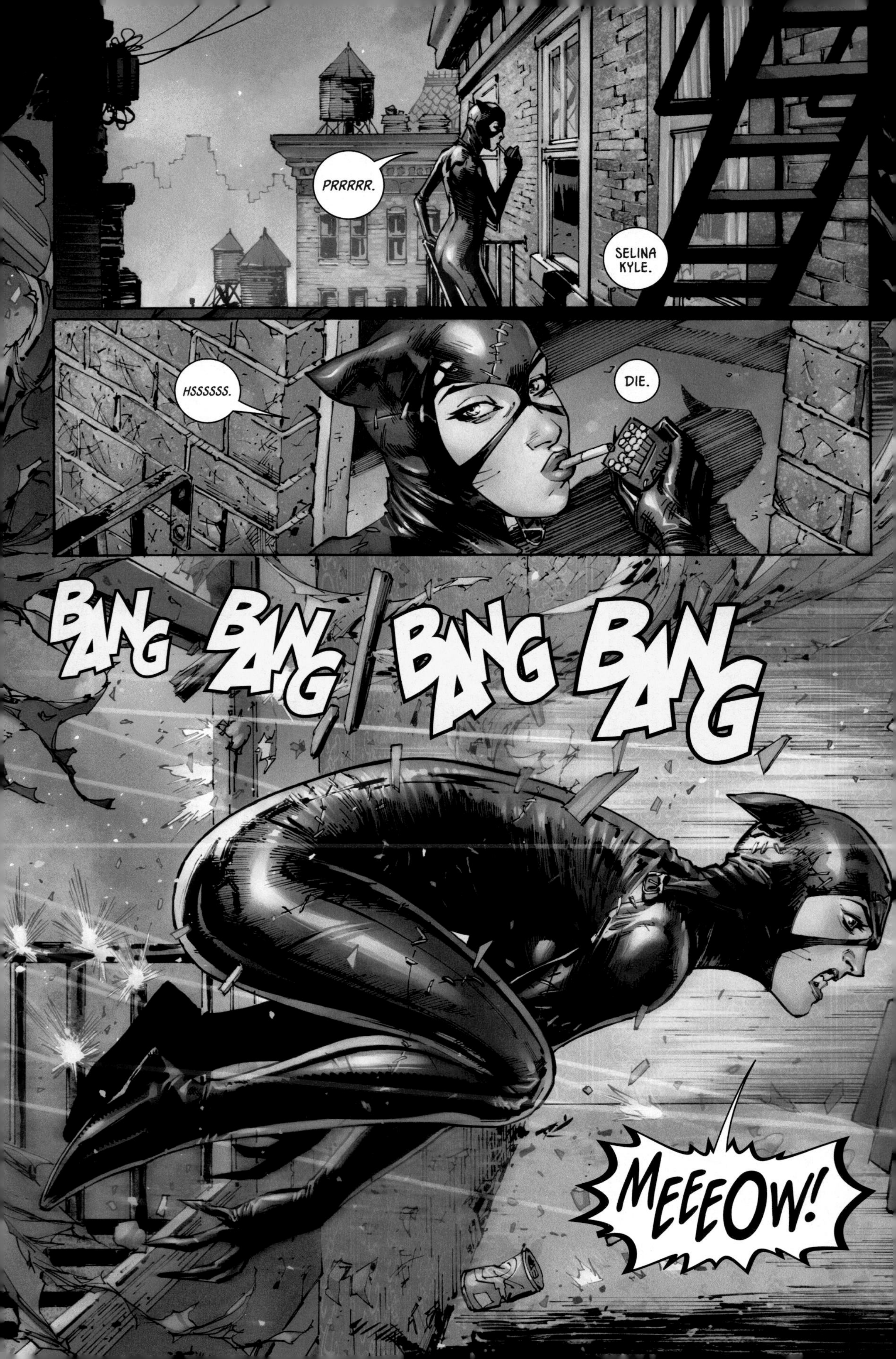
PRRRRR.
SELINA KYLE.
HSSSSSS.
DIE.
BANG BANG BANG BANG
MEEEOW!

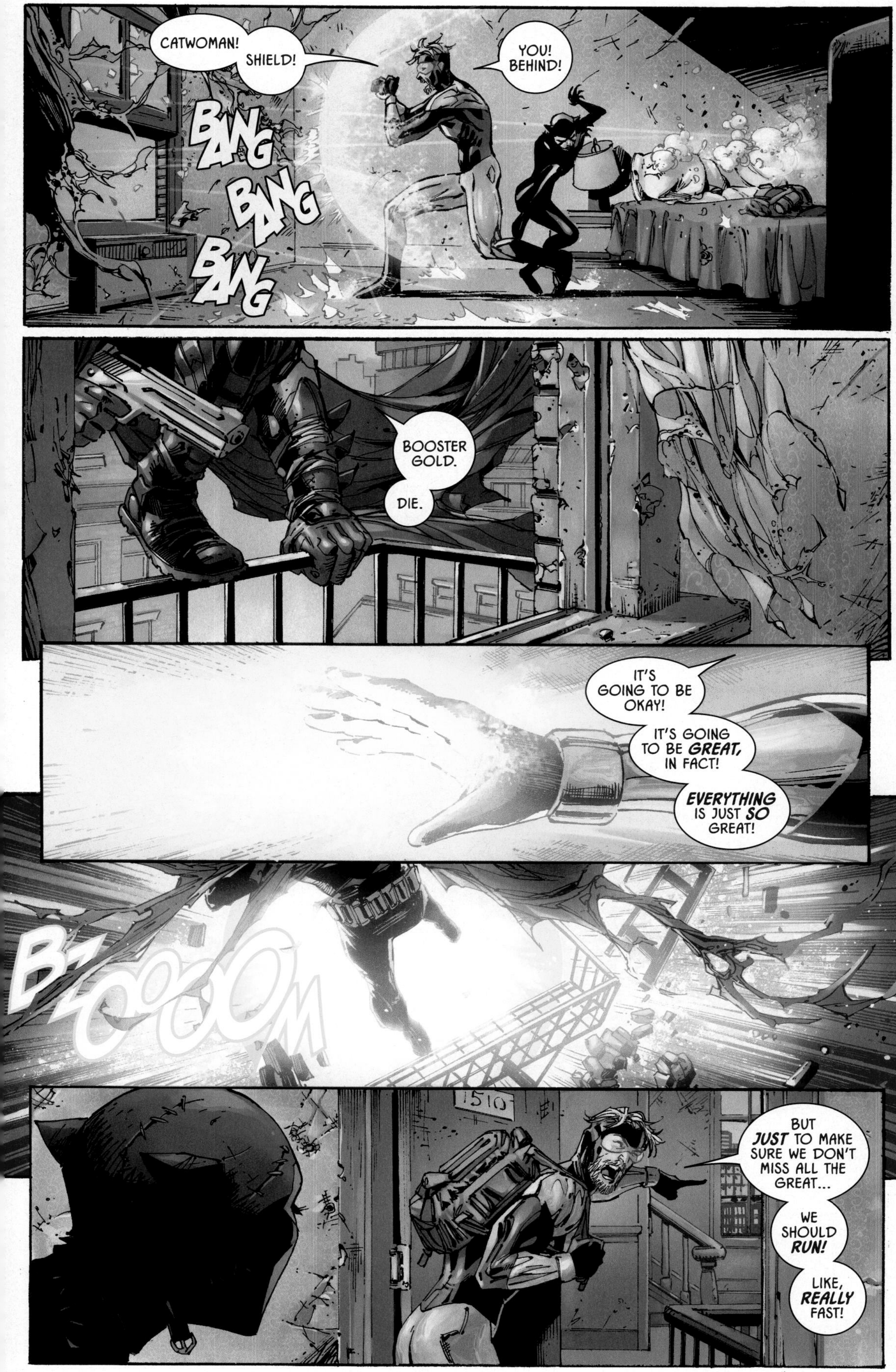
CATWOMAN!
SHIELD!
YOU! BEHIND!
BANG BANG BANG
BOOSTER GOLD.
DIE.
IT'S GOING TO BE OKAY!
IT'S GOING TO BE GREAT, IN FACT!
EVERYTHING IS JUST SO GREAT!
BZOOOOM
1510
BUT JUST TO MAKE SURE WE DON'T MISS ALL THE GREAT...
WE SHOULD RUN!
LIKE, REALLY FAST!

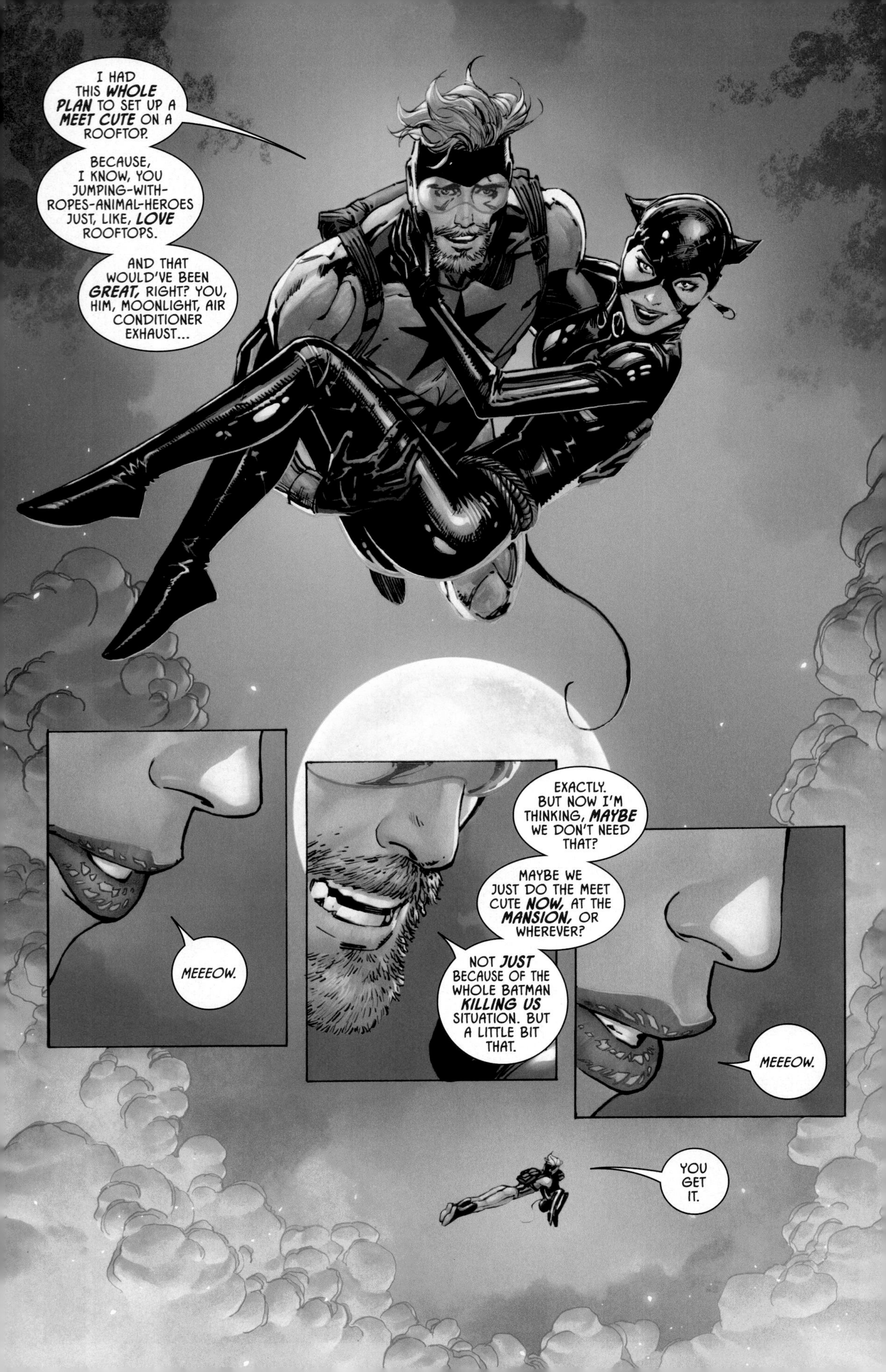
I HAD THIS WHOLE PLAN TO SET UP A MEET CUTE ON A ROOFTOP.
BECAUSE, I KNOW, YOU JUMPING-WITH-ROPES-ANIMAL-HEROES JUST, LIKE, LOVE ROOFTOPS.
AND THAT WOULD'VE BEEN GREAT, RIGHT? YOU, HIM, MOONLIGHT, AIR CONDITIONER EXHAUST...
MEEEOW.
EXACTLY. BUT NOW I'M THINKING, MAYBE WE DON'T NEED THAT?
MAYBE WE JUST DO THE MEET CUTE NOW, AT THE MANSION, OR WHEREVER?
NOT JUST BECAUSE OF THE WHOLE BATMAN KILLING US SITUATION. BUT A LITTLE BIT THAT.
MEEEOW.
YOU GET IT.

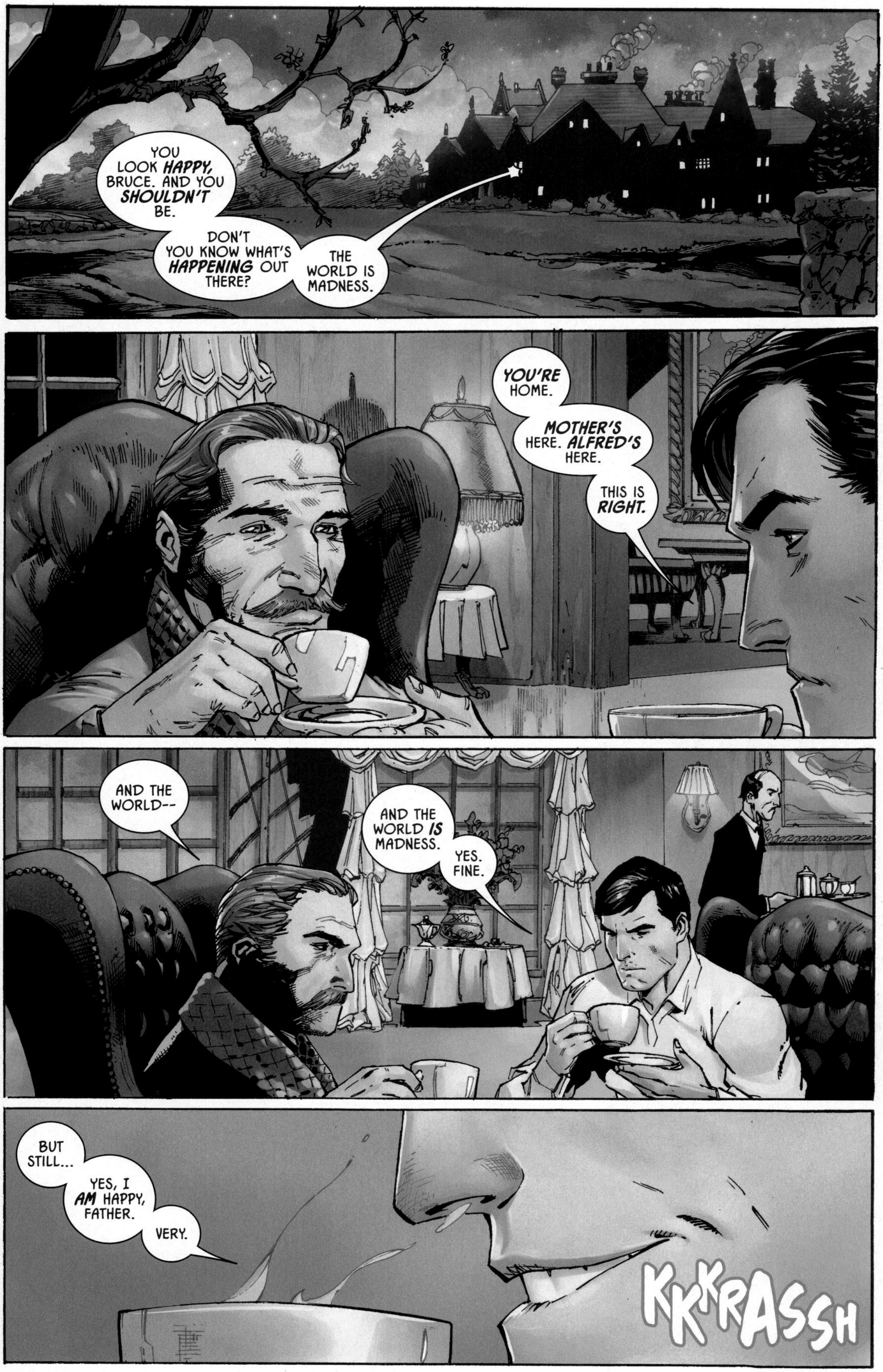
YOU LOOK HAPPY, BRUCE. AND YOU SHOULDN'T BE.
DON'T YOU KNOW WHAT'S HAPPENING OUT THERE?
THE WORLD IS MADNESS.
YOU'RE HOME.
MOTHER'S HERE. ALFRED'S HERE.
THIS IS RIGHT.
AND THE WORLD--
AND THE WORLD IS MADNESS.
YES. FINE.
BUT STILL...
YES, I AM HAPPY, FATHER.
VERY.
KKKRASSH

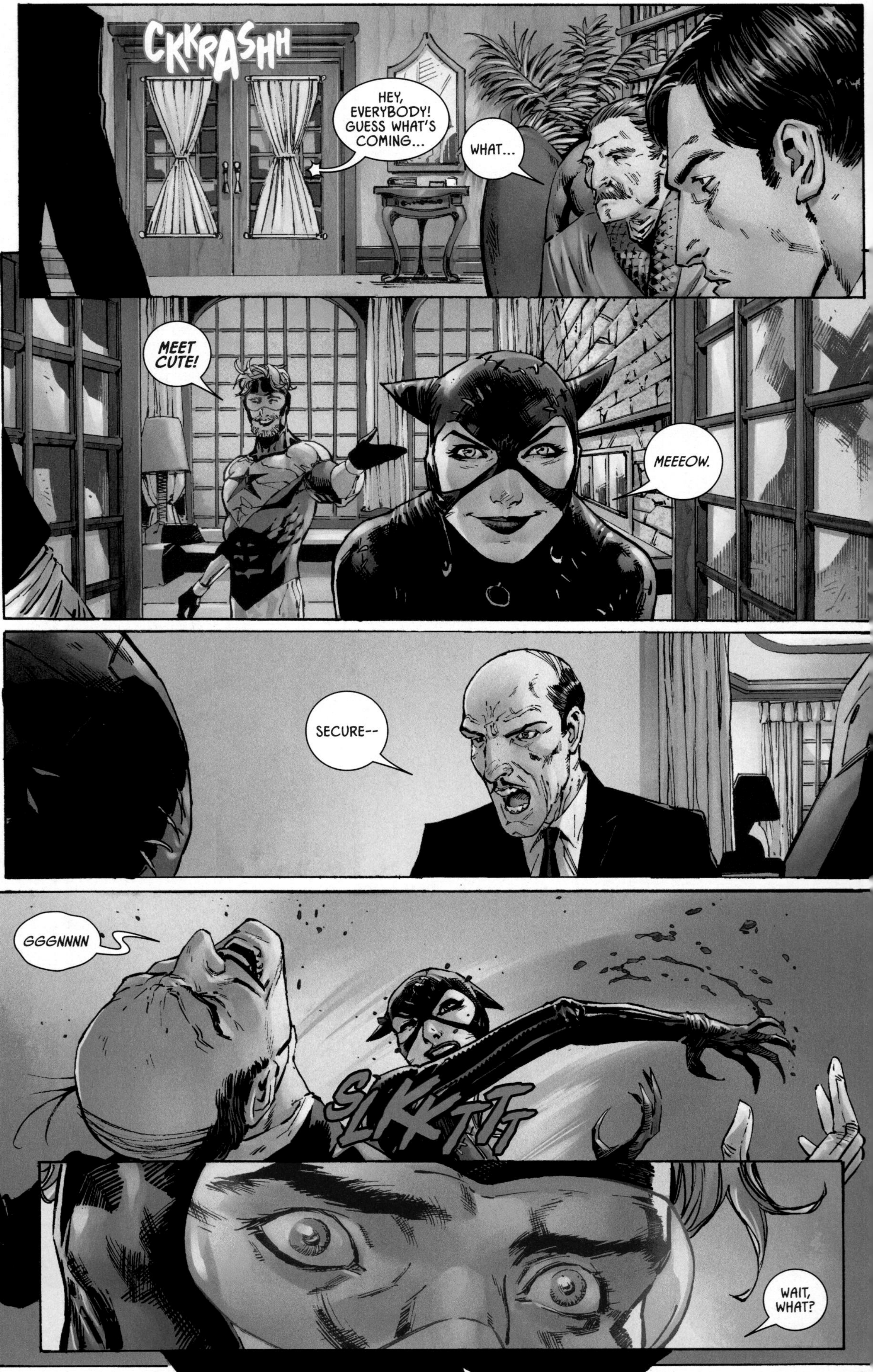
CKKRASHH
HEY, EVERYBODY! GUESS WHAT'S COMING...
WHAT...
MEET CUTE!
MEEEOW.
SECURE--
GGGNNNN
SLKTTT
WAIT, WHAT?

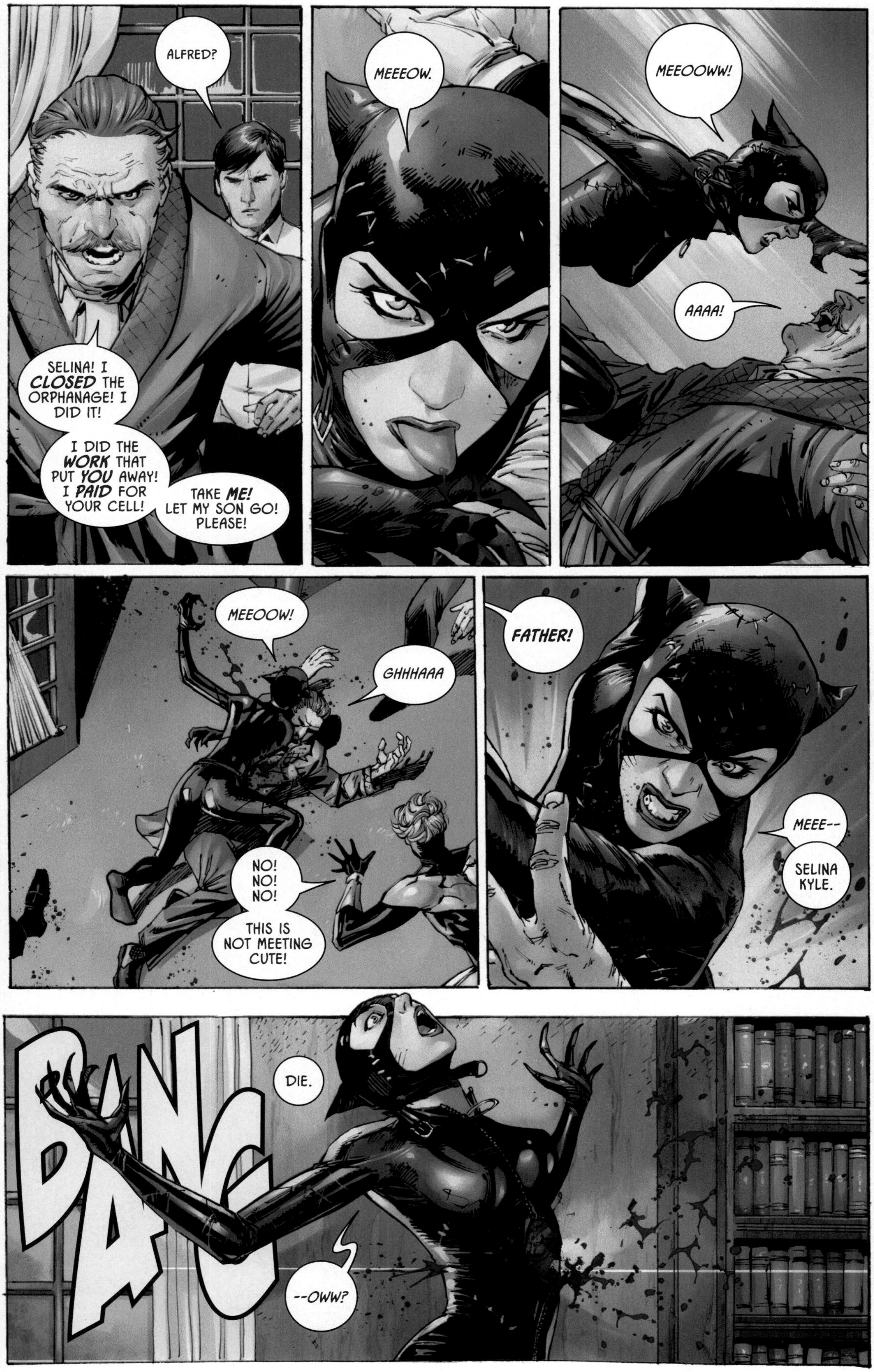
ALFRED?
SELINA! I CLOSED THE ORPHANAGE! I DID IT!
I DID THE WORK THAT PUT YOU AWAY! I PAID FOR YOUR CELL!
TAKE ME! LET MY SON GO! PLEASE!
MEEEOW.
MEEOOWW!
AAAA!
MEEOOW!
GHHHAAA
NO! NO! NO!
THIS IS NOT MEETING CUTE!
FATHER!
MEEE--
SELINA KYLE.
BANG
DIE.
--OWW?

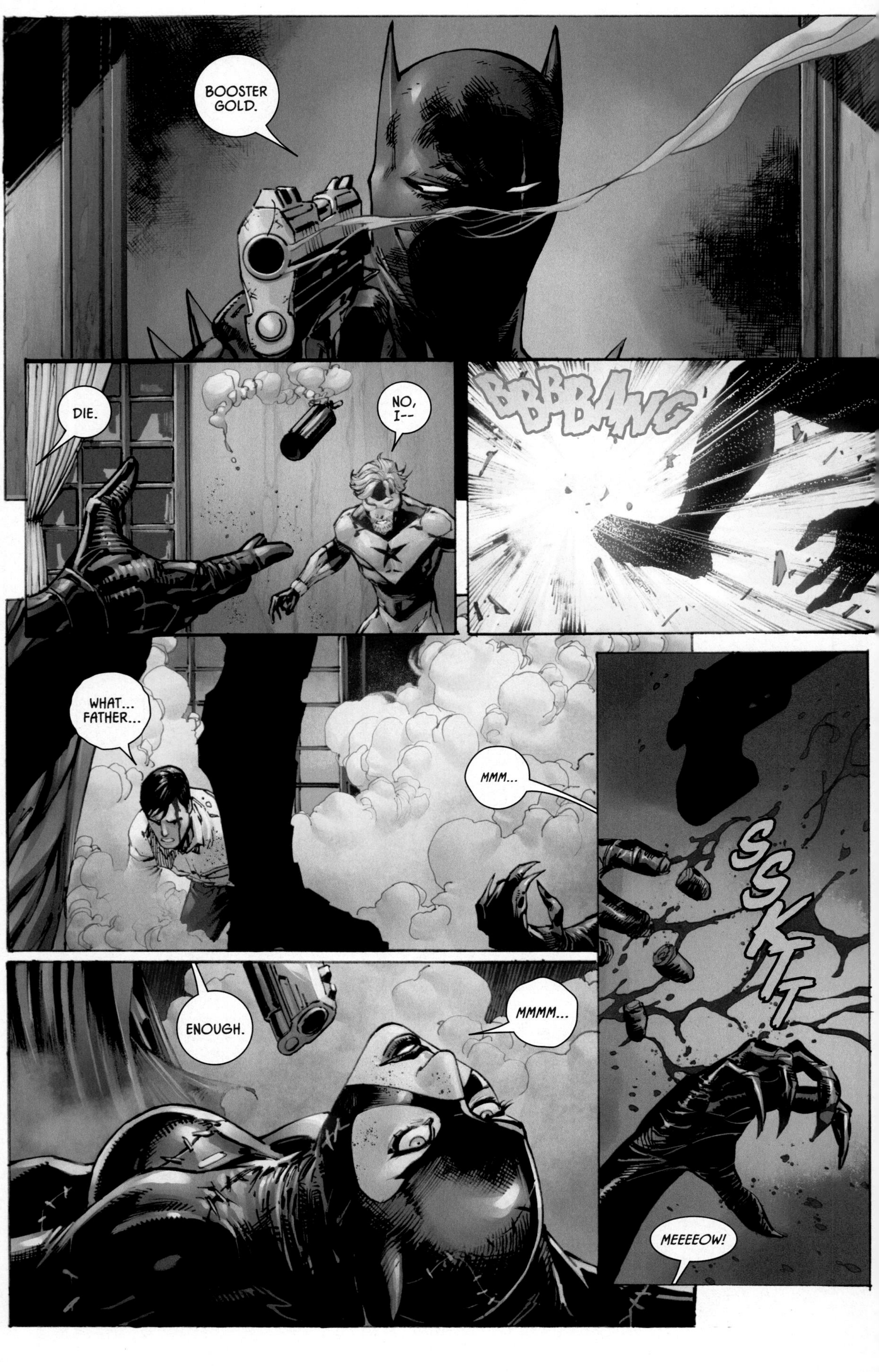
BOOSTER GOLD.
DIE.
NO, I--
BBBBANG
WHAT... FATHER...
MMM...
SSKTT
ENOUGH.
MMMM...
MEEEEOW!

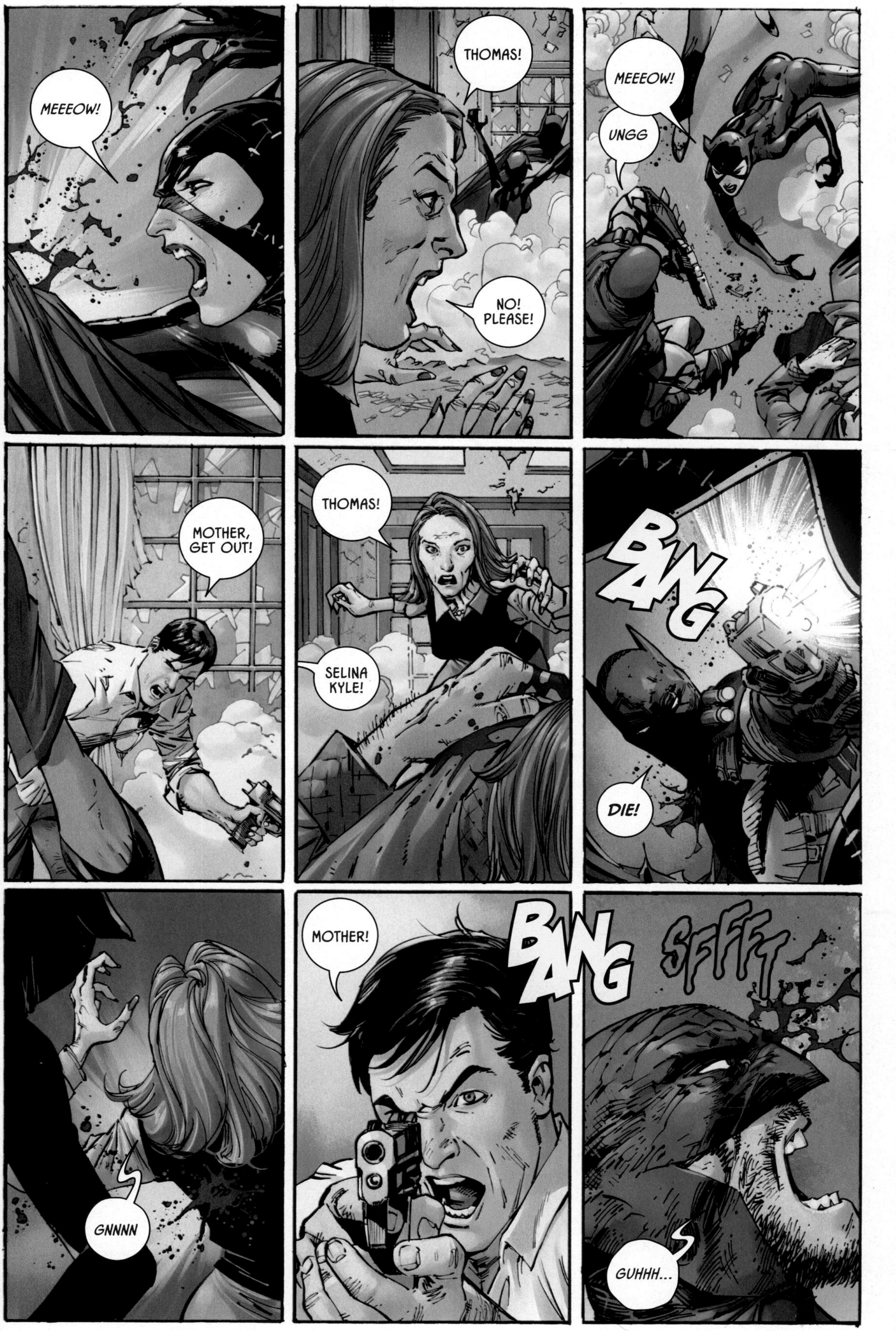
MEEEOW!
THOMAS!
NO! PLEASE!
MEEEOW!
UNGG
MOTHER, GET OUT!
THOMAS!
SELINA KYLE!
BANG
DIE!
GNNNN
MOTHER!
BANG
SFFFT
GUHHH...

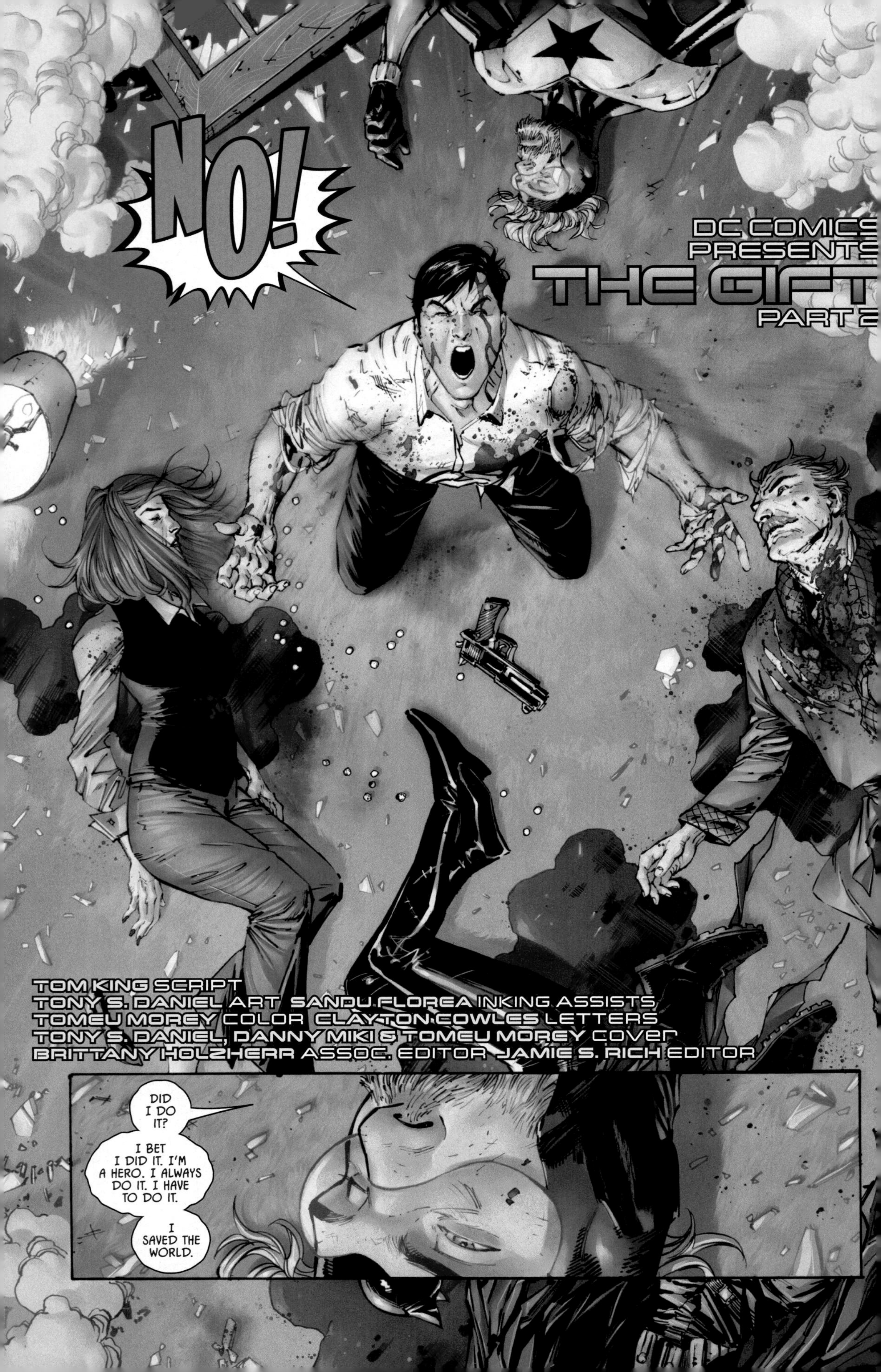

NO!
DC COMICS PRESENTS
THE GIFT
PART 2
TOM KING SCRIPT
TONY S. DANIEL ART SANDU FLOREA INKING ASSISTS
TOMEU MOREY COLOR CLAYTON COWLES LETTERS
TONY S. DANIEL, DANNY MIKI & TOMEU MOREY COVER
BRITTANY HOLZHERR ASSOC. EDITOR JAMIE S. RICH EDITOR
DID I DO IT?
I BET I DID IT. I'M A HERO. I ALWAYS DO IT. I HAVE TO DO IT.
I SAVED THE WORLD.

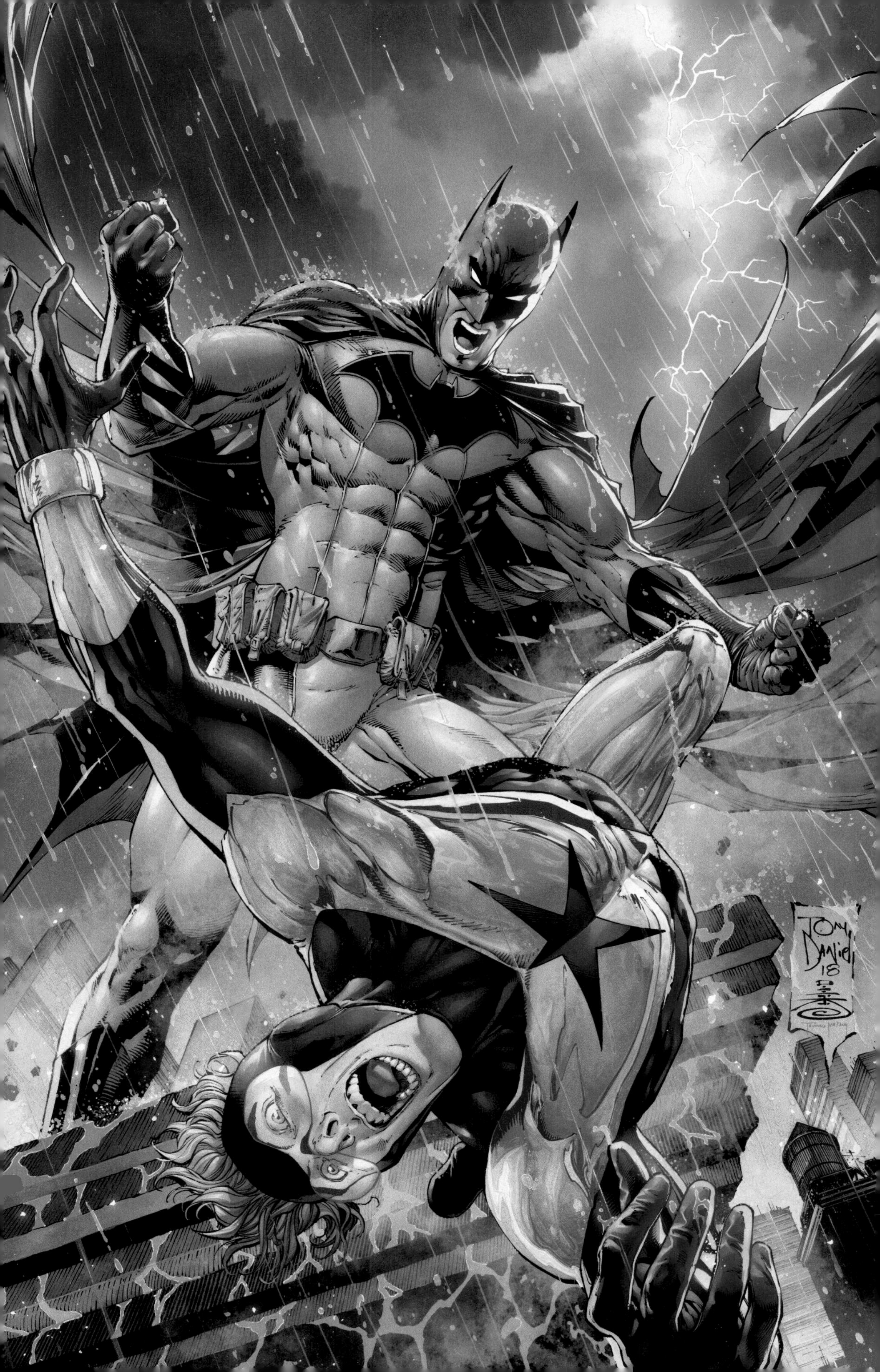

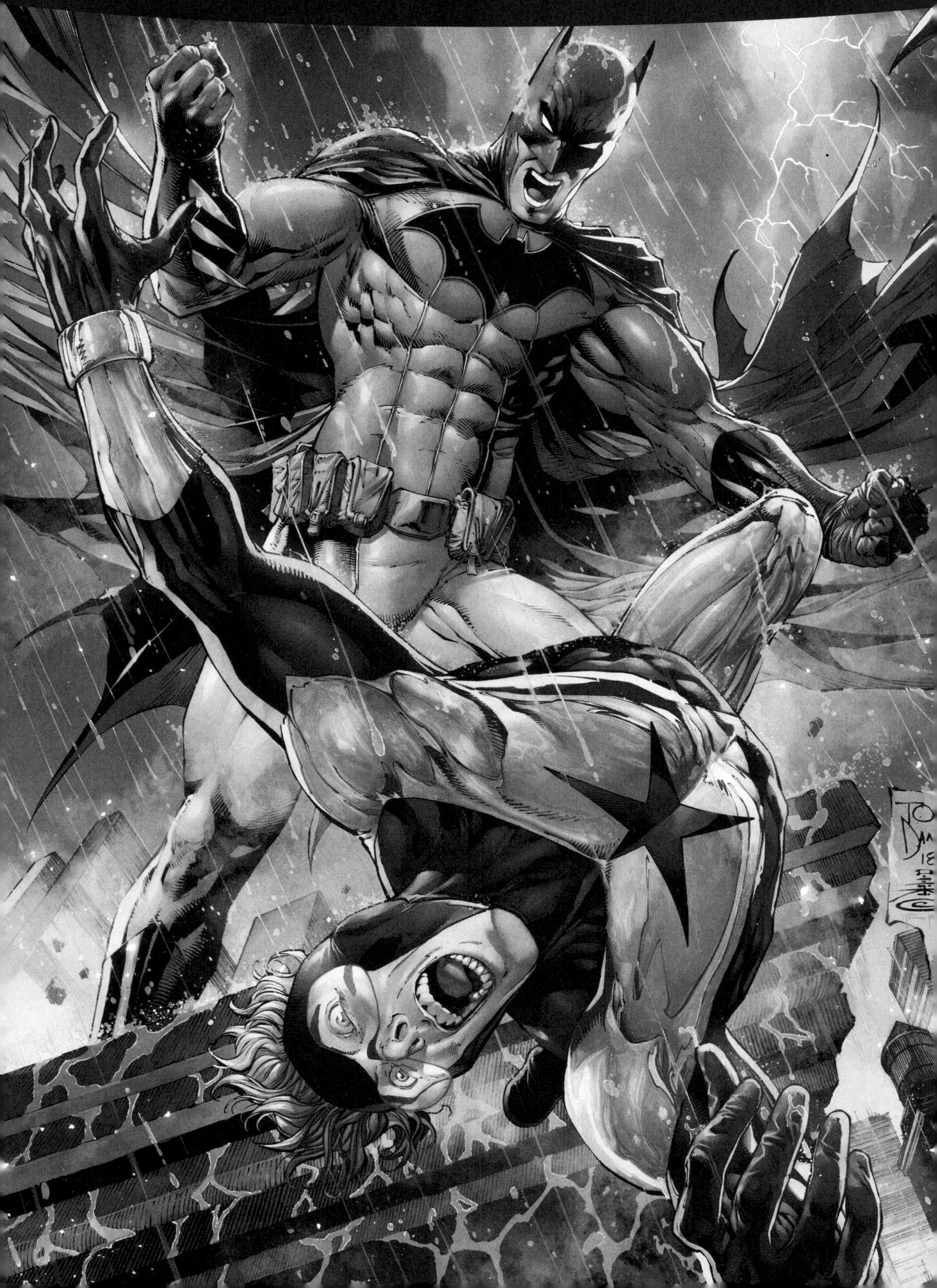

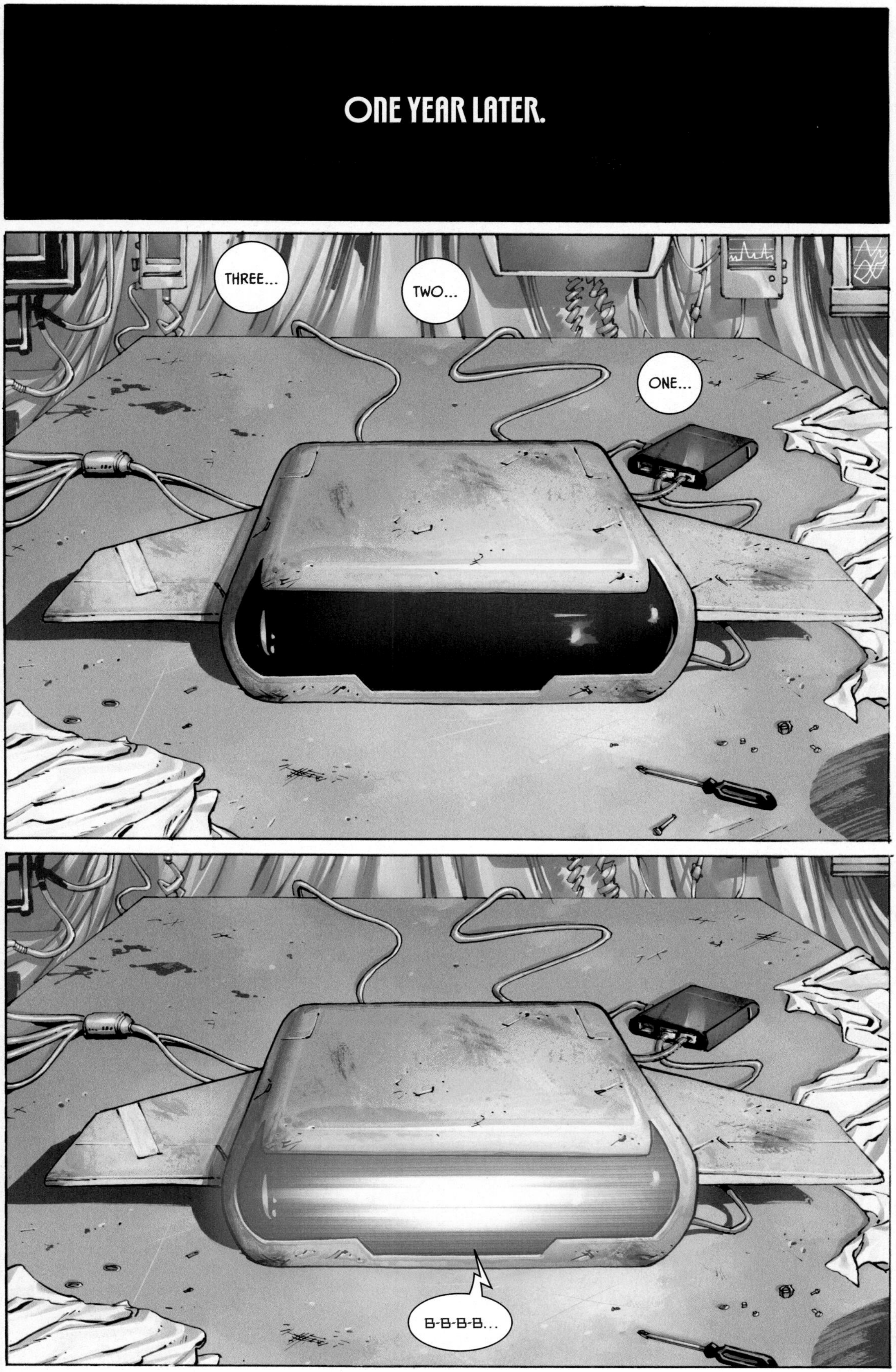
ONE YEAR LATER.
THREE...
TWO...
ONE...
B-B-B-B...

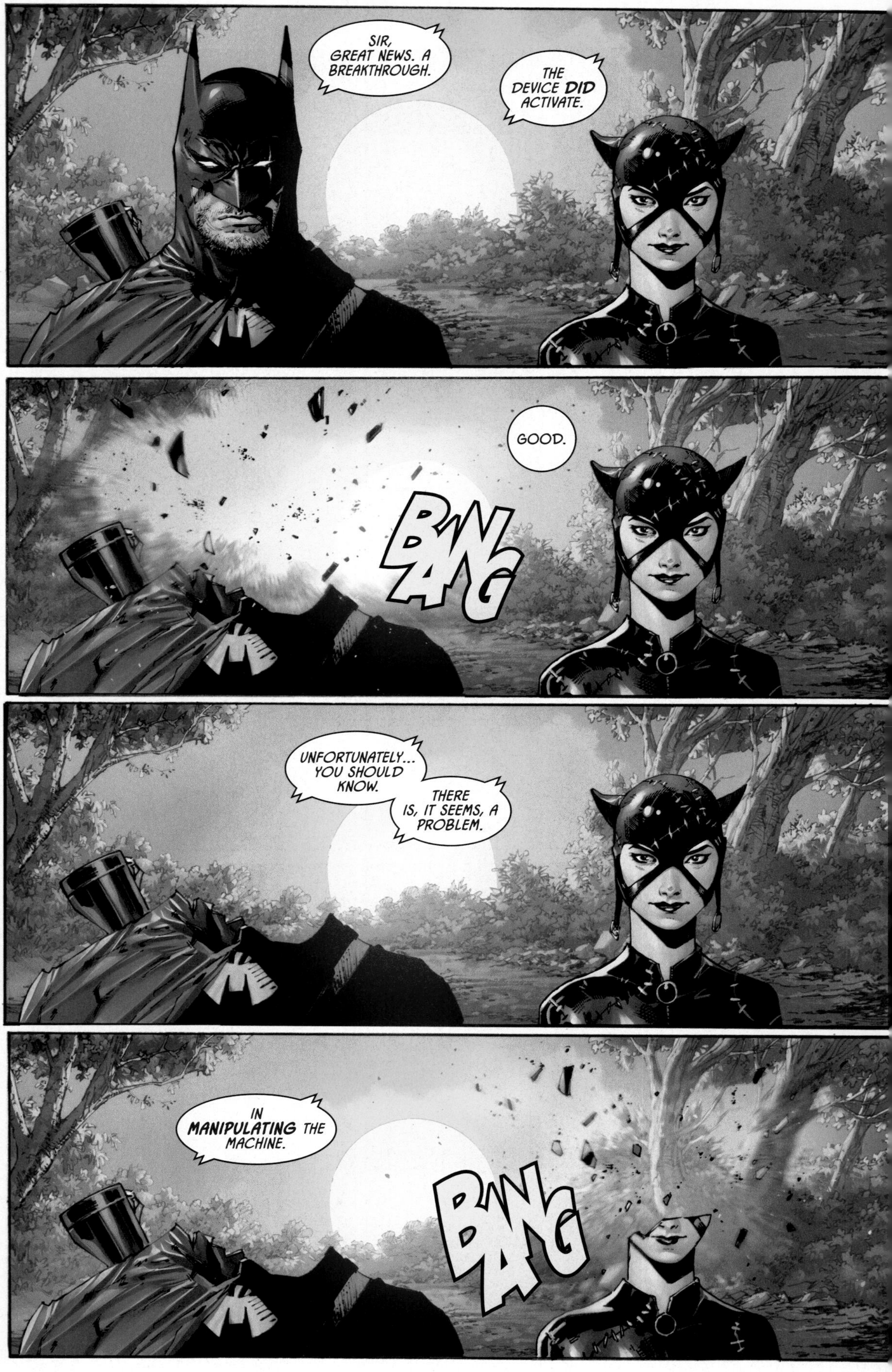
SIR, GREAT NEWS. A BREAKTHROUGH.
THE DEVICE DID ACTIVATE.
GOOD.
BANG
UNFORTUNATELY... YOU SHOULD KNOW.
THERE IS, IT SEEMS, A PROBLEM.
IN MANIPULATING THE MACHINE.
BANG

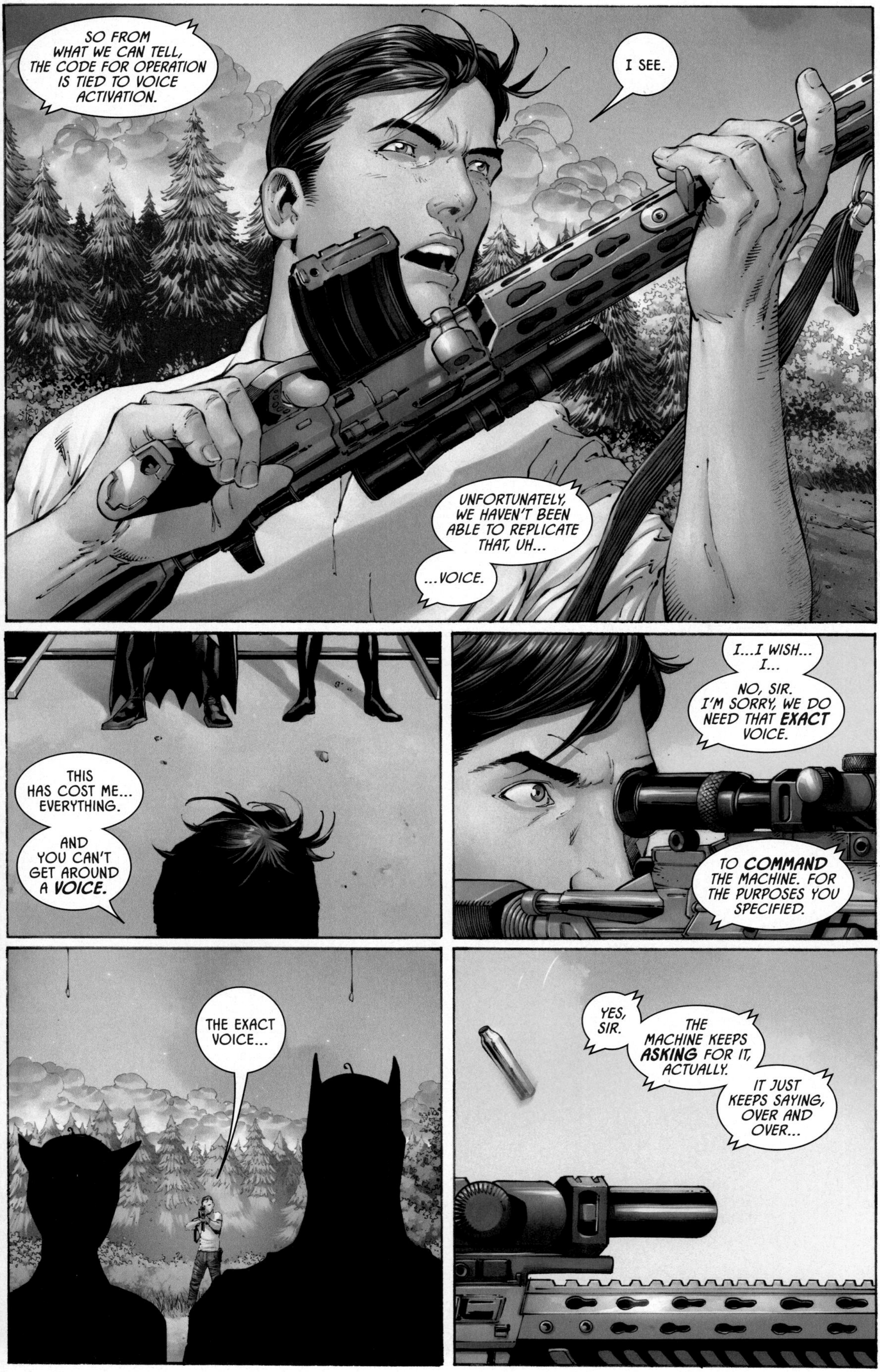
SO FROM WHAT WE CAN TELL, THE CODE FOR OPERATION IS TIED TO VOICE ACTIVATION.
I SEE.
UNFORTUNATELY, WE HAVEN'T BEEN ABLE TO REPLICATE THAT, UH...
...VOICE.
THIS HAS COST ME... EVERYTHING.
AND YOU CAN'T GET AROUND A **VOICE.**
I...I WISH... I...
NO, SIR. I'M SORRY, WE DO NEED THAT **EXACT** VOICE.
TO **COMMAND** THE MACHINE. FOR THE PURPOSES YOU SPECIFIED.
THE EXACT VOICE...
YES, SIR.
THE MACHINE KEEPS **ASKING** FOR IT, ACTUALLY.
IT JUST KEEPS SAYING, OVER AND OVER...

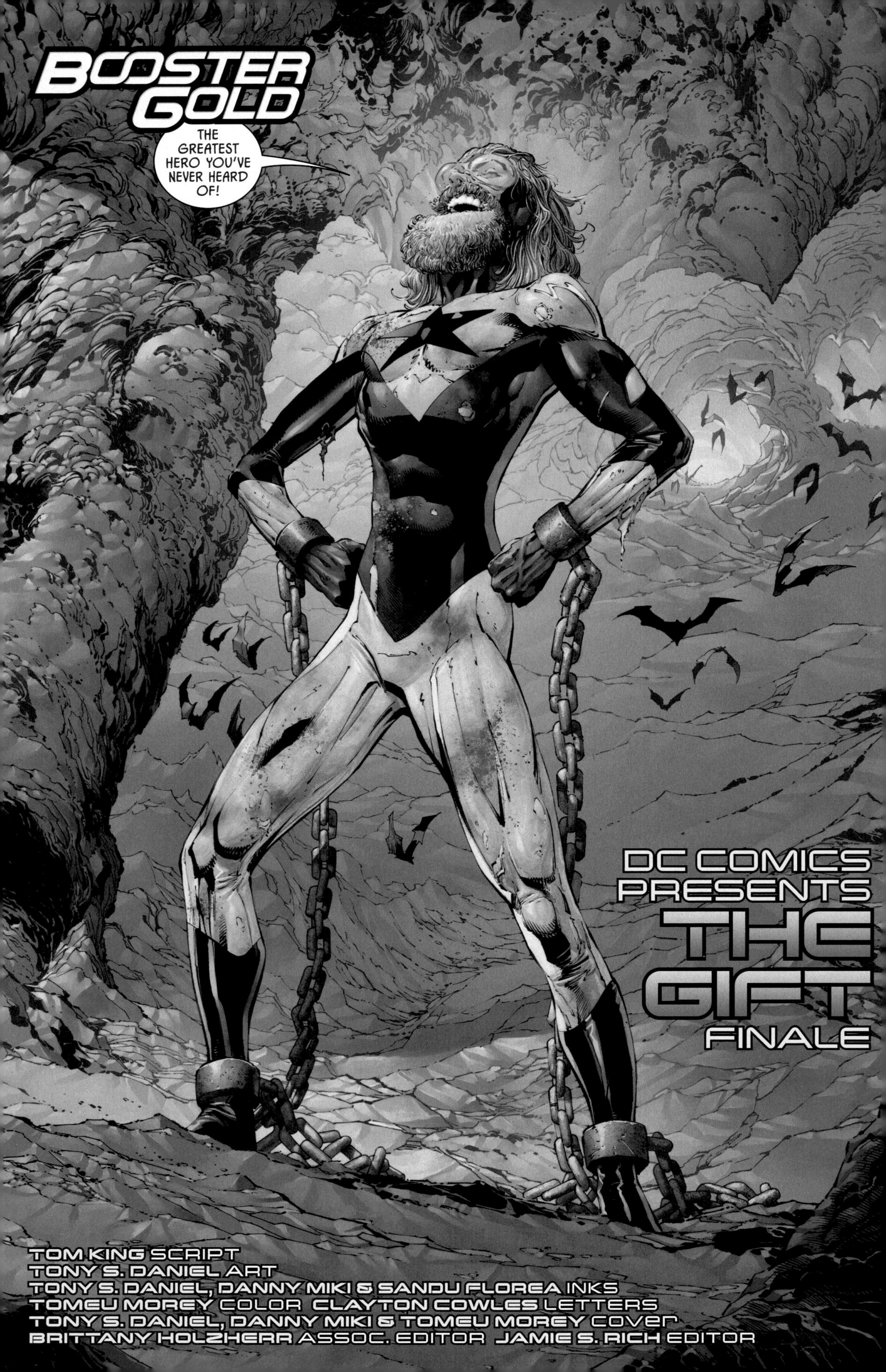
BOOSTER GOLD
THE GREATEST HERO YOU'VE NEVER HEARD OF!
DC COMICS PRESENTS
THE GIFT
FINALE
TOM KING SCRIPT
TONY S. DANIEL ART
TONY S. DANIEL, DANNY MIKI & SANDU FLOREA INKS
TOMEU MOREY COLOR CLAYTON COWLES LETTERS
TONY S. DANIEL, DANNY MIKI & TOMEU MOREY COVER
BRITTANY HOLZHERR ASSOC. EDITOR JAMIE S. RICH EDITOR

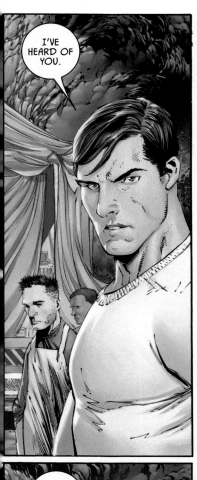

I'VE HEARD OF YOU.

YOU'RE THE MAN WHO BROUGHT THE BATMAN AND THE CATWOMAN INTO MY HOME.

YOU'RE THE MAN WHO WATCHED AS THEY SLAUGHTERED MY PARENTS.

YOU'RE THE MAN WHO BROKE EVERYTHING.

BOOSTER GOLD!

THE GREATEST HERO ONLY ONE PERSON HAS HEARD OF!

GET HIM OUT OF THE CHAINS.

CLEAN HIM. DRESS HIM.

BRING HIM TO THE LIBRARY.

YES, SIR.

HEY, WANT TO HEAR A STORY?

IT'S GOT A REALLY HAPPY ENDING.

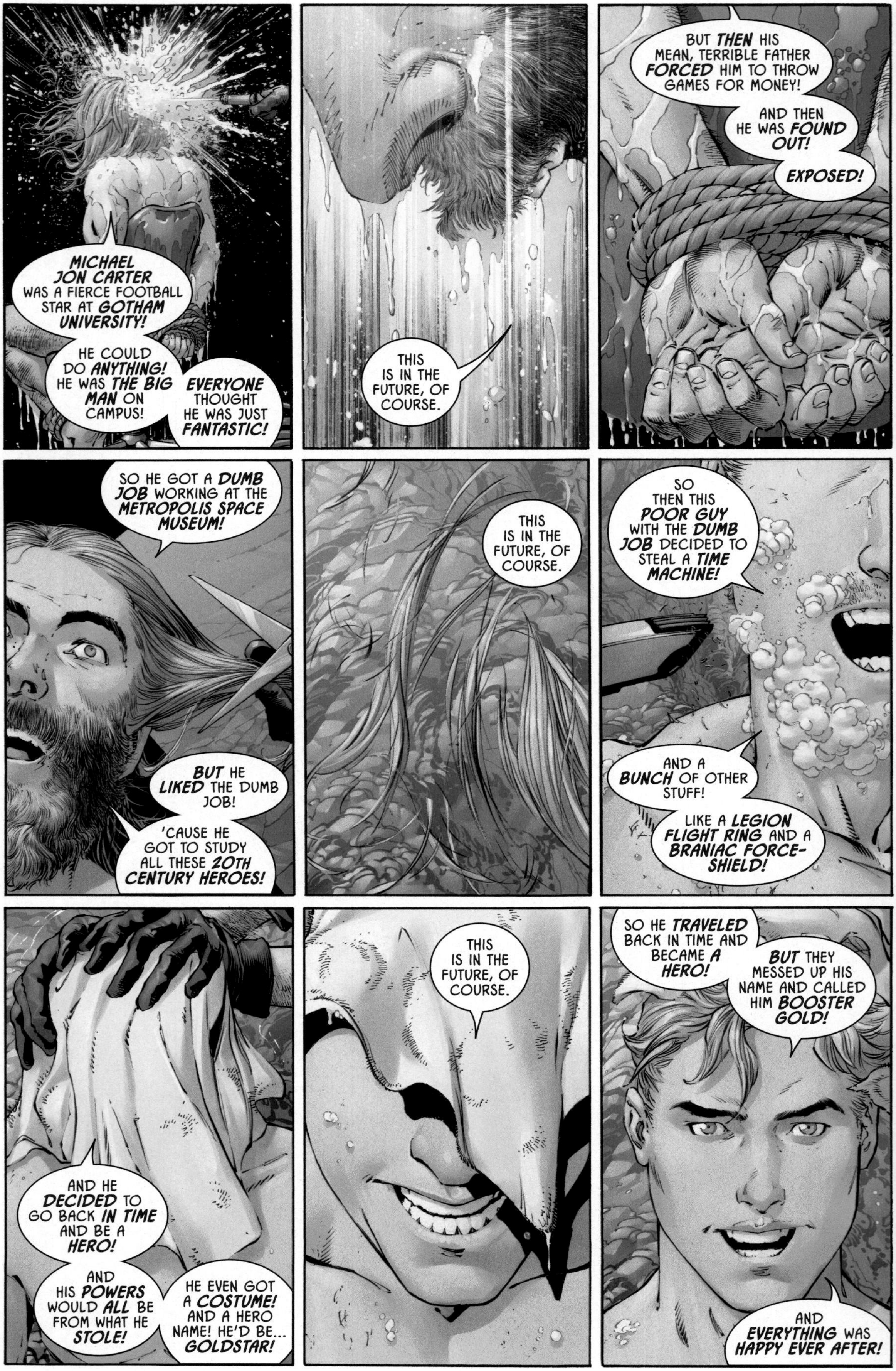
MICHAEL JON CARTER WAS A FIERCE FOOTBALL STAR AT GOTHAM UNIVERSITY!
HE COULD DO ANYTHING! HE WAS THE BIG MAN ON CAMPUS!
EVERYONE THOUGHT HE WAS JUST FANTASTIC!
THIS IS IN THE FUTURE, OF COURSE.
BUT THEN HIS MEAN, TERRIBLE FATHER FORCED HIM TO THROW GAMES FOR MONEY!
AND THEN HE WAS FOUND OUT!
EXPOSED!
SO HE GOT A DUMB JOB WORKING AT THE METROPOLIS SPACE MUSEUM!
BUT HE LIKED THE DUMB JOB!
'CAUSE HE GOT TO STUDY ALL THESE 20TH CENTURY HEROES!
THIS IS IN THE FUTURE, OF COURSE.
SO THEN THIS POOR GUY WITH THE DUMB JOB DECIDED TO STEAL A TIME MACHINE!
AND A BUNCH OF OTHER STUFF!
LIKE A LEGION FLIGHT RING AND A BRANIAC FORCE-SHIELD!
AND HE DECIDED TO GO BACK IN TIME AND BE A HERO!
AND HIS POWERS WOULD ALL BE FROM WHAT HE STOLE!
HE EVEN GOT A COSTUME! AND A HERO NAME! HE'D BE... GOLDSTAR!
THIS IS IN THE FUTURE, OF COURSE.
SO HE TRAVELED BACK IN TIME AND BECAME A HERO!
BUT THEY MESSED UP HIS NAME AND CALLED HIM BOOSTER GOLD!
AND EVERYTHING WAS HAPPY EVER AFTER!

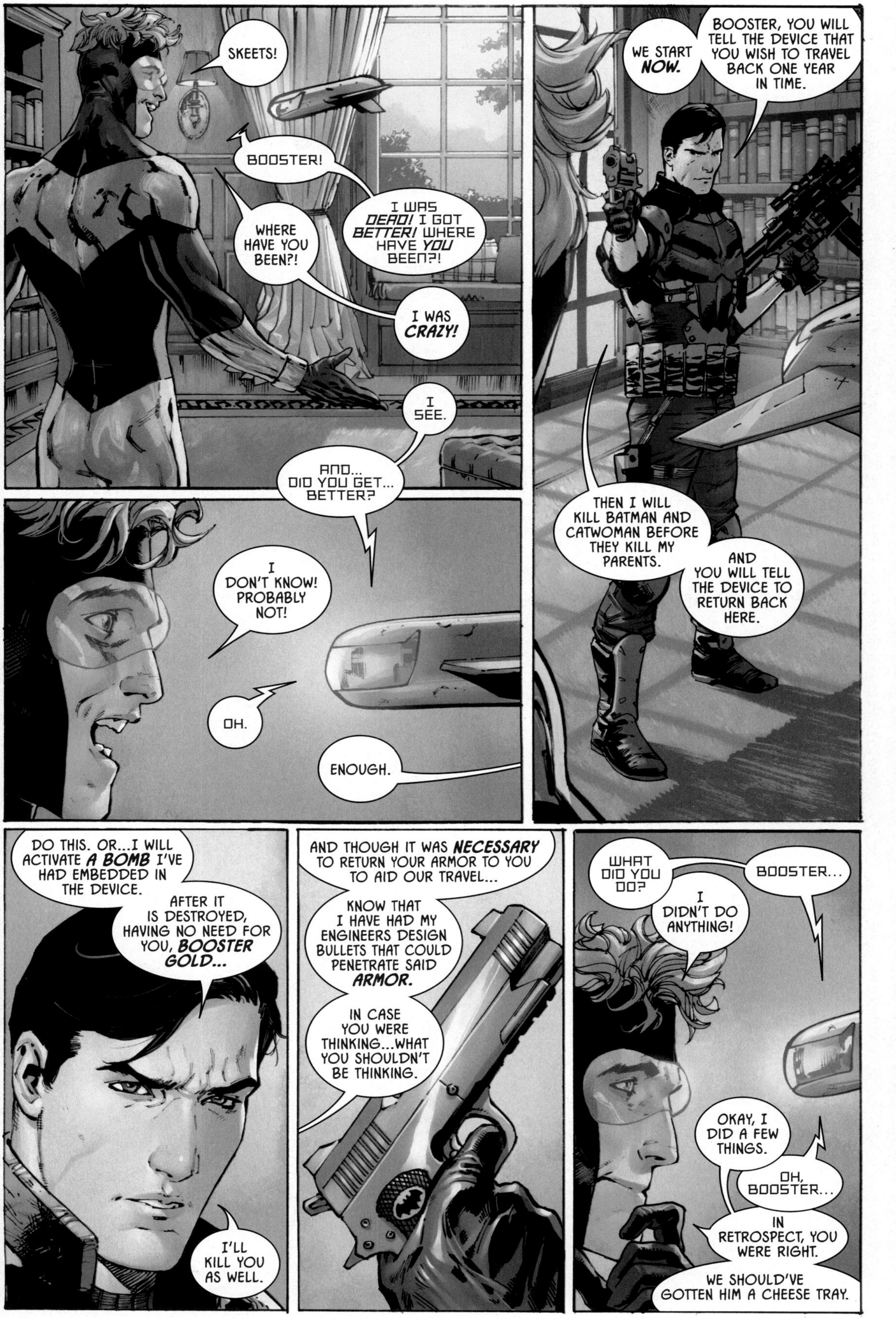
SKEETS!
BOOSTER!
WHERE HAVE YOU BEEN?!
I WAS *DEAD!* I GOT *BETTER!* WHERE HAVE *YOU* BEEN?!
I WAS *CRAZY!*
I SEE.
AND... DID YOU GET... BETTER?
WE START *NOW.*
BOOSTER, YOU WILL TELL THE DEVICE THAT YOU WISH TO TRAVEL BACK ONE YEAR IN TIME.
THEN I WILL KILL BATMAN AND CATWOMAN BEFORE THEY KILL MY PARENTS.
AND YOU WILL TELL THE DEVICE TO RETURN BACK HERE.
I DON'T KNOW! PROBABLY NOT!
OH.
ENOUGH.
DO THIS. OR...I WILL ACTIVATE *A BOMB* I'VE HAD EMBEDDED IN THE DEVICE.
AFTER IT IS DESTROYED, HAVING NO NEED FOR YOU, *BOOSTER GOLD...*
I'LL KILL YOU AS WELL.
AND THOUGH IT WAS *NECESSARY* TO RETURN YOUR ARMOR TO YOU TO AID OUR TRAVEL...
KNOW THAT I HAVE HAD MY ENGINEERS DESIGN BULLETS THAT COULD PENETRATE SAID *ARMOR.*
IN CASE YOU WERE THINKING...WHAT YOU SHOULDN'T BE THINKING.
WHAT DID YOU DO?
BOOSTER...
I DIDN'T DO ANYTHING!
OKAY, I DID A FEW THINGS.
OH, BOOSTER...
IN RETROSPECT, YOU WERE RIGHT.
WE SHOULD'VE GOTTEN HIM A CHEESE TRAY.

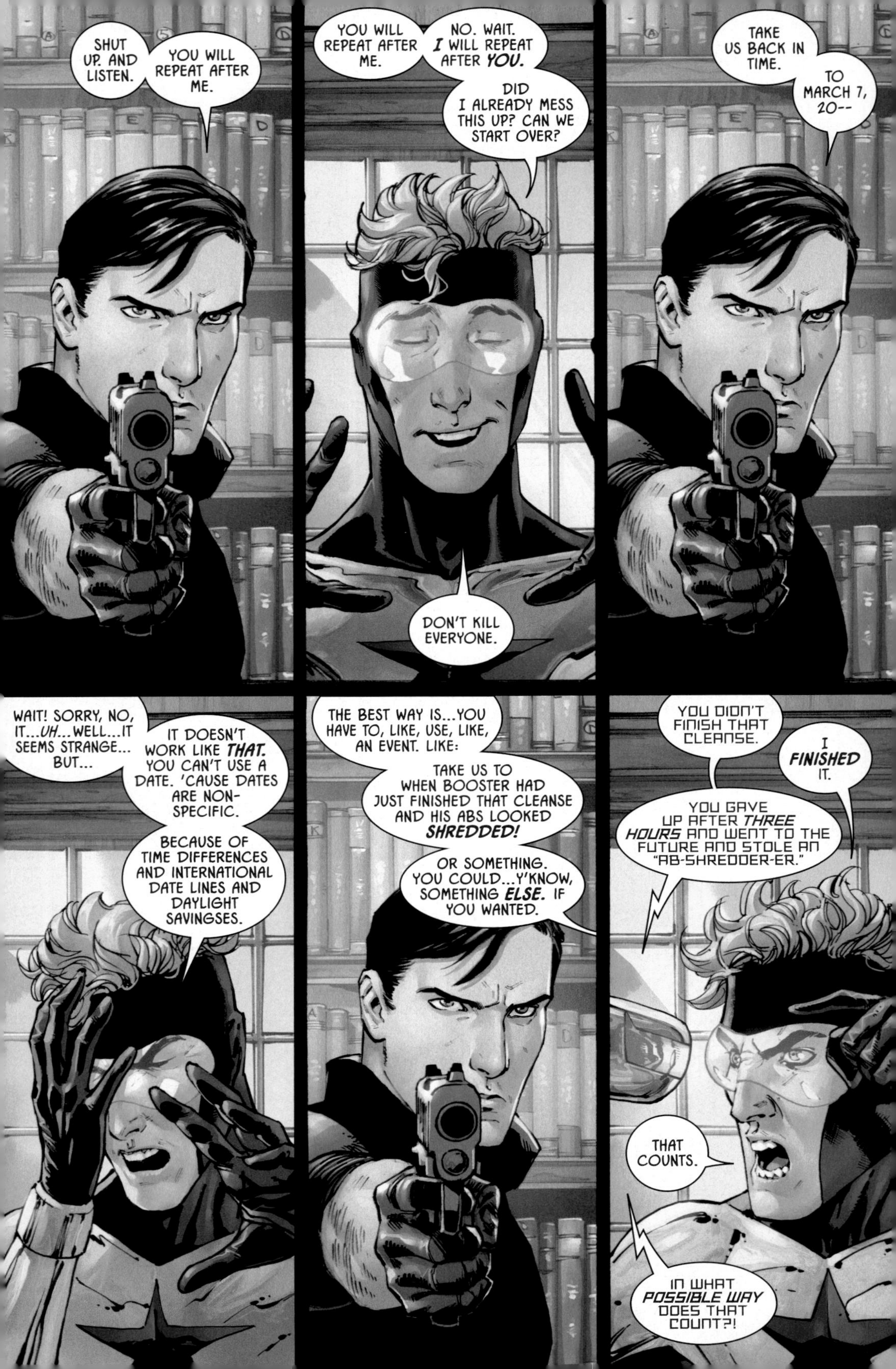
SHUT UP. AND LISTEN.
YOU WILL REPEAT AFTER ME.
YOU WILL REPEAT AFTER ME.
NO. WAIT. I WILL REPEAT AFTER YOU.
DID I ALREADY MESS THIS UP? CAN WE START OVER?
DON'T KILL EVERYONE.
TAKE US BACK IN TIME.
TO MARCH 7, 20--
WAIT! SORRY, NO, IT...UH...WELL...IT SEEMS STRANGE... BUT...
IT DOESN'T WORK LIKE THAT. YOU CAN'T USE A DATE. 'CAUSE DATES ARE NON-SPECIFIC.
BECAUSE OF TIME DIFFERENCES AND INTERNATIONAL DATE LINES AND DAYLIGHT SAVINGSES.
THE BEST WAY IS...YOU HAVE TO, LIKE, USE, LIKE, AN EVENT. LIKE:
TAKE US TO WHEN BOOSTER HAD JUST FINISHED THAT CLEANSE AND HIS ABS LOOKED SHREDDED!
OR SOMETHING. YOU COULD...Y'KNOW, SOMETHING ELSE. IF YOU WANTED.
YOU DIDN'T FINISH THAT CLEANSE.
I FINISHED IT.
YOU GAVE UP AFTER THREE HOURS AND WENT TO THE FUTURE AND STOLE AN "AB-SHREDDER-ER."
THAT COUNTS.
IN WHAT POSSIBLE WAY DOES THAT COUNT?!

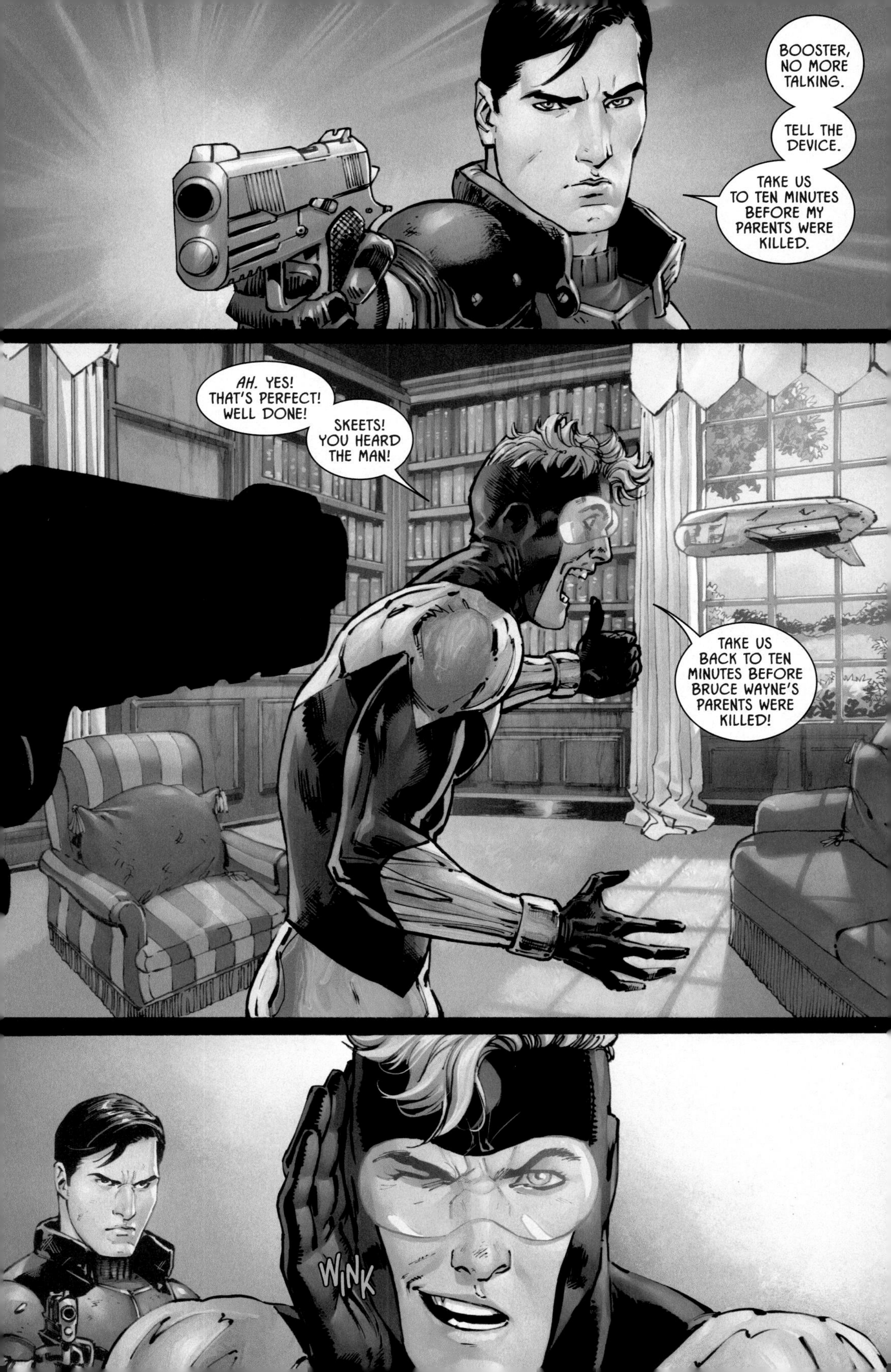

BOOSTER, NO MORE TALKING.
TELL THE DEVICE.
TAKE US TO TEN MINUTES BEFORE MY PARENTS WERE KILLED.
AH. YES! THAT'S PERFECT! WELL DONE!
SKEETS! YOU HEARD THE MAN!
TAKE US BACK TO TEN MINUTES BEFORE BRUCE WAYNE'S PARENTS WERE KILLED!
WINK

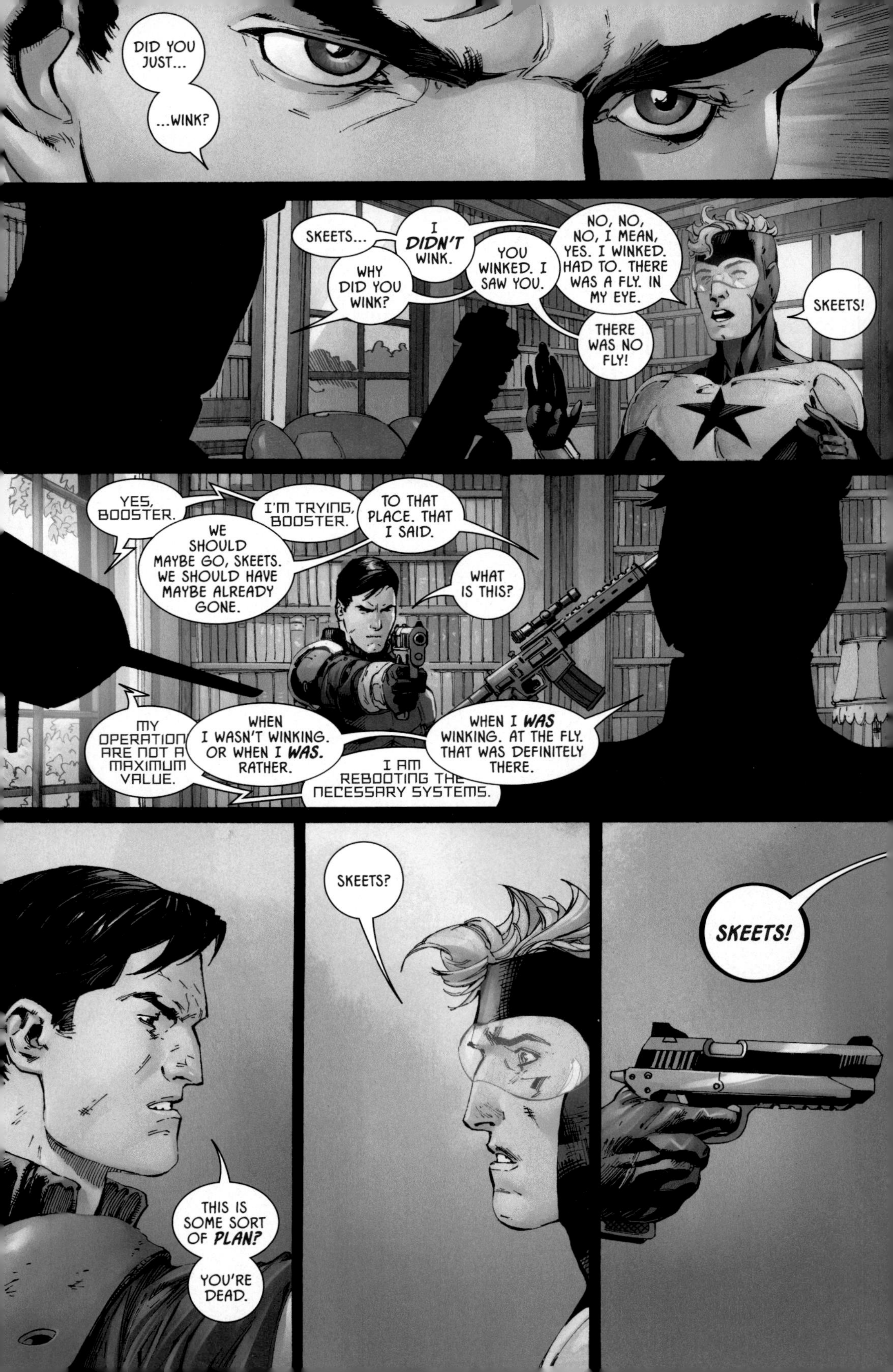
DID YOU JUST...
...WINK?
SKEETS...
I DIDN'T WINK.
WHY DID YOU WINK?
YOU WINKED. I SAW YOU.
NO, NO, NO, I MEAN, YES. I WINKED. HAD TO. THERE WAS A FLY. IN MY EYE.
THERE WAS NO FLY!
SKEETS!
YES, BOOSTER.
I'M TRYING, BOOSTER.
WE SHOULD MAYBE GO, SKEETS. WE SHOULD HAVE MAYBE ALREADY GONE.
TO THAT PLACE. THAT I SAID.
WHAT IS THIS?
MY OPERATION ARE NOT A MAXIMUM VALUE.
WHEN I WASN'T WINKING. OR WHEN I WAS. RATHER.
WHEN I WAS WINKING. AT THE FLY. THAT WAS DEFINITELY THERE.
I AM REBOOTING THE NECESSARY SYSTEMS.
SKEETS?
SKEETS!
THIS IS SOME SORT OF PLAN?
YOU'RE DEAD.

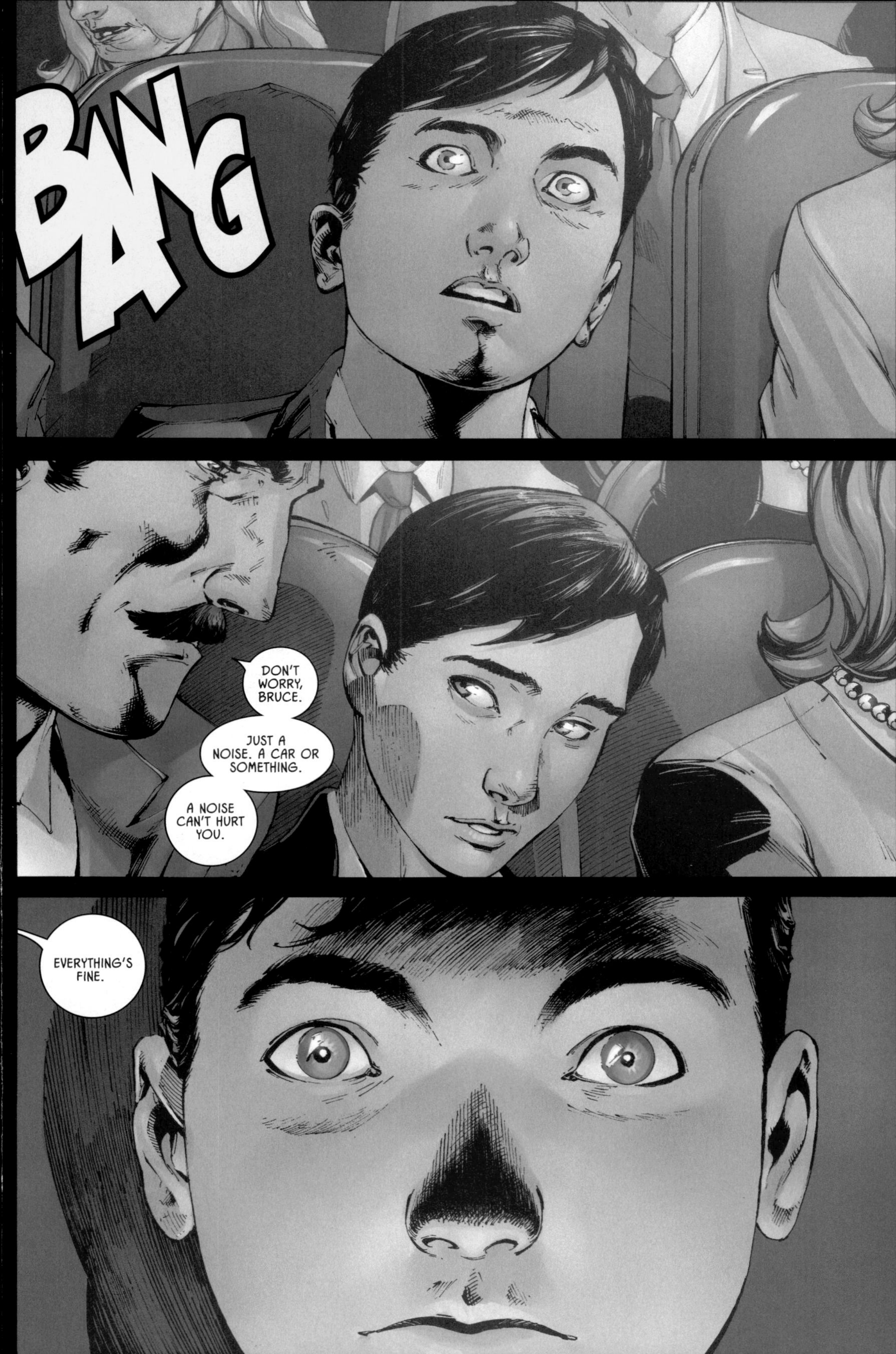
BANG
DON'T WORRY, BRUCE.
JUST A NOISE. A CAR OR SOMETHING.
A NOISE CAN'T HURT YOU.
EVERYTHING'S FINE.

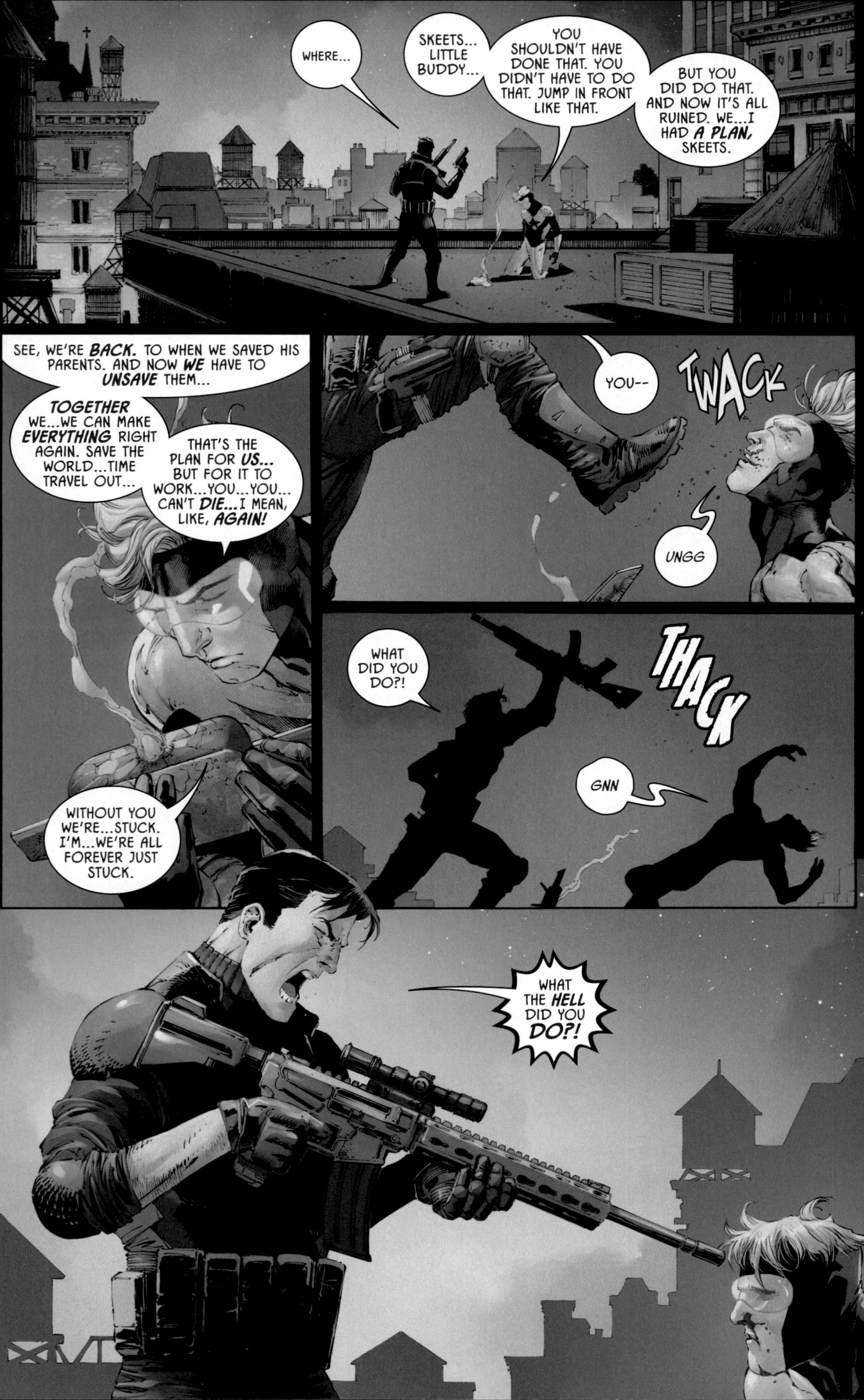
WHERE...
SKEETS... LITTLE BUDDY...
YOU SHOULDN'T HAVE DONE THAT. YOU DIDN'T HAVE TO DO THAT. JUMP IN FRONT LIKE THAT.
BUT YOU DID DO THAT. AND NOW IT'S ALL RUINED. WE...I HAD A PLAN, SKEETS.
SEE, WE'RE BACK. TO WHEN WE SAVED HIS PARENTS. AND NOW WE HAVE TO UNSAVE THEM...
TOGETHER WE...WE CAN MAKE EVERYTHING RIGHT AGAIN. SAVE THE WORLD...TIME TRAVEL OUT...
THAT'S THE PLAN FOR US... BUT FOR IT TO WORK...YOU...YOU... CAN'T DIE...I MEAN, LIKE, AGAIN!
WITHOUT YOU WE'RE...STUCK. I'M...WE'RE ALL FOREVER JUST STUCK.
YOU--
TWACK
UNGG
WHAT DID YOU DO?!
THACK
GNN
WHAT THE HELL DID YOU DO?!

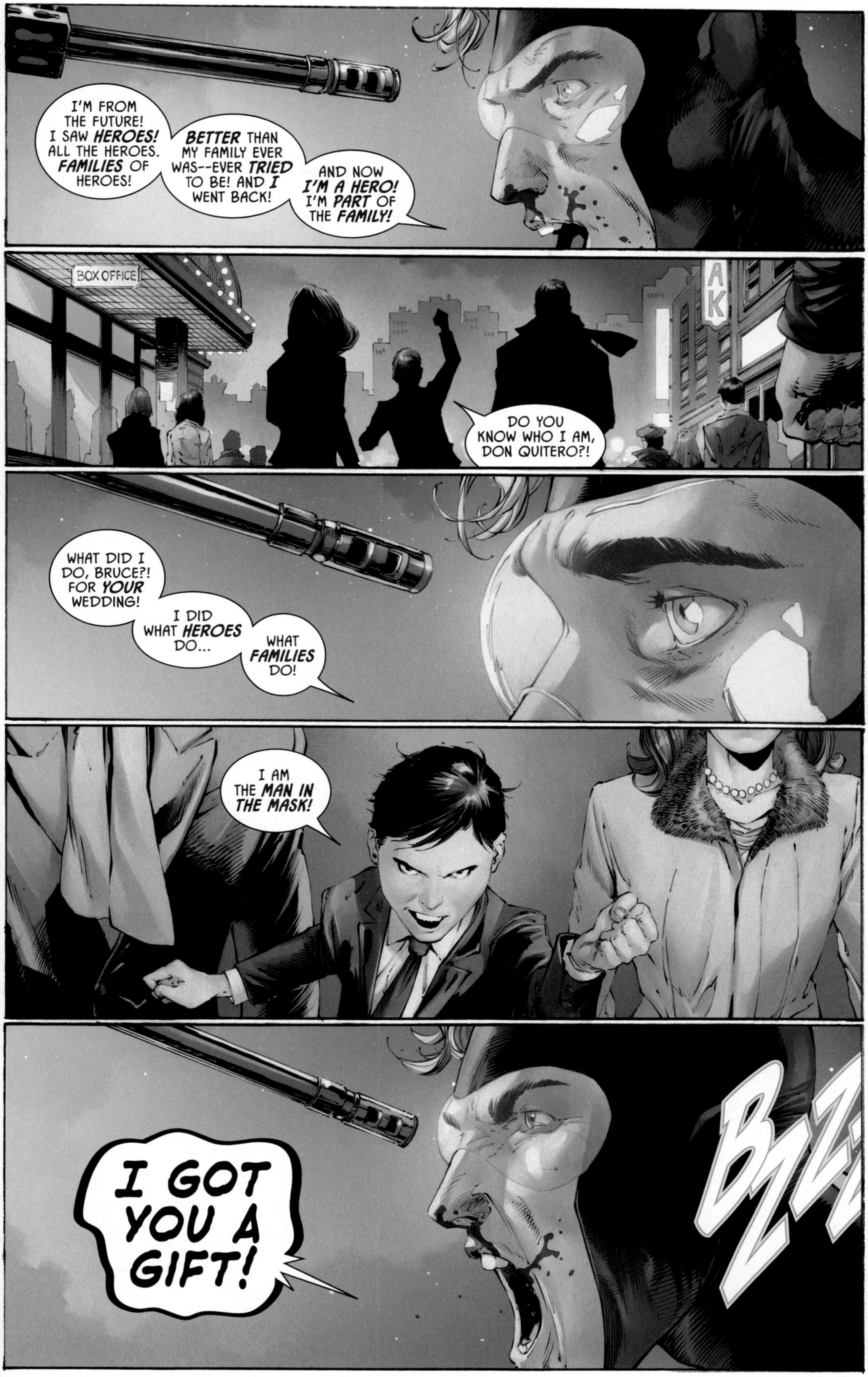
I'M FROM THE FUTURE! I SAW HEROES! ALL THE HEROES. FAMILIES OF HEROES!
BETTER THAN MY FAMILY EVER WAS--EVER TRIED TO BE! AND I WENT BACK!
AND NOW I'M A HERO! I'M PART OF THE FAMILY!
BOX OFFICE
AK
DO YOU KNOW WHO I AM, DON QUITERO?!
WHAT DID I DO, BRUCE?! FOR YOUR WEDDING!
I DID WHAT HEROES DO...
WHAT FAMILIES DO!
I AM THE MAN IN THE MASK!
I GOT YOU A GIFT!
BZZ

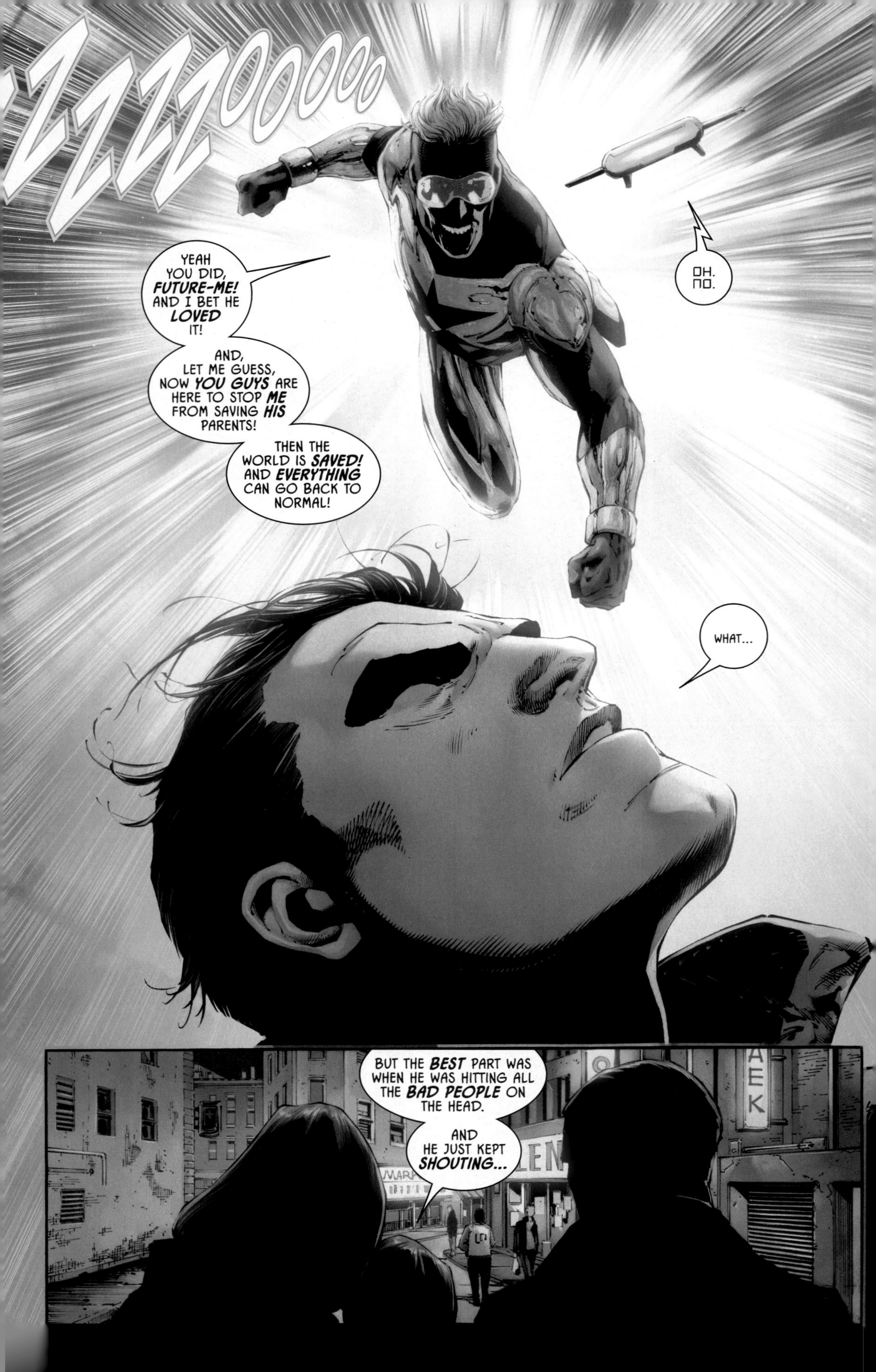
ZZZZOOOOO
YEAH YOU DID, **FUTURE-ME!** AND I BET HE **LOVED** IT!
AND, LET ME GUESS, NOW **YOU GUYS** ARE HERE TO STOP **ME** FROM SAVING **HIS** PARENTS!
THEN THE WORLD IS **SAVED!** AND **EVERYTHING** CAN GO BACK TO NORMAL!
OH. NO.
WHAT...
BUT THE **BEST** PART WAS WHEN HE WAS HITTING ALL THE **BAD PEOPLE** ON THE HEAD.
AND HE JUST KEPT **SHOUTING...**

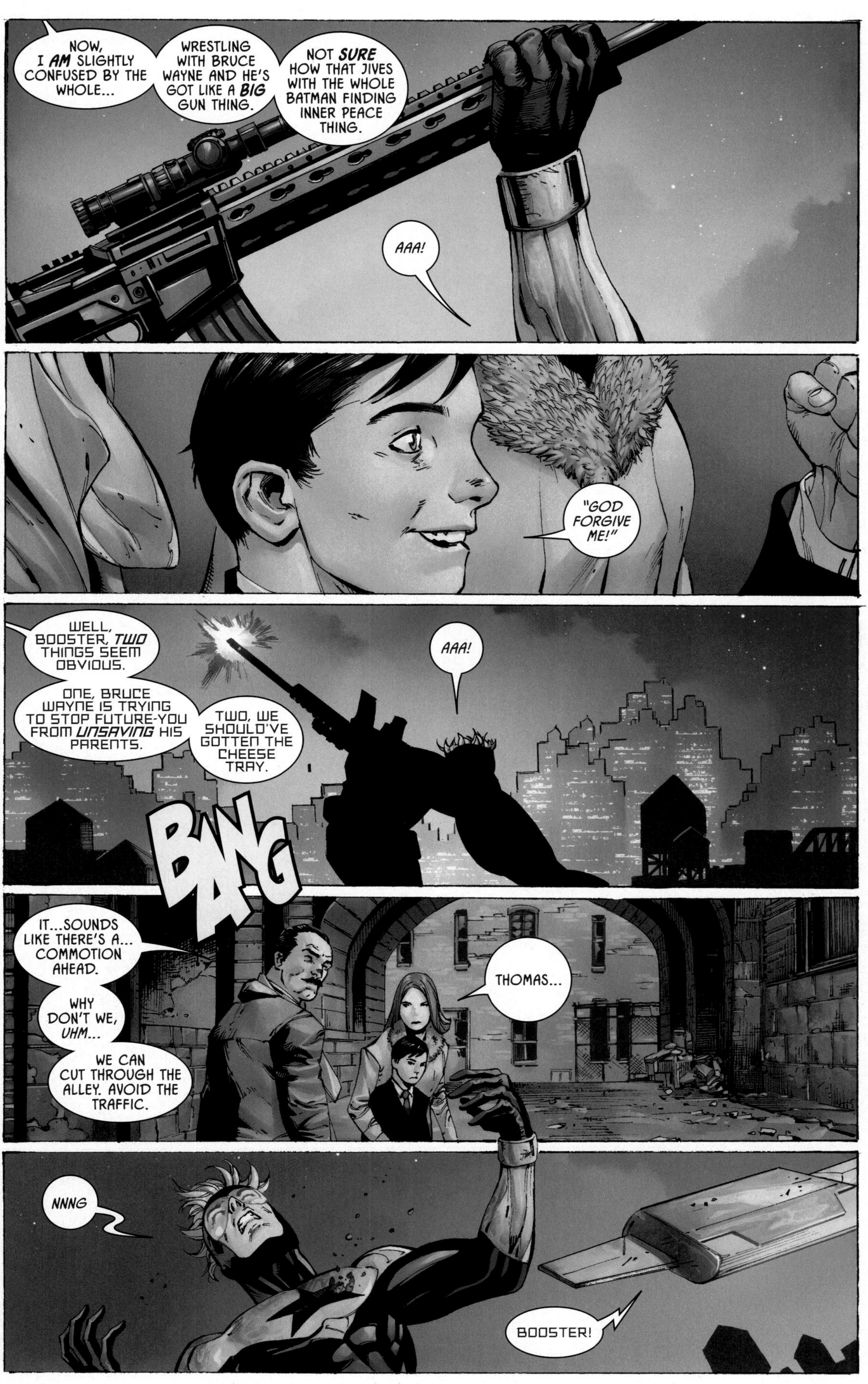
NOW, I AM SLIGHTLY CONFUSED BY THE WHOLE...
WRESTLING WITH BRUCE WAYNE AND HE'S GOT LIKE A BIG GUN THING.
NOT SURE HOW THAT JIVES WITH THE WHOLE BATMAN FINDING INNER PEACE THING.
AAA!
"GOD FORGIVE ME!"
WELL, BOOSTER, TWO THINGS SEEM OBVIOUS.
ONE, BRUCE WAYNE IS TRYING TO STOP FUTURE-YOU FROM UNSAVING HIS PARENTS.
TWO, WE SHOULD'VE GOTTEN THE CHEESE TRAY.
AAA!
BANG
IT...SOUNDS LIKE THERE'S A... COMMOTION AHEAD.
WHY DON'T WE, UHM...
WE CAN CUT THROUGH THE ALLEY. AVOID THE TRAFFIC.
THOMAS...
NNNG
BOOSTER!

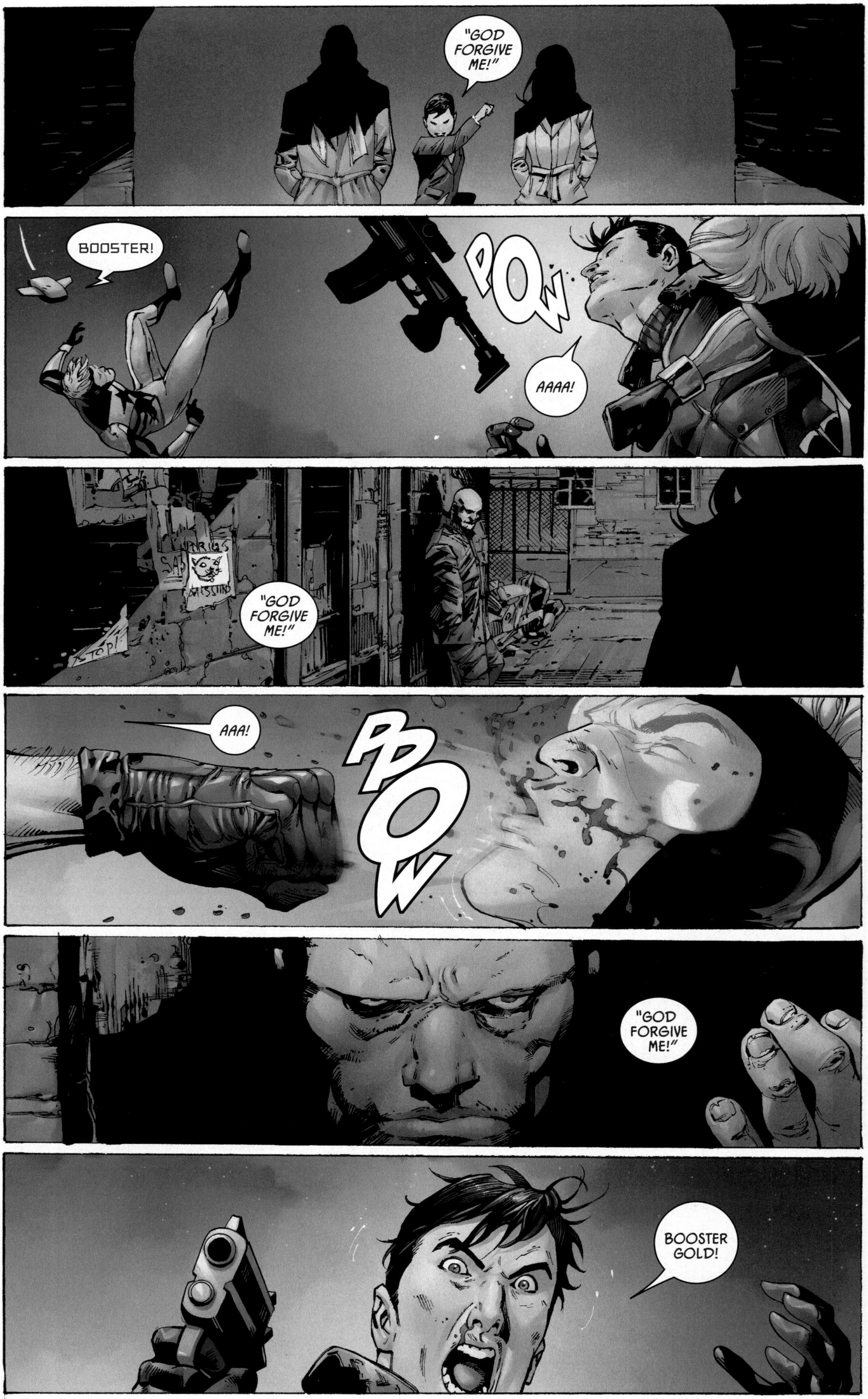
"GOD FORGIVE ME!"
BOOSTER!
POW
AAAA!
"GOD FORGIVE ME!"
AAA!
POW
"GOD FORGIVE ME!"
BOOSTER GOLD!

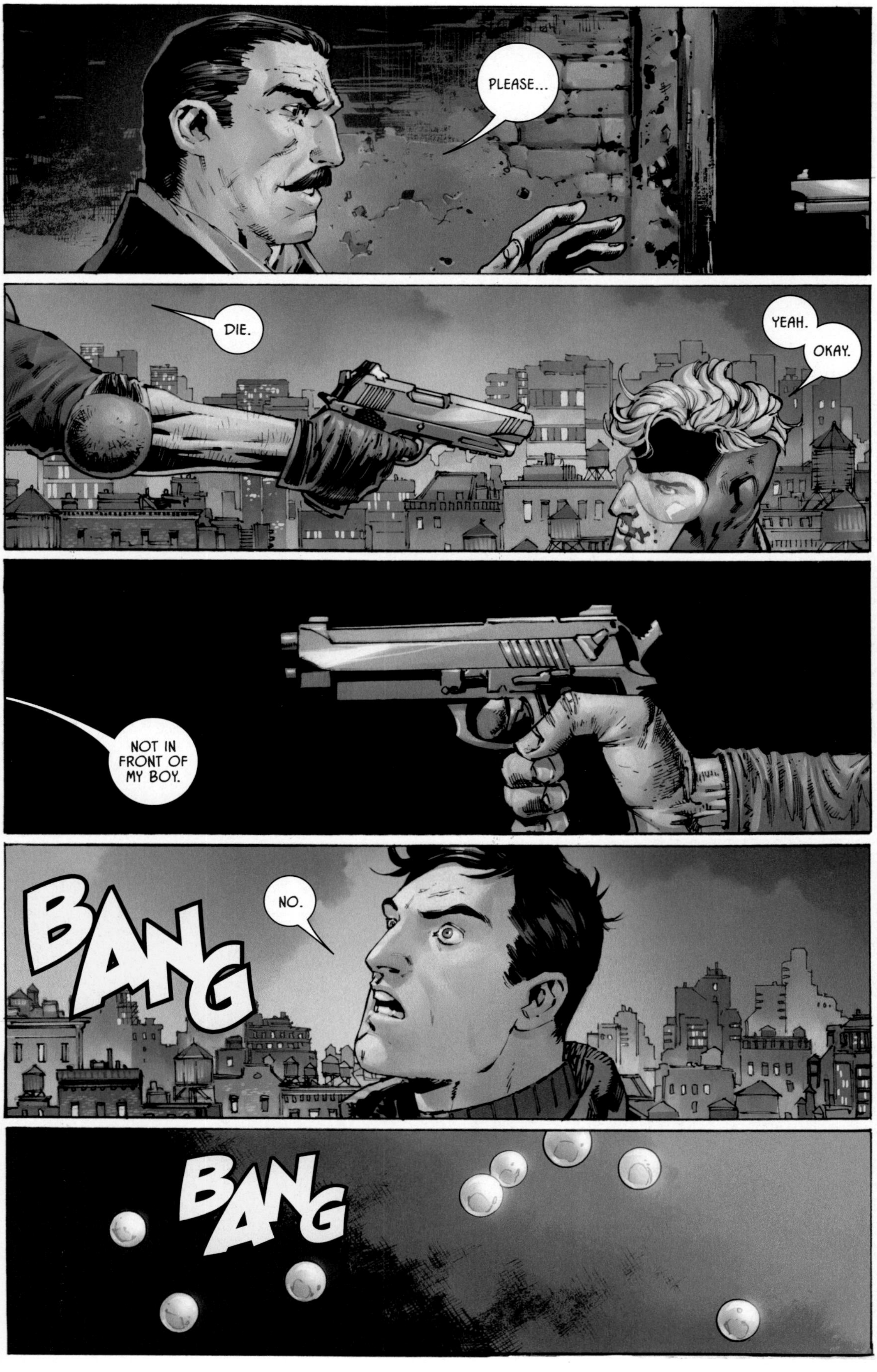
PLEASE...
DIE.
YEAH.
OKAY.
NOT IN FRONT OF MY BOY.
BANG
NO.
BANG

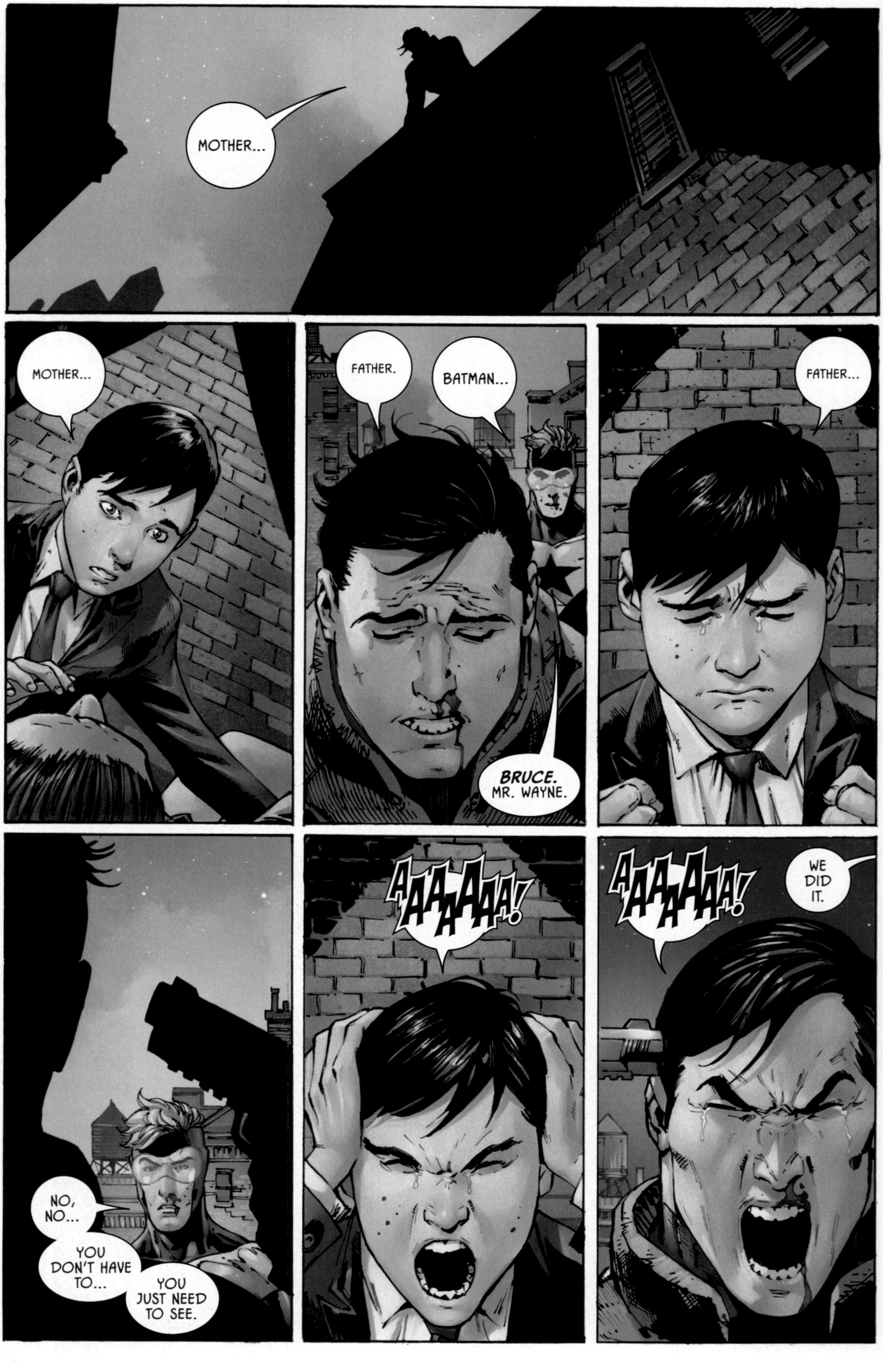
MOTHER...
MOTHER...
FATHER.
BATMAN...
BRUCE. MR. WAYNE.
FATHER...
NO, NO...
YOU DON'T HAVE TO...
YOU JUST NEED TO SEE.
AAAAAAA!
AAAAAAA!
WE DID IT.

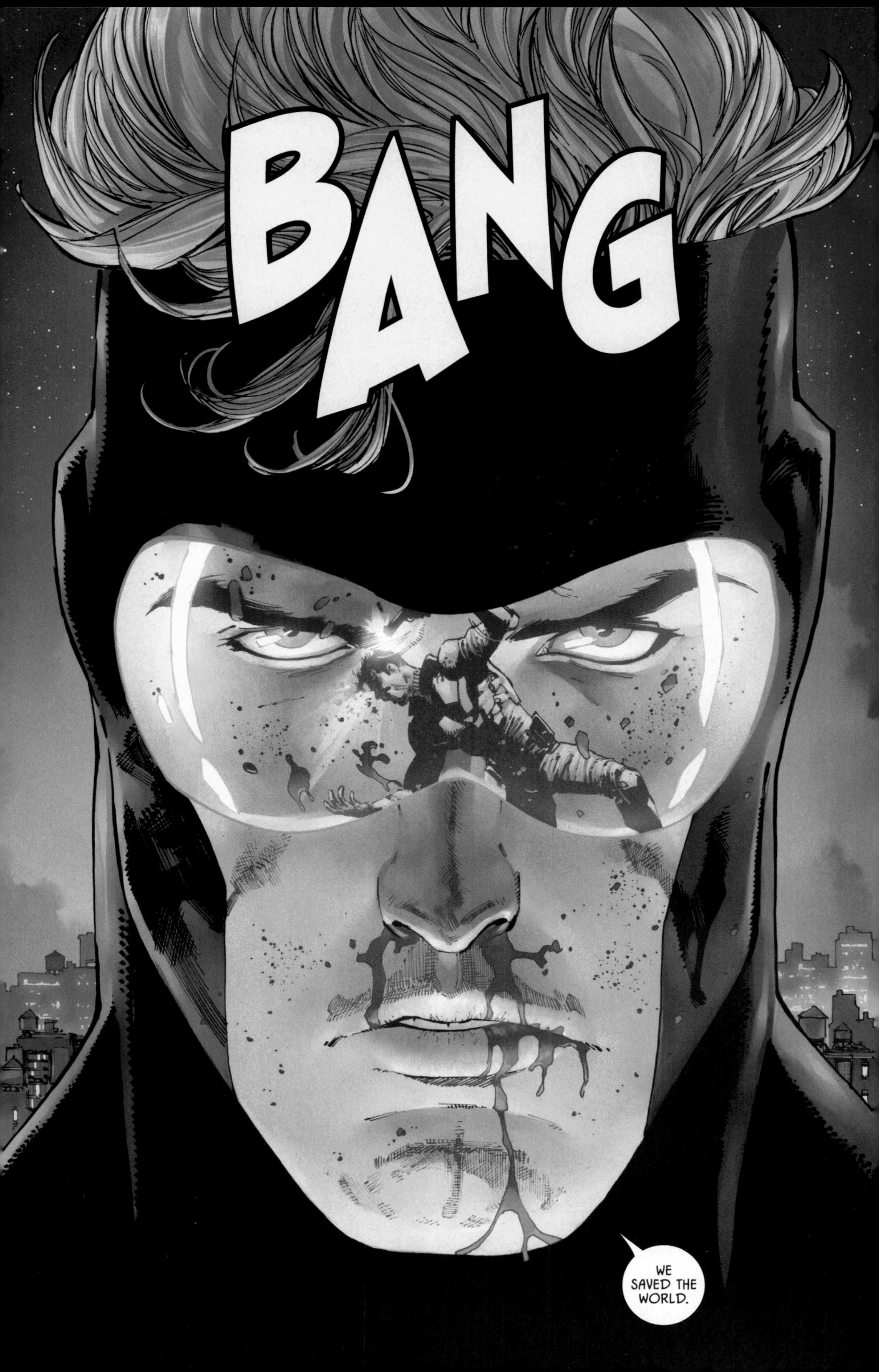
BANG
WE SAVED THE WORLD.

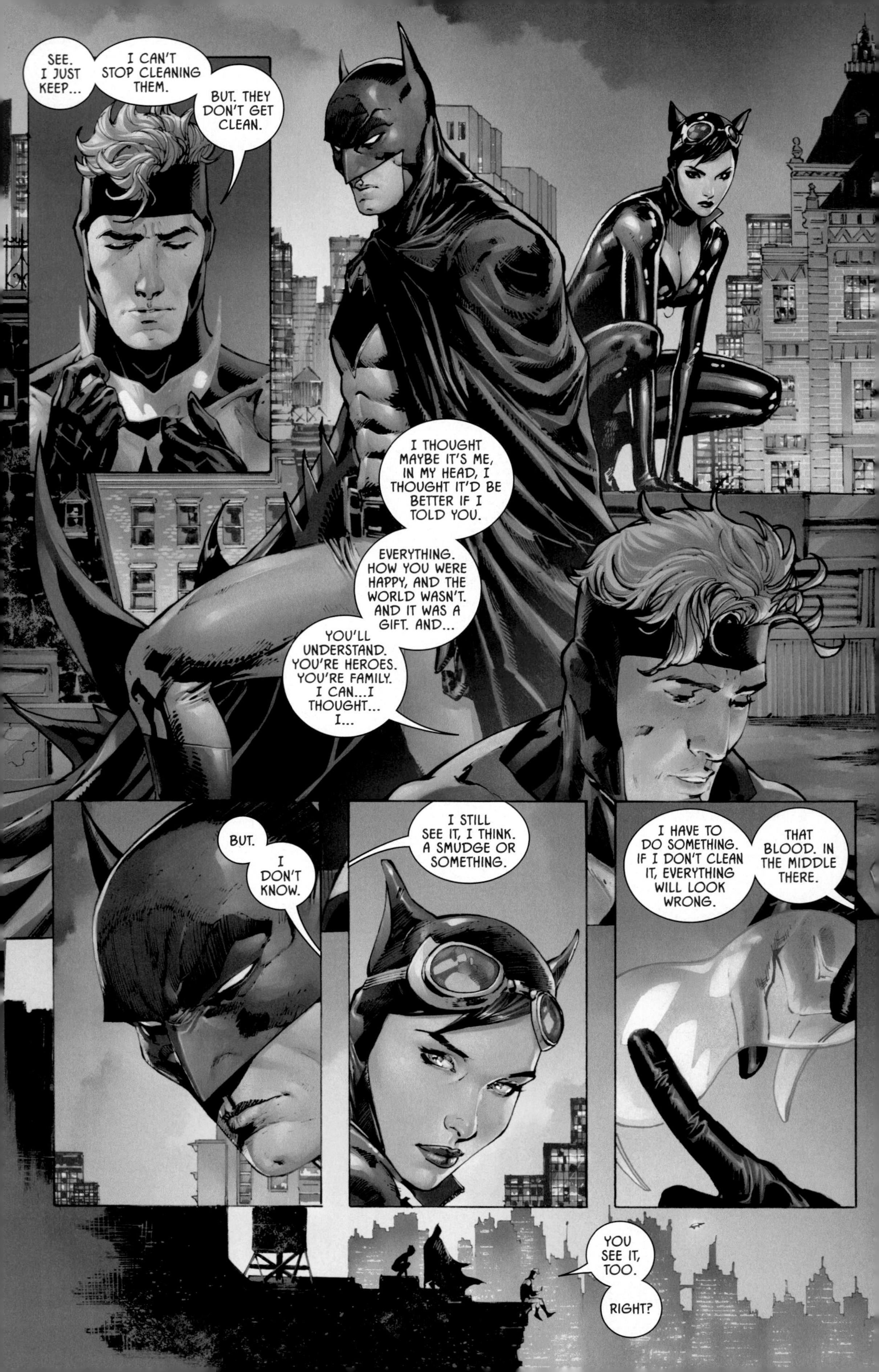
SEE. I JUST KEEP...
I CAN'T STOP CLEANING THEM.
BUT. THEY DON'T GET CLEAN.
I THOUGHT MAYBE IT'S ME, IN MY HEAD, I THOUGHT IT'D BE BETTER IF I TOLD YOU.
EVERYTHING. HOW YOU WERE HAPPY, AND THE WORLD WASN'T. AND IT WAS A GIFT. AND...
YOU'LL UNDERSTAND. YOU'RE HEROES. YOU'RE FAMILY. I CAN...I THOUGHT... I...
BUT.
I DON'T KNOW.
I STILL SEE IT, I THINK. A SMUDGE OR SOMETHING.
I HAVE TO DO SOMETHING. IF I DON'T CLEAN IT, EVERYTHING WILL LOOK WRONG.
THAT BLOOD. IN THE MIDDLE THERE.
YOU SEE IT, TOO.
RIGHT?

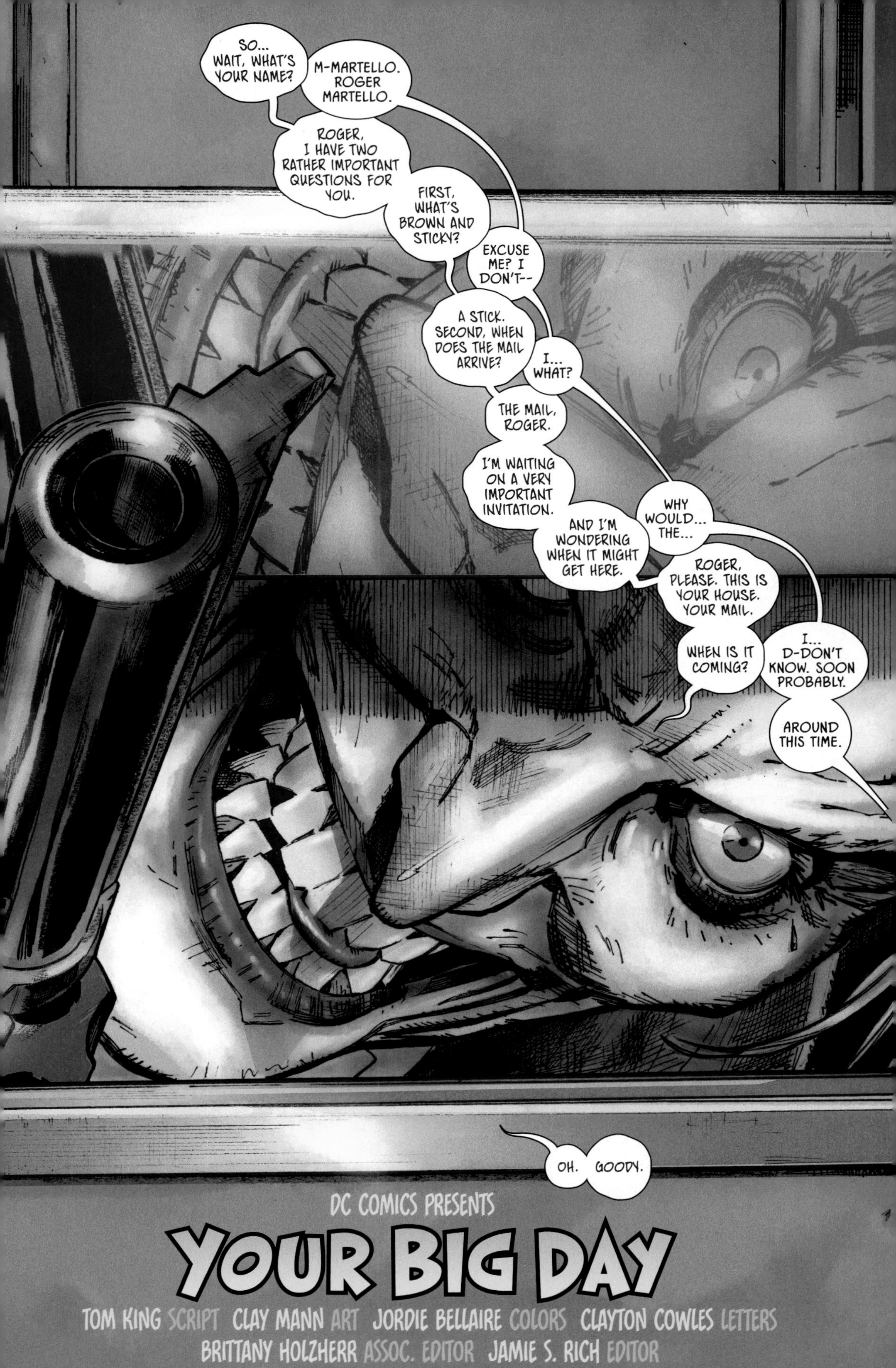
SO... WAIT, WHAT'S YOUR NAME?
M-MARTELLO. ROGER MARTELLO.
ROGER, I HAVE TWO RATHER IMPORTANT QUESTIONS FOR YOU.
FIRST, WHAT'S BROWN AND STICKY?
EXCUSE ME? I DON'T--
A STICK. SECOND, WHEN DOES THE MAIL ARRIVE?
I... WHAT?
THE MAIL, ROGER.
I'M WAITING ON A VERY IMPORTANT INVITATION.
AND I'M WONDERING WHEN IT MIGHT GET HERE.
WHY WOULD... THE...
ROGER, PLEASE. THIS IS YOUR HOUSE. YOUR MAIL.
WHEN IS IT COMING?
I... D-DON'T KNOW. SOON PROBABLY.
AROUND THIS TIME.
OH. GOODY.

DC COMICS PRESENTS

YOUR BIG DAY

TOM KING SCRIPT CLAY MANN ART JORDIE BELLAIRE COLORS CLAYTON COWLES LETTERS
BRITTANY HOLZHERR ASSOC. EDITOR JAMIE S. RICH EDITOR

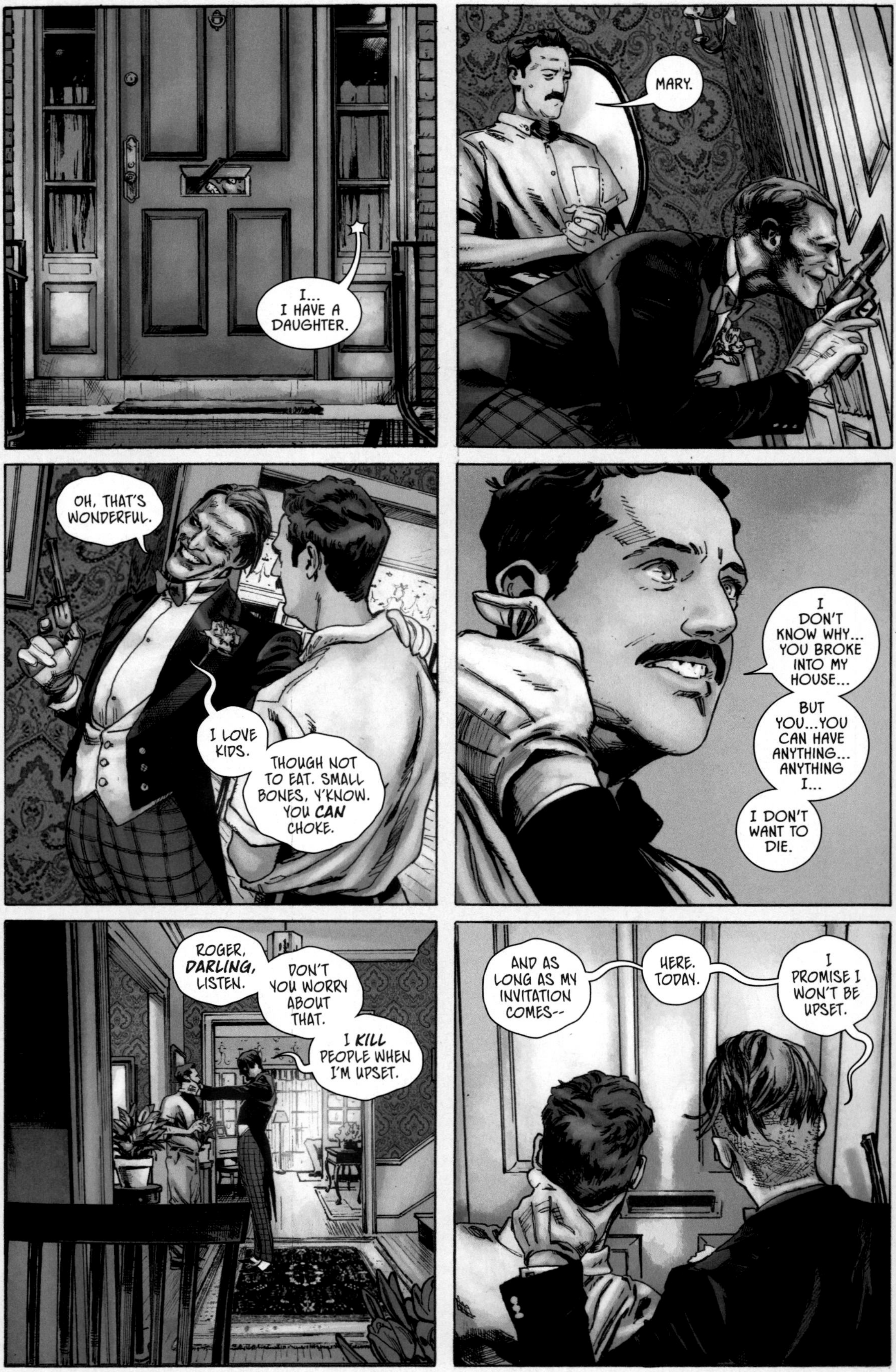
I... I HAVE A DAUGHTER.
MARY.
OH, THAT'S WONDERFUL.
I LOVE KIDS.
THOUGH NOT TO EAT. SMALL BONES, Y'KNOW. YOU CAN CHOKE.
I DON'T KNOW WHY... YOU BROKE INTO MY HOUSE...
BUT YOU...YOU CAN HAVE ANYTHING... ANYTHING I...
I DON'T WANT TO DIE.
ROGER, DARLING, LISTEN.
DON'T YOU WORRY ABOUT THAT.
I KILL PEOPLE WHEN I'M UPSET.
AND AS LONG AS MY INVITATION COMES--
HERE. TODAY.
I PROMISE I WON'T BE UPSET.

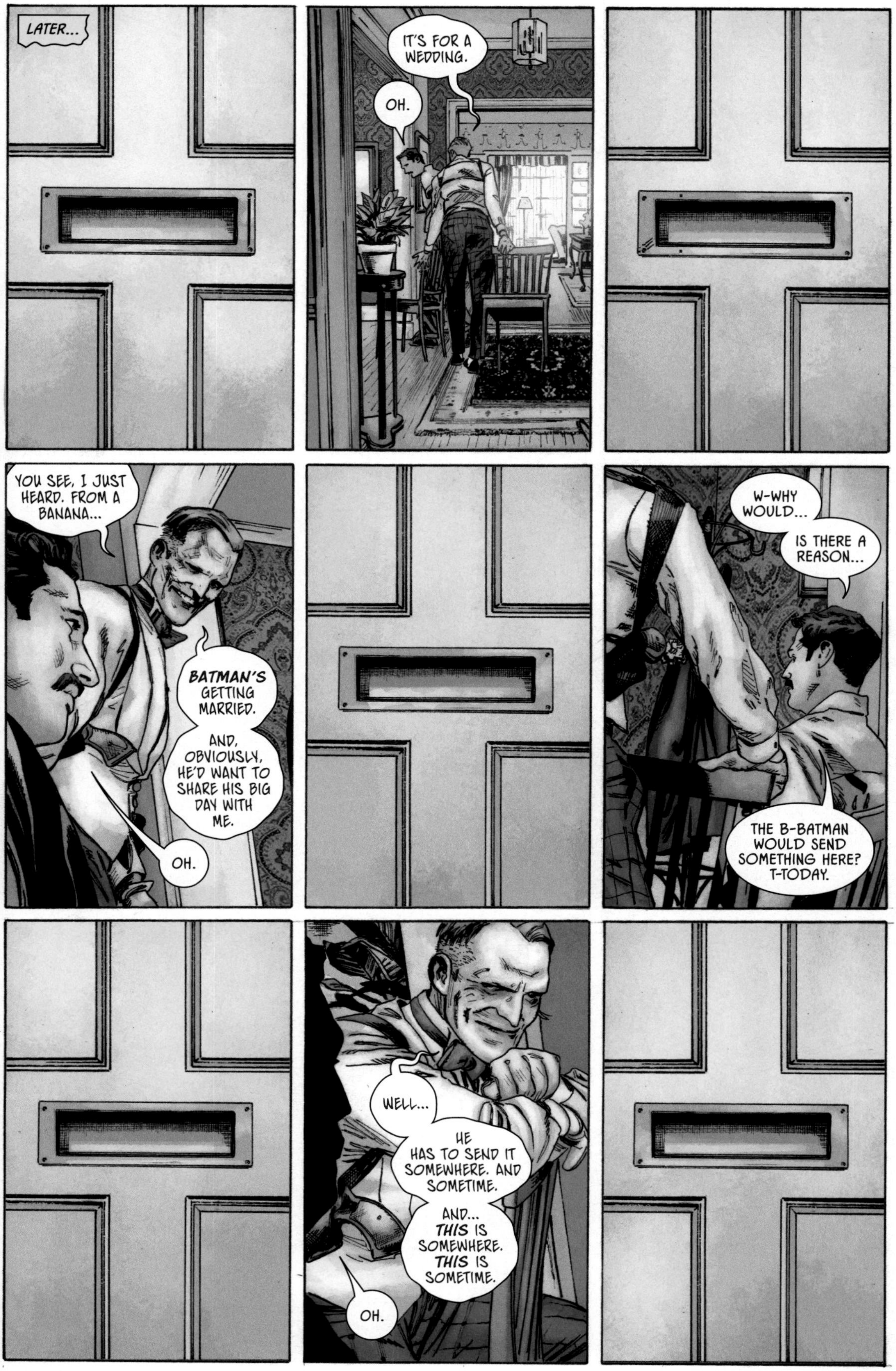
LATER...
IT'S FOR A WEDDING.
OH.
YOU SEE, I JUST HEARD. FROM A BANANA...
BATMAN'S GETTING MARRIED.
AND, OBVIOUSLY, HE'D WANT TO SHARE HIS BIG DAY WITH ME.
OH.
W-WHY WOULD...
IS THERE A REASON...
THE B-BATMAN WOULD SEND SOMETHING HERE? T-TODAY.
WELL...
HE HAS TO SEND IT SOMEWHERE. AND SOMETIME.
AND... THIS IS SOMEWHERE. THIS IS SOMETIME.
OH.

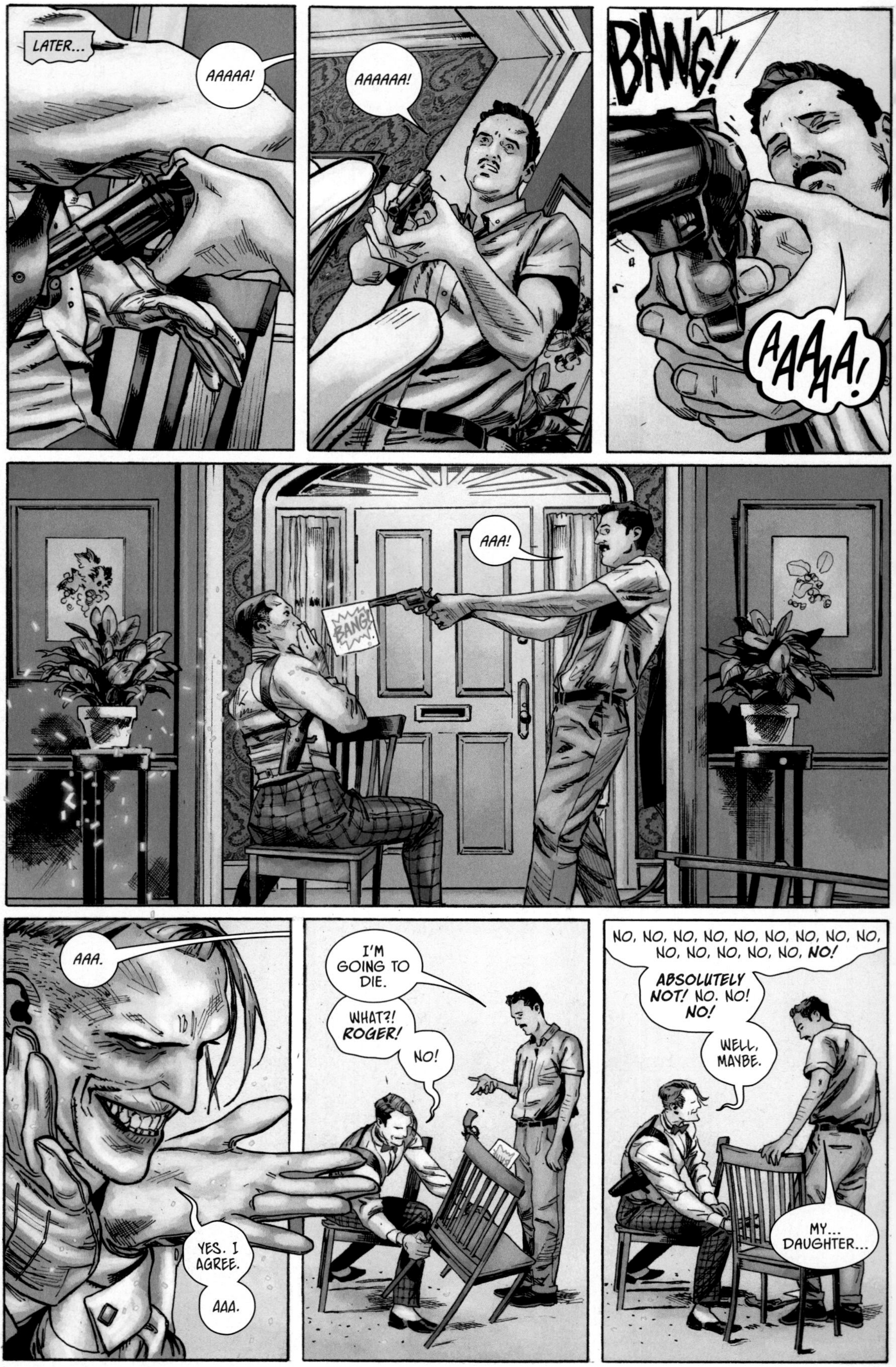
LATER...
AAAAA!
AAAAAA!
BANG!
AAAAA!
AAA!
BANG!
AAA.
YES. I AGREE.
AAA.
I'M GOING TO DIE.
WHAT?! ROGER!
NO!
NO, NO, NO, NO, NO, NO, NO, NO, NO, NO, NO, NO, NO, NO, NO!
ABSOLUTELY NOT! NO. NO! NO!
WELL, MAYBE.
MY... DAUGHTER...

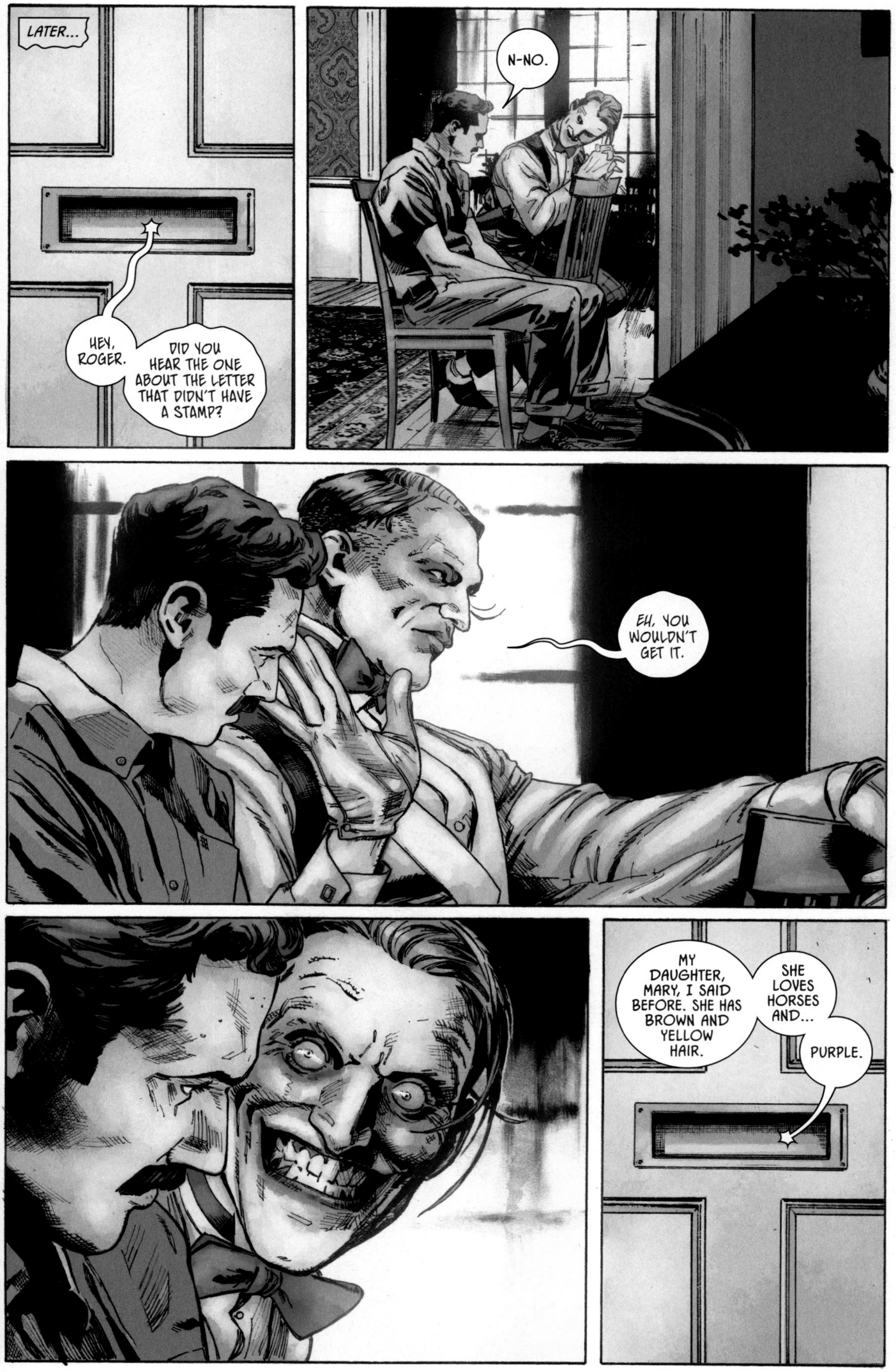
LATER...
HEY, ROGER.
DID YOU HEAR THE ONE ABOUT THE LETTER THAT DIDN'T HAVE A STAMP?
N-NO.
EH, YOU WOULDN'T GET IT.
MY DAUGHTER, MARY, I SAID BEFORE. SHE HAS BROWN AND YELLOW HAIR.
SHE LOVES HORSES AND...
PURPLE.

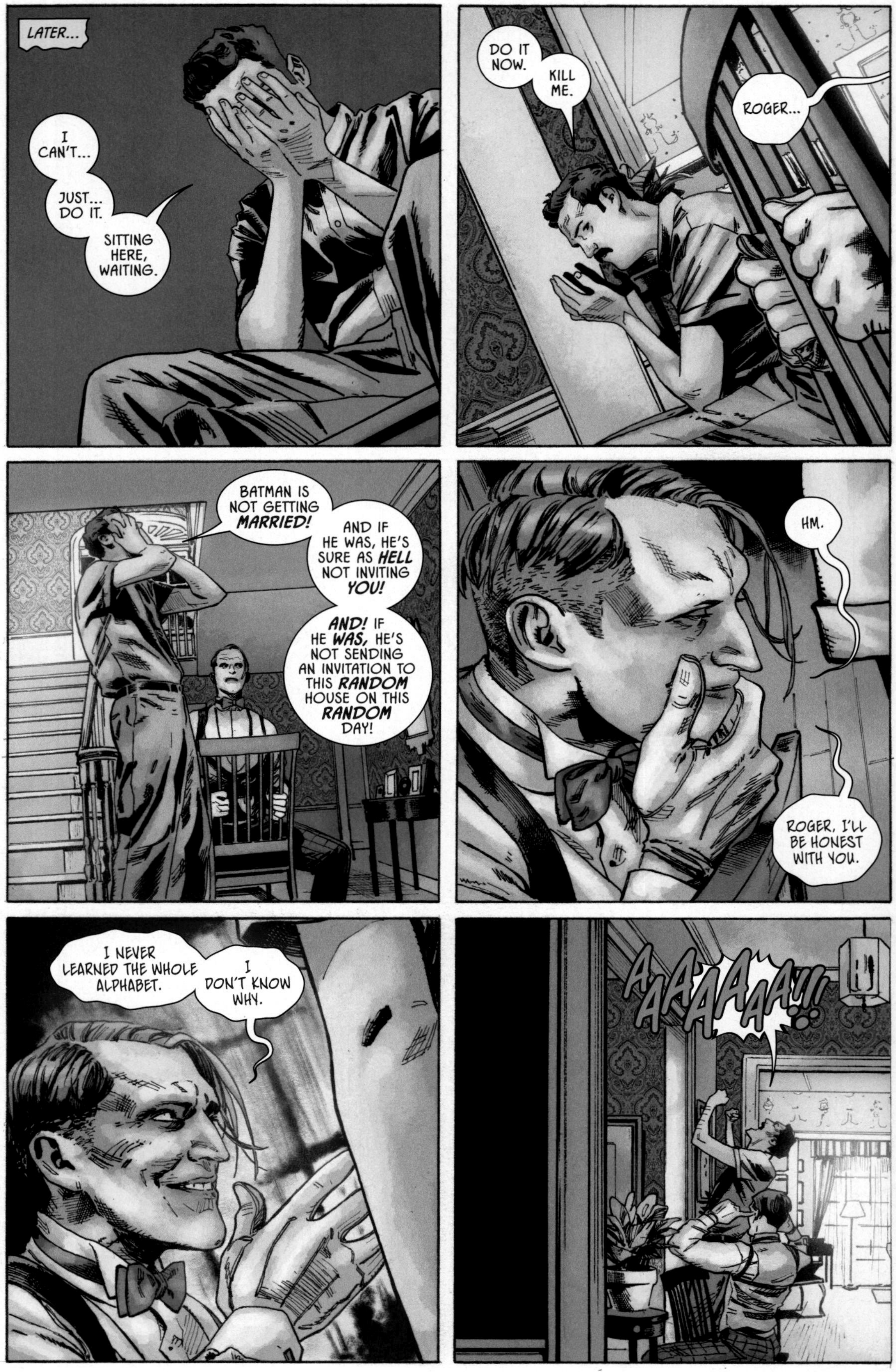
LATER...
I CAN'T...
JUST... DO IT.
SITTING HERE, WAITING.
DO IT NOW.
KILL ME.
ROGER...
BATMAN IS NOT GETTING *MARRIED!*
AND IF HE WAS, HE'S SURE AS *HELL* NOT INVITING *YOU!*
AND! IF HE *WAS,* HE'S NOT SENDING AN INVITATION TO THIS *RANDOM* HOUSE ON THIS *RANDOM* DAY!
HM.
ROGER, I'LL BE HONEST WITH YOU.
I NEVER LEARNED THE WHOLE ALPHABET.
I DON'T KNOW WHY.
AAAAAAAA!!!

LATER...

SRKREE

SKRRFFF

SKKKKKK

SKKRFFFF

FNNFT

SHOULD WE LOOK? WE HAVE TO LOOK!

I MEAN, I DON'T KNOW ABOUT YOU, ROGER...

BUT THE TENSION IS JUST *KILLING* ME!

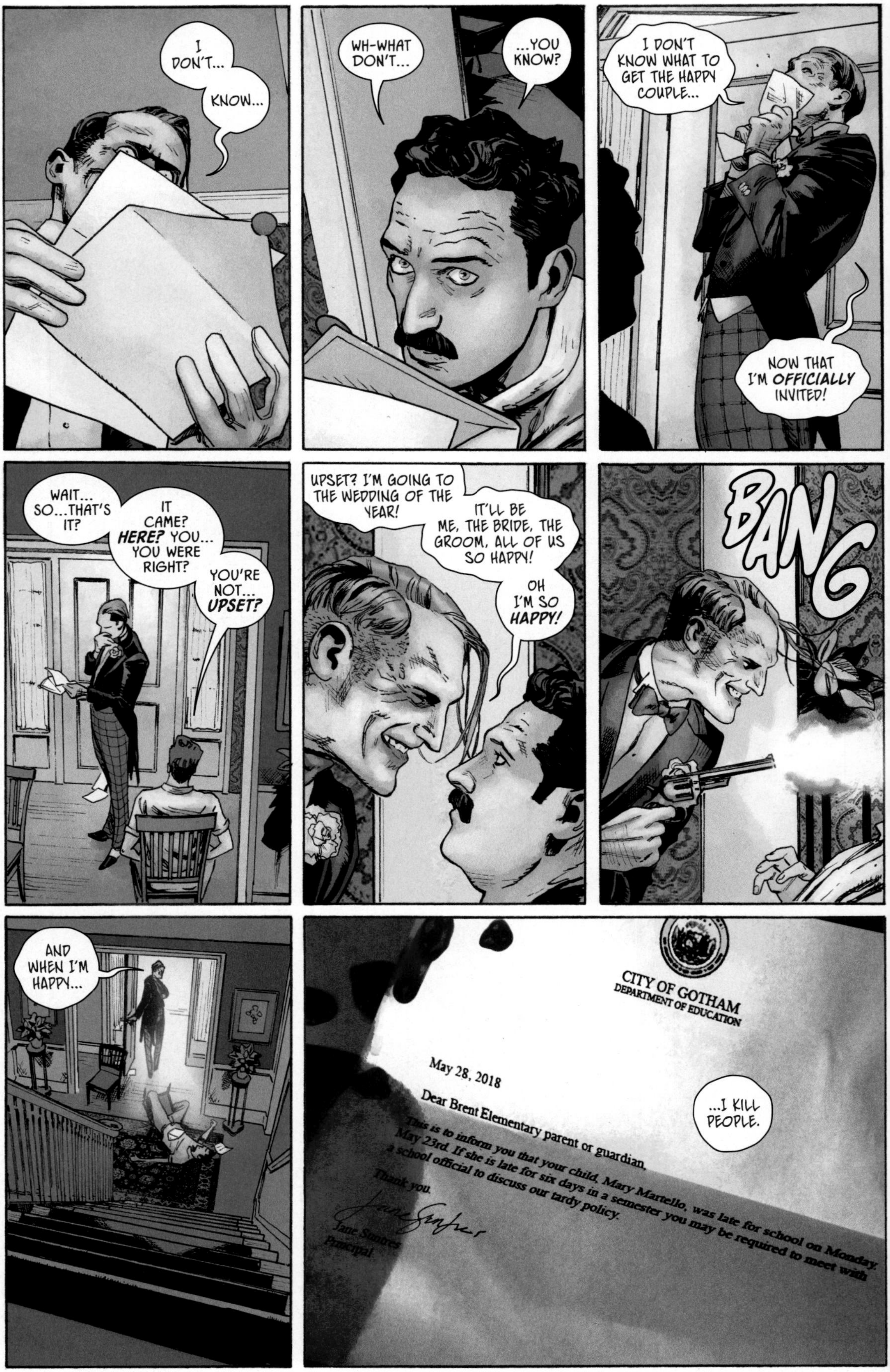
I DON'T...
KNOW...
WH-WHAT DON'T...
...YOU KNOW?
I DON'T KNOW WHAT TO GET THE HAPPY COUPLE...
NOW THAT I'M OFFICIALLY INVITED!
WAIT... SO...THAT'S IT?
IT CAME? HERE? YOU... YOU WERE RIGHT?
YOU'RE NOT... UPSET?
UPSET? I'M GOING TO THE WEDDING OF THE YEAR!
IT'LL BE ME, THE BRIDE, THE GROOM, ALL OF US SO HAPPY!
OH I'M SO HAPPY!
BANG
AND WHEN I'M HAPPY...
CITY OF GOTHAM
DEPARTMENT OF EDUCATION
May 28, 2018
Dear Brent Elementary parent or guardian,
This is to inform you that your child, Mary Martello, was late for school on Monday, May 23rd. If she is late for six days in a semester you may be required to meet with a school official to discuss our tardy policy.
Thank you.
Jane Suntres
Principal
...I KILL PEOPLE.

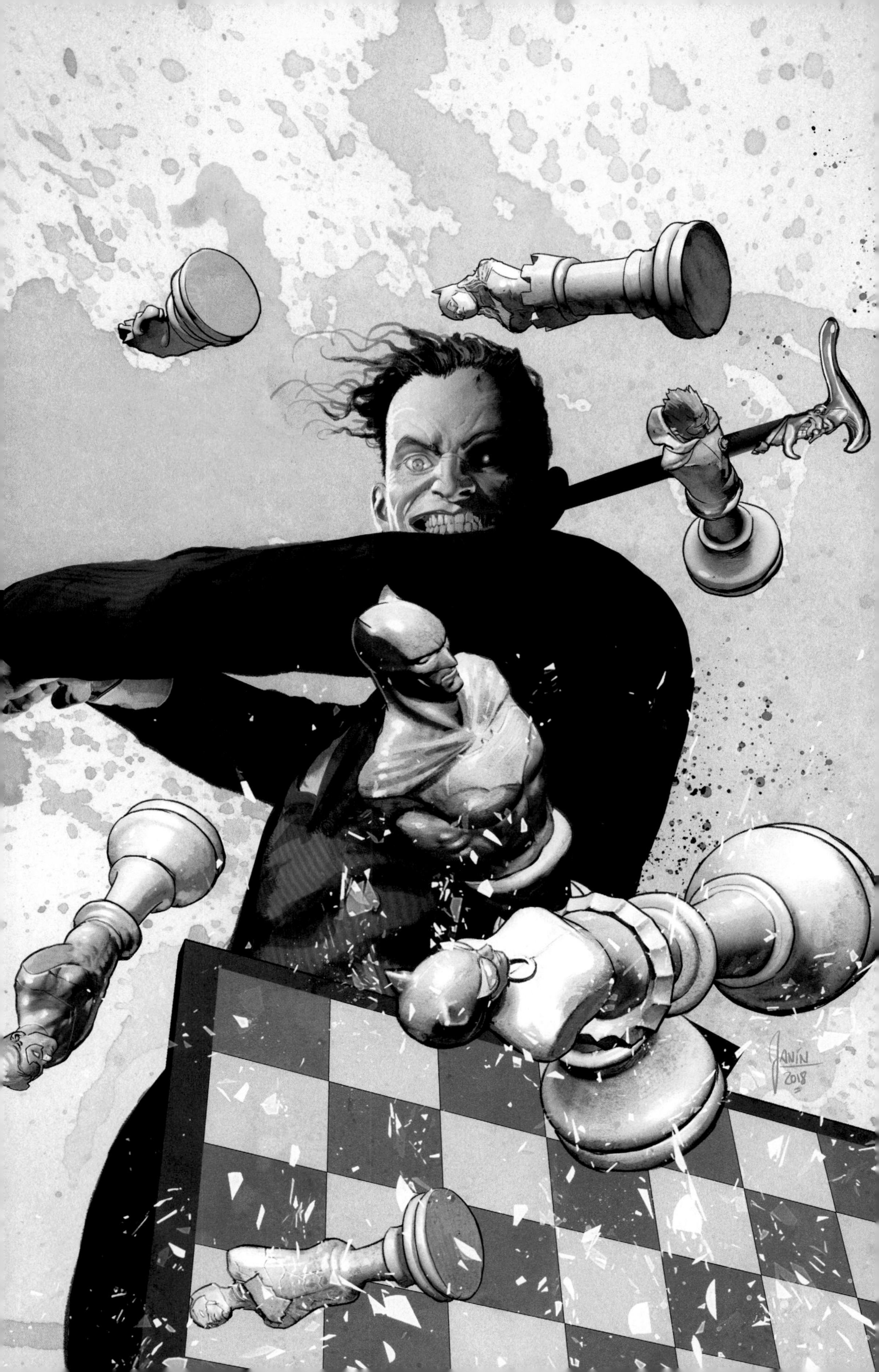
JANÍN
2018

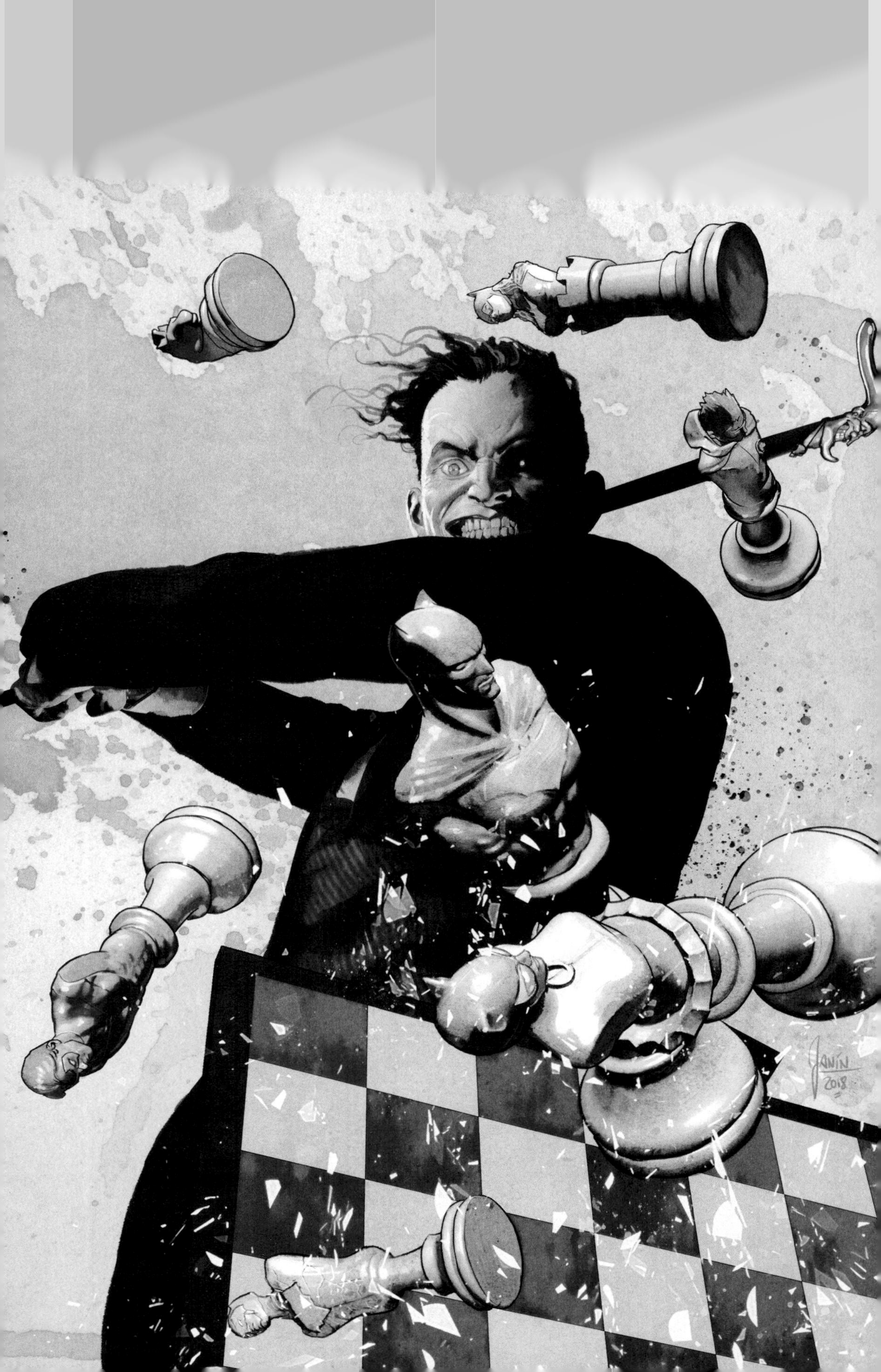
JANÍN
2018

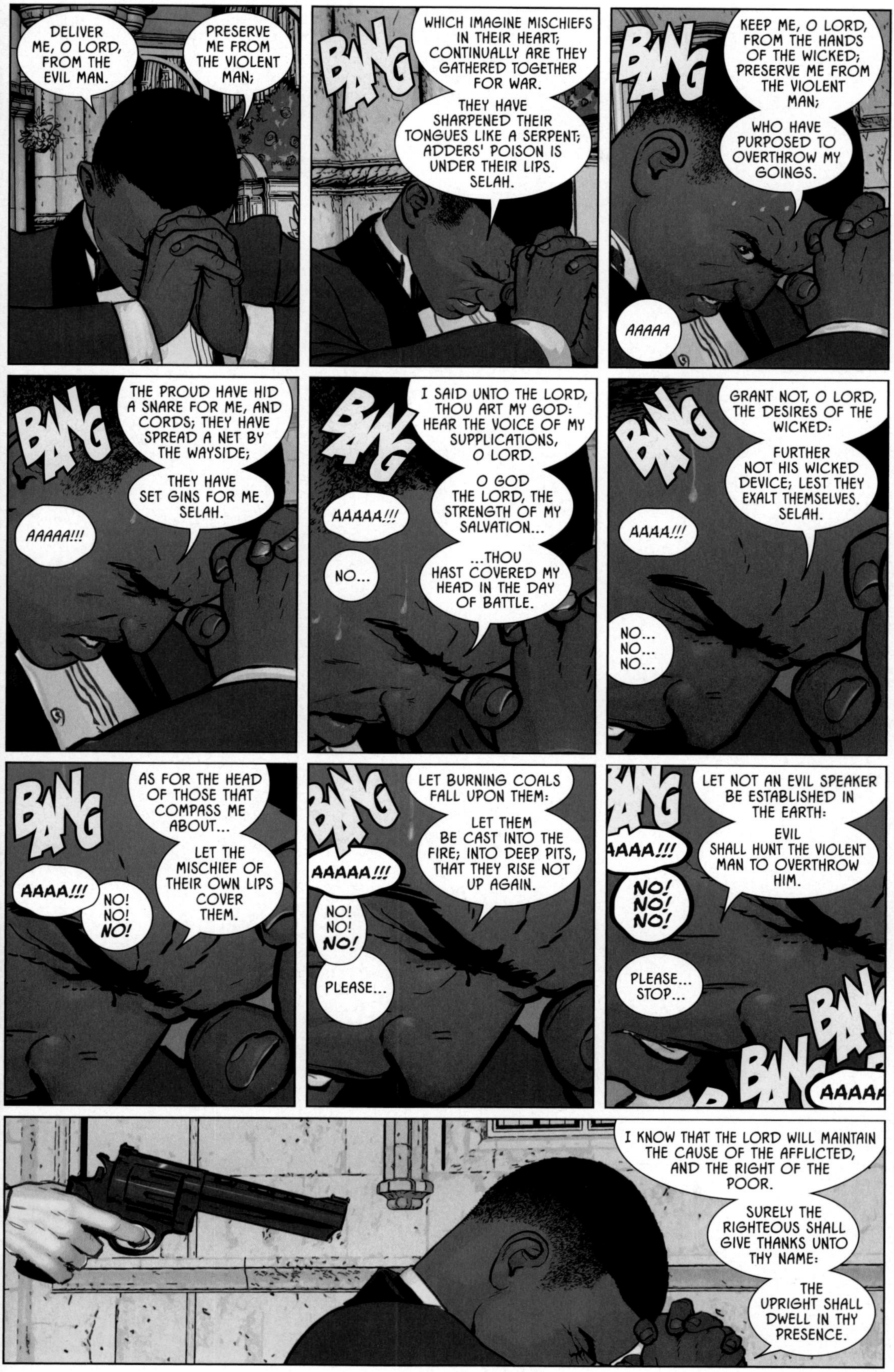
DELIVER ME, O LORD, FROM THE EVIL MAN.
PRESERVE ME FROM THE VIOLENT MAN;
BANG
WHICH IMAGINE MISCHIEFS IN THEIR HEART; CONTINUALLY ARE THEY GATHERED TOGETHER FOR WAR.
THEY HAVE SHARPENED THEIR TONGUES LIKE A SERPENT; ADDERS' POISON IS UNDER THEIR LIPS. SELAH.
BANG
KEEP ME, O LORD, FROM THE HANDS OF THE WICKED; PRESERVE ME FROM THE VIOLENT MAN;
WHO HAVE PURPOSED TO OVERTHROW MY GOINGS.
AAAAA
BANG
THE PROUD HAVE HID A SNARE FOR ME, AND CORDS; THEY HAVE SPREAD A NET BY THE WAYSIDE;
THEY HAVE SET GINS FOR ME. SELAH.
AAAAA!!!
BANG
I SAID UNTO THE LORD, THOU ART MY GOD: HEAR THE VOICE OF MY SUPPLICATIONS, O LORD.
O GOD THE LORD, THE STRENGTH OF MY SALVATION...
...THOU HAST COVERED MY HEAD IN THE DAY OF BATTLE.
AAAAA!!!
NO...
BANG
GRANT NOT, O LORD, THE DESIRES OF THE WICKED:
FURTHER NOT HIS WICKED DEVICE; LEST THEY EXALT THEMSELVES. SELAH.
AAAA!!!
NO... NO... NO...
BANG
AS FOR THE HEAD OF THOSE THAT COMPASS ME ABOUT...
LET THE MISCHIEF OF THEIR OWN LIPS COVER THEM.
AAAA!!!
NO! NO! NO!
BANG
LET BURNING COALS FALL UPON THEM:
LET THEM BE CAST INTO THE FIRE; INTO DEEP PITS, THAT THEY RISE NOT UP AGAIN.
AAAAA!!!
NO! NO! NO!
PLEASE...
BANG
LET NOT AN EVIL SPEAKER BE ESTABLISHED IN THE EARTH:
EVIL SHALL HUNT THE VIOLENT MAN TO OVERTHROW HIM.
AAAA!!!
NO! NO! NO!
PLEASE... STOP...
BANG
BANG
AAAAA
I KNOW THAT THE LORD WILL MAINTAIN THE CAUSE OF THE AFFLICTED, AND THE RIGHT OF THE POOR.
SURELY THE RIGHTEOUS SHALL GIVE THANKS UNTO THY NAME:
THE UPRIGHT SHALL DWELL IN THY PRESENCE.

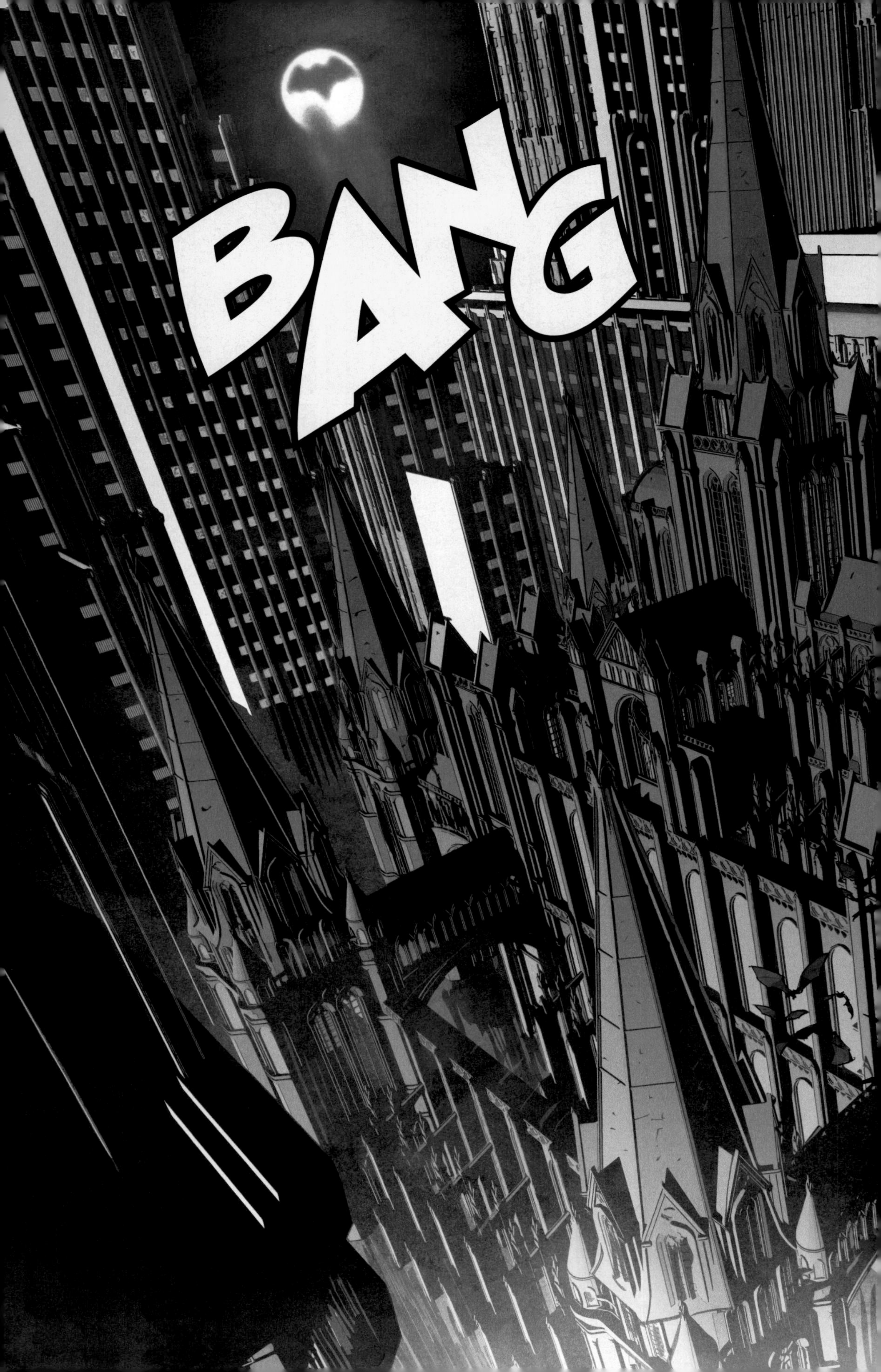
BANG

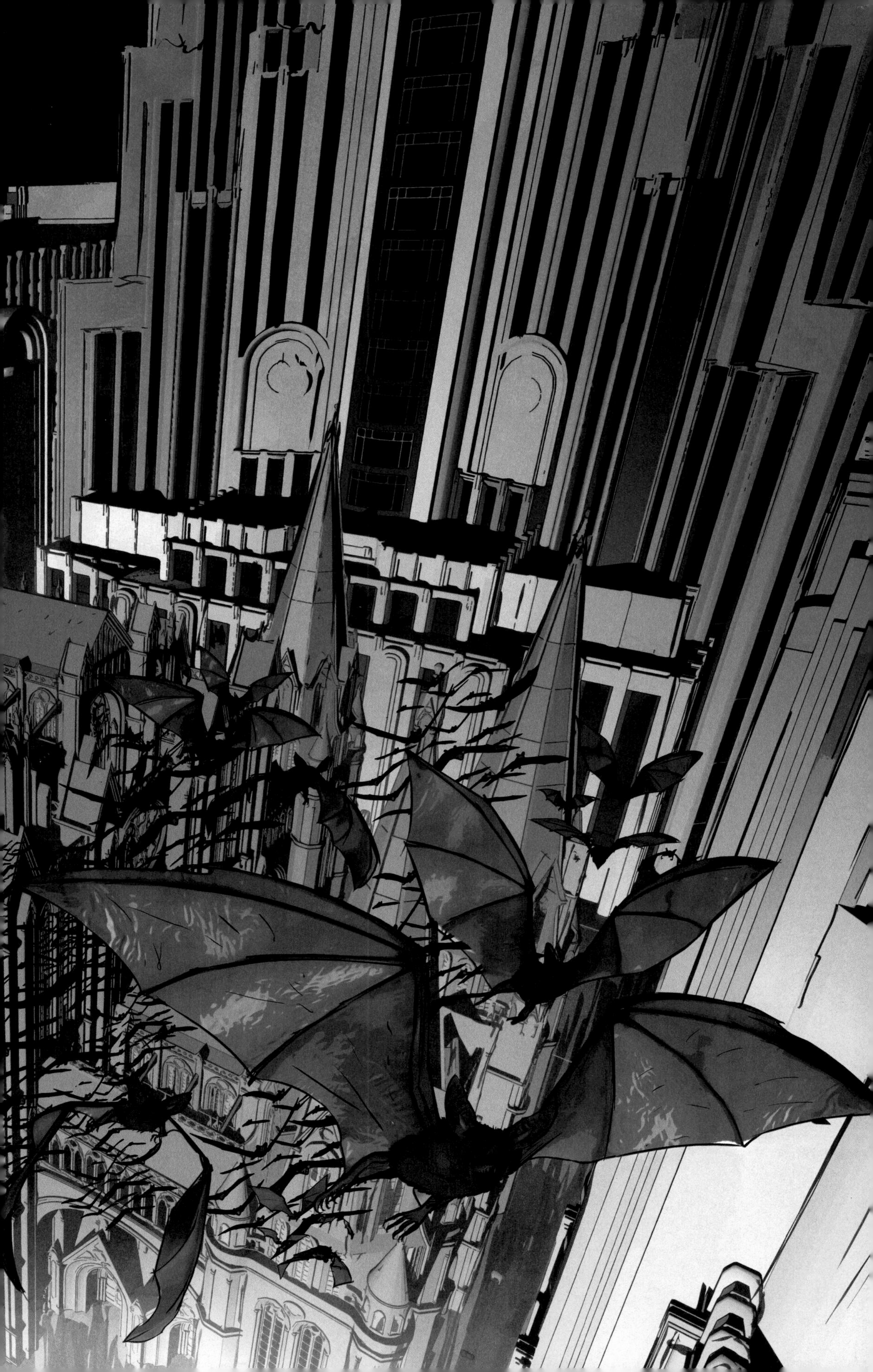

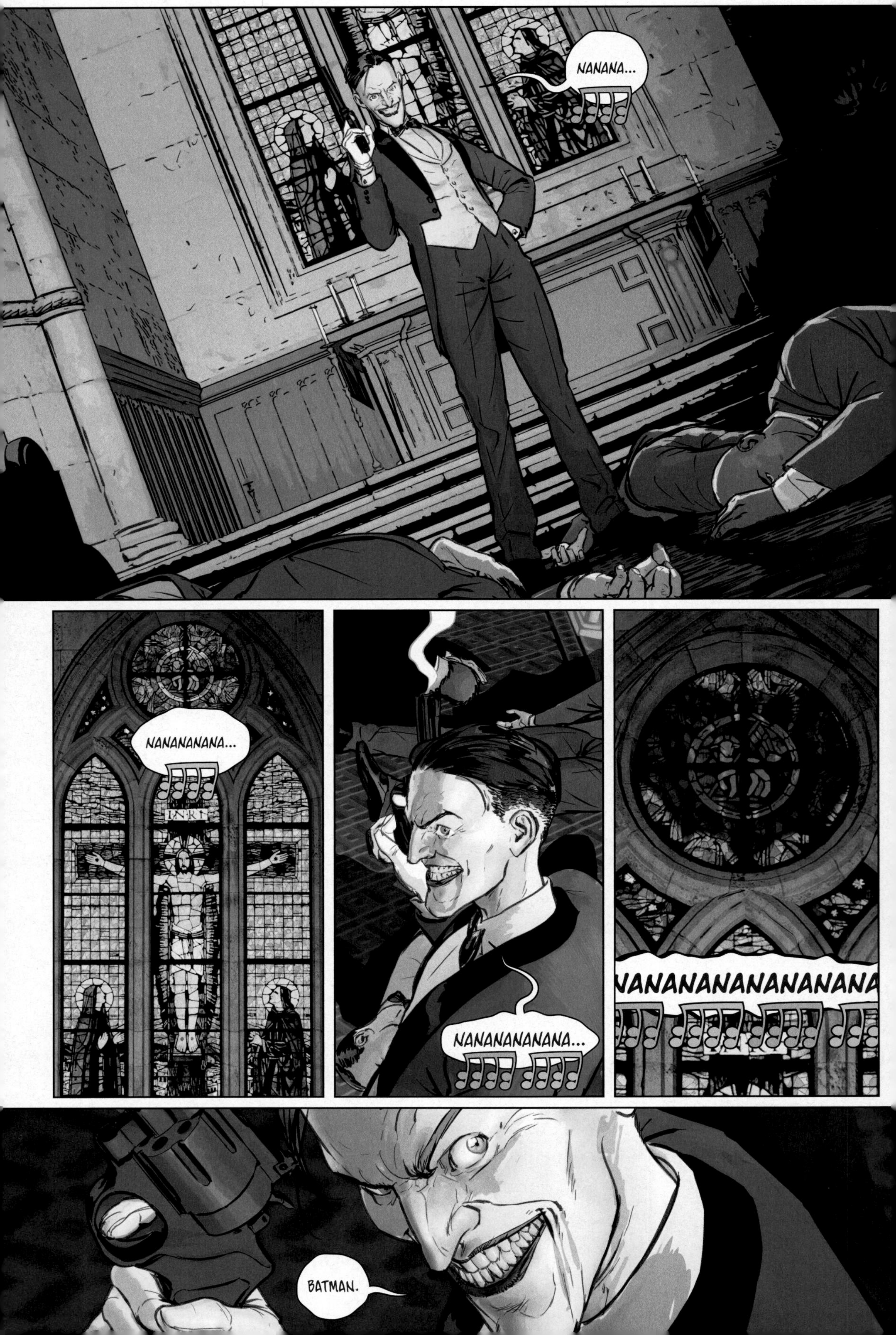
NANANA...
NANANANANA...
NANANANANA...
NANANANANANANANA
BATMAN.

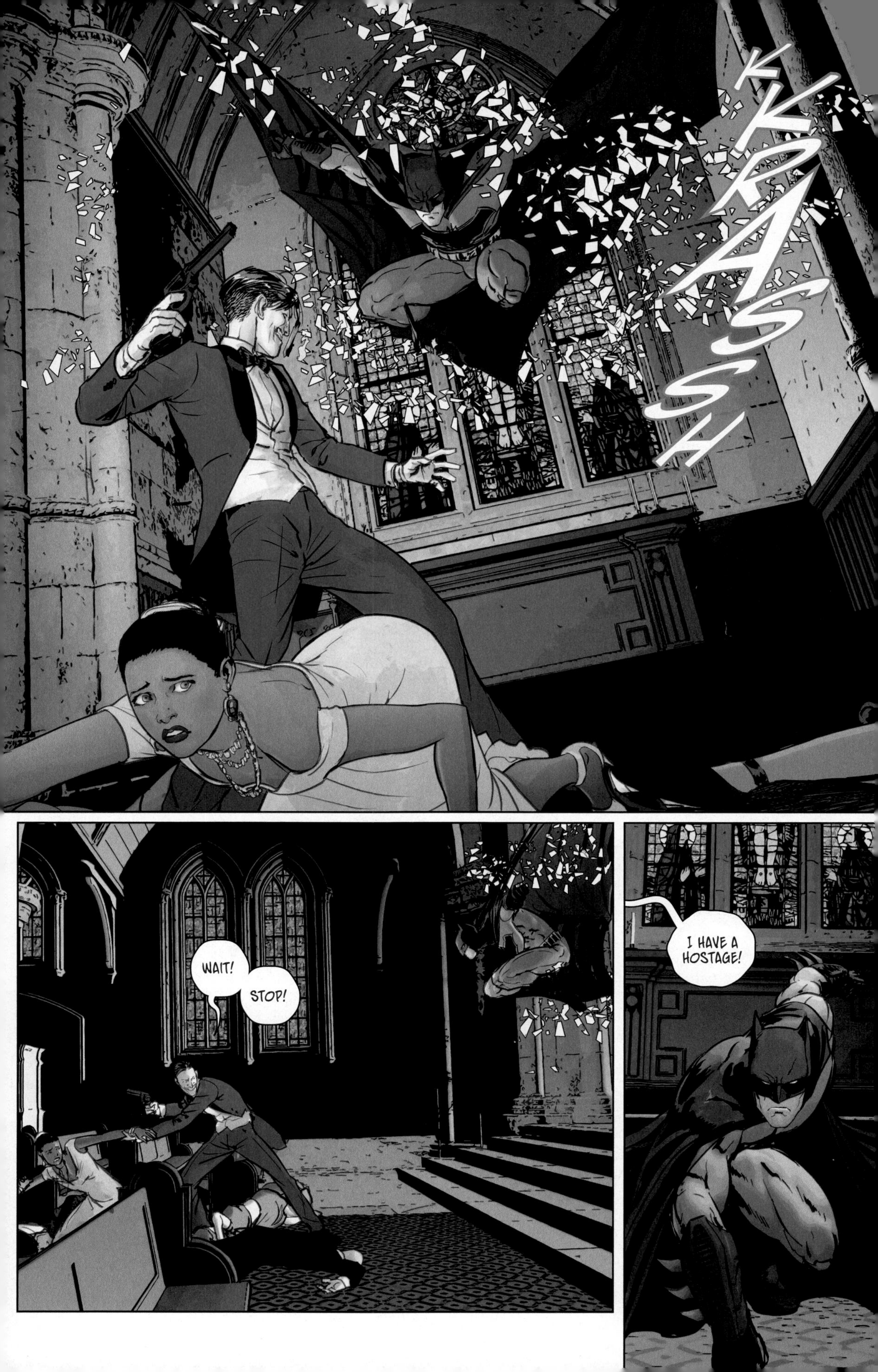
KKRASSH
WAIT!
STOP!
I HAVE A HOSTAGE!

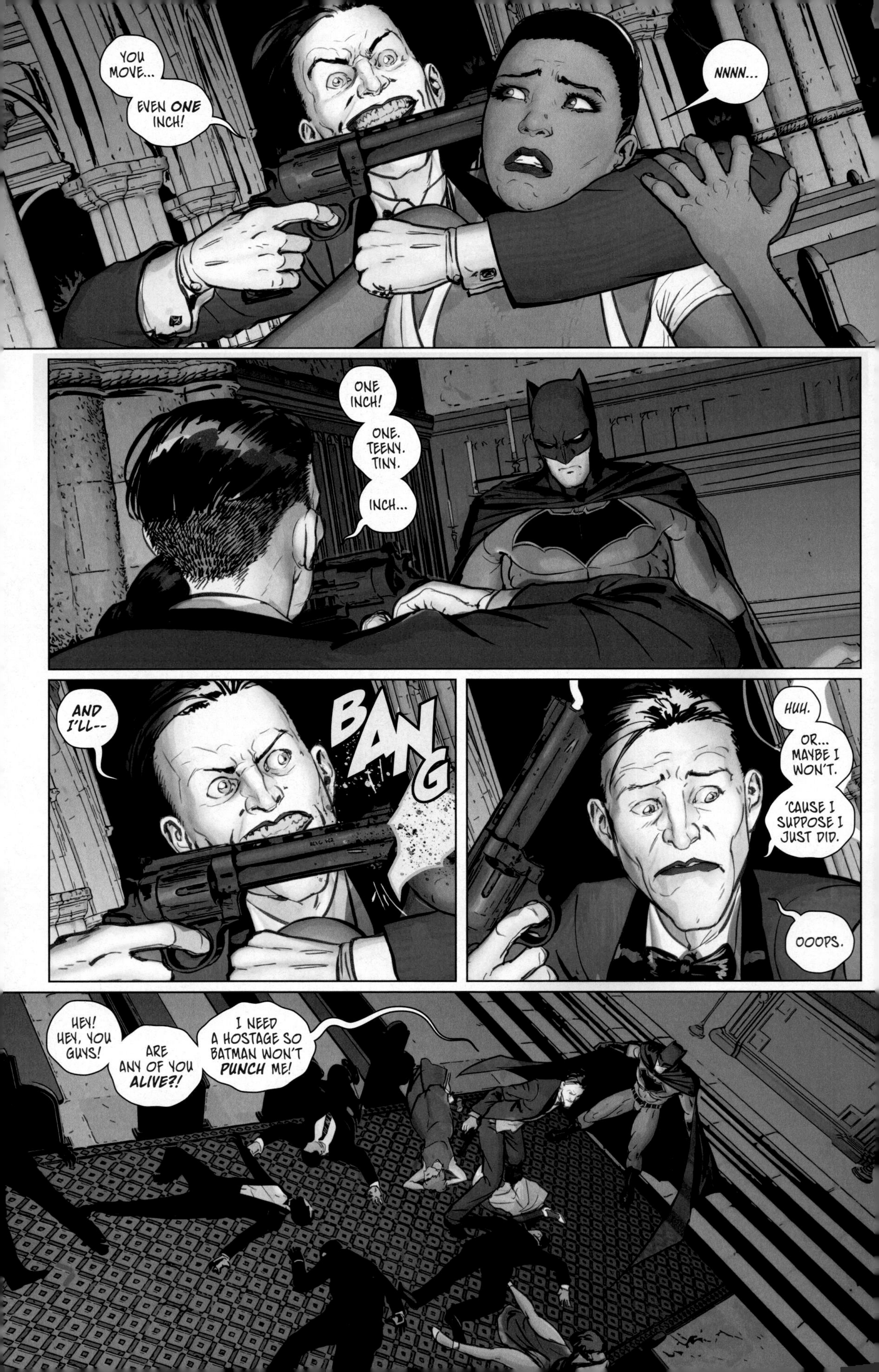
YOU MOVE...
EVEN ONE INCH!
NNNN...
ONE INCH!
ONE. TEENY. TINY.
INCH...
AND I'LL--
BANG
HUH.
OR... MAYBE I WON'T.
'CAUSE I SUPPOSE I JUST DID.
OOOPS.
HEY! HEY, YOU GUYS!
ARE ANY OF YOU ALIVE?!
I NEED A HOSTAGE SO BATMAN WON'T PUNCH ME!

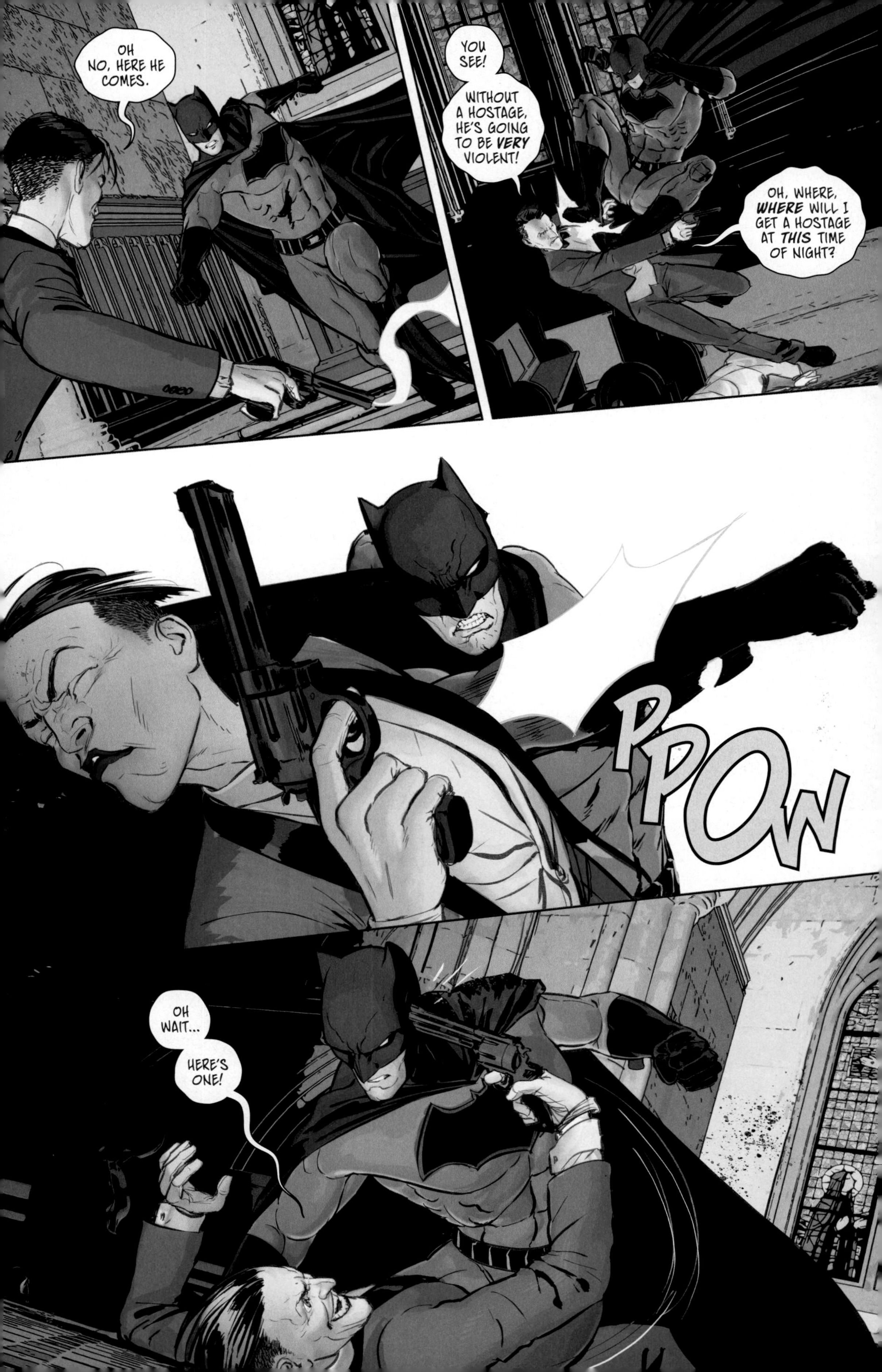
OH NO, HERE HE COMES.
YOU SEE!
WITHOUT A HOSTAGE, HE'S GOING TO BE VERY VIOLENT!
OH, WHERE, WHERE WILL I GET A HOSTAGE AT THIS TIME OF NIGHT?
PPOW
OH WAIT...
HERE'S ONE!

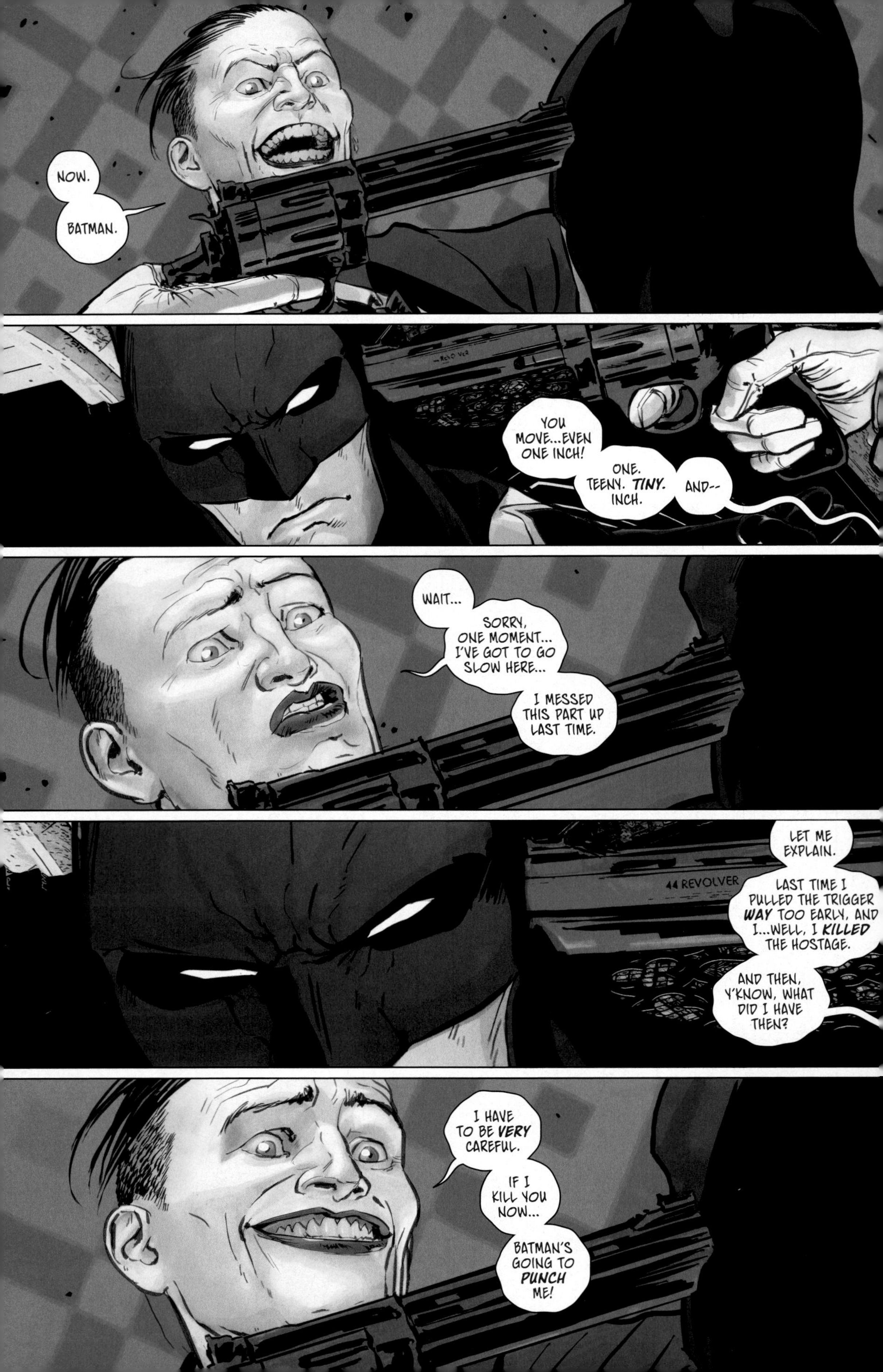
NOW.
BATMAN.
YOU MOVE...EVEN ONE INCH!
ONE. TEENY. TINY. INCH.
AND--
WAIT...
SORRY, ONE MOMENT... I'VE GOT TO GO SLOW HERE...
I MESSED THIS PART UP LAST TIME.
44 REVOLVER
LET ME EXPLAIN.
LAST TIME I PULLED THE TRIGGER WAY TOO EARLY, AND I...WELL, I KILLED THE HOSTAGE.
AND THEN, Y'KNOW, WHAT DID I HAVE THEN?
I HAVE TO BE VERY CAREFUL.
IF I KILL YOU NOW...
BATMAN'S GOING TO PUNCH ME!

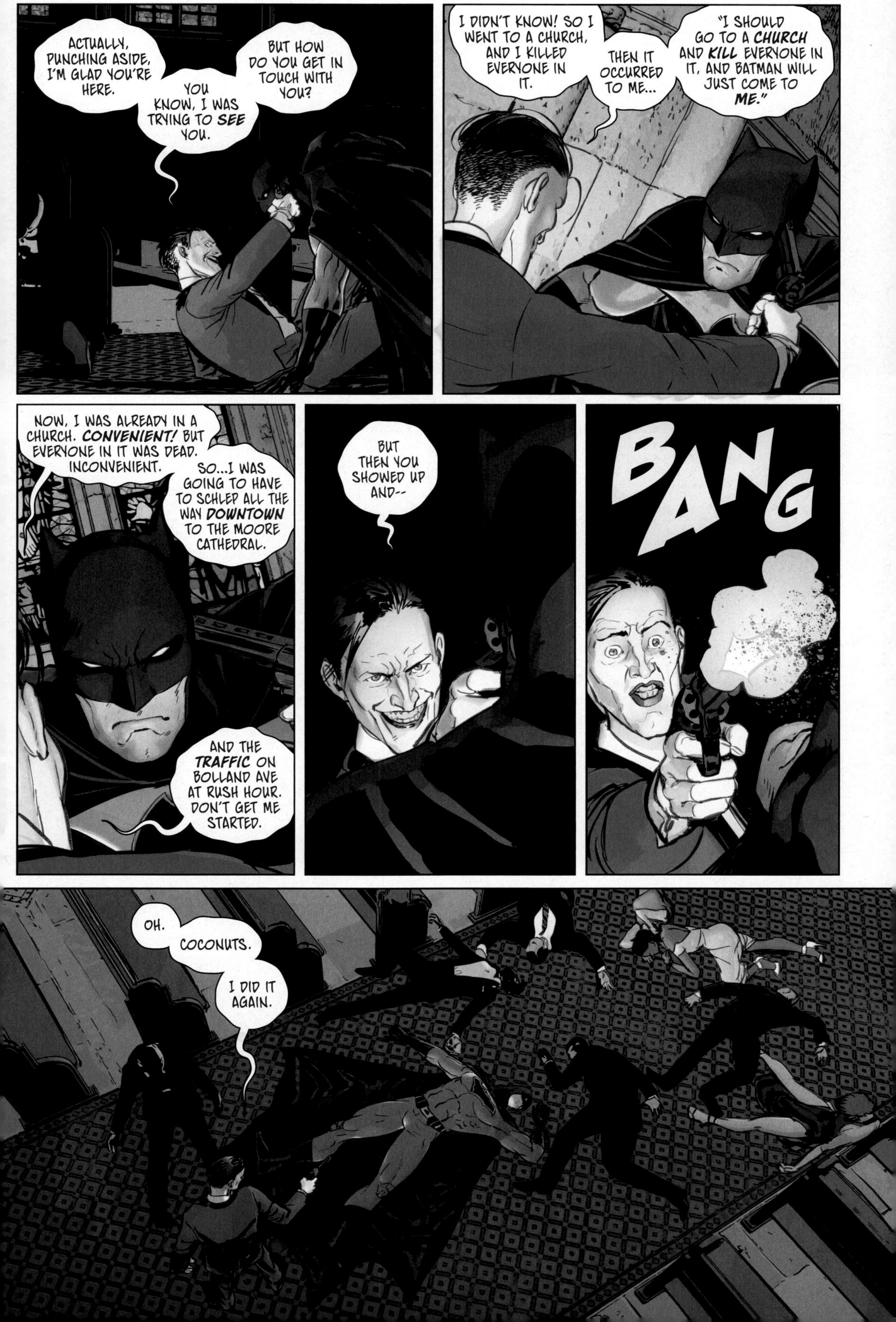
ACTUALLY, PUNCHING ASIDE, I'M GLAD YOU'RE HERE.
YOU KNOW, I WAS TRYING TO SEE YOU.
BUT HOW DO YOU GET IN TOUCH WITH YOU?
I DIDN'T KNOW! SO I WENT TO A CHURCH, AND I KILLED EVERYONE IN IT.
THEN IT OCCURRED TO ME...
"I SHOULD GO TO A CHURCH AND KILL EVERYONE IN IT, AND BATMAN WILL JUST COME TO ME."
NOW, I WAS ALREADY IN A CHURCH. CONVENIENT! BUT EVERYONE IN IT WAS DEAD. INCONVENIENT.
SO...I WAS GOING TO HAVE TO SCHLEP ALL THE WAY DOWNTOWN TO THE MOORE CATHEDRAL.
AND THE TRAFFIC ON BOLLAND AVE AT RUSH HOUR. DON'T GET ME STARTED.
BUT THEN YOU SHOWED UP AND--
BANG
OH.
COCONUTS.
I DID IT AGAIN.

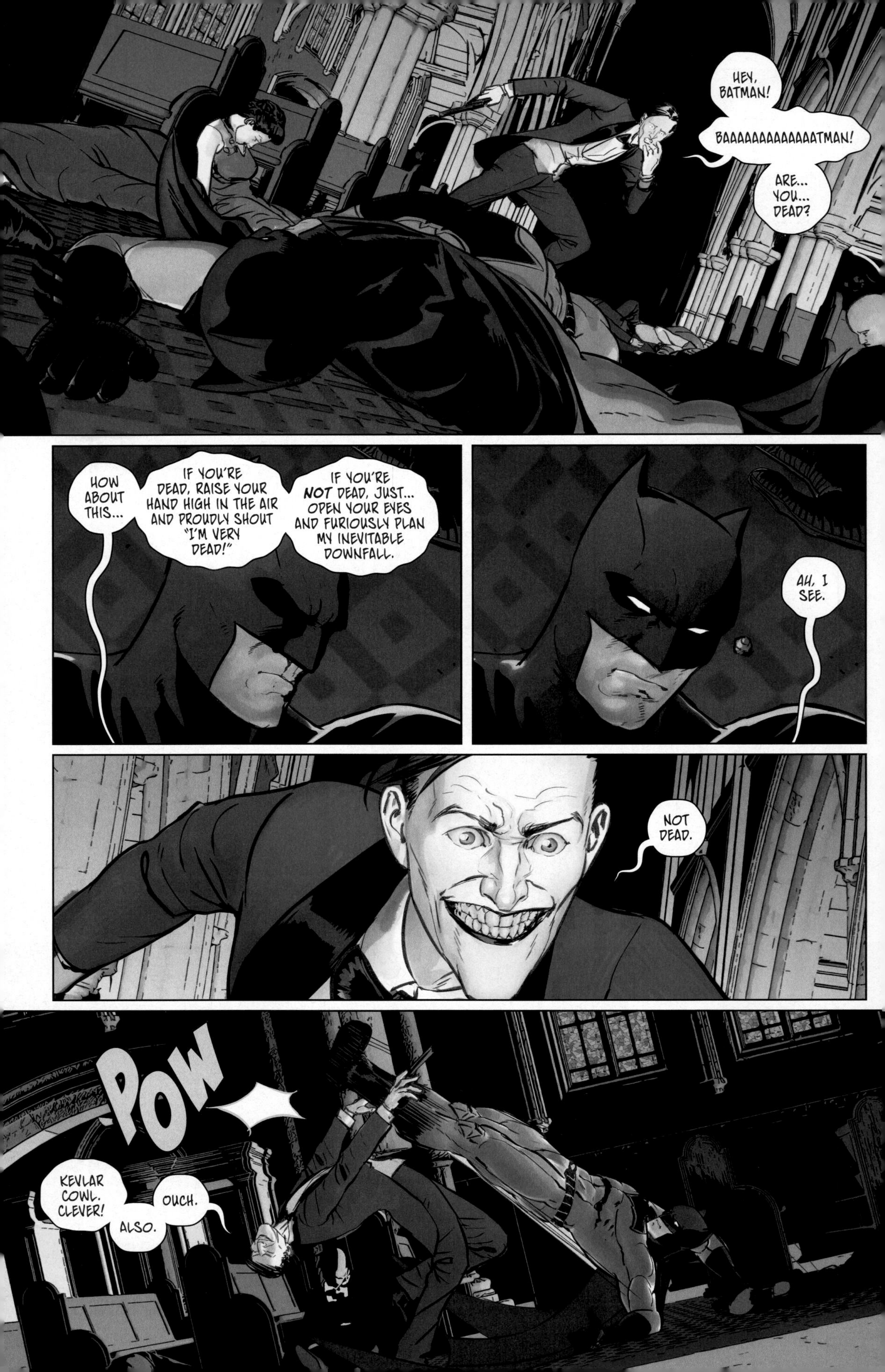
HEY, BATMAN!
BAAAAAAAAAAAAATMAN!
ARE... YOU... DEAD?
HOW ABOUT THIS...
IF YOU'RE DEAD, RAISE YOUR HAND HIGH IN THE AIR AND PROUDLY SHOUT "I'M VERY DEAD!"
IF YOU'RE **NOT** DEAD, JUST... OPEN YOUR EYES AND FURIOUSLY PLAN MY INEVITABLE DOWNFALL.
AH, I SEE.
NOT DEAD.
POW
KEVLAR COWL. CLEVER!
ALSO.
OUCH.

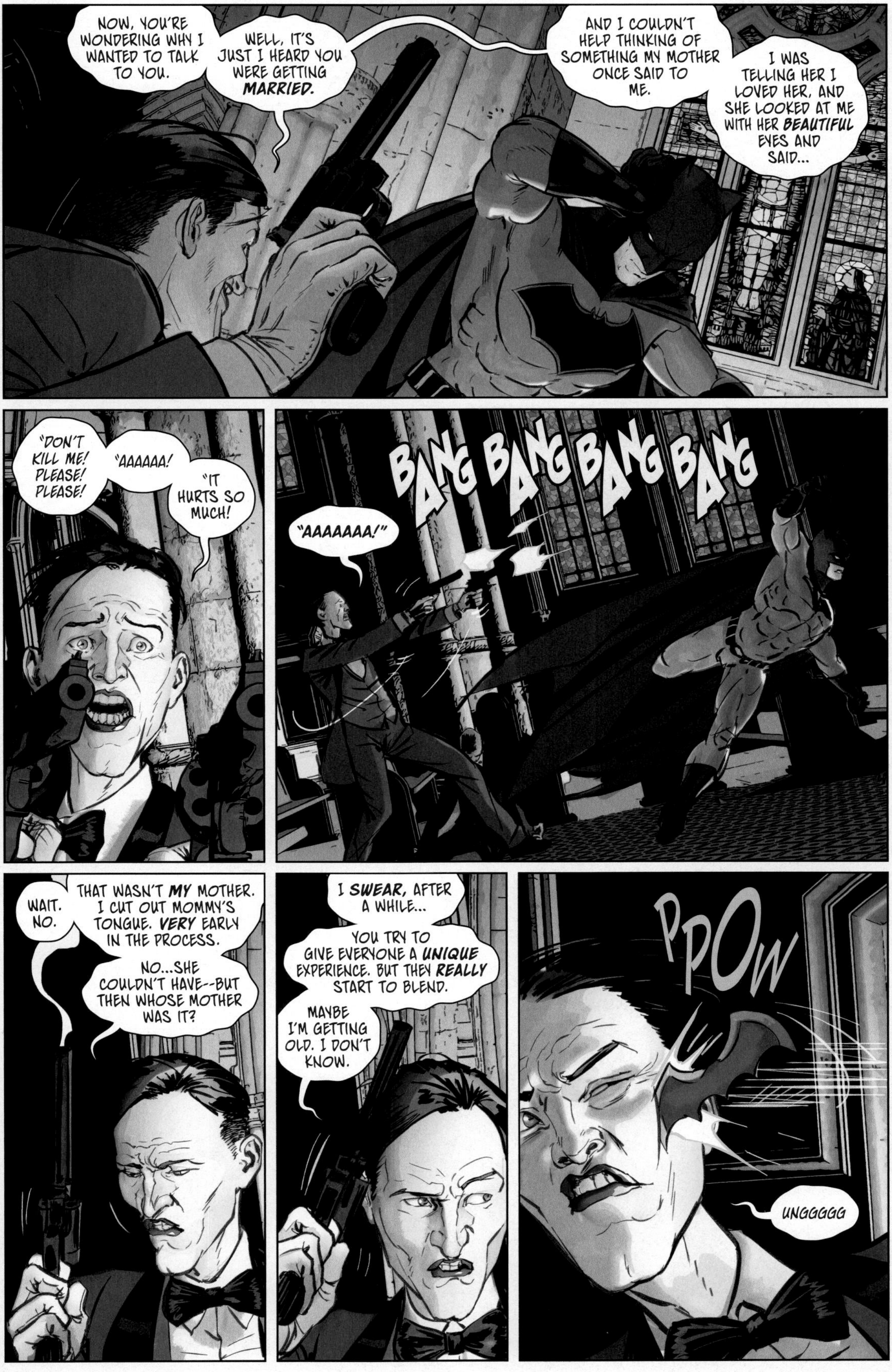
NOW, YOU'RE WONDERING WHY I WANTED TO TALK TO YOU.
WELL, IT'S JUST I HEARD YOU WERE GETTING MARRIED.
AND I COULDN'T HELP THINKING OF SOMETHING MY MOTHER ONCE SAID TO ME.
I WAS TELLING HER I LOVED HER, AND SHE LOOKED AT ME WITH HER BEAUTIFUL EYES AND SAID...
"DON'T KILL ME! PLEASE! PLEASE!
"AAAAAA!
"IT HURTS SO MUCH!
BANG BANG BANG BANG
"AAAAAAA!"
WAIT. NO.
THAT WASN'T MY MOTHER. I CUT OUT MOMMY'S TONGUE. VERY EARLY IN THE PROCESS.
NO...SHE COULDN'T HAVE--BUT THEN WHOSE MOTHER WAS IT?
I SWEAR, AFTER A WHILE...
YOU TRY TO GIVE EVERYONE A UNIQUE EXPERIENCE. BUT THEY REALLY START TO BLEND.
MAYBE I'M GETTING OLD. I DON'T KNOW.
PPOW
UNGGGGG

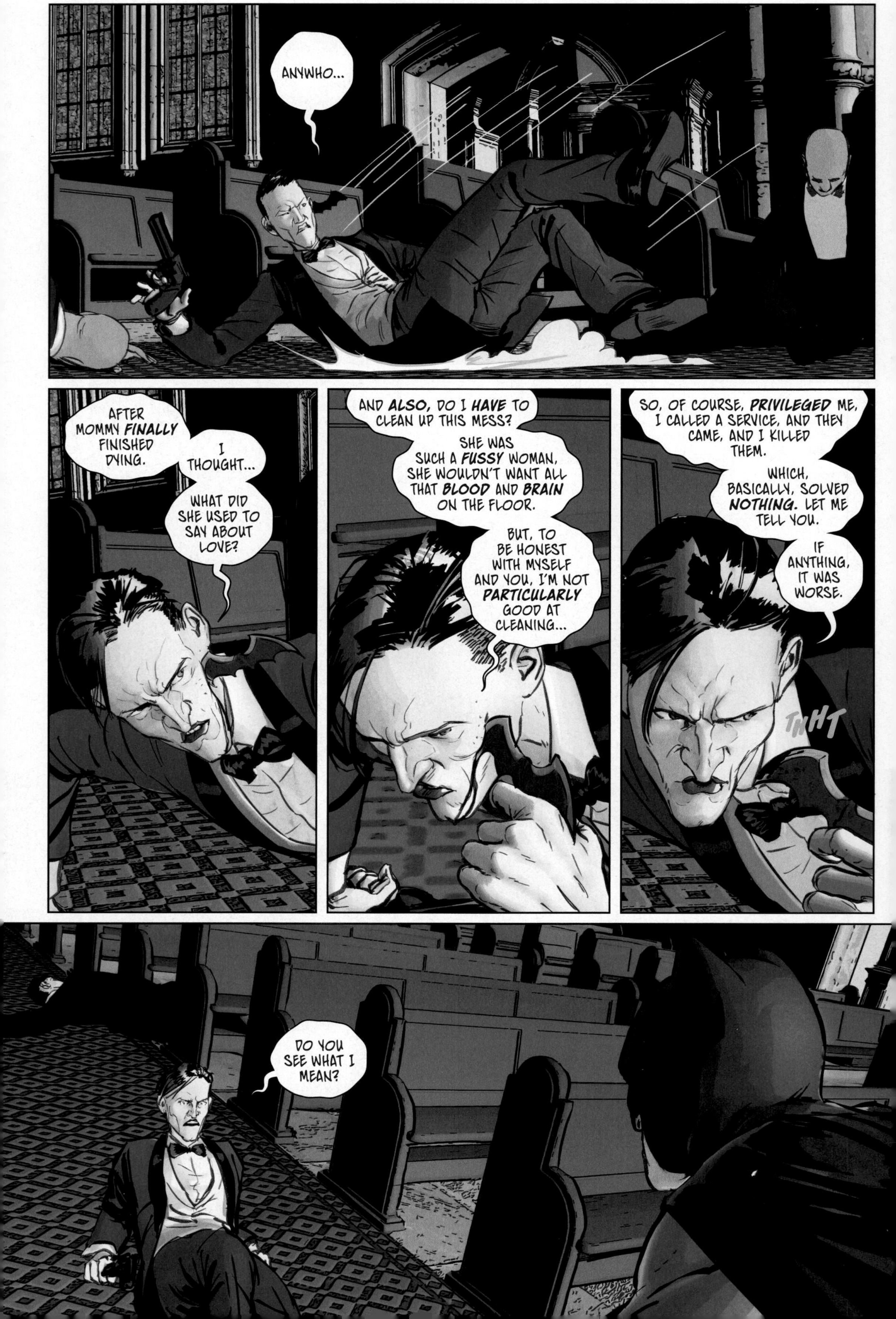
ANYWHO...
AFTER MOMMY FINALLY FINISHED DYING.
I THOUGHT...
WHAT DID SHE USED TO SAY ABOUT LOVE?
AND ALSO, DO I HAVE TO CLEAN UP THIS MESS?
SHE WAS SUCH A FUSSY WOMAN, SHE WOULDN'T WANT ALL THAT BLOOD AND BRAIN ON THE FLOOR.
BUT, TO BE HONEST WITH MYSELF AND YOU, I'M NOT PARTICULARLY GOOD AT CLEANING...
SO, OF COURSE, PRIVILEGED ME, I CALLED A SERVICE, AND THEY CAME, AND I KILLED THEM.
WHICH, BASICALLY, SOLVED NOTHING. LET ME TELL YOU.
IF ANYTHING, IT WAS WORSE.
THHT
DO YOU SEE WHAT I MEAN?

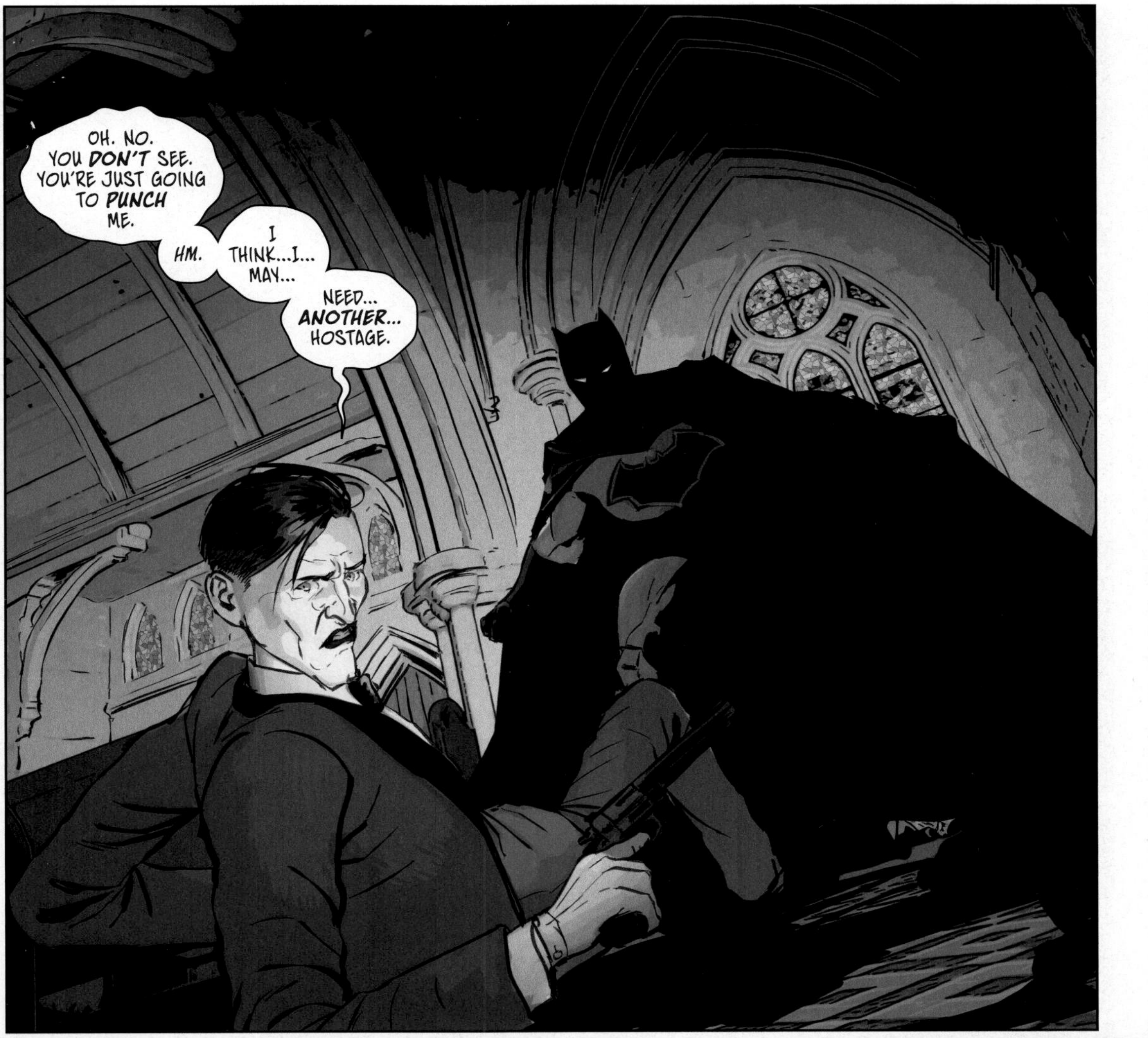
OH. NO. YOU DON'T SEE. YOU'RE JUST GOING TO PUNCH ME.
HM.
I THINK...I... MAY...
NEED... ANOTHER... HOSTAGE.

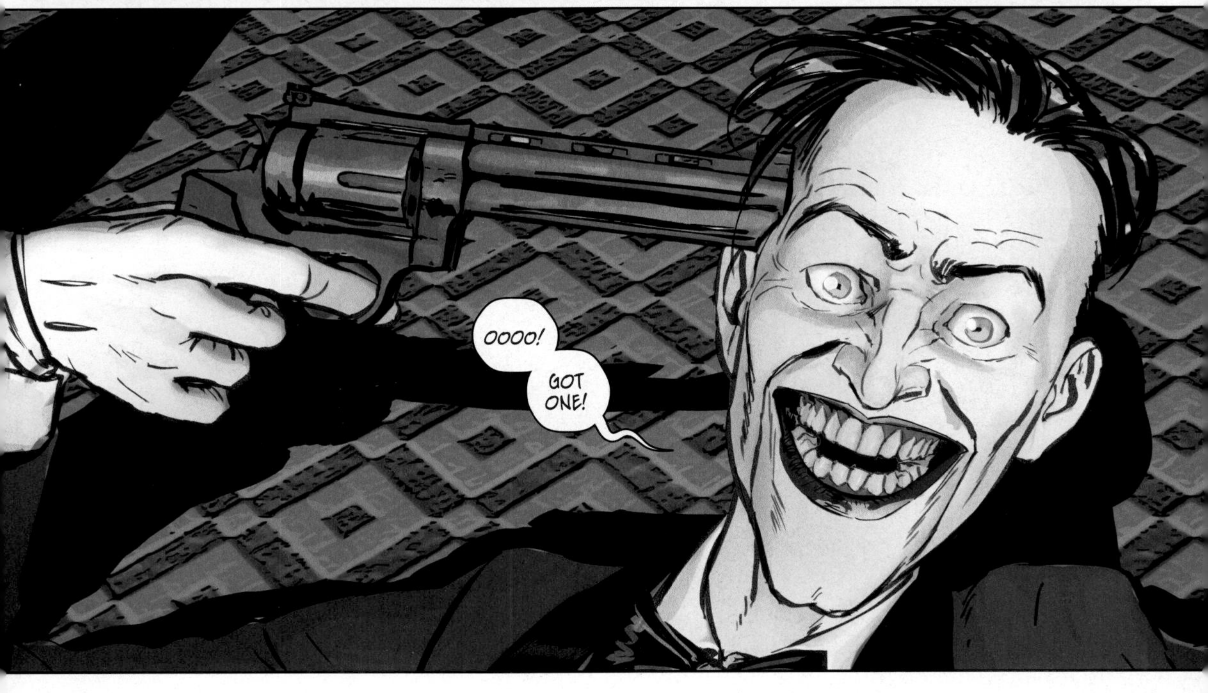
OOOO!
GOT ONE!

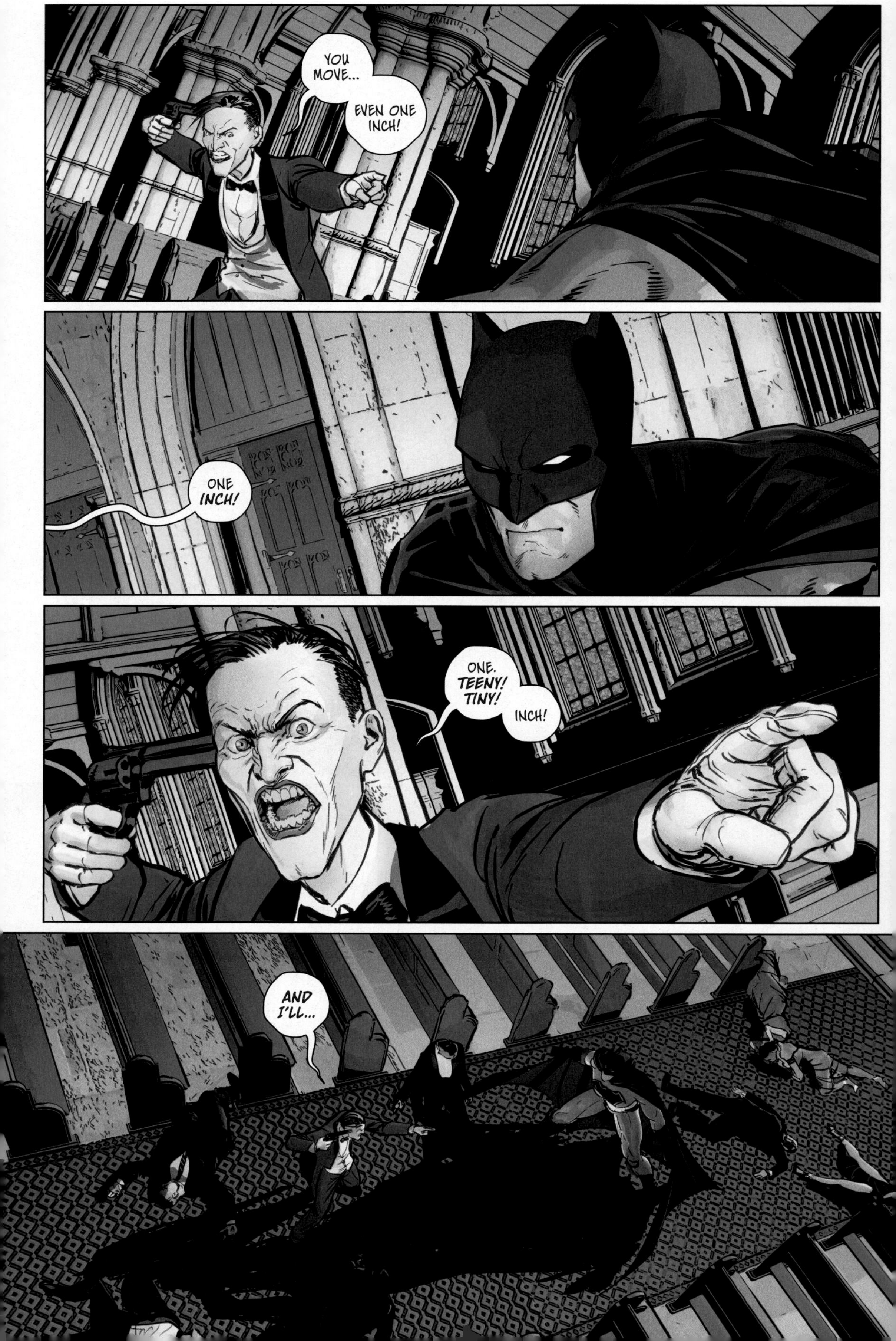
YOU MOVE...
EVEN ONE INCH!
ONE INCH!
ONE. TEENY! TINY!
INCH!
AND I'LL...

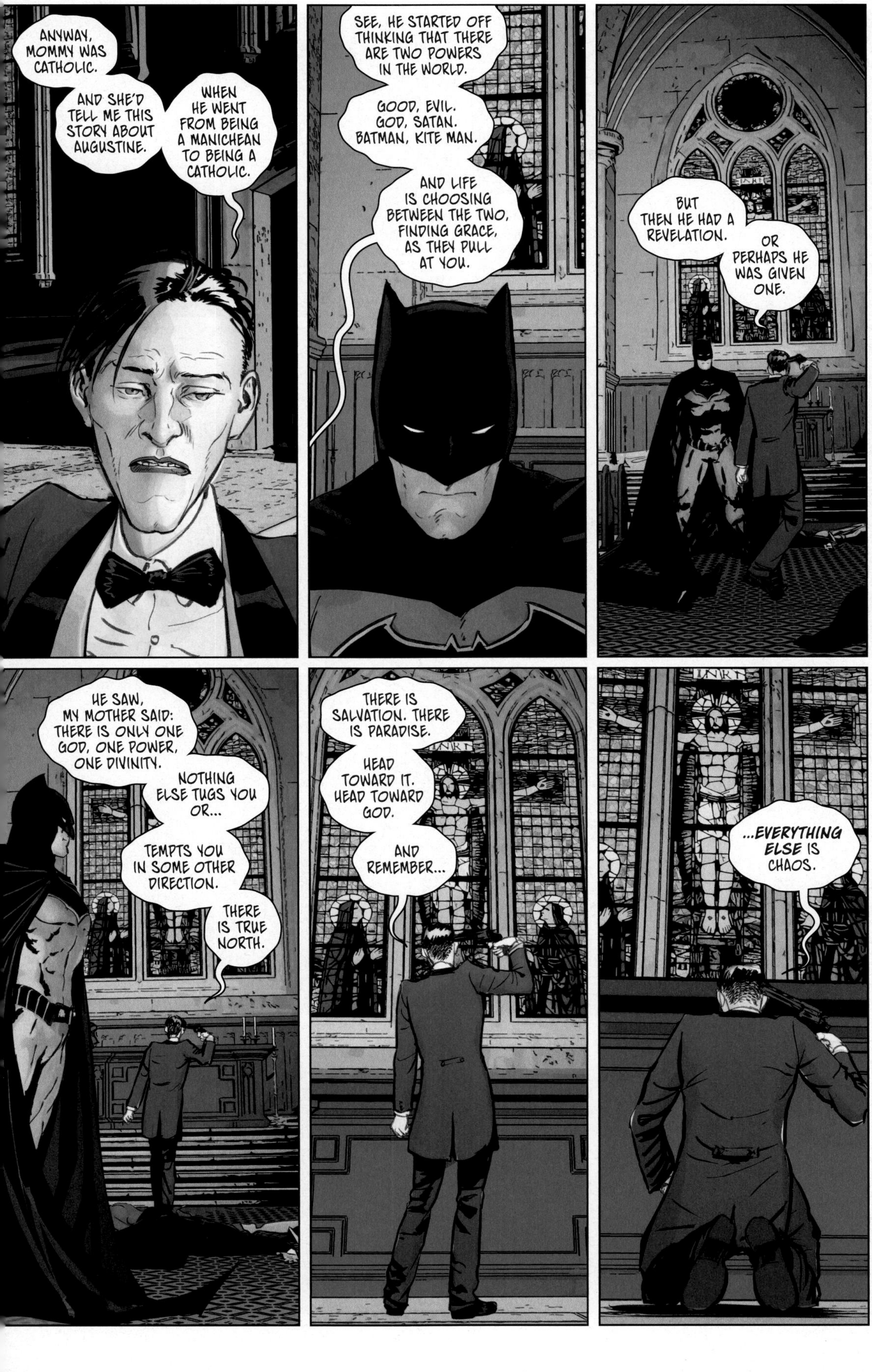
ANYWAY, MOMMY WAS CATHOLIC.
AND SHE'D TELL ME THIS STORY ABOUT AUGUSTINE.
WHEN HE WENT FROM BEING A MANICHEAN TO BEING A CATHOLIC.
SEE, HE STARTED OFF THINKING THAT THERE ARE TWO POWERS IN THE WORLD.
GOOD, EVIL. GOD, SATAN. BATMAN, KITE MAN.
AND LIFE IS CHOOSING BETWEEN THE TWO, FINDING GRACE, AS THEY PULL AT YOU.
BUT THEN HE HAD A REVELATION.
OR PERHAPS HE WAS GIVEN ONE.
HE SAW, MY MOTHER SAID: THERE IS ONLY ONE GOD, ONE POWER, ONE DIVINITY.
NOTHING ELSE TUGS YOU OR...
TEMPTS YOU IN SOME OTHER DIRECTION.
THERE IS TRUE NORTH.
THERE IS SALVATION. THERE IS PARADISE.
HEAD TOWARD IT. HEAD TOWARD GOD.
AND REMEMBER...
...**EVERYTHING ELSE** IS CHAOS.

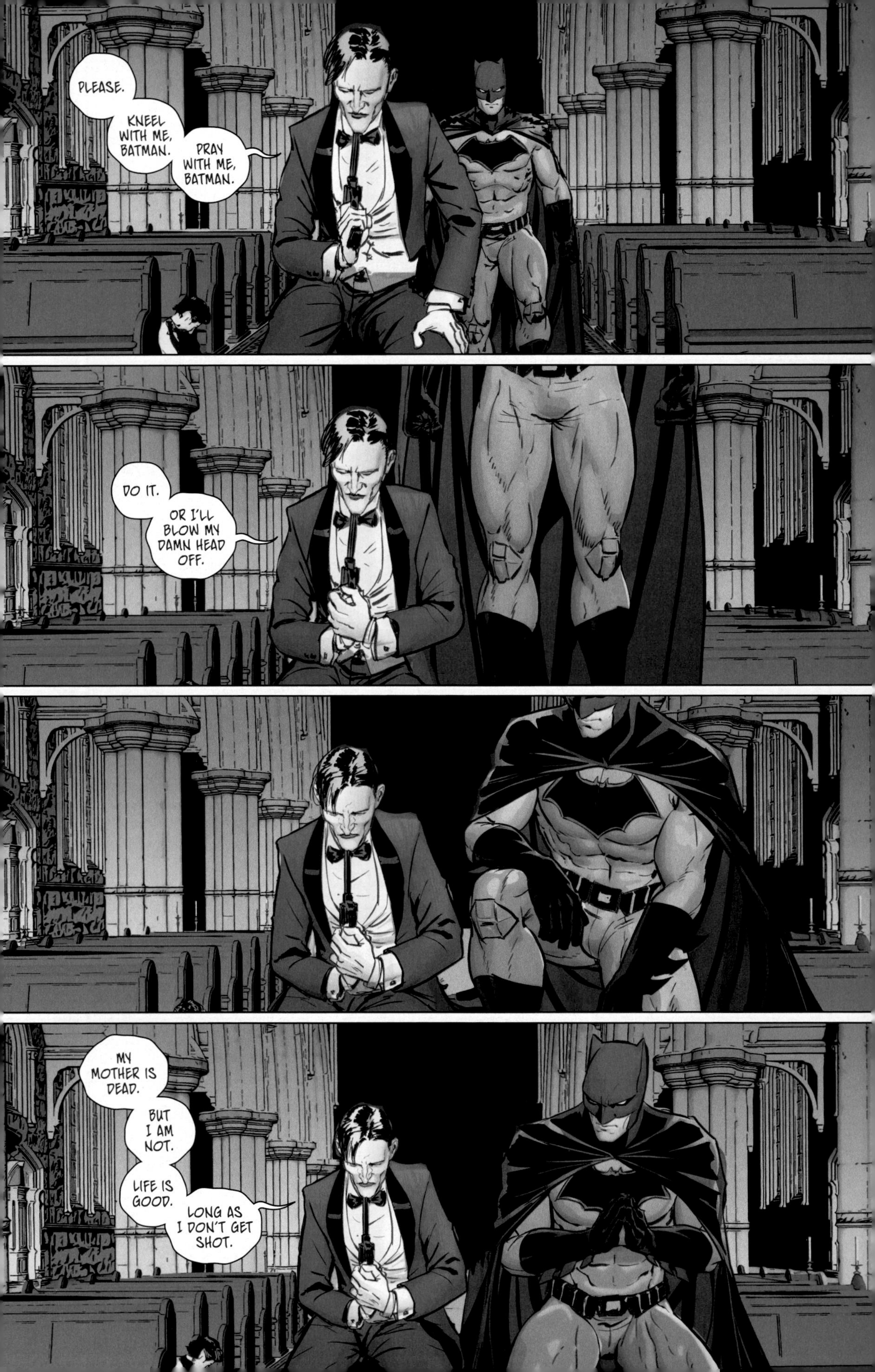
PLEASE.
KNEEL WITH ME, BATMAN.
PRAY WITH ME, BATMAN.
DO IT.
OR I'LL BLOW MY DAMN HEAD OFF.
MY MOTHER IS DEAD.
BUT I AM NOT.
LIFE IS GOOD.
LONG AS I DON'T GET SHOT.

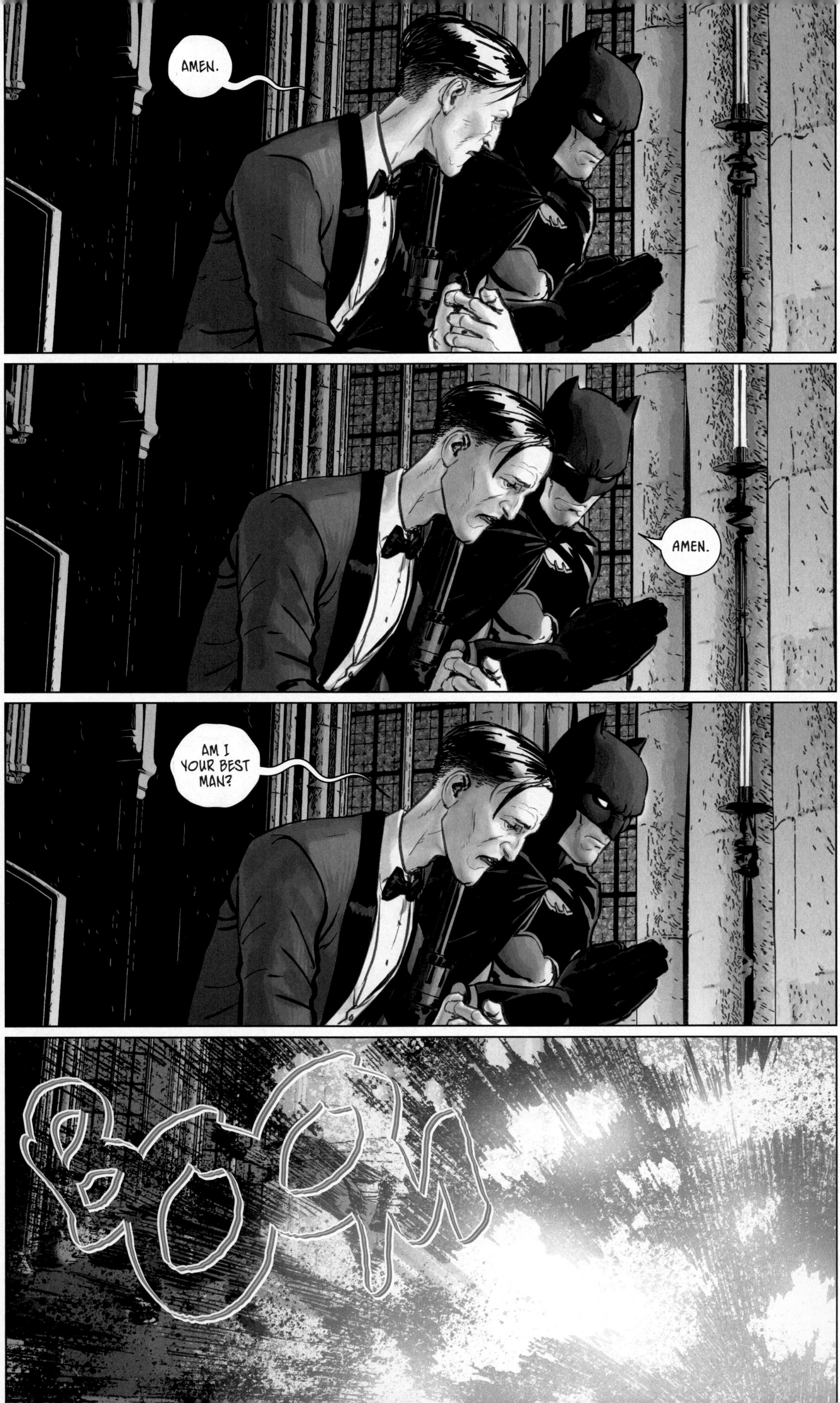
AMEN.
AMEN.
AM I YOUR BEST MAN?
BOOM

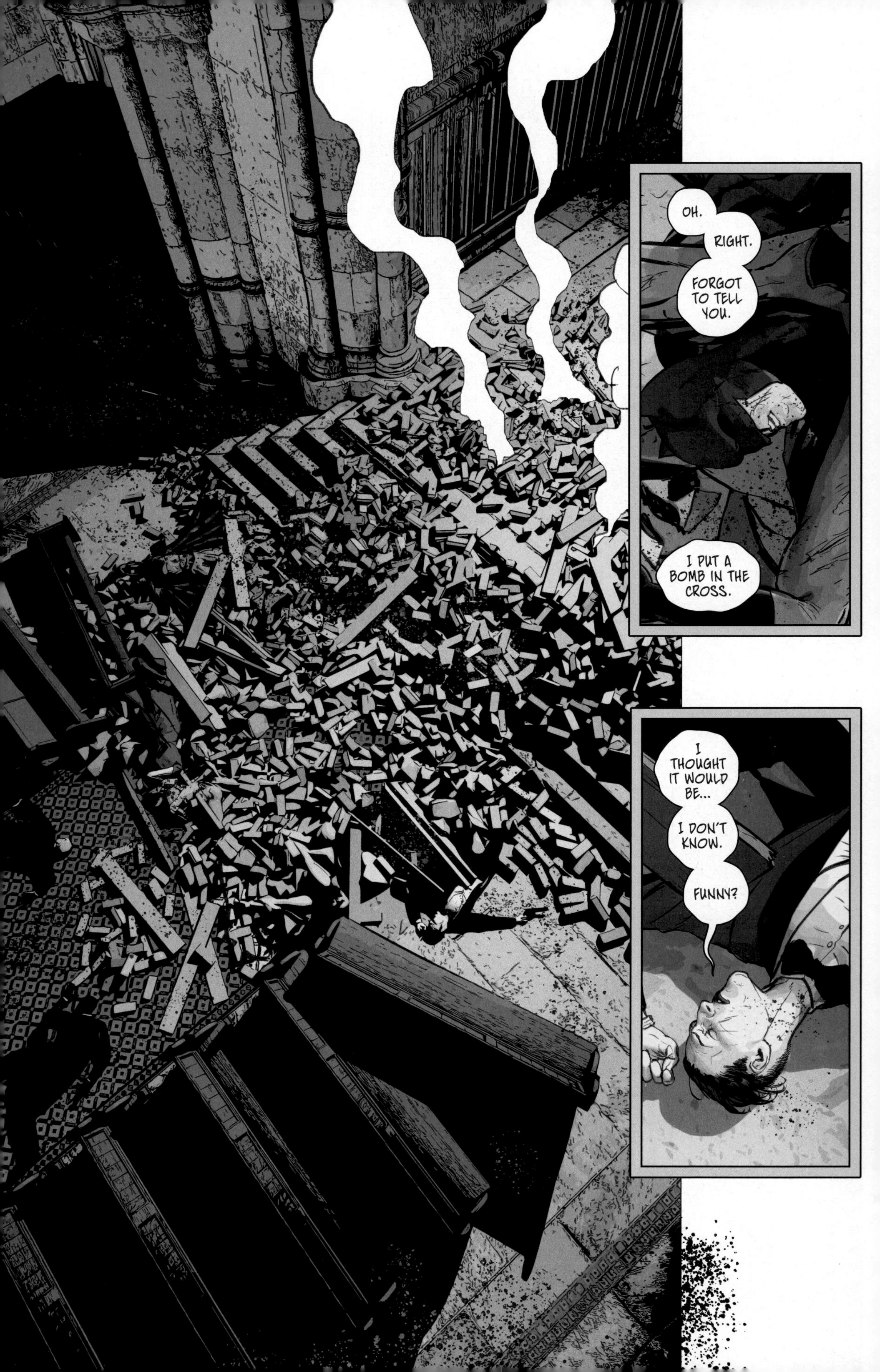
OH.
RIGHT.
FORGOT TO TELL YOU.
I PUT A BOMB IN THE CROSS.
I THOUGHT IT WOULD BE...
I DON'T KNOW.
FUNNY?

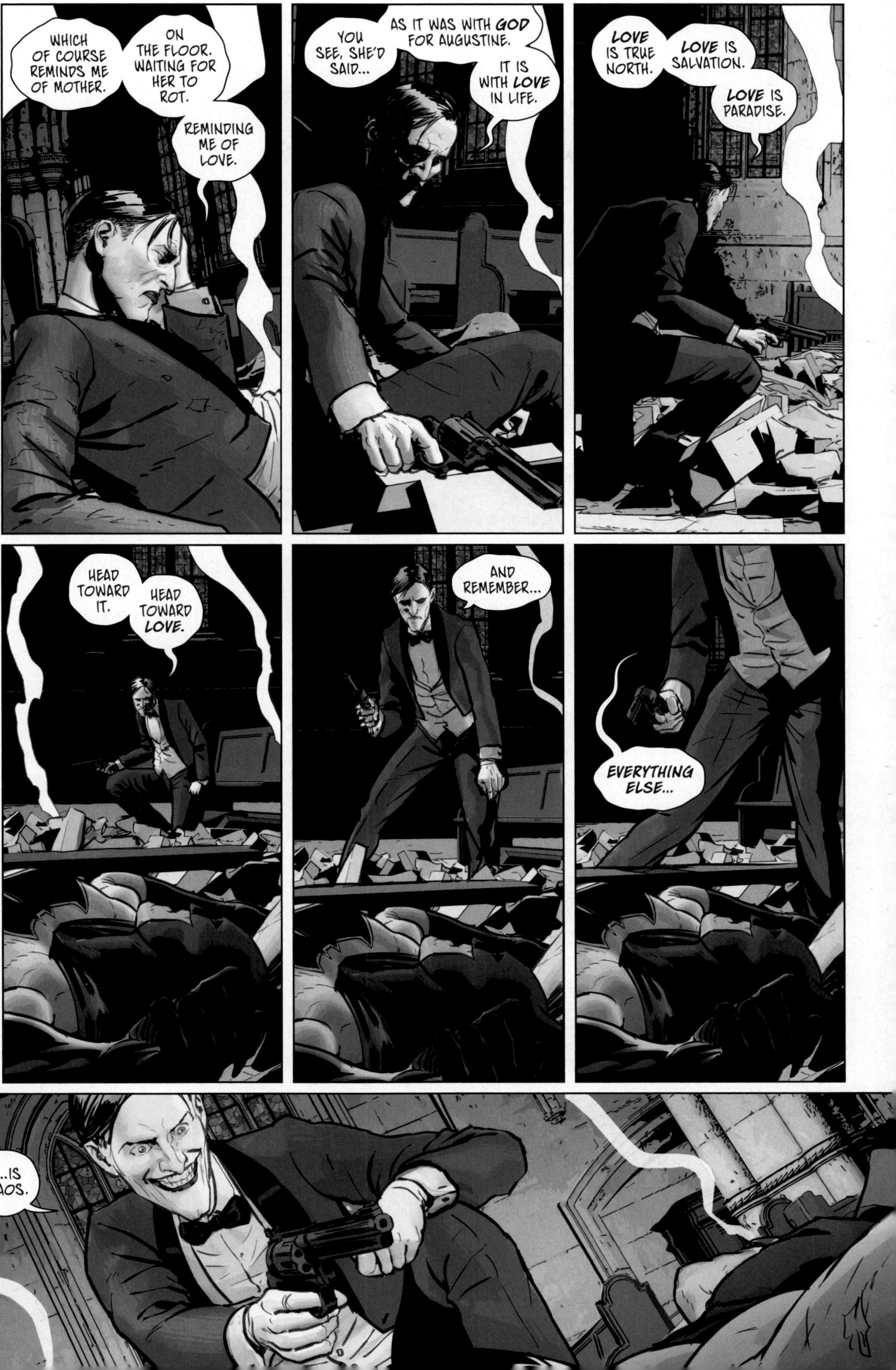
WHICH OF COURSE REMINDS ME OF MOTHER.
ON THE FLOOR. WAITING FOR HER TO ROT.
REMINDING ME OF LOVE.
YOU SEE, SHE'D SAID...
AS IT WAS WITH GOD FOR AUGUSTINE.
IT IS WITH LOVE IN LIFE.
LOVE IS TRUE NORTH.
LOVE IS SALVATION.
LOVE IS PARADISE.
HEAD TOWARD IT.
HEAD TOWARD LOVE.
AND REMEMBER...
EVERYTHING ELSE...
...IS CHAOS.

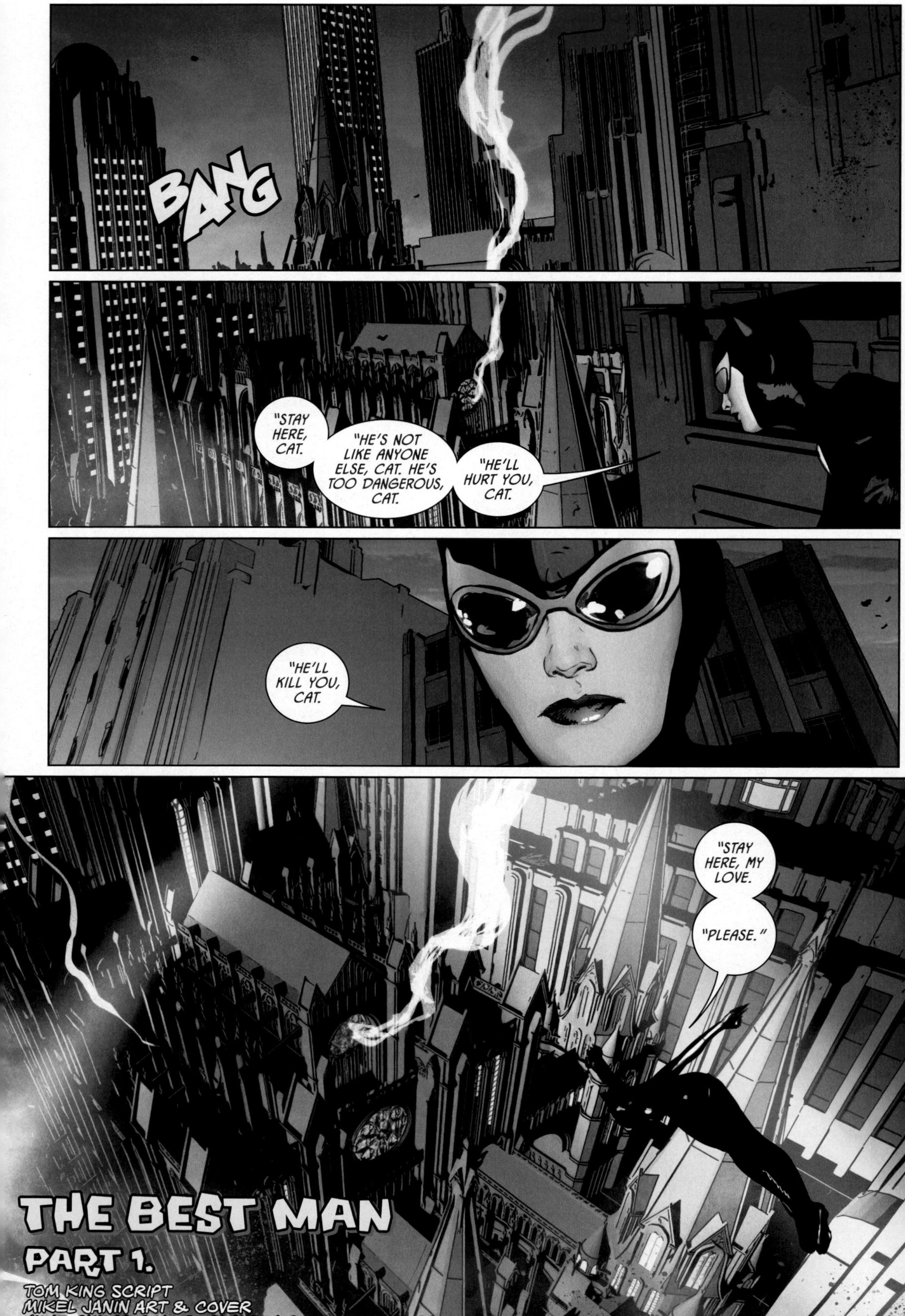
BANG
"STAY HERE, CAT.
"HE'S NOT LIKE ANYONE ELSE, CAT. HE'S TOO DANGEROUS, CAT.
"HE'LL HURT YOU, CAT.
"HE'LL KILL YOU, CAT.
"STAY HERE, MY LOVE.
"PLEASE."
THE BEST MAN
PART 1.
TOM KING SCRIPT
MIKEL JANIN ART & COVER
JUNE CHUNG COLOR CLAYTON COWLES LETTERS
BRITTANY HOLZHERR ASSOC. EDITOR JAMIE S. RICH EDITOR

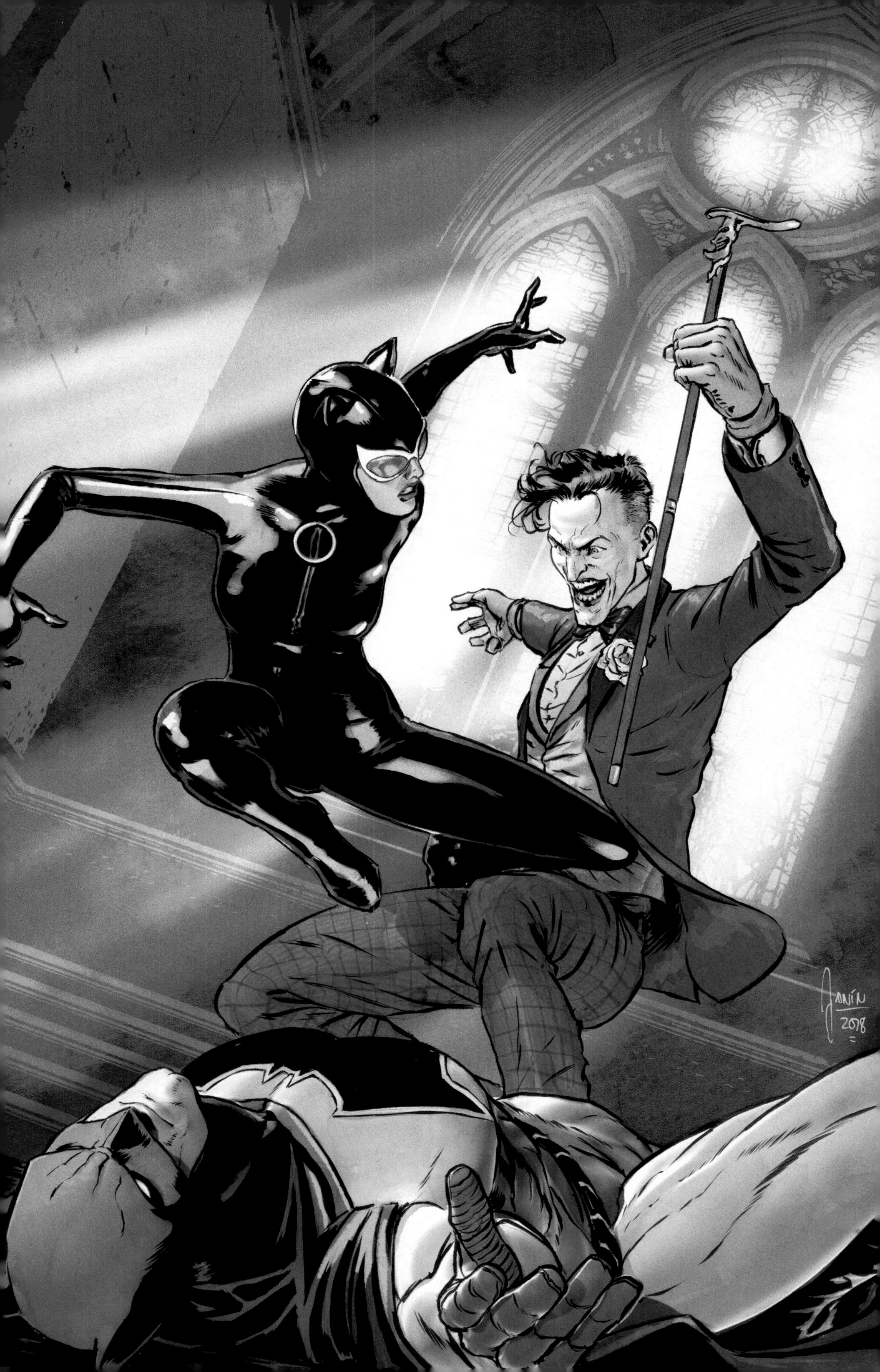

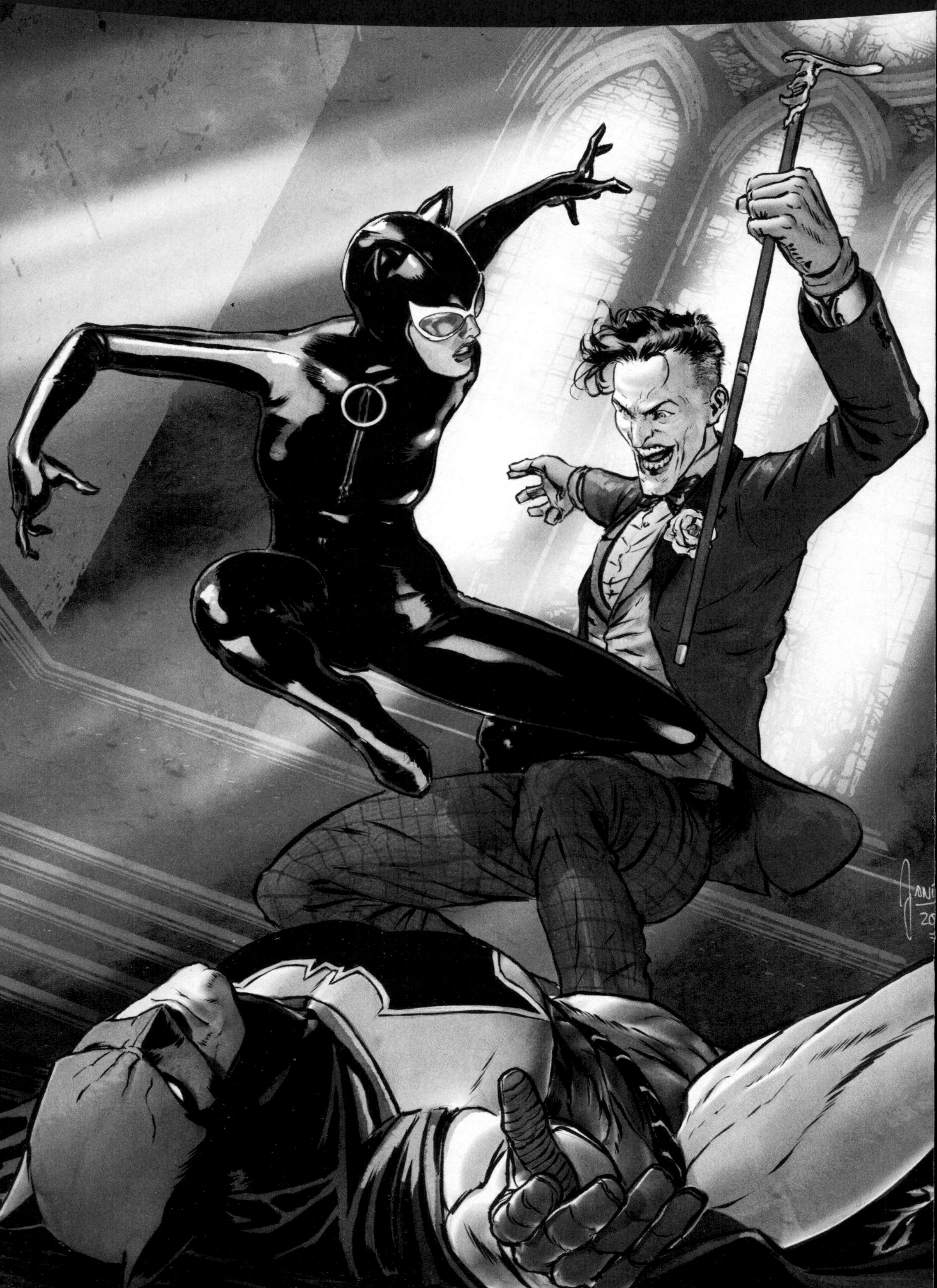

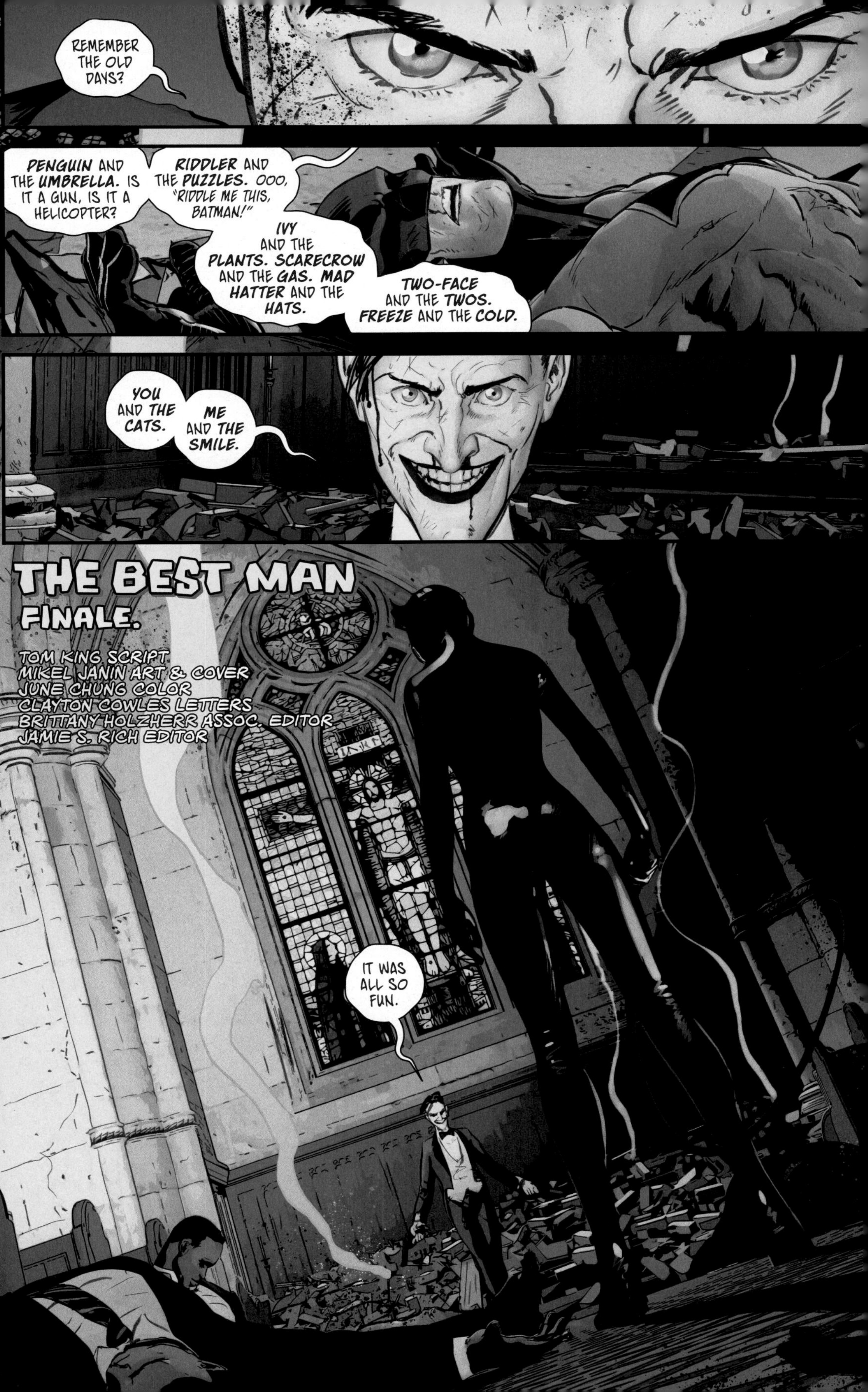
REMEMBER THE OLD DAYS?
PENGUIN AND THE UMBRELLA. IS IT A GUN, IS IT A HELICOPTER?
RIDDLER AND THE PUZZLES. OOO, "RIDDLE ME THIS, BATMAN!"
IVY AND THE PLANTS. SCARECROW AND THE GAS. MAD HATTER AND THE HATS.
TWO-FACE AND THE TWOS. FREEZE AND THE COLD.
YOU AND THE CATS.
ME AND THE SMILE.
THE BEST MAN
FINALE.
TOM KING SCRIPT
MIKEL JANIN ART & COVER
JUNE CHUNG COLOR
CLAYTON COWLES LETTERS
BRITTANY HOLZHERR ASSOC. EDITOR
JAMIE S. RICH EDITOR
IT WAS ALL SO FUN.

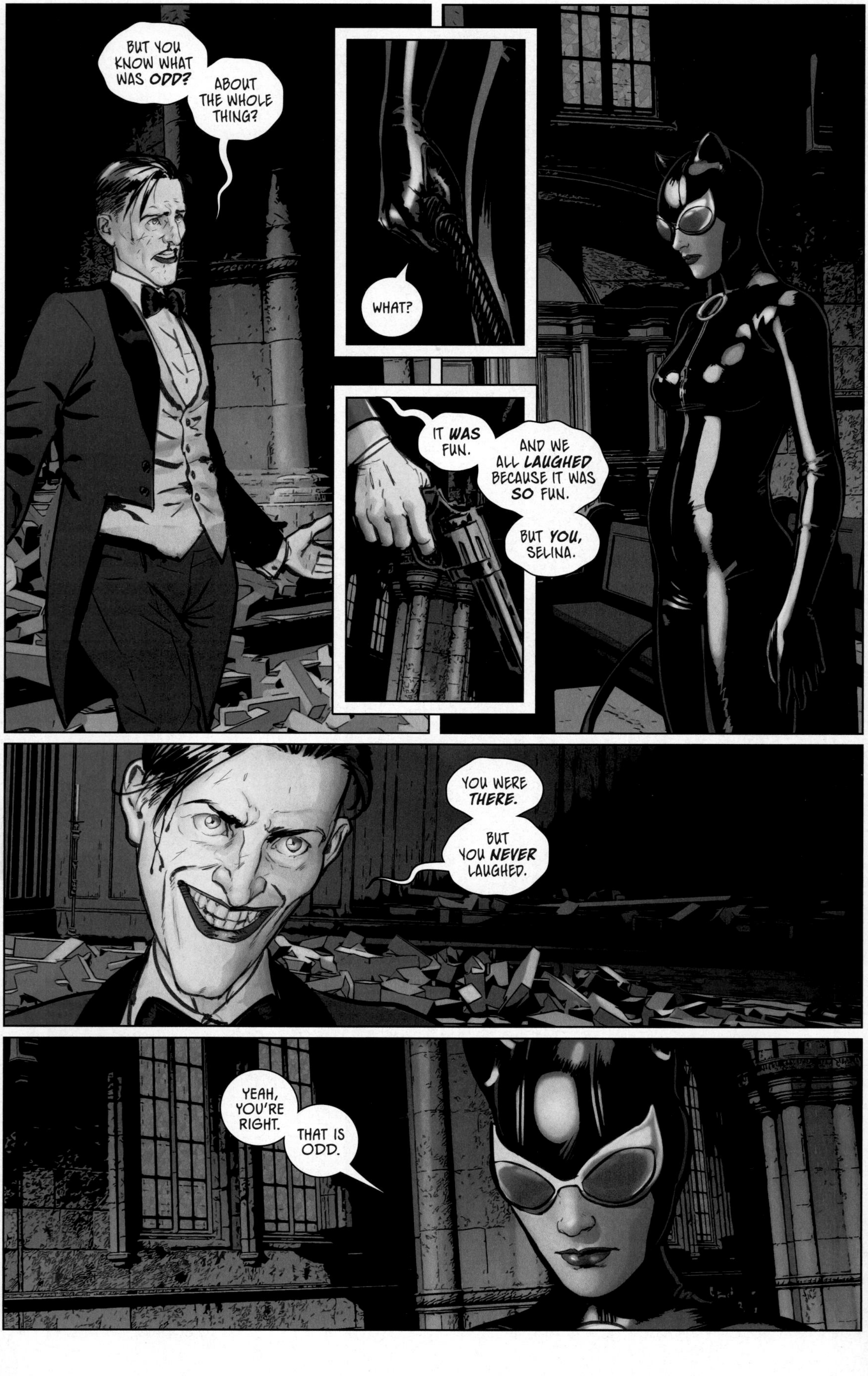

BUT YOU KNOW WHAT WAS ODD?
ABOUT THE WHOLE THING?
WHAT?
IT WAS FUN.
AND WE ALL LAUGHED BECAUSE IT WAS SO FUN.
BUT YOU, SELINA.
YOU WERE THERE.
BUT YOU NEVER LAUGHED.
YEAH, YOU'RE RIGHT.
THAT IS ODD.

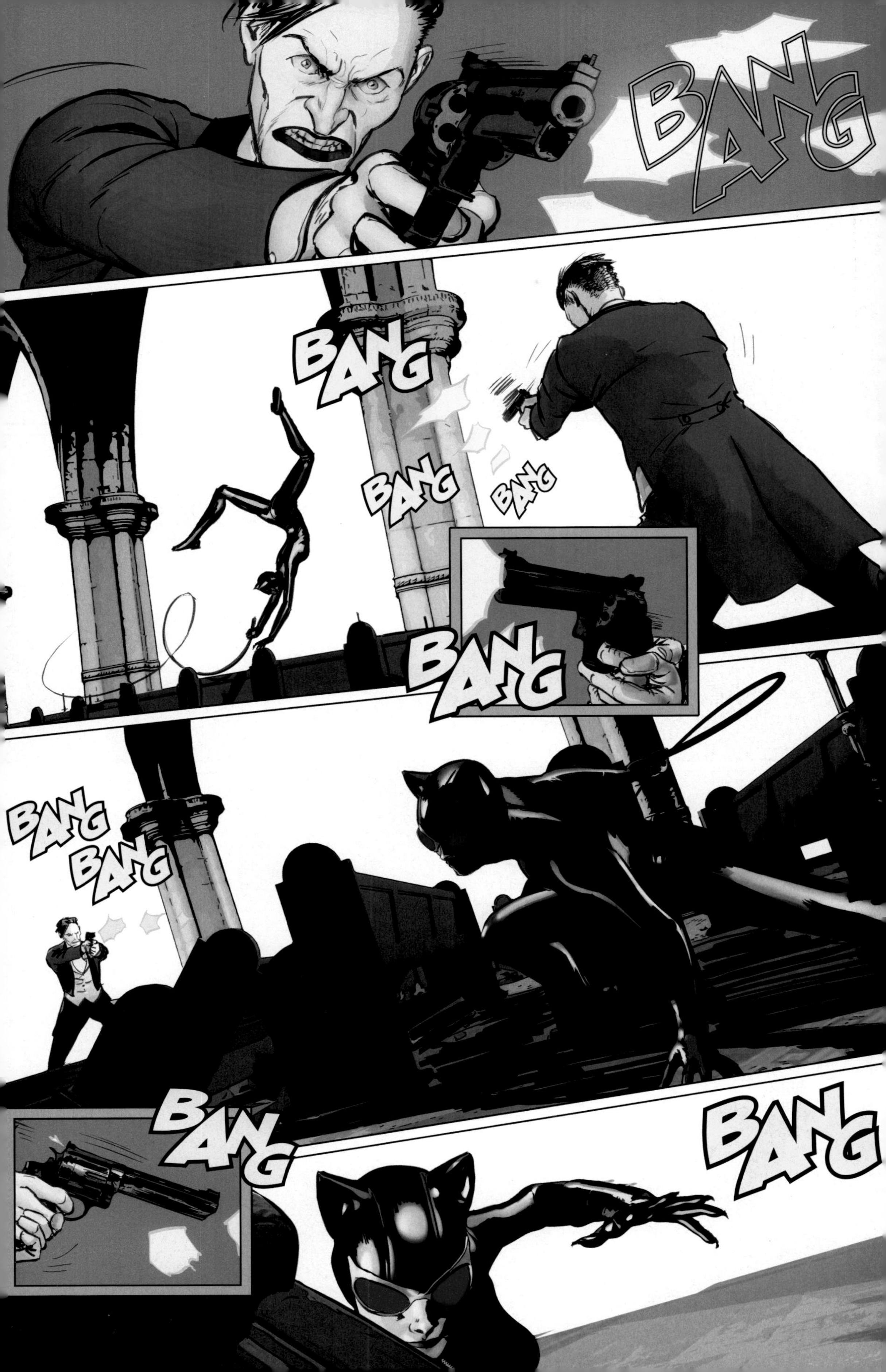
BANG
BANG
BANG
BANG
BANG
BANG
BANG
BANG
BANG

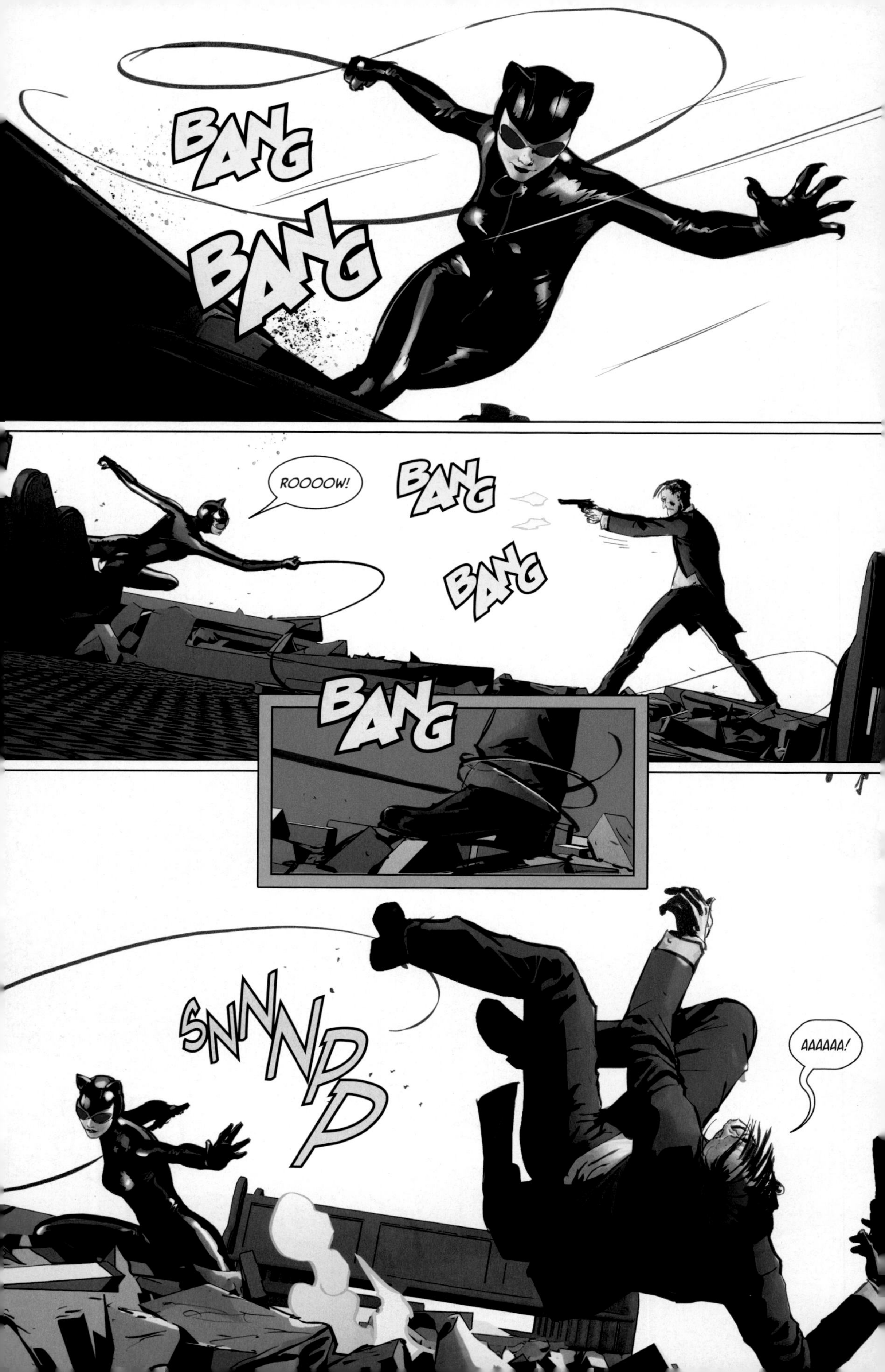
BANG
BANG
ROOOOW!
BANG
BANG
BANG
SNNNPP
AAAAAA!

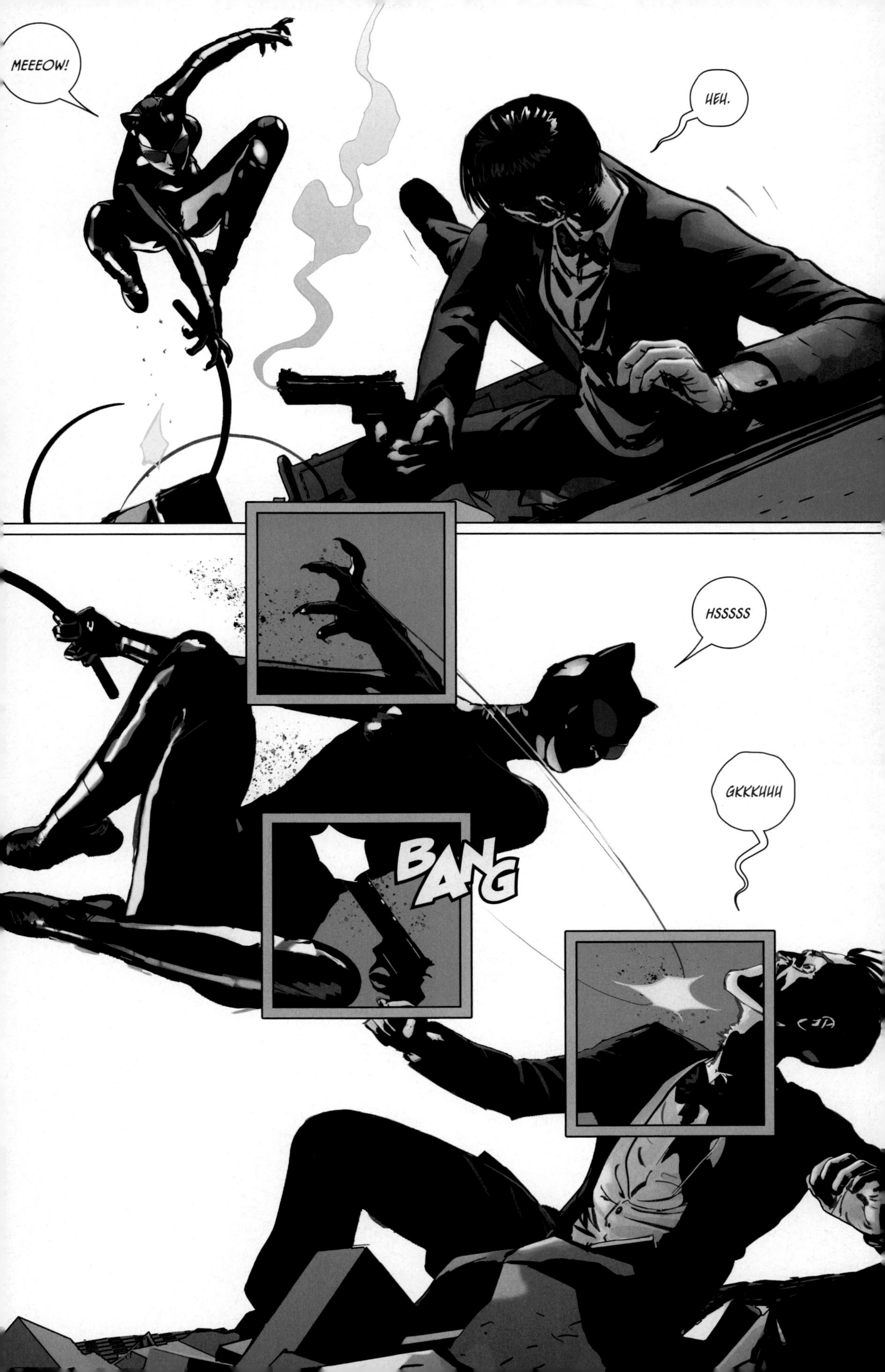
MEEEOW!
HEH.
HSSSSS
GKKKHHH
BANG

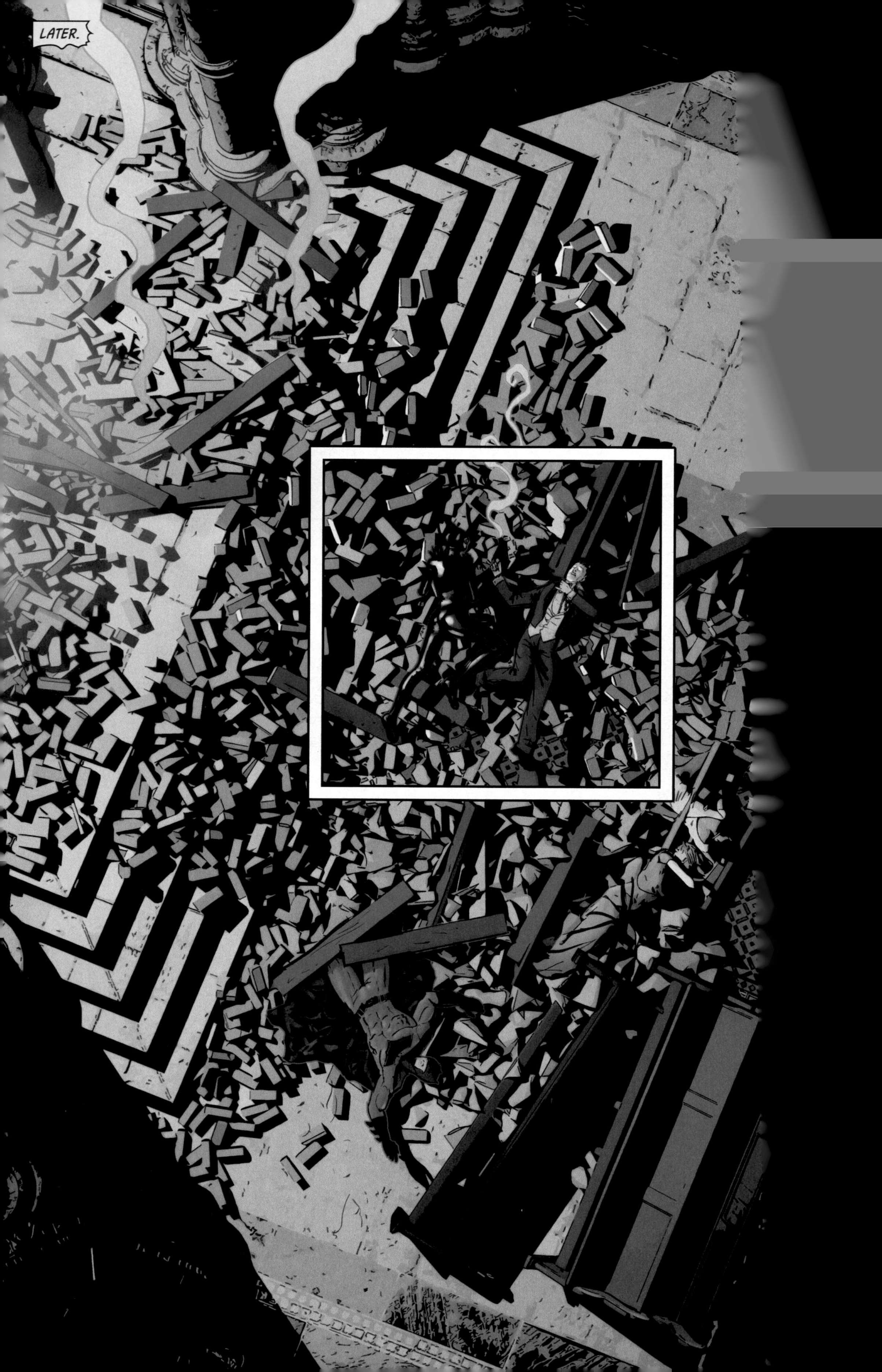
LATER.

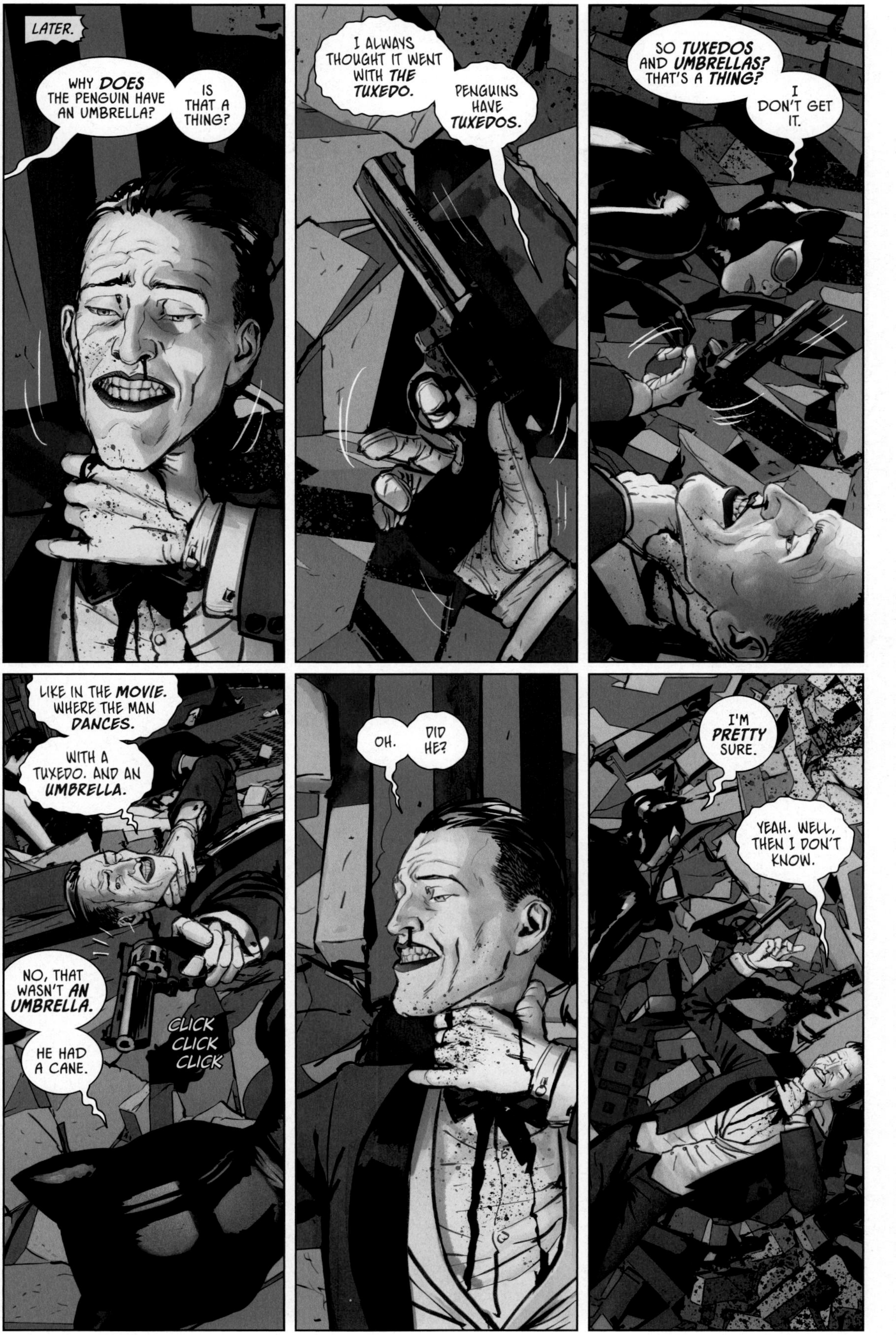
LATER.
WHY DOES THE PENGUIN HAVE AN UMBRELLA?
IS THAT A THING?
I ALWAYS THOUGHT IT WENT WITH THE TUXEDO.
PENGUINS HAVE TUXEDOS.
SO TUXEDOS AND UMBRELLAS? THAT'S A THING?
I DON'T GET IT.
LIKE IN THE MOVIE. WHERE THE MAN DANCES.
WITH A TUXEDO. AND AN UMBRELLA.
NO, THAT WASN'T AN UMBRELLA.
HE HAD A CANE.
CLICK CLICK CLICK
OH.
DID HE?
I'M PRETTY SURE.
YEAH. WELL, THEN I DON'T KNOW.

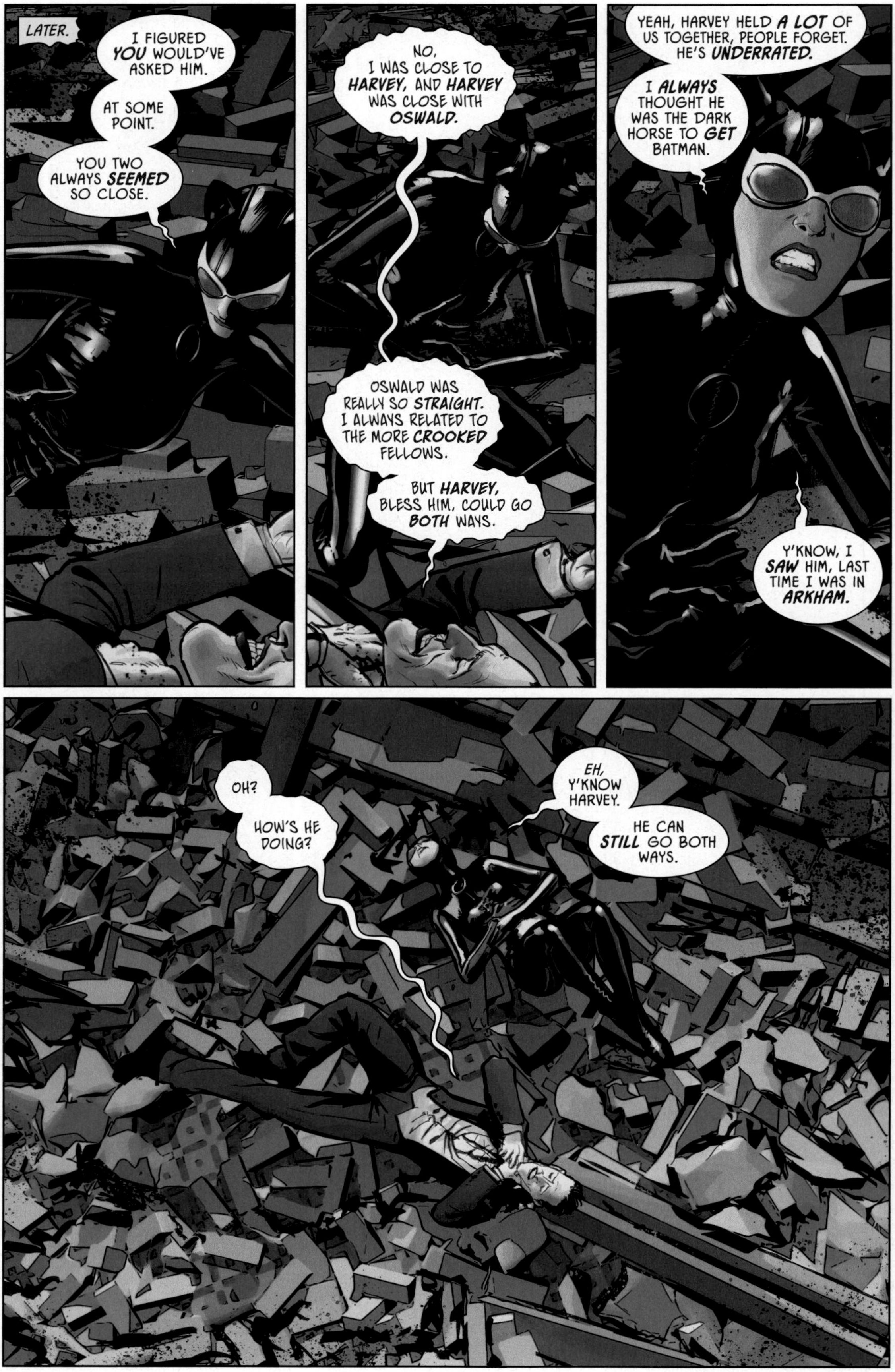
LATER.
I FIGURED YOU WOULD'VE ASKED HIM.
AT SOME POINT.
YOU TWO ALWAYS SEEMED SO CLOSE.
NO, I WAS CLOSE TO HARVEY, AND HARVEY WAS CLOSE WITH OSWALD.
OSWALD WAS REALLY SO STRAIGHT. I ALWAYS RELATED TO THE MORE CROOKED FELLOWS.
BUT HARVEY, BLESS HIM, COULD GO BOTH WAYS.
YEAH, HARVEY HELD A LOT OF US TOGETHER, PEOPLE FORGET. HE'S UNDERRATED.
I ALWAYS THOUGHT HE WAS THE DARK HORSE TO GET BATMAN.
Y'KNOW, I SAW HIM, LAST TIME I WAS IN ARKHAM.
OH?
HOW'S HE DOING?
EH, Y'KNOW HARVEY.
HE CAN STILL GO BOTH WAYS.

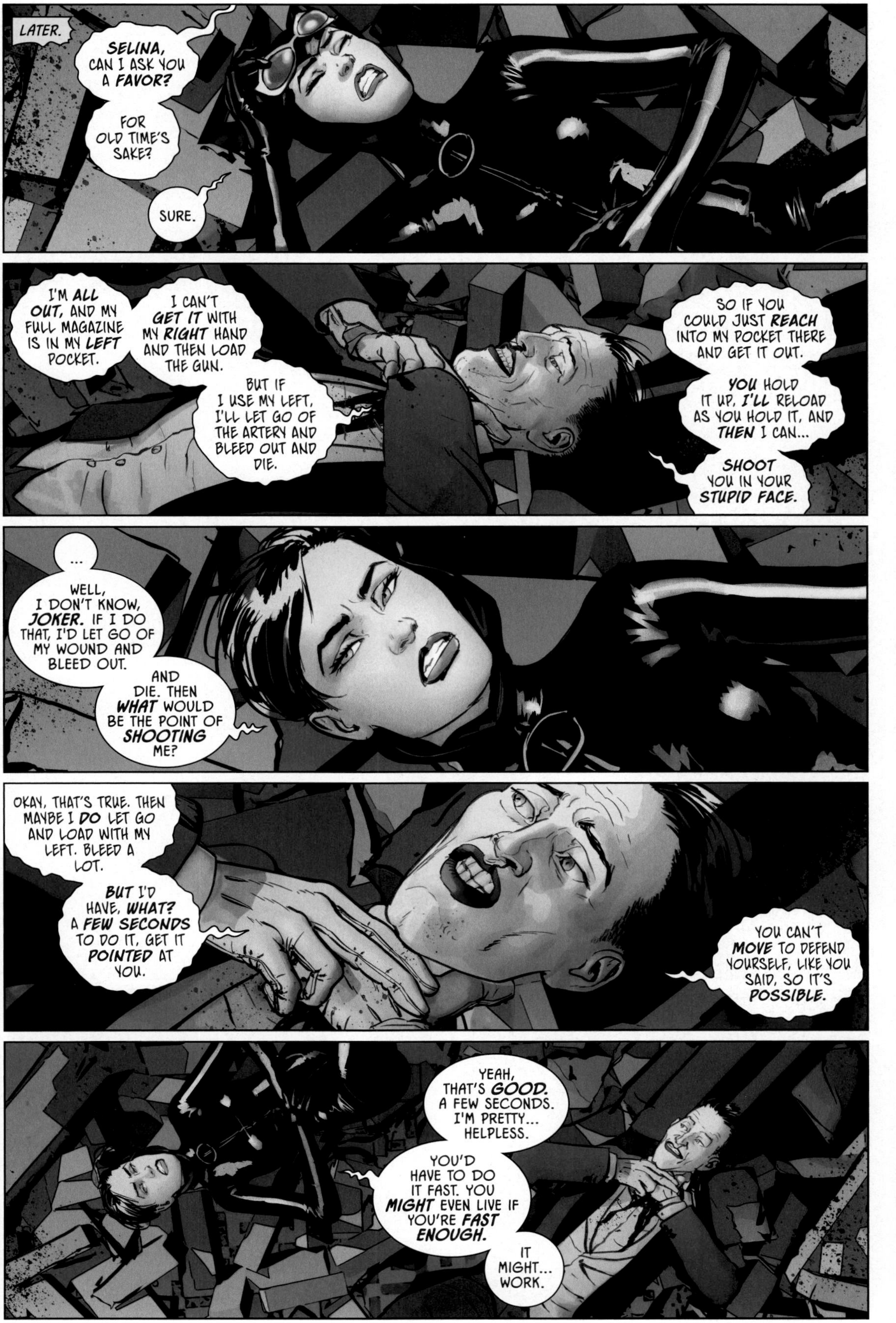
LATER.
SELINA, CAN I ASK YOU A FAVOR?
FOR OLD TIME'S SAKE?
SURE.
I'M ALL OUT, AND MY FULL MAGAZINE IS IN MY LEFT POCKET.
I CAN'T GET IT WITH MY RIGHT HAND AND THEN LOAD THE GUN.
BUT IF I USE MY LEFT, I'LL LET GO OF THE ARTERY AND BLEED OUT AND DIE.
SO IF YOU COULD JUST REACH INTO MY POCKET THERE AND GET IT OUT.
YOU HOLD IT UP, I'LL RELOAD AS YOU HOLD IT, AND THEN I CAN...
SHOOT YOU IN YOUR STUPID FACE.
...
WELL, I DON'T KNOW, JOKER. IF I DO THAT, I'D LET GO OF MY WOUND AND BLEED OUT.
AND DIE. THEN WHAT WOULD BE THE POINT OF SHOOTING ME?
OKAY, THAT'S TRUE. THEN MAYBE I DO LET GO AND LOAD WITH MY LEFT. BLEED A LOT.
BUT I'D HAVE, WHAT? A FEW SECONDS TO DO IT, GET IT POINTED AT YOU.
YOU CAN'T MOVE TO DEFEND YOURSELF, LIKE YOU SAID, SO IT'S POSSIBLE.
YEAH, THAT'S GOOD. A FEW SECONDS. I'M PRETTY... HELPLESS.
YOU'D HAVE TO DO IT FAST. YOU MIGHT EVEN LIVE IF YOU'RE FAST ENOUGH.
IT MIGHT... WORK.

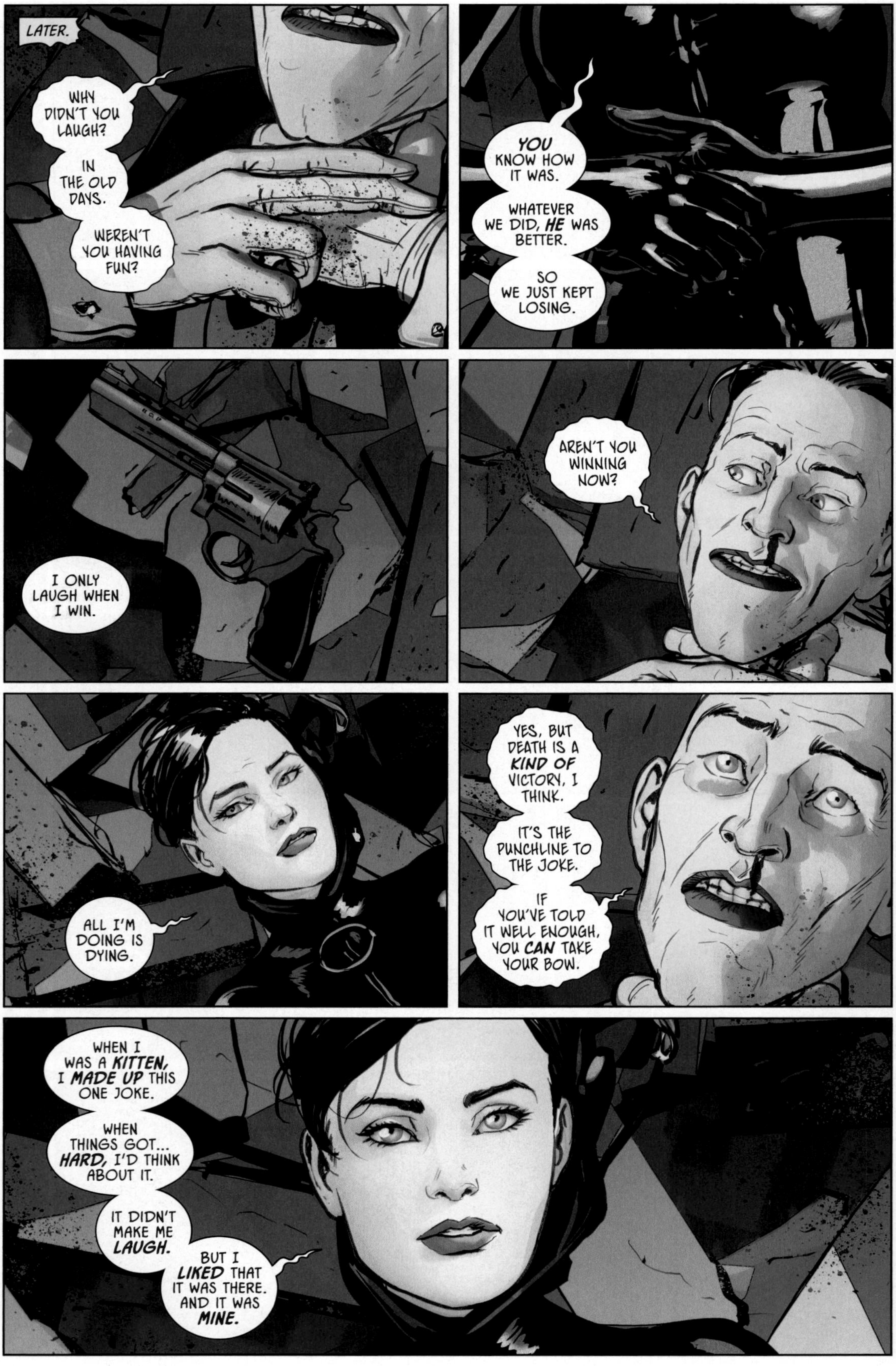
LATER.
WHY DIDN'T YOU LAUGH?
IN THE OLD DAYS.
WEREN'T YOU HAVING FUN?
YOU KNOW HOW IT WAS.
WHATEVER WE DID, HE WAS BETTER.
SO WE JUST KEPT LOSING.
I ONLY LAUGH WHEN I WIN.
AREN'T YOU WINNING NOW?
ALL I'M DOING IS DYING.
YES, BUT DEATH IS A KIND OF VICTORY, I THINK.
IT'S THE PUNCHLINE TO THE JOKE.
IF YOU'VE TOLD IT WELL ENOUGH, YOU CAN TAKE YOUR BOW.
WHEN I WAS A KITTEN, I MADE UP THIS ONE JOKE.
WHEN THINGS GOT... HARD, I'D THINK ABOUT IT.
IT DIDN'T MAKE ME LAUGH.
BUT I LIKED THAT IT WAS THERE. AND IT WAS MINE.

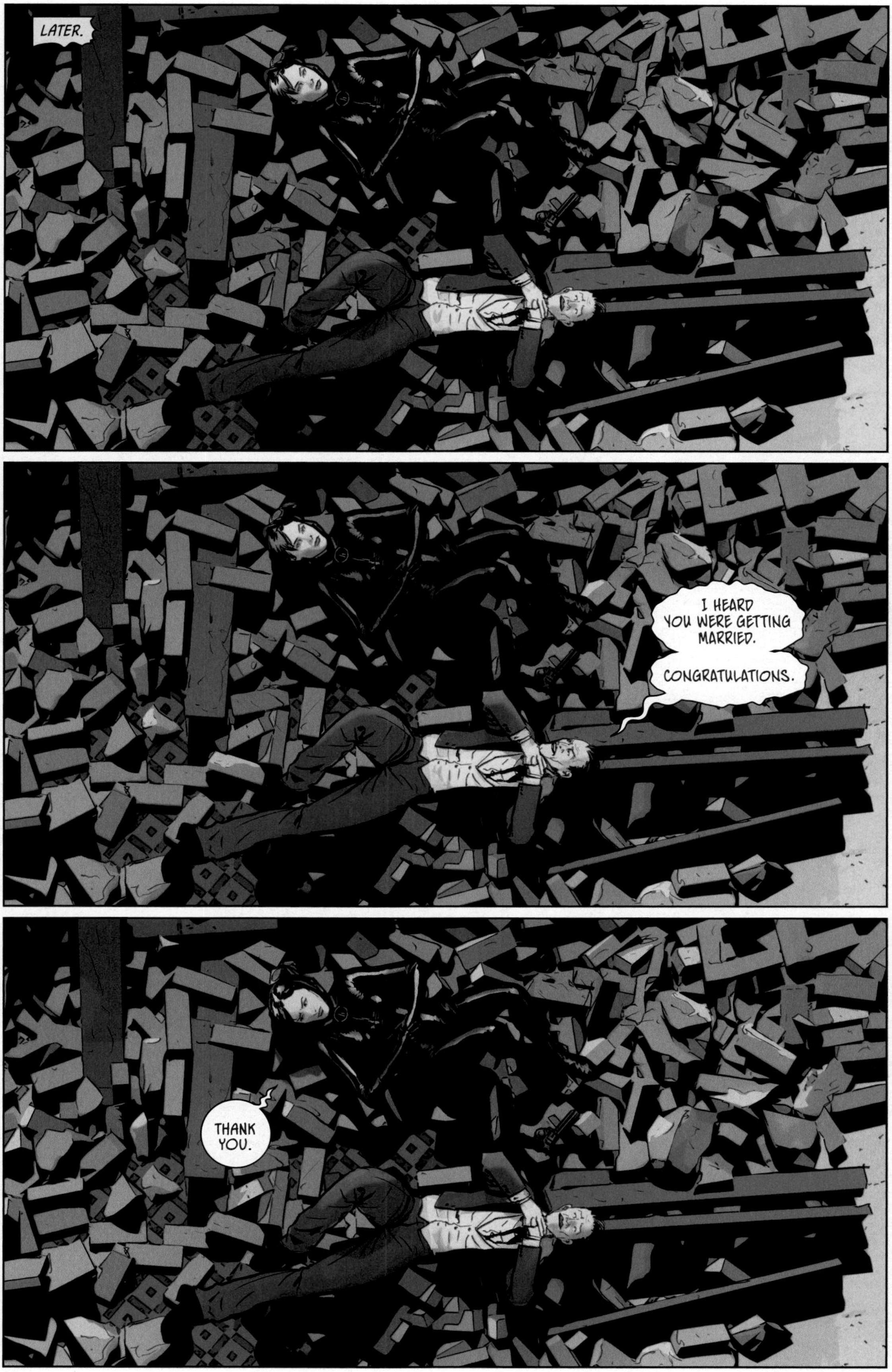
LATER.
I HEARD YOU WERE GETTING MARRIED.
CONGRATULATIONS.
THANK YOU.

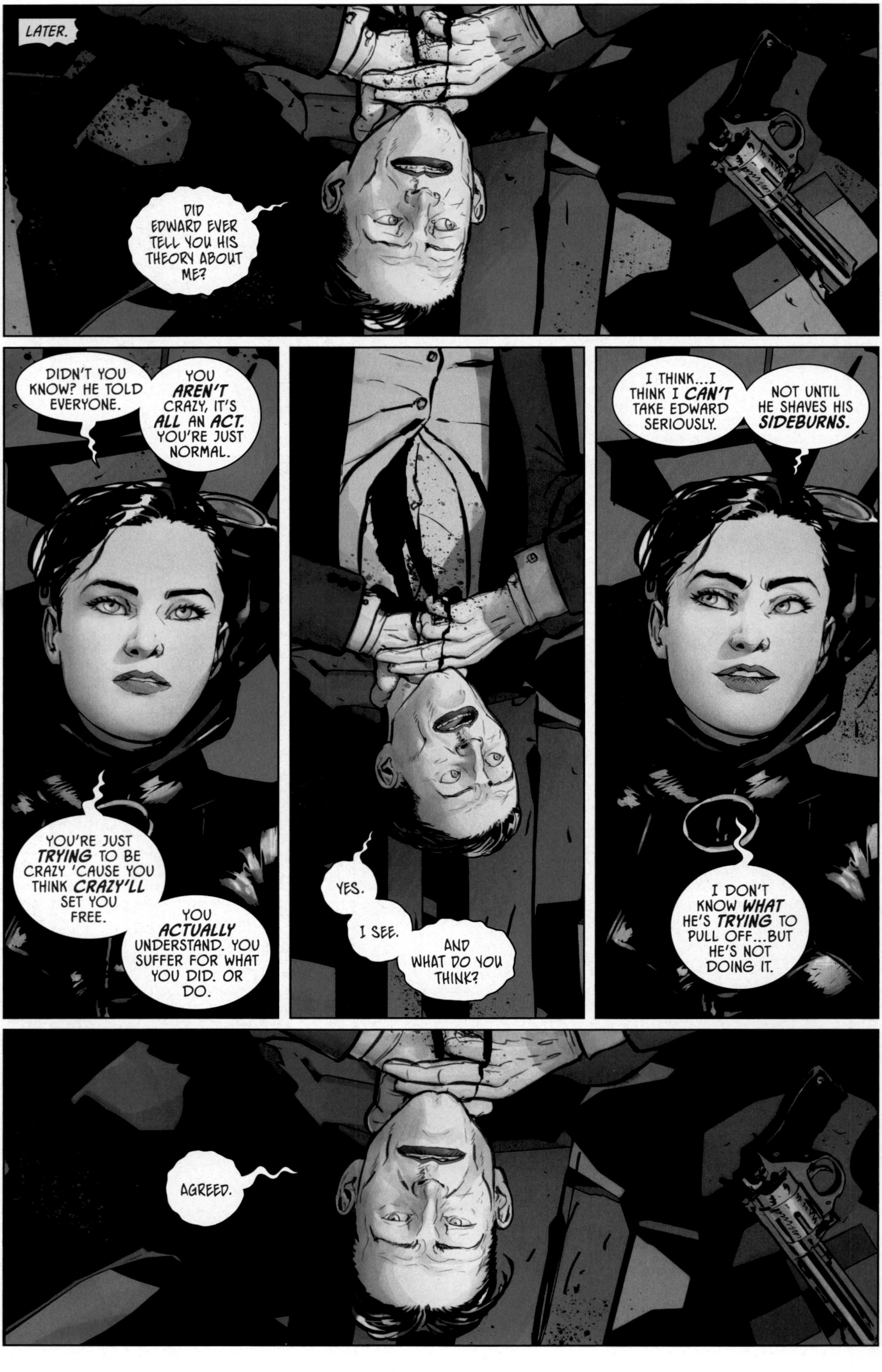
LATER.
DID EDWARD EVER TELL YOU HIS THEORY ABOUT ME?
DIDN'T YOU KNOW? HE TOLD EVERYONE.
YOU AREN'T CRAZY, IT'S ALL AN ACT. YOU'RE JUST NORMAL.
YOU'RE JUST TRYING TO BE CRAZY 'CAUSE YOU THINK CRAZY'LL SET YOU FREE.
YOU ACTUALLY UNDERSTAND. YOU SUFFER FOR WHAT YOU DID. OR DO.
YES.
I SEE.
AND WHAT DO YOU THINK?
I THINK...I THINK I CAN'T TAKE EDWARD SERIOUSLY.
NOT UNTIL HE SHAVES HIS SIDEBURNS.
I DON'T KNOW WHAT HE'S TRYING TO PULL OFF...BUT HE'S NOT DOING IT.
AGREED.

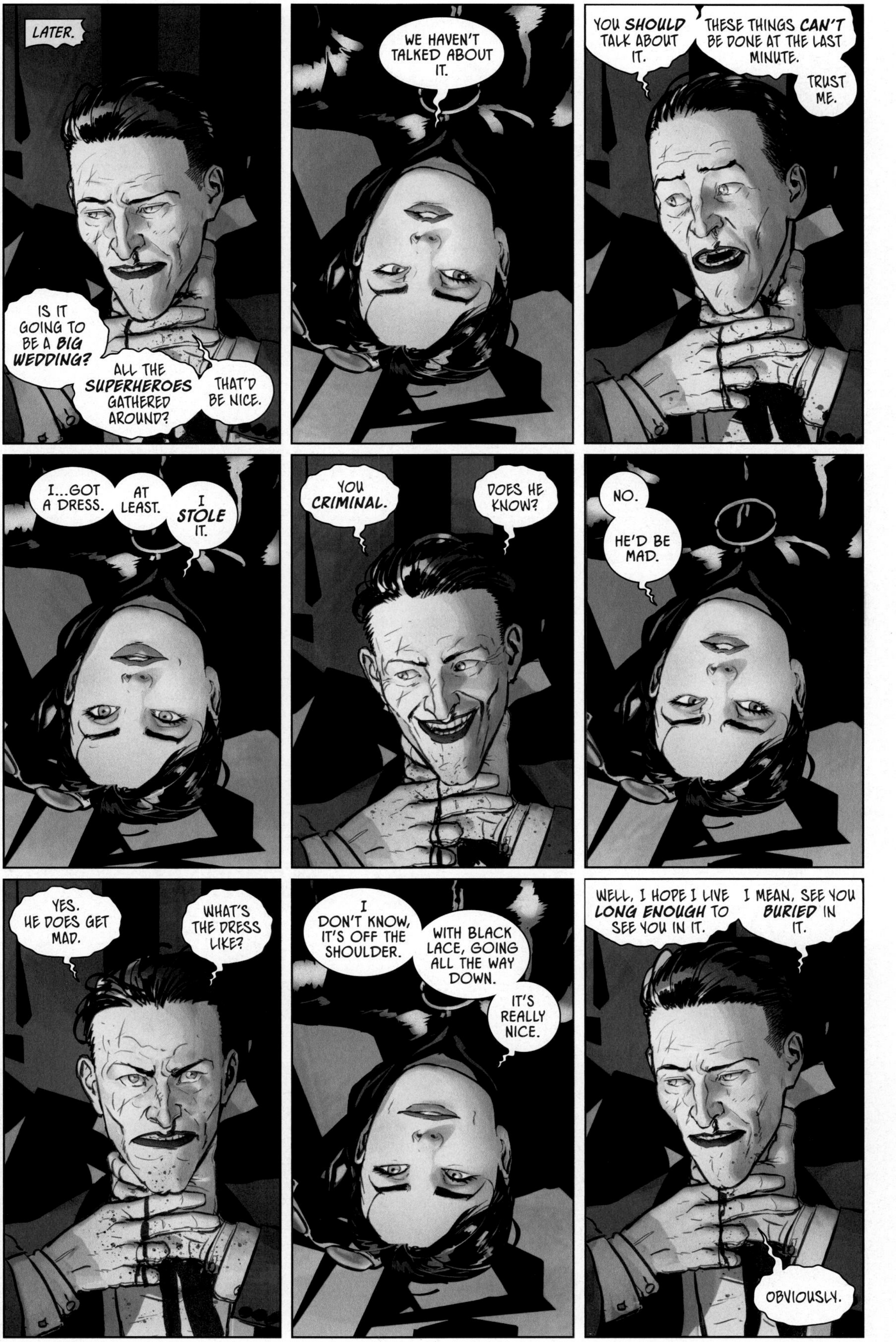
LATER.
IS IT GOING TO BE A BIG WEDDING?
ALL THE SUPERHEROES GATHERED AROUND?
THAT'D BE NICE.
WE HAVEN'T TALKED ABOUT IT.
YOU SHOULD TALK ABOUT IT.
THESE THINGS CAN'T BE DONE AT THE LAST MINUTE.
TRUST ME.
I...GOT A DRESS.
AT LEAST.
I STOLE IT.
YOU CRIMINAL.
DOES HE KNOW?
NO.
HE'D BE MAD.
YES. HE DOES GET MAD.
WHAT'S THE DRESS LIKE?
I DON'T KNOW, IT'S OFF THE SHOULDER.
WITH BLACK LACE, GOING ALL THE WAY DOWN.
IT'S REALLY NICE.
WELL, I HOPE I LIVE LONG ENOUGH TO SEE YOU IN IT.
I MEAN, SEE YOU BURIED IN IT.
OBVIOUSLY.

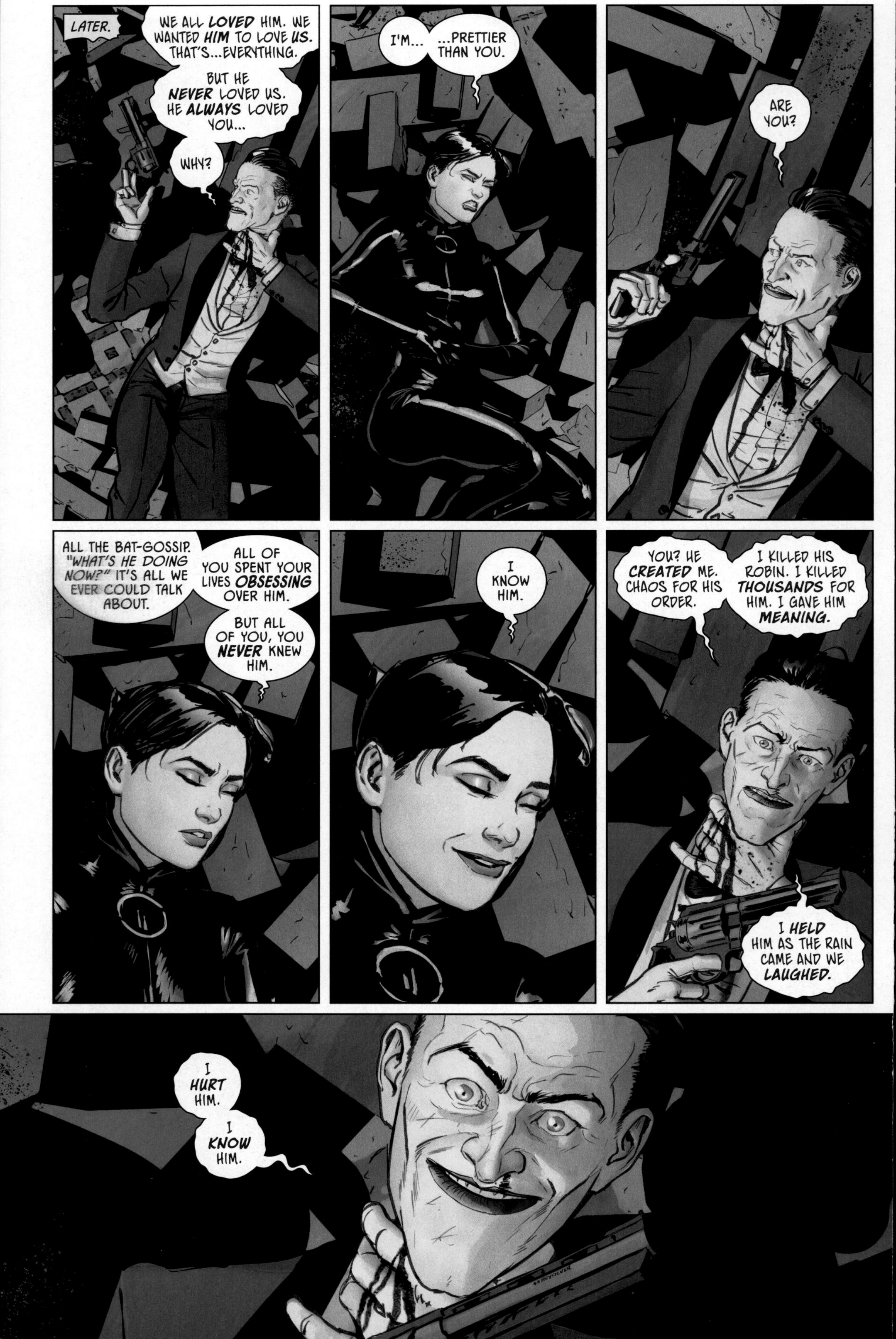
LATER.
WE ALL LOVED HIM. WE WANTED HIM TO LOVE US. THAT'S...EVERYTHING.
BUT HE NEVER LOVED US. HE ALWAYS LOVED YOU...
WHY?
I'M...
...PRETTIER THAN YOU.
ARE YOU?
ALL THE BAT-GOSSIP. "WHAT'S HE DOING NOW?" IT'S ALL WE EVER COULD TALK ABOUT.
ALL OF YOU SPENT YOUR LIVES OBSESSING OVER HIM.
BUT ALL OF YOU, YOU NEVER KNEW HIM.
I KNOW HIM.
YOU? HE CREATED ME. CHAOS FOR HIS ORDER.
I KILLED HIS ROBIN. I KILLED THOUSANDS FOR HIM. I GAVE HIM MEANING.
I HELD HIM AS THE RAIN CAME AND WE LAUGHED.
I HURT HIM.
I KNOW HIM.

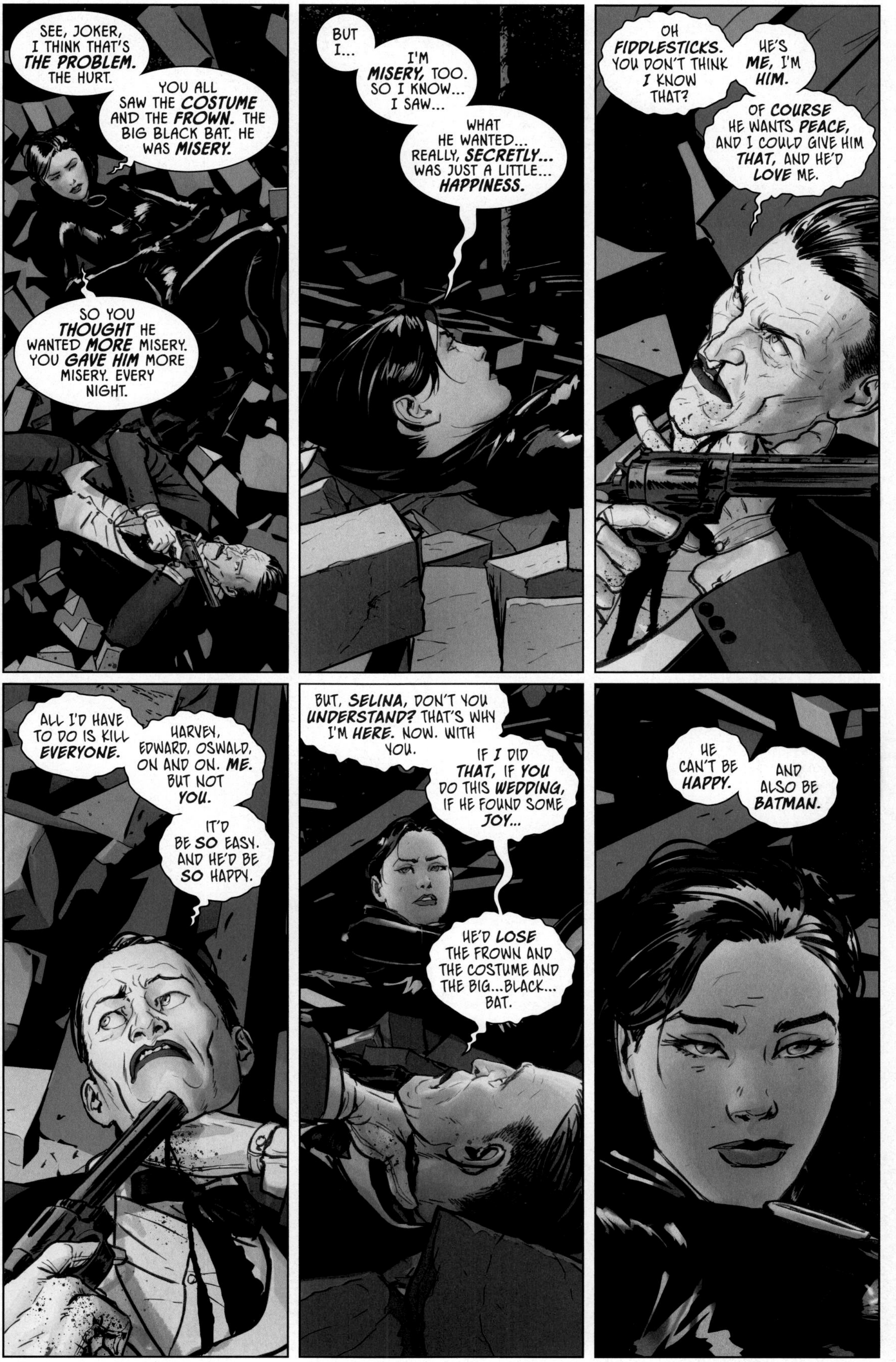
SEE, JOKER, I THINK THAT'S THE PROBLEM. THE HURT.
YOU ALL SAW THE COSTUME AND THE FROWN. THE BIG BLACK BAT. HE WAS MISERY.
SO YOU THOUGHT HE WANTED MORE MISERY. YOU GAVE HIM MORE MISERY. EVERY NIGHT.
BUT I...
I'M MISERY, TOO. SO I KNOW... I SAW...
WHAT HE WANTED... REALLY, SECRETLY... WAS JUST A LITTLE... HAPPINESS.
OH FIDDLESTICKS. YOU DON'T THINK I KNOW THAT?
HE'S ME, I'M HIM.
OF COURSE HE WANTS PEACE, AND I COULD GIVE HIM THAT, AND HE'D LOVE ME.
ALL I'D HAVE TO DO IS KILL EVERYONE.
HARVEY, EDWARD, OSWALD, ON AND ON. ME. BUT NOT YOU.
IT'D BE SO EASY. AND HE'D BE SO HAPPY.
BUT, SELINA, DON'T YOU UNDERSTAND? THAT'S WHY I'M HERE. NOW. WITH YOU.
IF I DID THAT, IF YOU DO THIS WEDDING, IF HE FOUND SOME JOY...
HE'D LOSE THE FROWN AND THE COSTUME AND THE BIG...BLACK... BAT.
HE CAN'T BE HAPPY.
AND ALSO BE BATMAN.

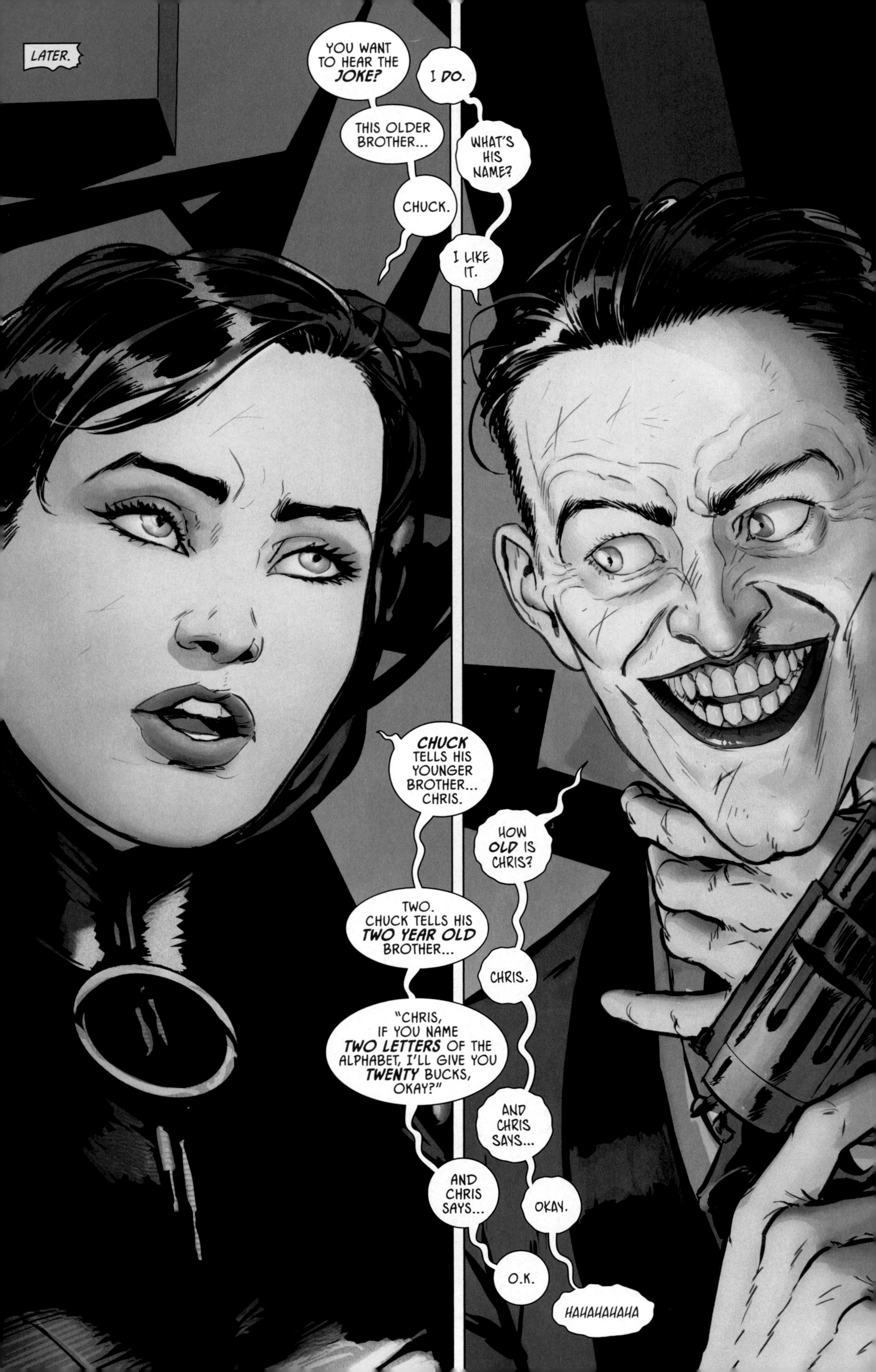

LATER.
YOU WANT TO HEAR THE JOKE?
I DO.
THIS OLDER BROTHER...
WHAT'S HIS NAME?
CHUCK.
I LIKE IT.
CHUCK TELLS HIS YOUNGER BROTHER... CHRIS.
HOW OLD IS CHRIS?
TWO. CHUCK TELLS HIS TWO YEAR OLD BROTHER...
CHRIS.
"CHRIS, IF YOU NAME TWO LETTERS OF THE ALPHABET, I'LL GIVE YOU TWENTY BUCKS, OKAY?"
AND CHRIS SAYS...
AND CHRIS SAYS...
OKAY.
O.K.
HAHAHAHAHA

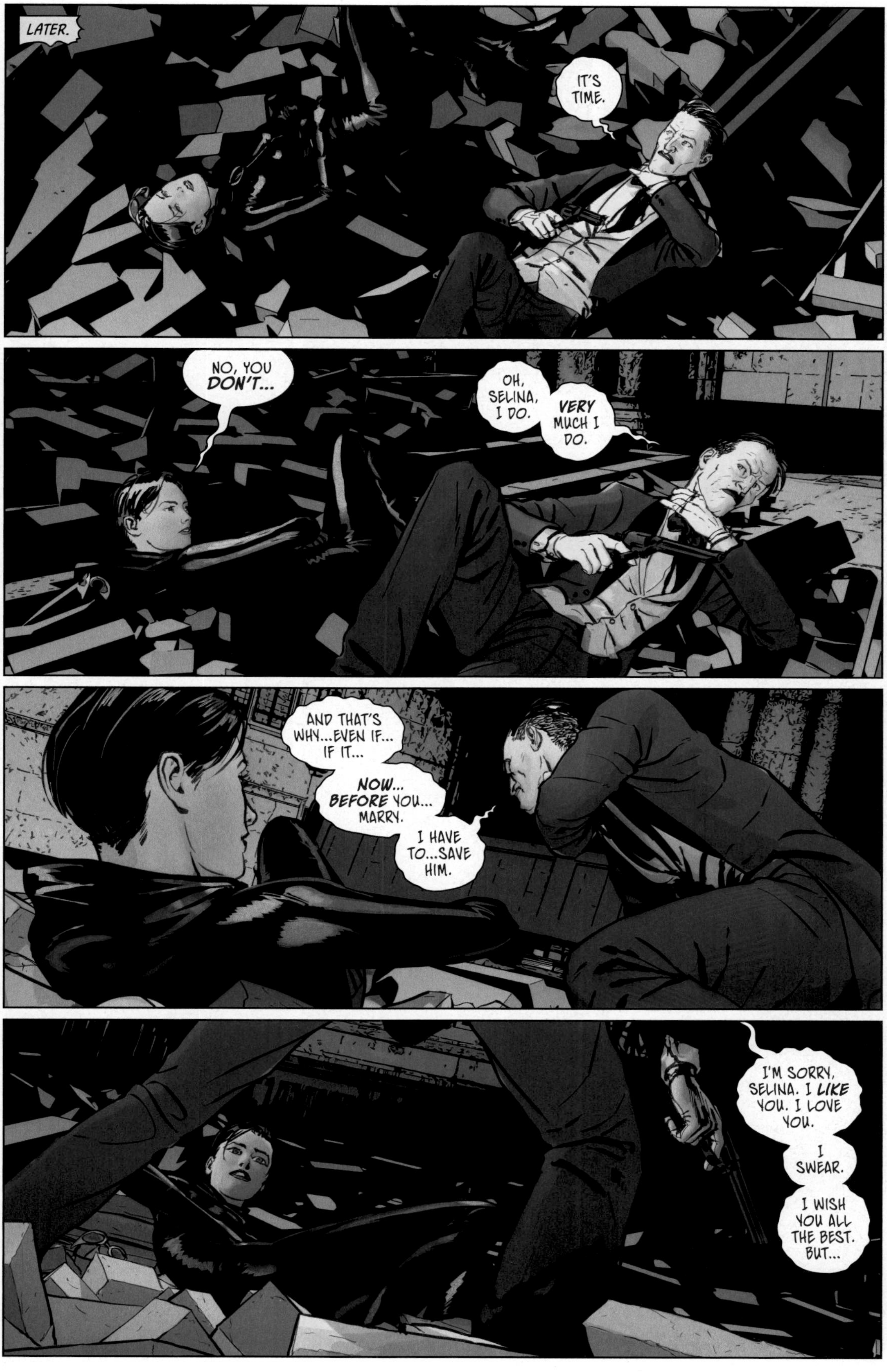
LATER.
IT'S TIME.
NO, YOU DON'T...
OH, SELINA, I DO.
VERY MUCH I DO.
AND THAT'S WHY...EVEN IF... IF IT...
NOW... BEFORE YOU... MARRY.
I HAVE TO...SAVE HIM.
I'M SORRY, SELINA. I LIKE YOU. I LOVE YOU.
I SWEAR.
I WISH YOU ALL THE BEST. BUT...

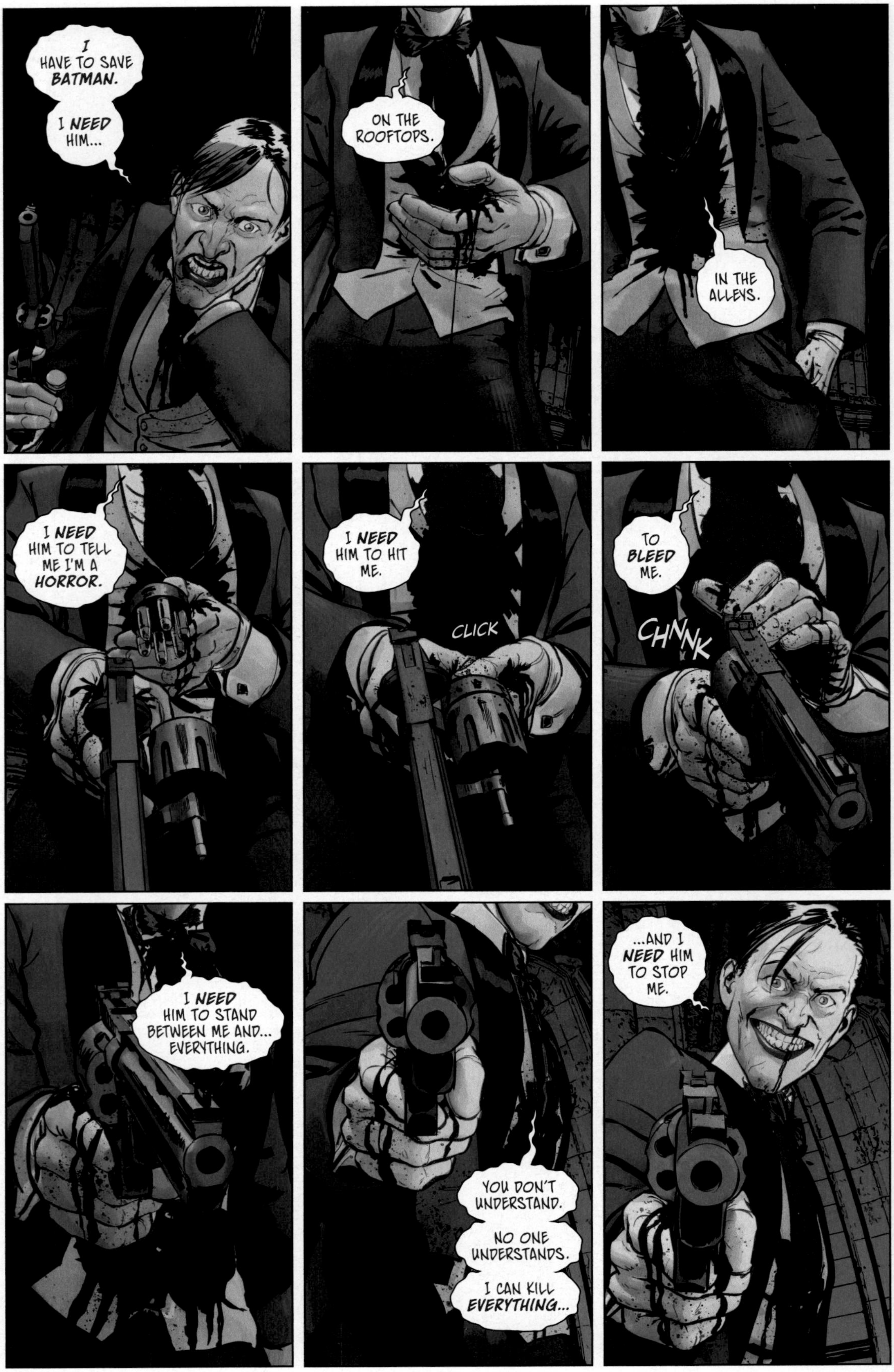
I HAVE TO SAVE BATMAN.
I NEED HIM...
ON THE ROOFTOPS.
IN THE ALLEYS.
I NEED HIM TO TELL ME I'M A HORROR.
I NEED HIM TO HIT ME.
CLICK
TO BLEED ME.
CHNNK
I NEED HIM TO STAND BETWEEN ME AND... EVERYTHING.
YOU DON'T UNDERSTAND.
NO ONE UNDERSTANDS.
I CAN KILL EVERYTHING...
...AND I NEED HIM TO STOP ME.

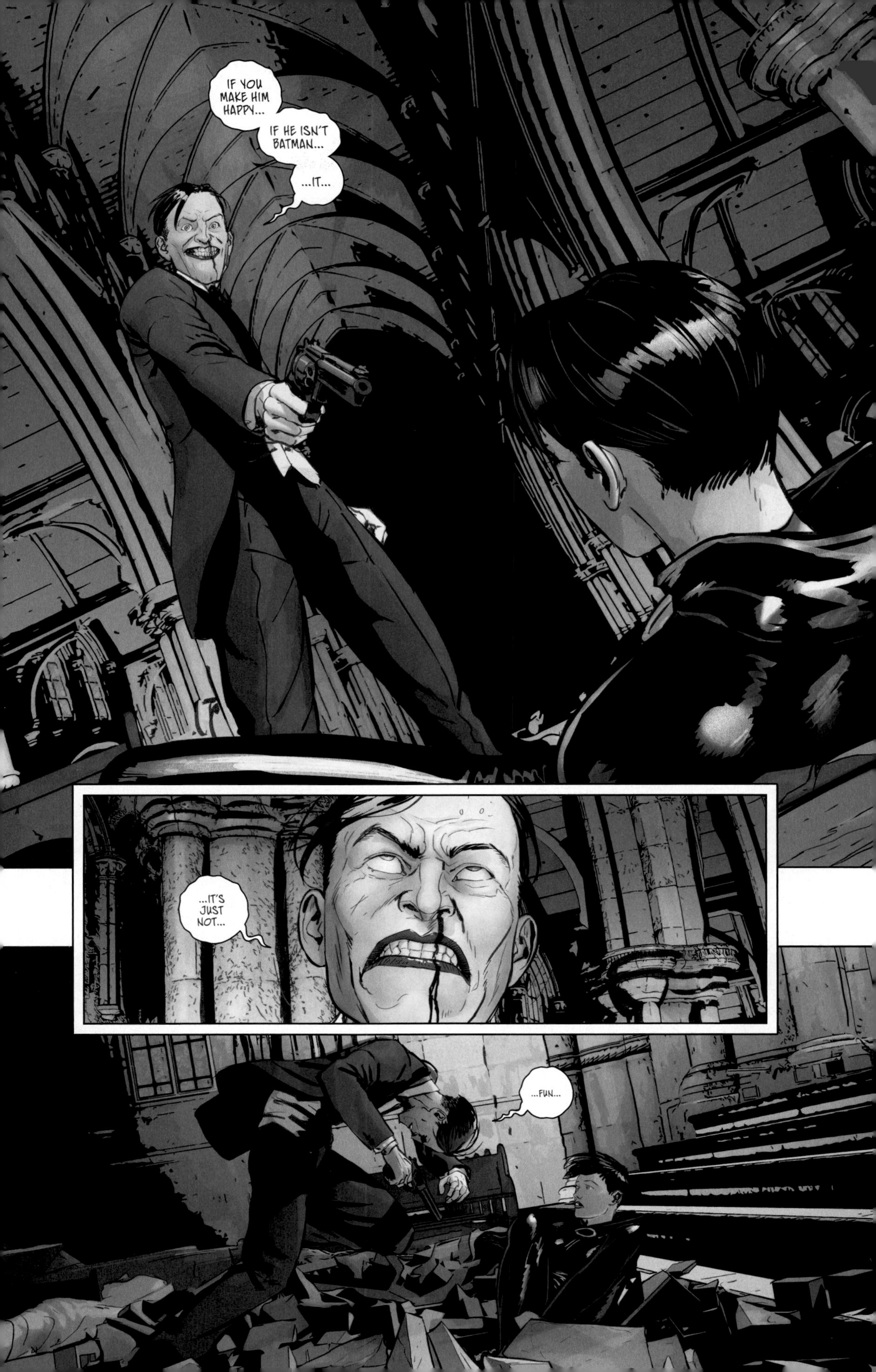
IF YOU MAKE HIM HAPPY...
IF HE ISN'T BATMAN...
...IT...
...IT'S JUST NOT...
...FUN...

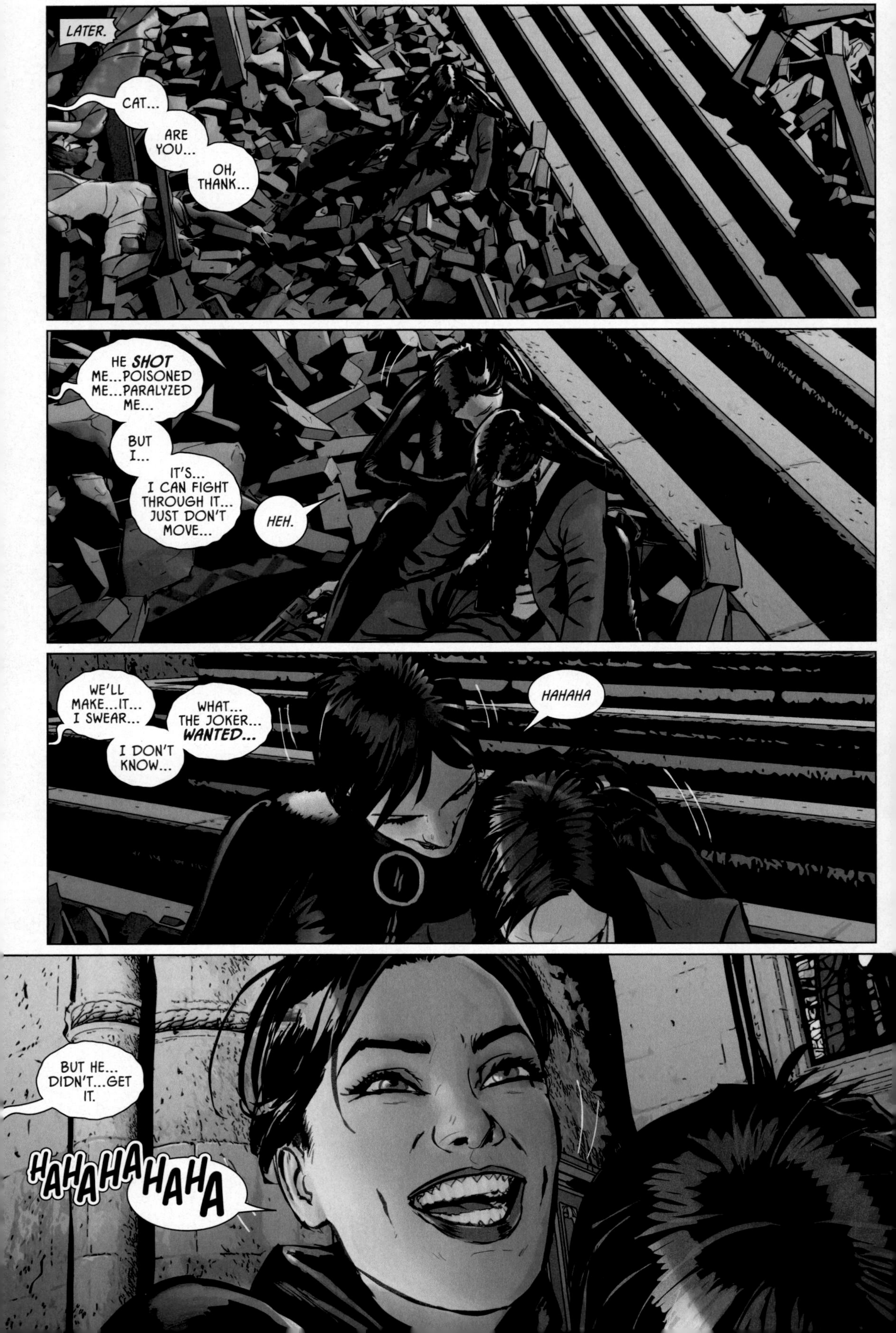
LATER.
CAT...
ARE YOU...
OH, THANK...
HE SHOT ME...POISONED ME...PARALYZED ME...
BUT I...
IT'S... I CAN FIGHT THROUGH IT... JUST DON'T MOVE...
HEH.
WE'LL MAKE...IT... I SWEAR...
I DON'T KNOW...
WHAT... THE JOKER... WANTED...
HAHAHA
BUT HE... DIDN'T...GET IT.
HAHAHAHAHAHA

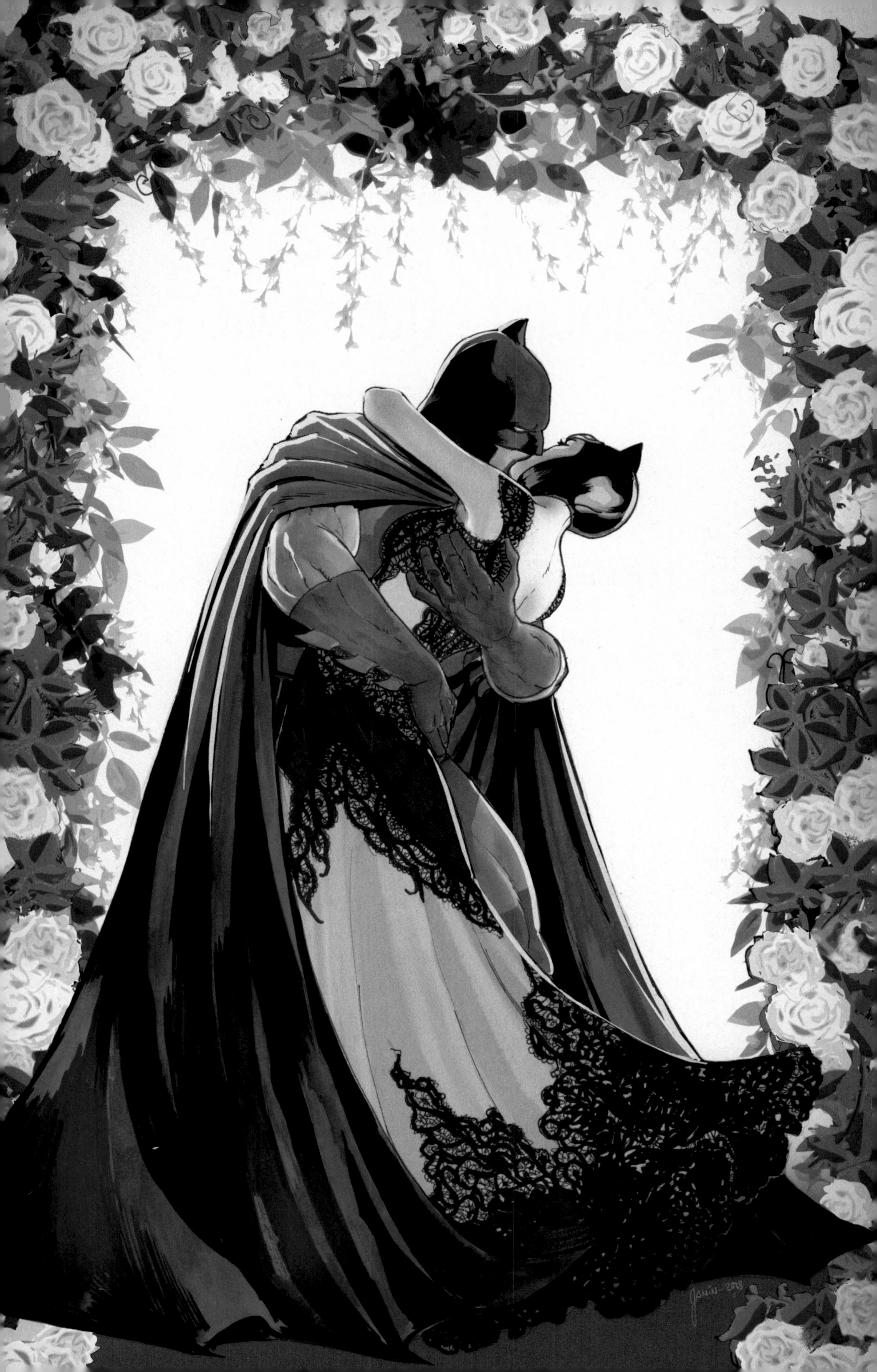

The Wedding of
Batman & Catwoman

July 4, 2018

Writer	Art & Cover
TOM KING	**MIKEL JANÍN**
Colorist	Letterer
JUNE CHUNG	CLAYTON COWLES

SPECIAL GUESTS

In order of appearance...

JOSÉ LUIS GARCÍA-LÓPEZ & TRISH MULVIHILL

BECKY CLOONAN

JASON FABOK & BRAD ANDERSON

FRANK MILLER & ALEX SINCLAIR

LEE BERMEJO

NEAL ADAMS & HI-FI

TONY S. DANIEL & TOMEU MOREY

AMANDA CONNER & PAUL MOUNTS

RAFAEL ALBUQUERQUE

ANDY KUBERT & ALEX SINCLAIR

TIM SALE & JOSÉ VILLARRUBIA

PAUL POPE & JOSÉ VILLARRUBIA

MITCH GERADS

CLAY MANN & JORDIE BELLAIRE

TY TEMPLETON & KEIREN SMITH

JOËLLE JONES & JORDIE BELLAIRE

DAVID FINCH & JORDIE BELLAIRE

JIM LEE, SCOTT WILLIAMS, & ALEX SINCLAIR

GREG CAPULLO & FCO PLASCENCIA

LEE WEEKS

Associate Editor	Editor
BRITTANY HOLZHERR	JAMIE S. RICH

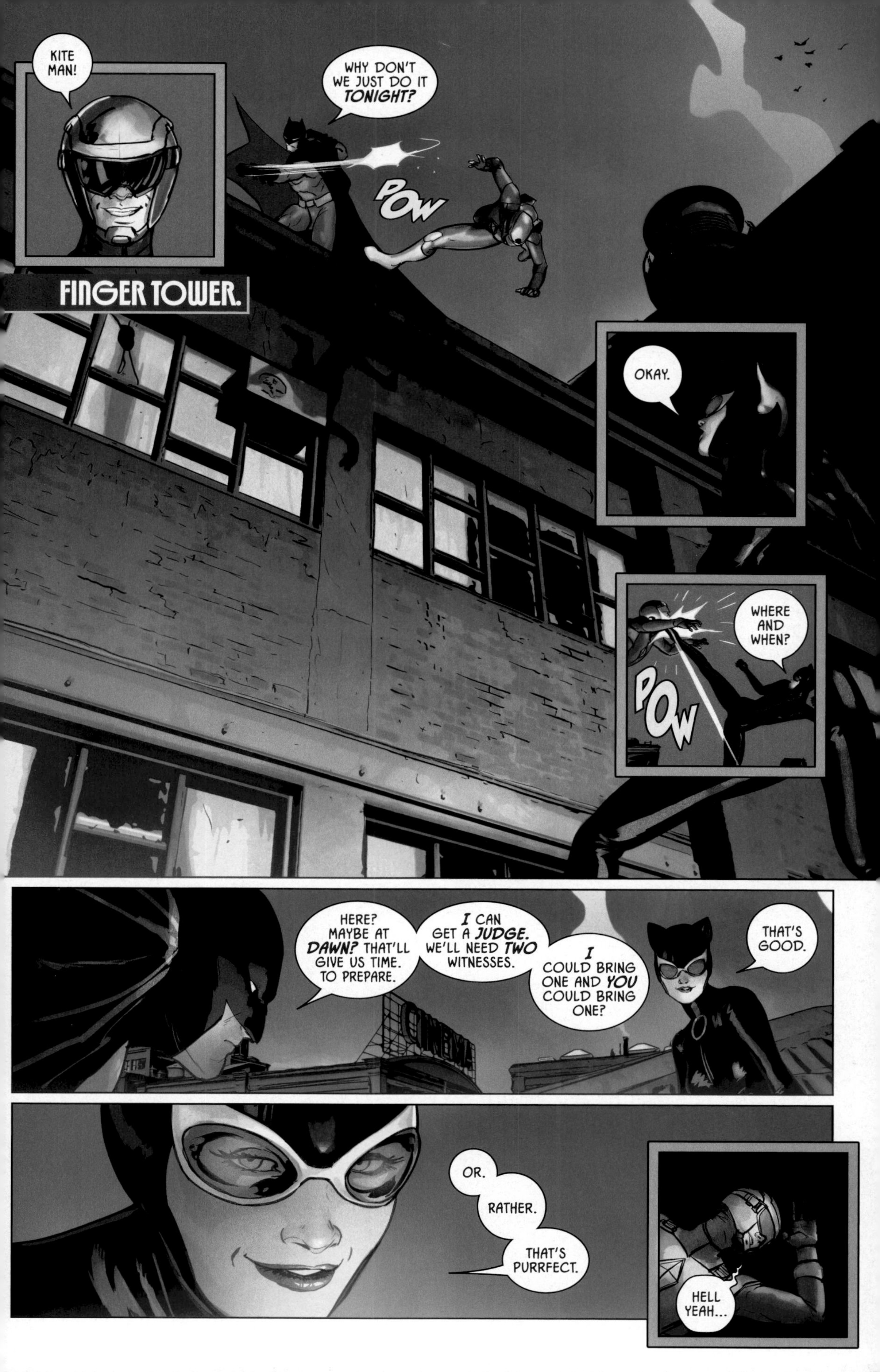

KITE MAN!
WHY DON'T WE JUST DO IT TONIGHT?
POW
FINGER TOWER.
OKAY.
WHERE AND WHEN?
POW
HERE? MAYBE AT DAWN? THAT'LL GIVE US TIME. TO PREPARE.
I CAN GET A JUDGE. WE'LL NEED TWO WITNESSES.
I COULD BRING ONE AND YOU COULD BRING ONE?
THAT'S GOOD.
CINEMA
OR.
RATHER.
THAT'S PURRFECT.
HELL YEAH...

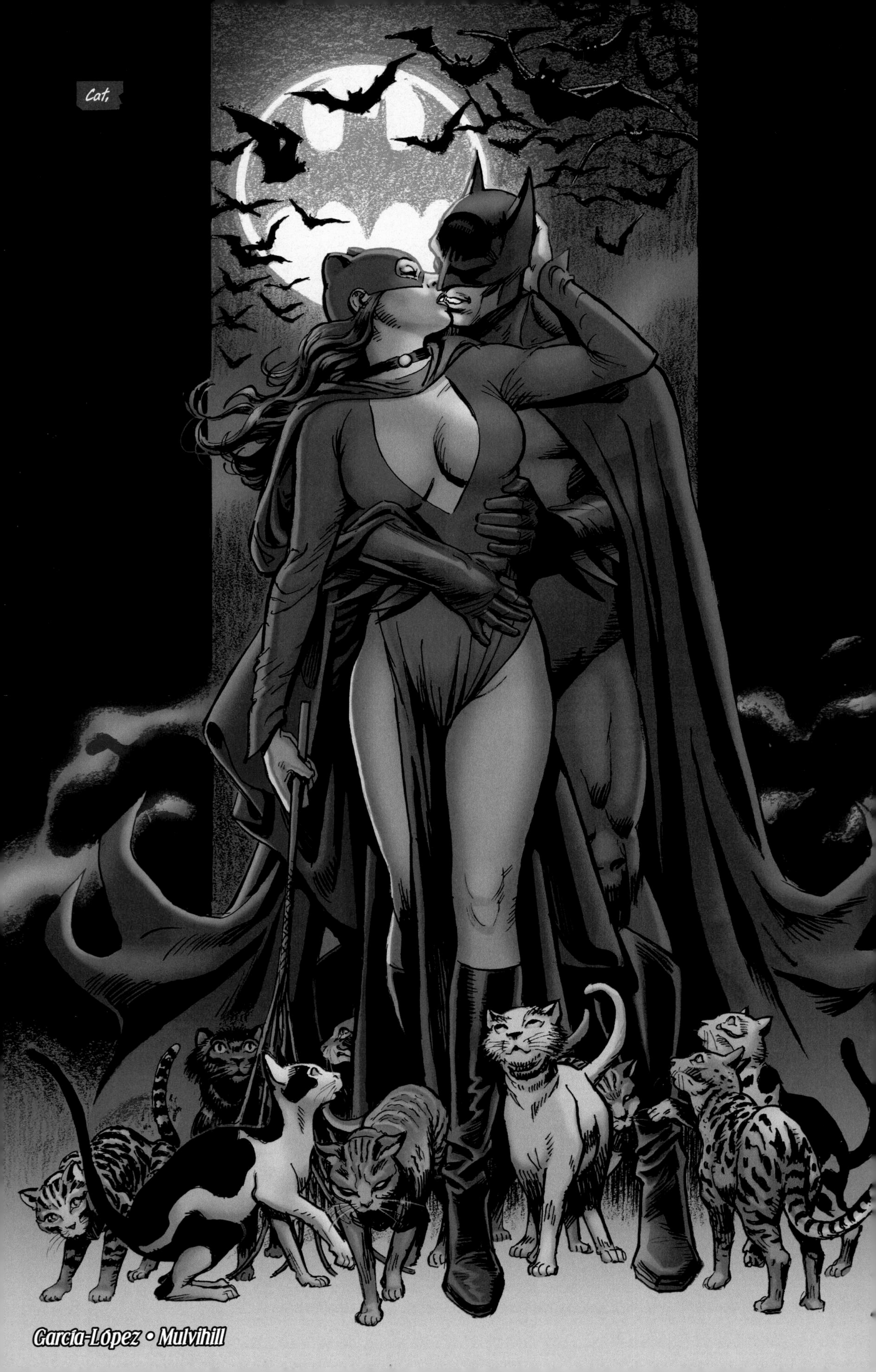
Cat.
Garcia-López • Mulvihill

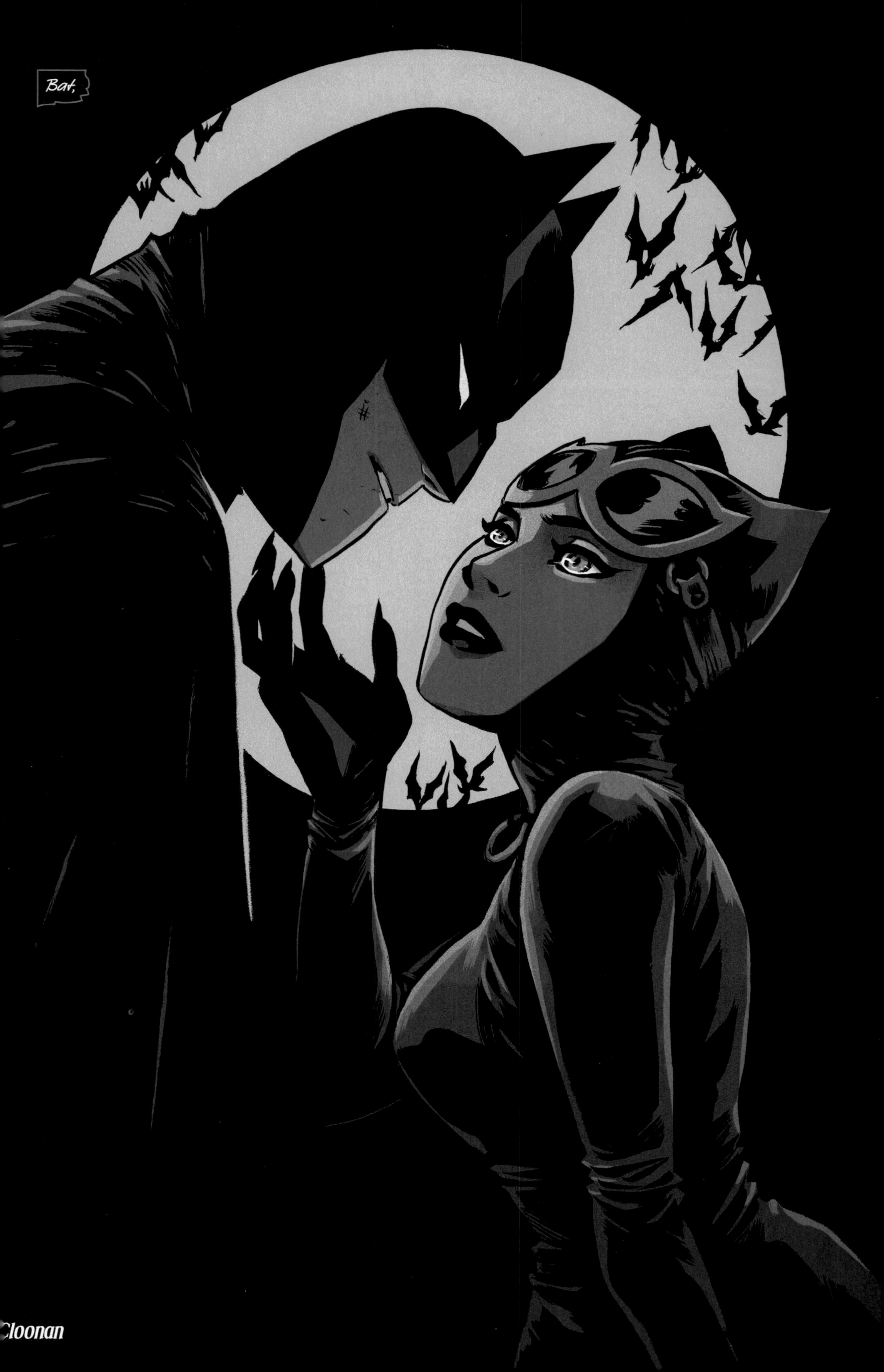
Bat,
Cloonan

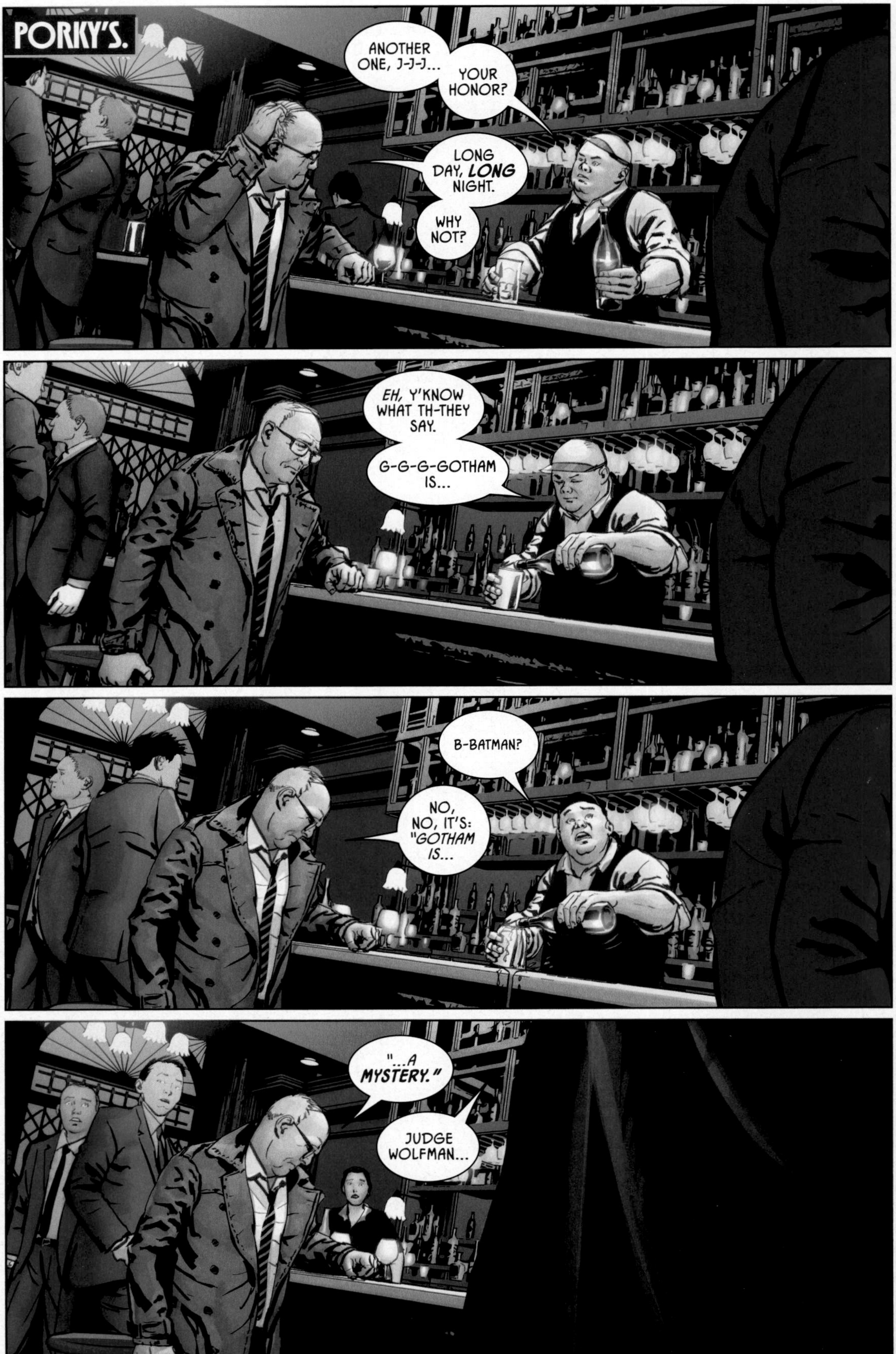
PORKY'S.
ANOTHER ONE, J-J-J...
YOUR HONOR?
LONG DAY, **LONG** NIGHT.
WHY NOT?
EH, Y'KNOW WHAT TH-THEY SAY.
G-G-G-GOTHAM IS...
B-BATMAN?
NO, NO, IT'S: "*GOTHAM IS...*
"...A ***MYSTERY.***"
JUDGE WOLFMAN...

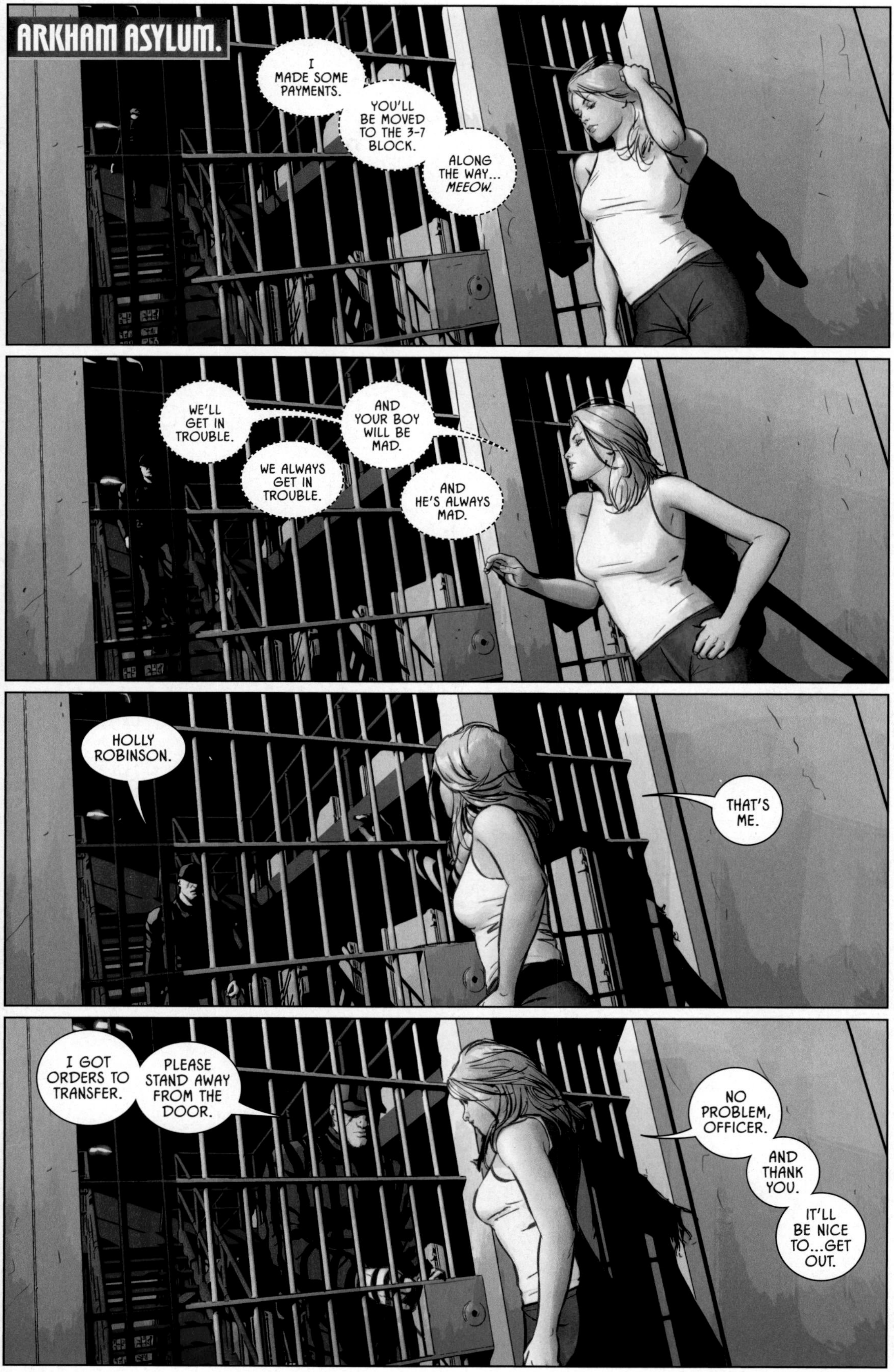
ARKHAM ASYLUM.
I MADE SOME PAYMENTS.
YOU'LL BE MOVED TO THE 3-7 BLOCK.
ALONG THE WAY... *MEEOW.*
WE'LL GET IN TROUBLE.
AND YOUR BOY WILL BE MAD.
WE ALWAYS GET IN TROUBLE.
AND HE'S ALWAYS MAD.
HOLLY ROBINSON.
THAT'S ME.
I GOT ORDERS TO TRANSFER.
PLEASE STAND AWAY FROM THE DOOR.
NO PROBLEM, OFFICER.
AND THANK YOU.
IT'LL BE NICE TO...GET OUT.

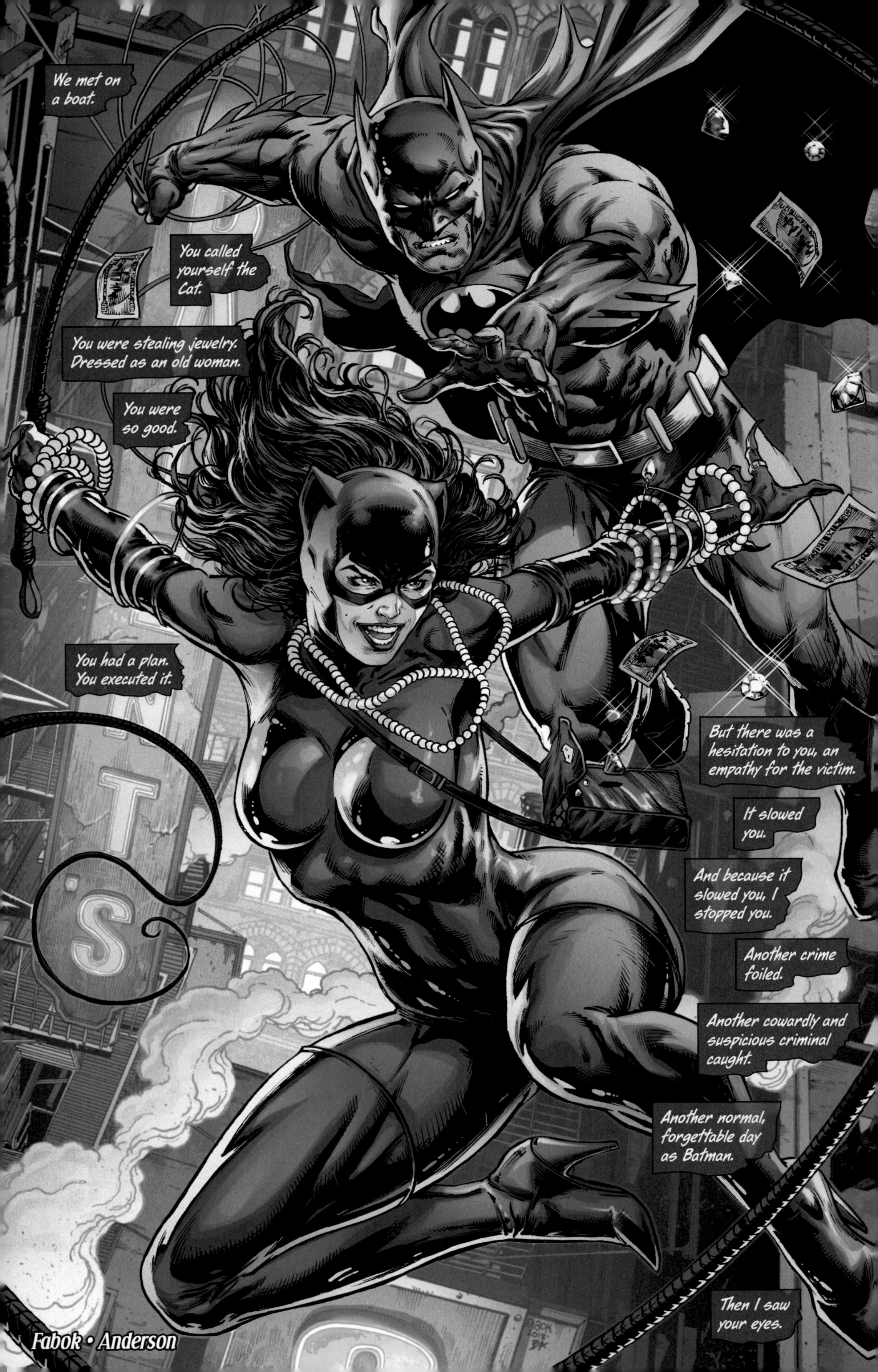
We met on a boat.
You called yourself the Cat.
You were stealing jewelry. Dressed as an old woman.
You were so good.
You had a plan. You executed it.
But there was a hesitation to you, an empathy for the victim.
It slowed you.
And because it slowed you, I stopped you.
Another crime foiled.
Another cowardly and suspicious criminal caught.
Another normal, forgettable day as Batman.
Then I saw your eyes.
Fabok • Anderson

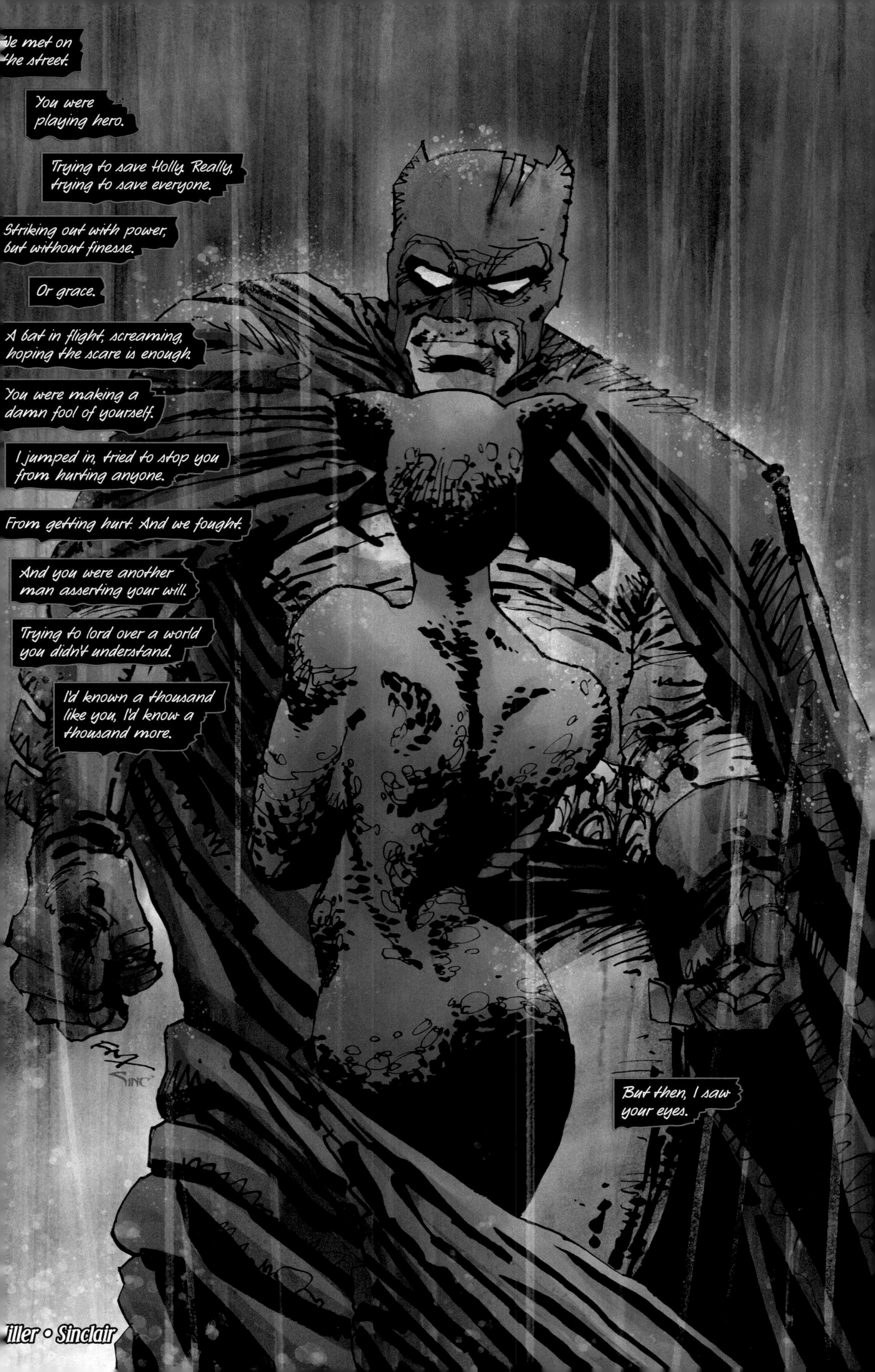
We met on the street.
You were playing hero.
Trying to save Holly. Really, trying to save everyone.
Striking out with power, but without finesse.
Or grace.
A bat in flight, screaming, hoping the scare is enough.
You were making a damn fool of yourself.
I jumped in, tried to stop you from hurting anyone.
From getting hurt. And we fought.
And you were another man asserting your will.
Trying to lord over a world you didn't understand.
I'd known a thousand like you, I'd know a thousand more.
But then, I saw your eyes.
FM
SINC
iller • Sinclair

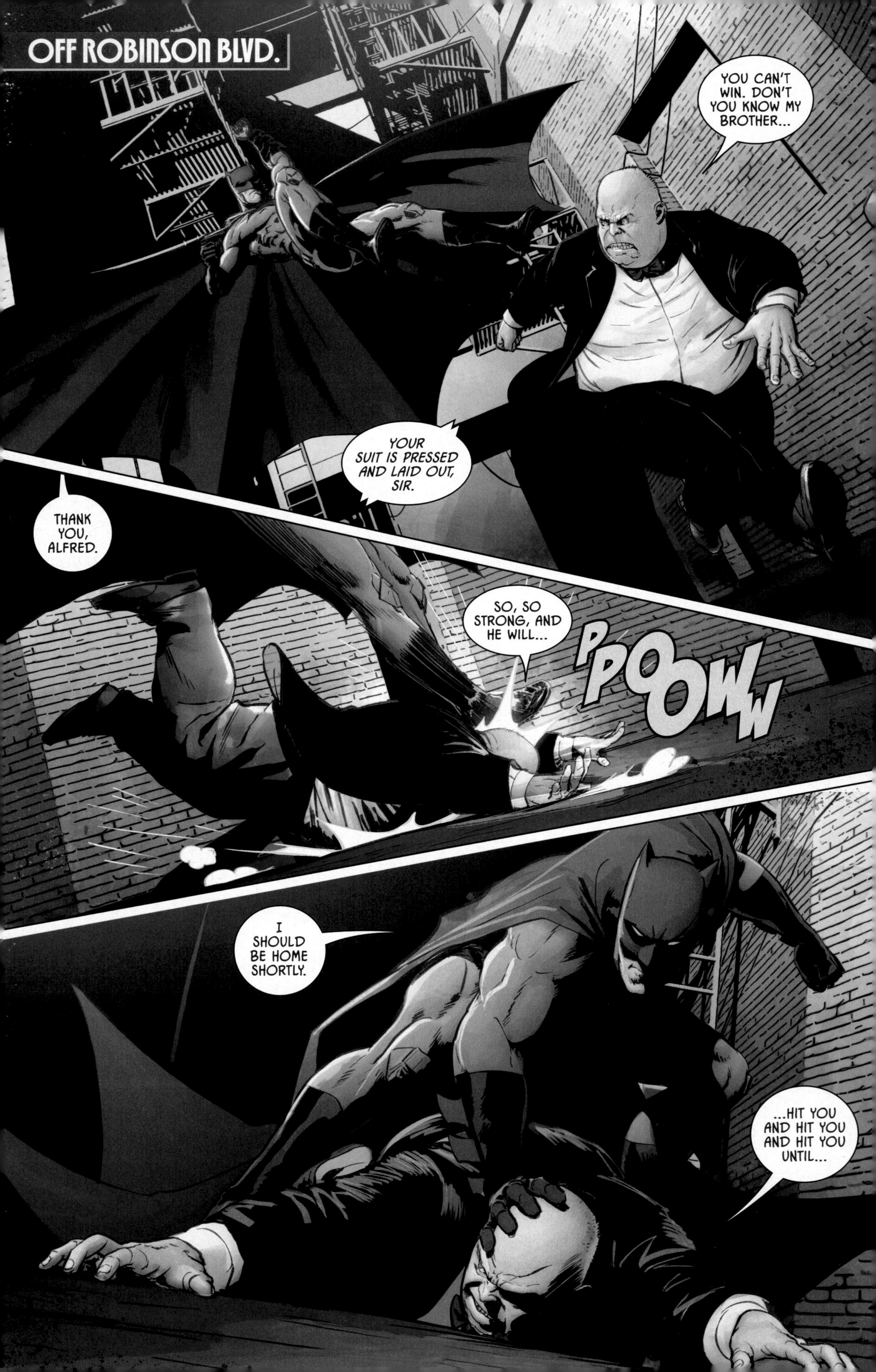
OFF ROBINSON BLVD.
YOU CAN'T WIN. DON'T YOU KNOW MY BROTHER...
YOUR SUIT IS PRESSED AND LAID OUT, SIR.
THANK YOU, ALFRED.
SO, SO STRONG, AND HE WILL...
PPOOWW
I SHOULD BE HOME SHORTLY.
...HIT YOU AND HIT YOU AND HIT YOU UNTIL...

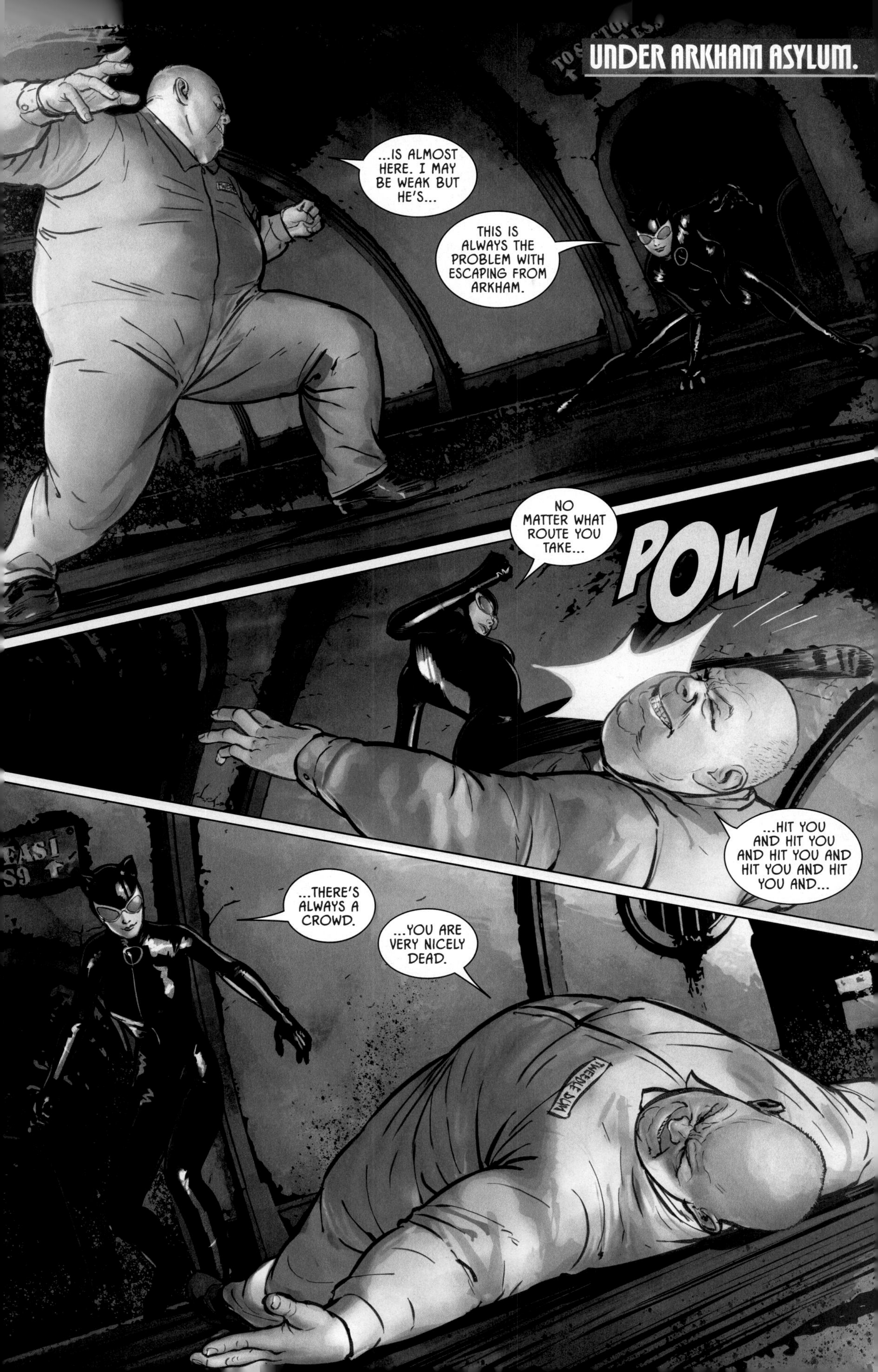
UNDER ARKHAM ASYLUM.
...IS ALMOST HERE. I MAY BE WEAK BUT HE'S...
THIS IS ALWAYS THE PROBLEM WITH ESCAPING FROM ARKHAM.
NO MATTER WHAT ROUTE YOU TAKE...
POW
...HIT YOU AND HIT YOU AND HIT YOU AND HIT YOU AND HIT YOU AND...
...THERE'S ALWAYS A CROWD.
...YOU ARE VERY NICELY DEAD.
TWEEDLE DUM

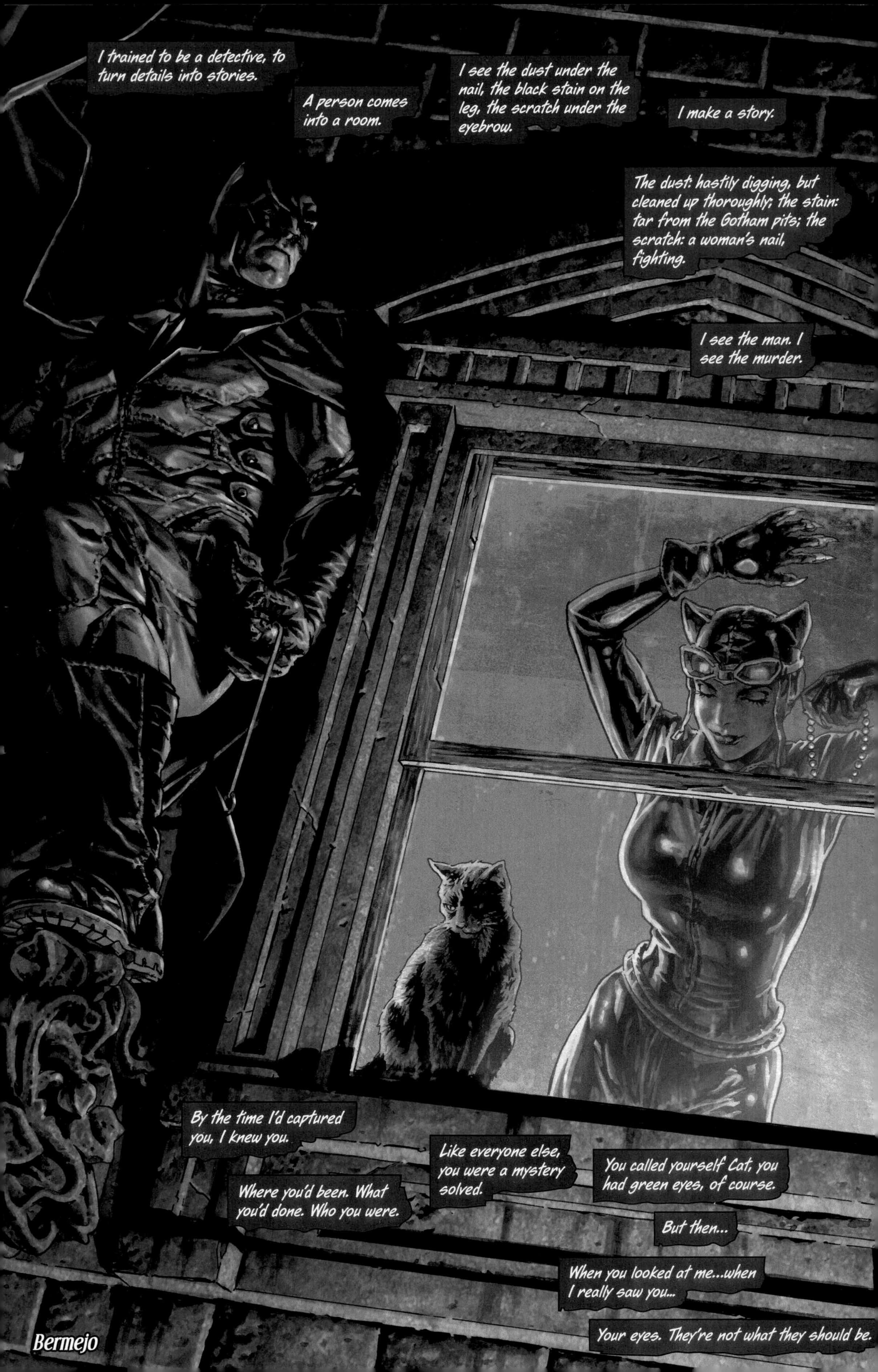
I trained to be a detective, to turn details into stories.
A person comes into a room.
I see the dust under the nail, the black stain on the leg, the scratch under the eyebrow.
I make a story.
The dust: hastily digging, but cleaned up thoroughly; the stain: tar from the Gotham pits; the scratch: a woman's nail, fighting.
I see the man. I see the murder.
By the time I'd captured you, I knew you.
Where you'd been. What you'd done. Who you were.
Like everyone else, you were a mystery solved.
You called yourself Cat, you had green eyes, of course.
But then...
When you looked at me...when I really saw you...
Your eyes. They're not what they should be.
Bermejo

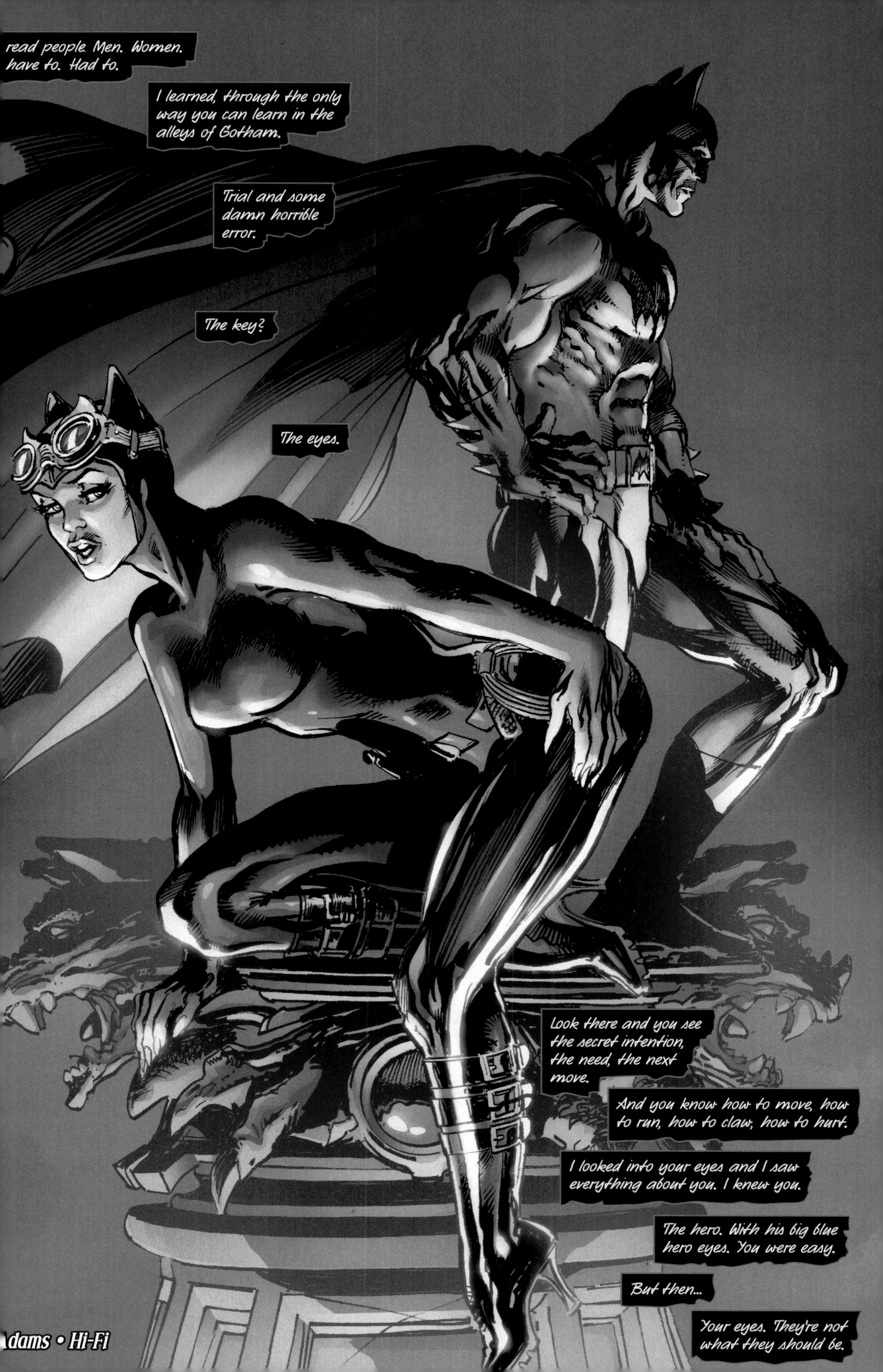

read people. Men. Women.
have to. Had to.
I learned, through the only way you can learn in the alleys of Gotham.
Trial and some damn horrible error.
The key?
The eyes.
Look there and you see the secret intention, the need, the next move.
And you know how to move, how to run, how to claw, how to hurt.
I looked into your eyes and I saw everything about you. I knew you.
The hero. With his big blue hero eyes. You were easy.
But then...
Your eyes. They're not what they should be.
Adams • Hi-Fi

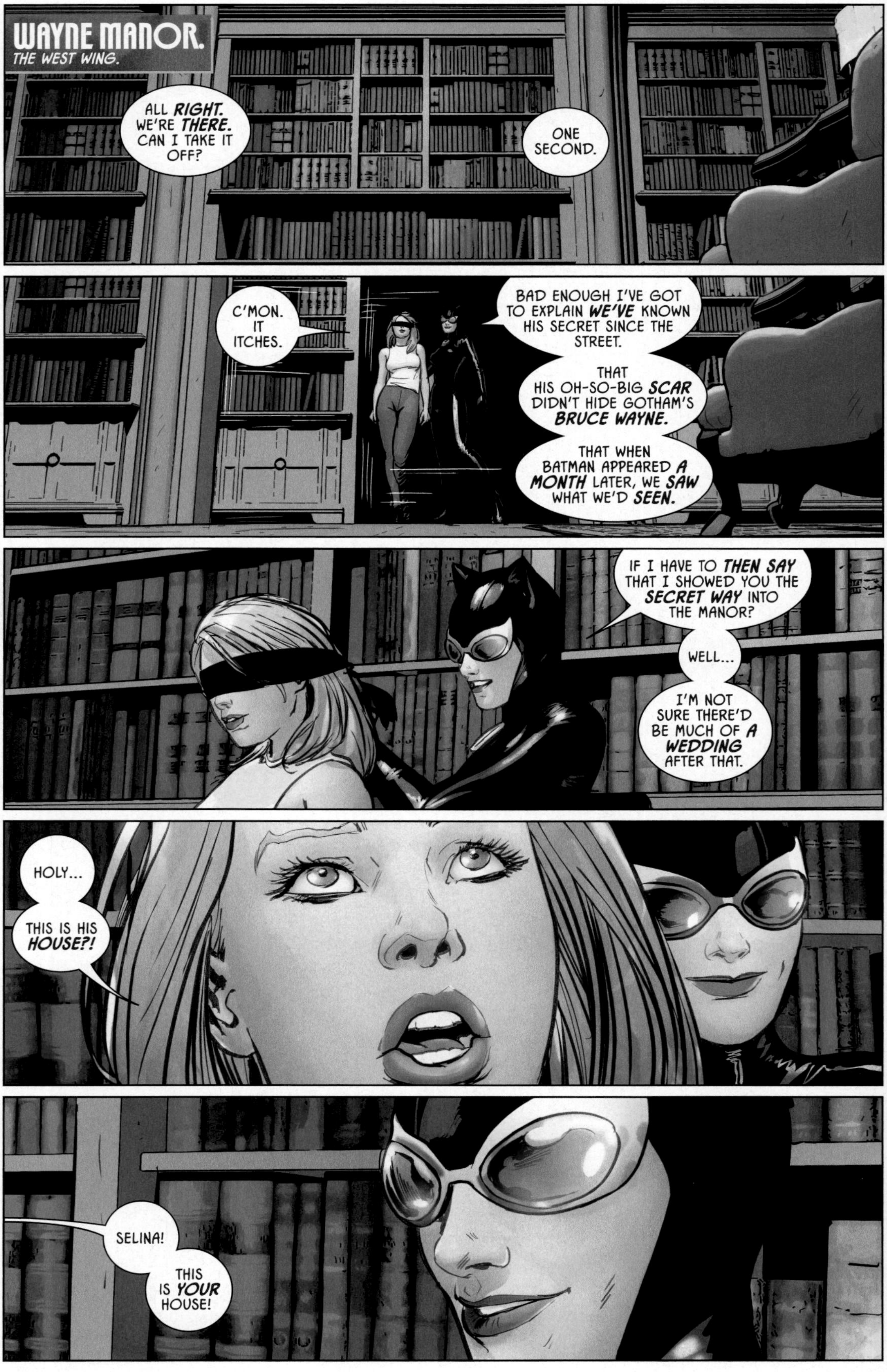
WAYNE MANOR.
THE WEST WING.
ALL RIGHT. WE'RE THERE. CAN I TAKE IT OFF?
ONE SECOND.
C'MON. IT ITCHES.
BAD ENOUGH I'VE GOT TO EXPLAIN WE'VE KNOWN HIS SECRET SINCE THE STREET.
THAT HIS OH-SO-BIG SCAR DIDN'T HIDE GOTHAM'S BRUCE WAYNE.
THAT WHEN BATMAN APPEARED A MONTH LATER, WE SAW WHAT WE'D SEEN.
IF I HAVE TO THEN SAY THAT I SHOWED YOU THE SECRET WAY INTO THE MANOR?
WELL...
I'M NOT SURE THERE'D BE MUCH OF A WEDDING AFTER THAT.
HOLY...
THIS IS HIS HOUSE?!
SELINA!
THIS IS YOUR HOUSE!

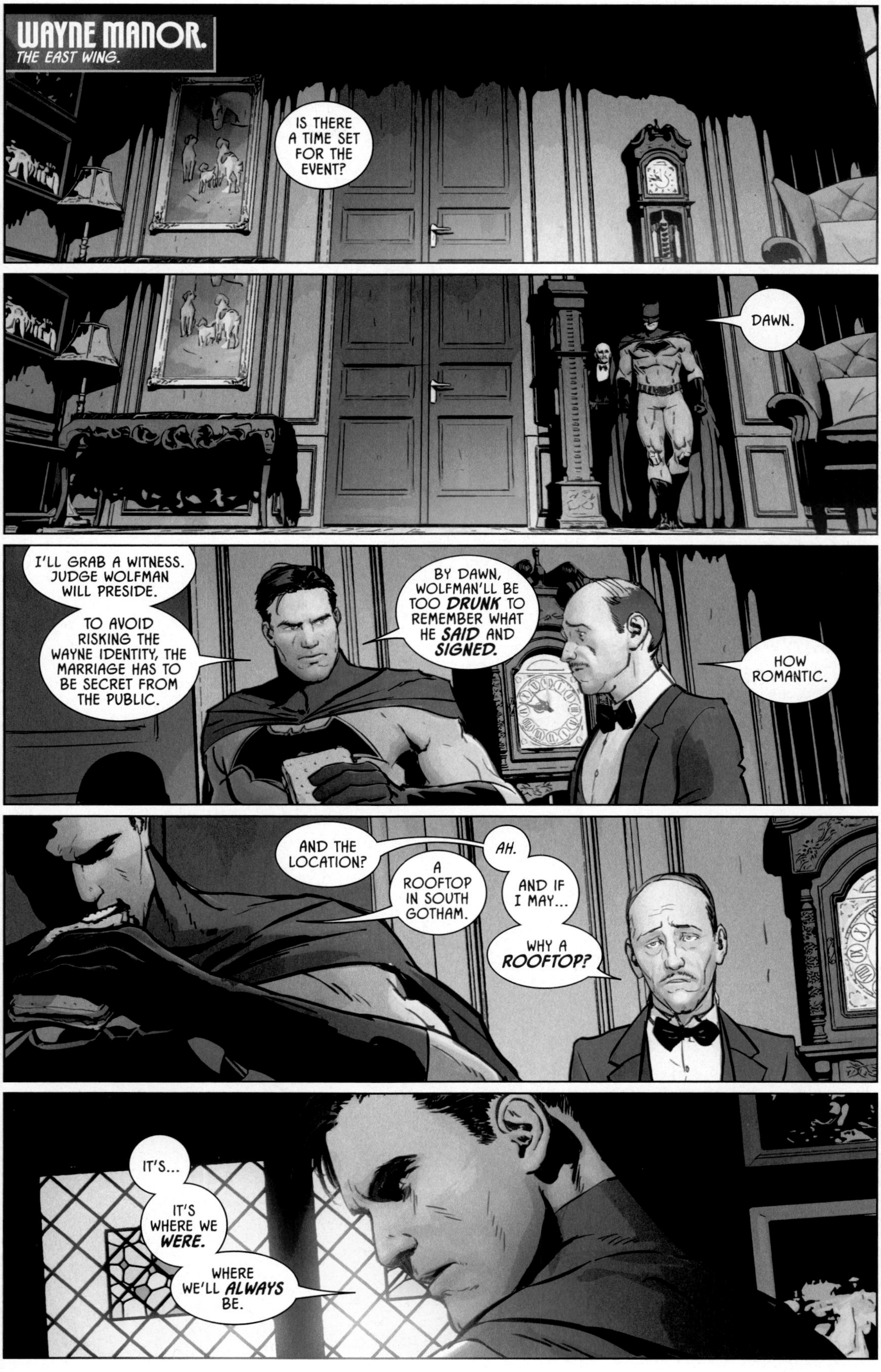
WAYNE MANOR.
THE EAST WING.
IS THERE A TIME SET FOR THE EVENT?
DAWN.
I'LL GRAB A WITNESS. JUDGE WOLFMAN WILL PRESIDE.
TO AVOID RISKING THE WAYNE IDENTITY, THE MARRIAGE HAS TO BE SECRET FROM THE PUBLIC.
BY DAWN, WOLFMAN'LL BE TOO DRUNK TO REMEMBER WHAT HE SAID AND SIGNED.
HOW ROMANTIC.
AND THE LOCATION?
A ROOFTOP IN SOUTH GOTHAM.
AH.
AND IF I MAY...
WHY A ROOFTOP?
IT'S...
IT'S WHERE WE WERE.
WHERE WE'LL ALWAYS BE.

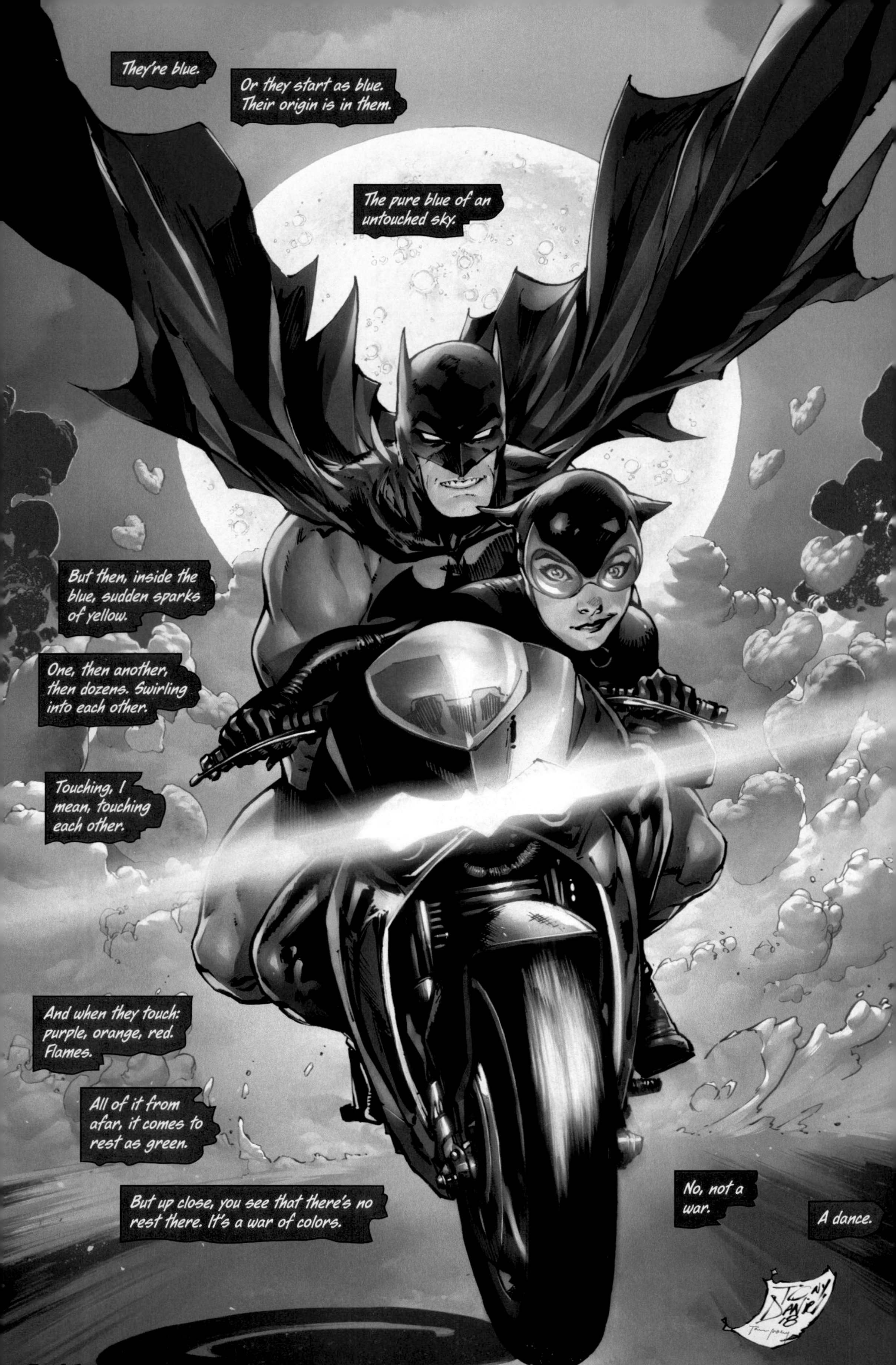

Daniel • Morey

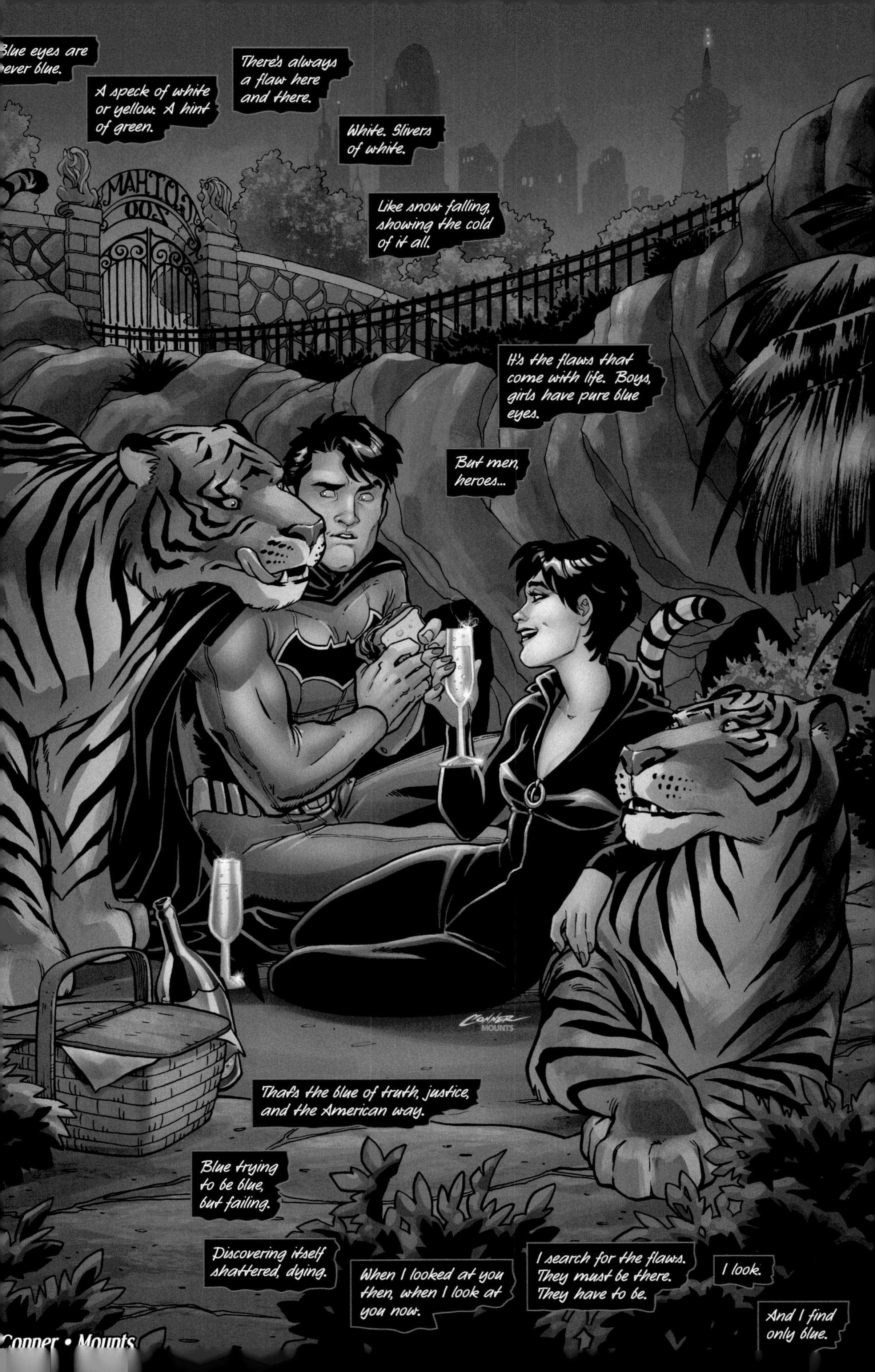
Blue eyes are
ever blue.
A speck of white or yellow. A hint of green.
There's always a flaw here and there.
White. Slivers of white.
Like snow falling, showing the cold of it all.
It's the flaws that come with life. Boys, girls have pure blue eyes.
But men, heroes...
That's the blue of truth, justice, and the American way.
Blue trying to be blue, but failing.
Discovering itself shattered, dying.
When I looked at you then, when I look at you now.
I search for the flaws. They must be there. They have to be.
I look.
And I find only blue.
CONNER MOUNTS
Conner • Mounts

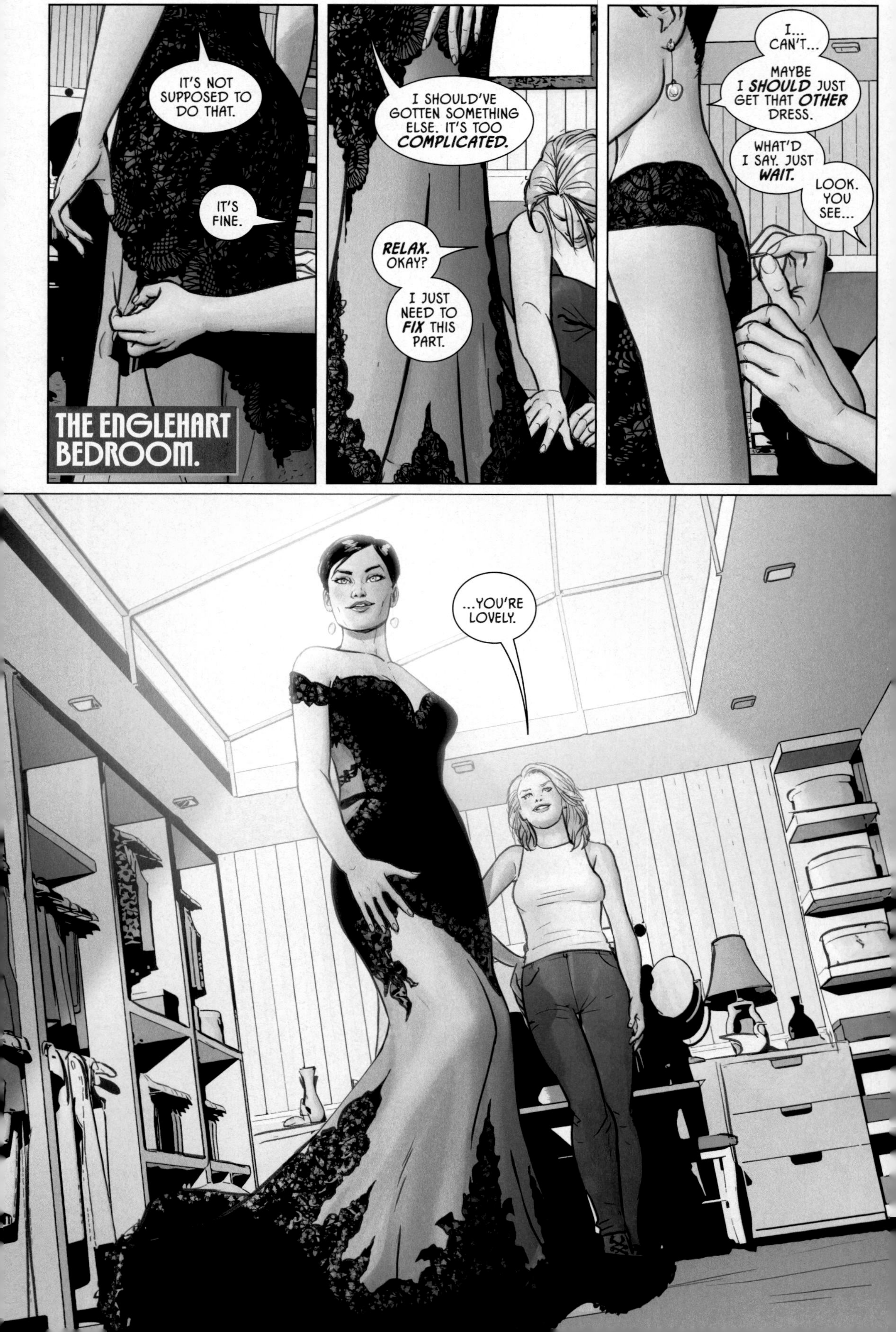
THE ENGLEHART BEDROOM.
IT'S NOT SUPPOSED TO DO THAT.
IT'S FINE.
I SHOULD'VE GOTTEN SOMETHING ELSE. IT'S TOO COMPLICATED.
RELAX. OKAY?
I JUST NEED TO FIX THIS PART.
I... CAN'T...
MAYBE I SHOULD JUST GET THAT OTHER DRESS.
WHAT'D I SAY. JUST WAIT.
LOOK. YOU SEE...
...YOU'RE LOVELY.

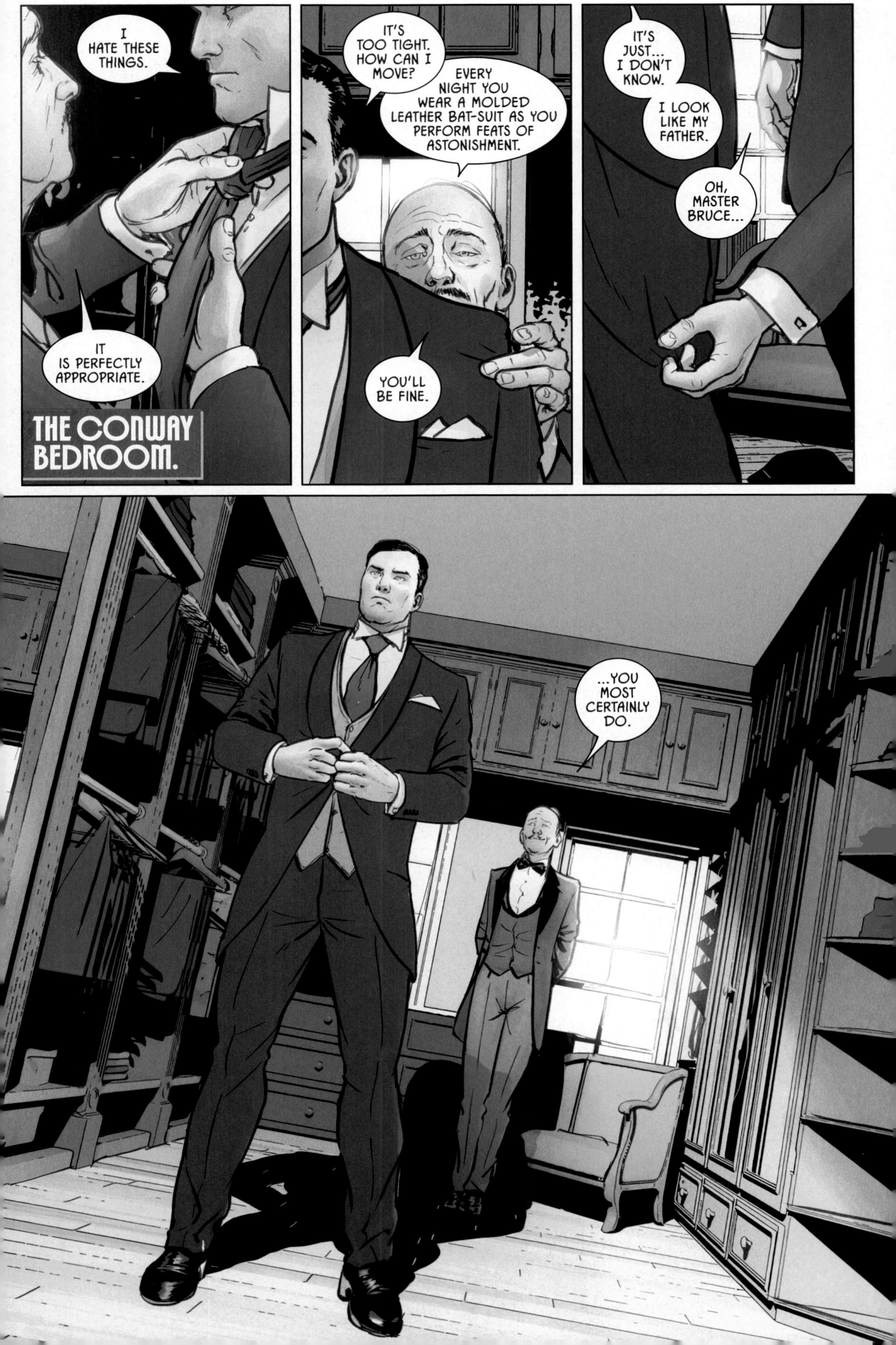
I HATE THESE THINGS.
IT IS PERFECTLY APPROPRIATE.
THE CONWAY BEDROOM.
IT'S TOO TIGHT. HOW CAN I MOVE?
EVERY NIGHT YOU WEAR A MOLDED LEATHER BAT-SUIT AS YOU PERFORM FEATS OF ASTONISHMENT.
YOU'LL BE FINE.
IT'S JUST... I DON'T KNOW.
I LOOK LIKE MY FATHER.
OH, MASTER BRUCE...
...YOU MOST CERTAINLY DO.

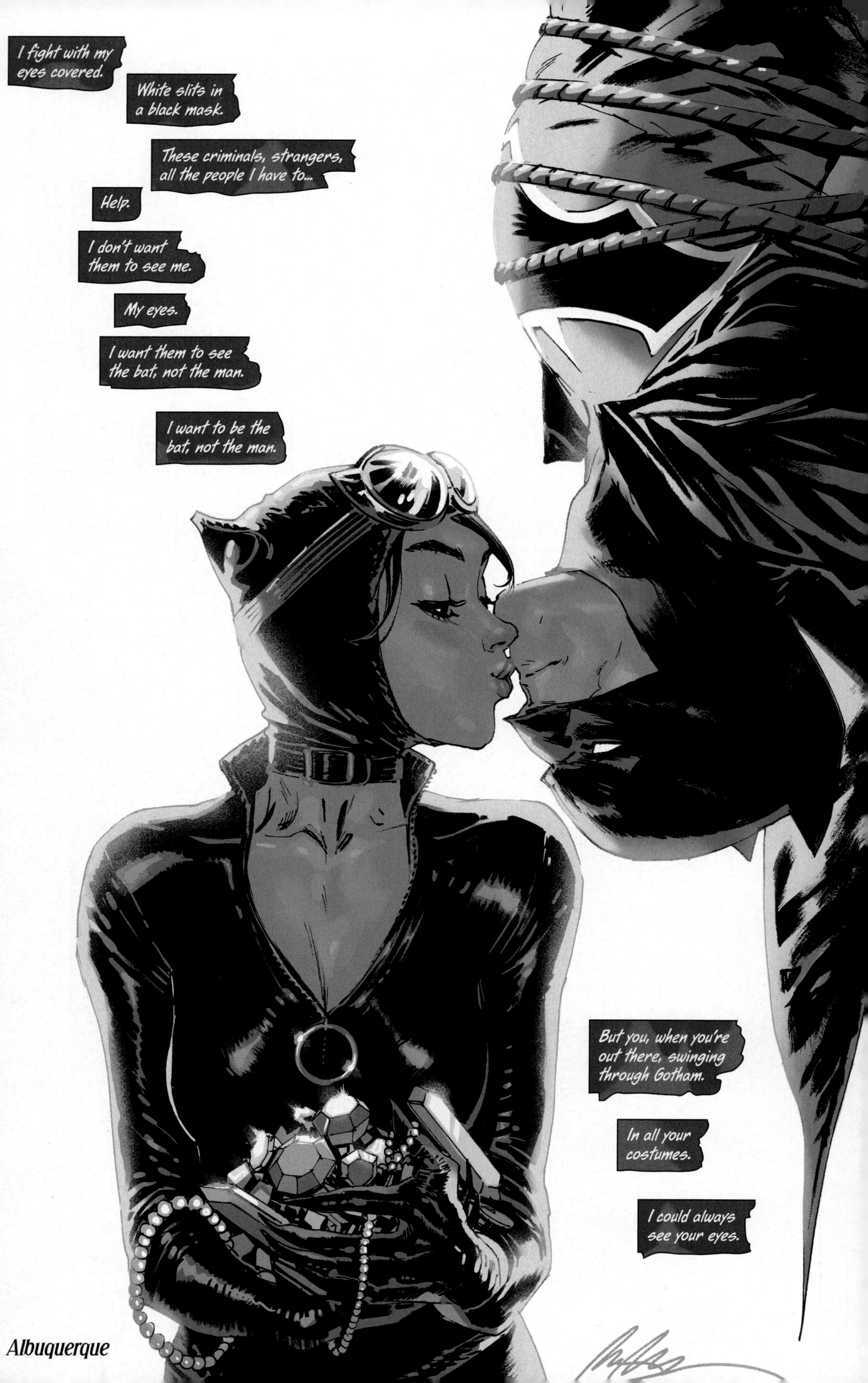
I fight with my eyes covered.
White slits in a black mask.
These criminals, strangers, all the people I have to...
Help.
I don't want them to see me.
My eyes.
I want them to see the bat, not the man.
I want to be the bat, not the man.
But you, when you're out there, swinging through Gotham.
In all your costumes.
I could always see your eyes.

Albuquerque

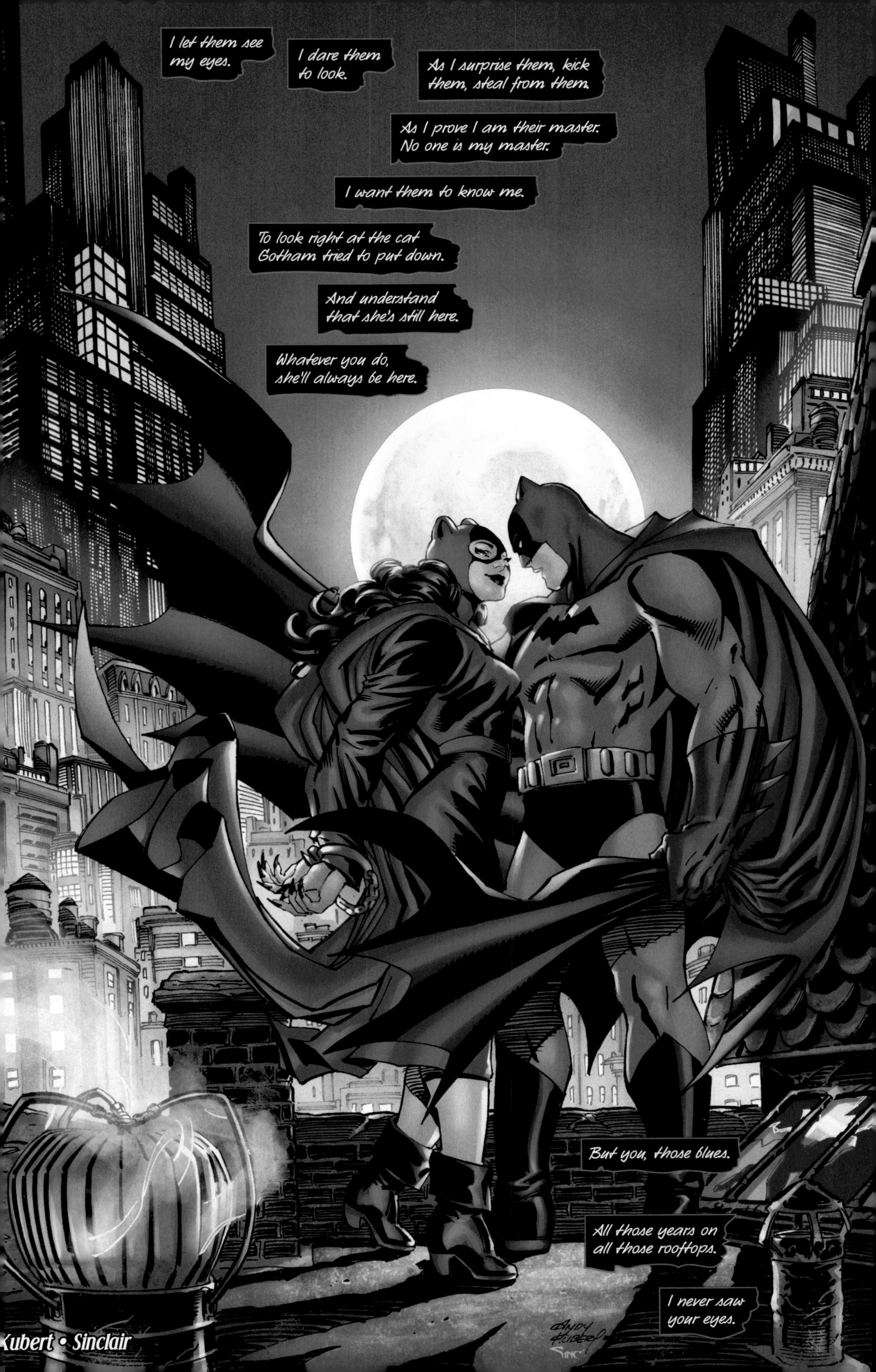
I let them see my eyes.
I dare them to look.
As I surprise them, kick them, steal from them.
As I prove I am their master. No one is my master.
I want them to know me.
To look right at the cat Gotham tried to put down.
And understand that she's still here.
Whatever you do, she'll always be here.
But you, those blues.
All those years on all those rooftops.
I never saw your eyes.
Kubert • Sinclair

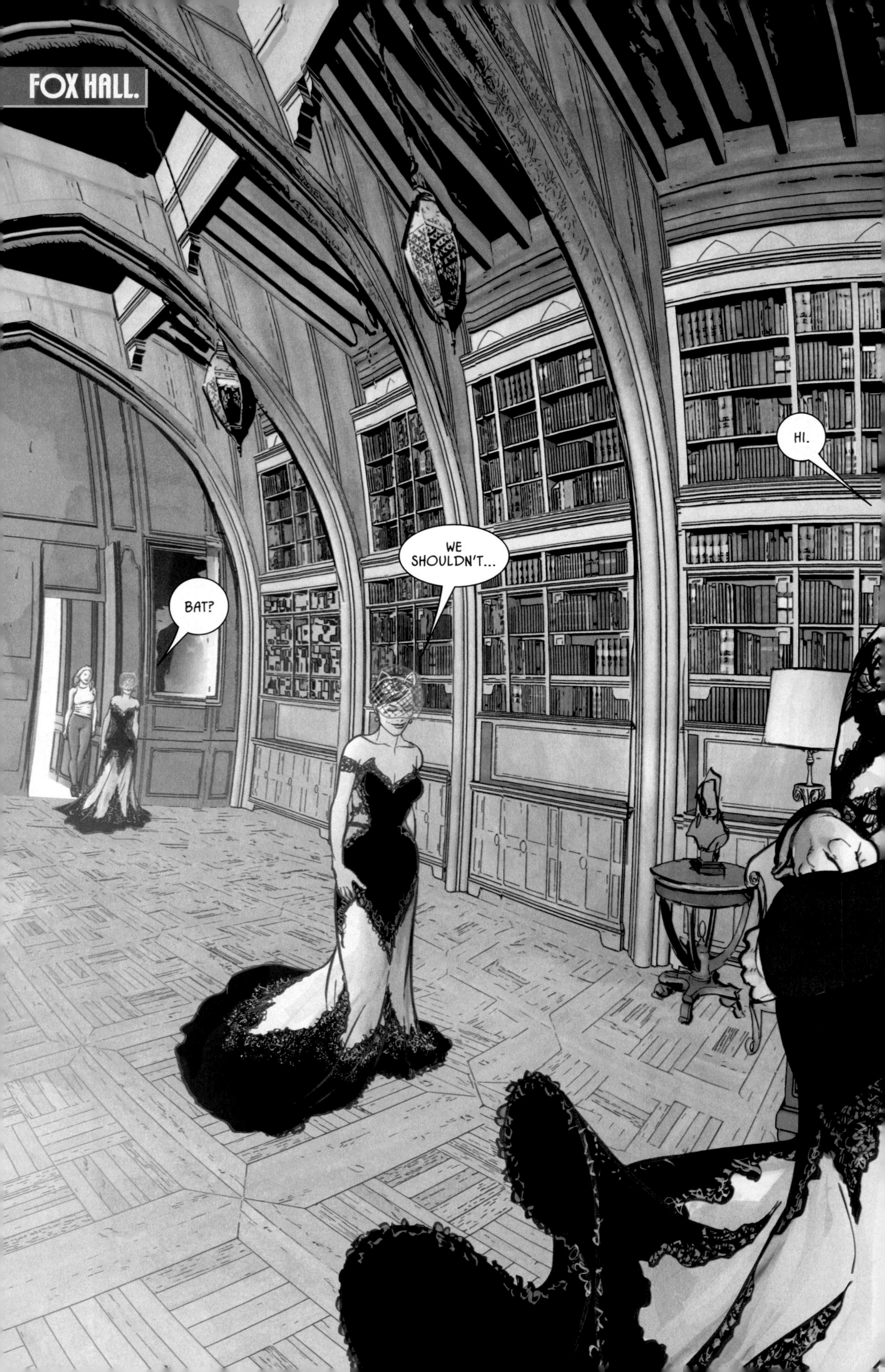
FOX HALL.
BAT?
WE SHOULDN'T...
HI.

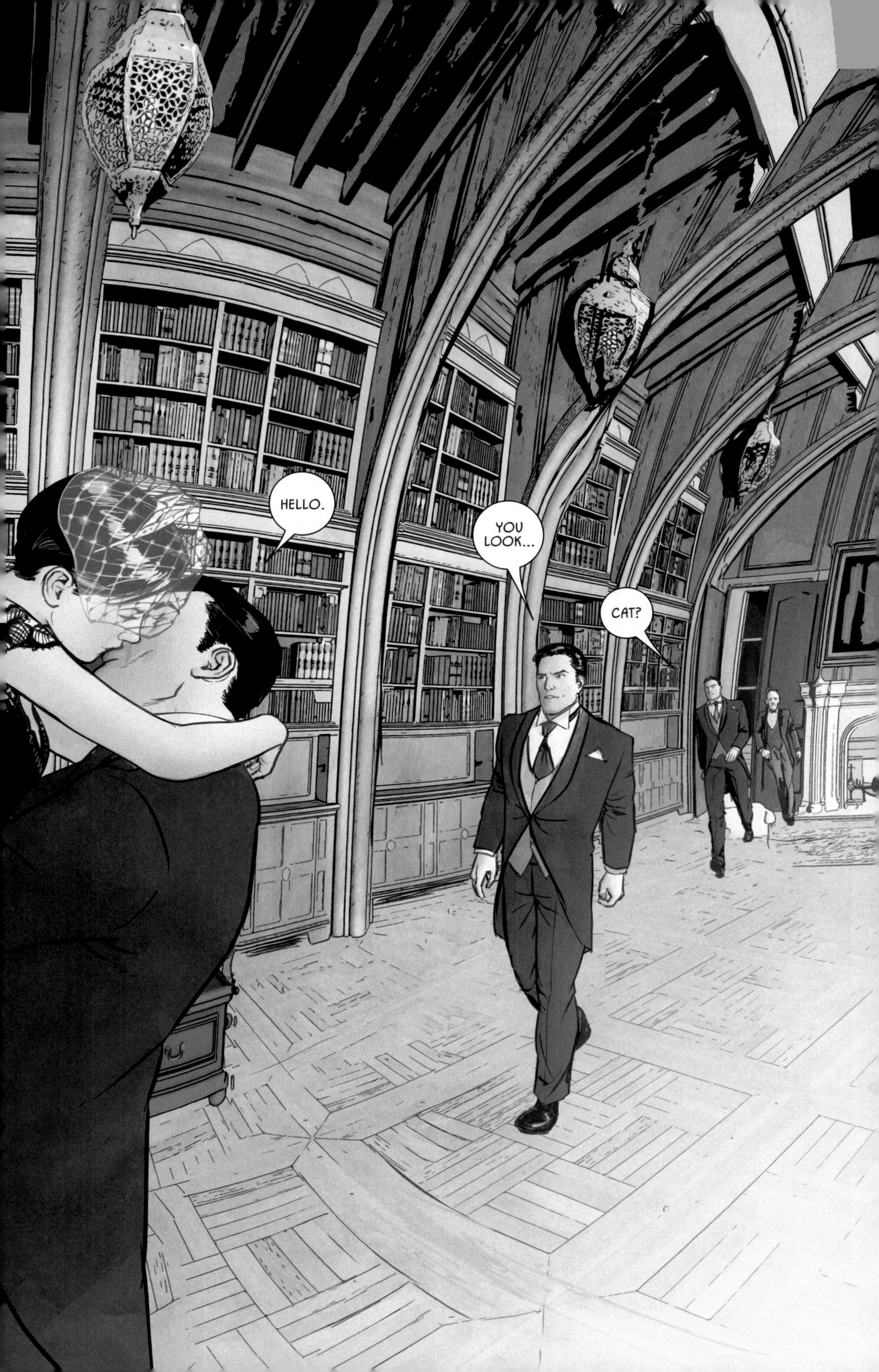
HELLO.
YOU LOOK...
CAT?

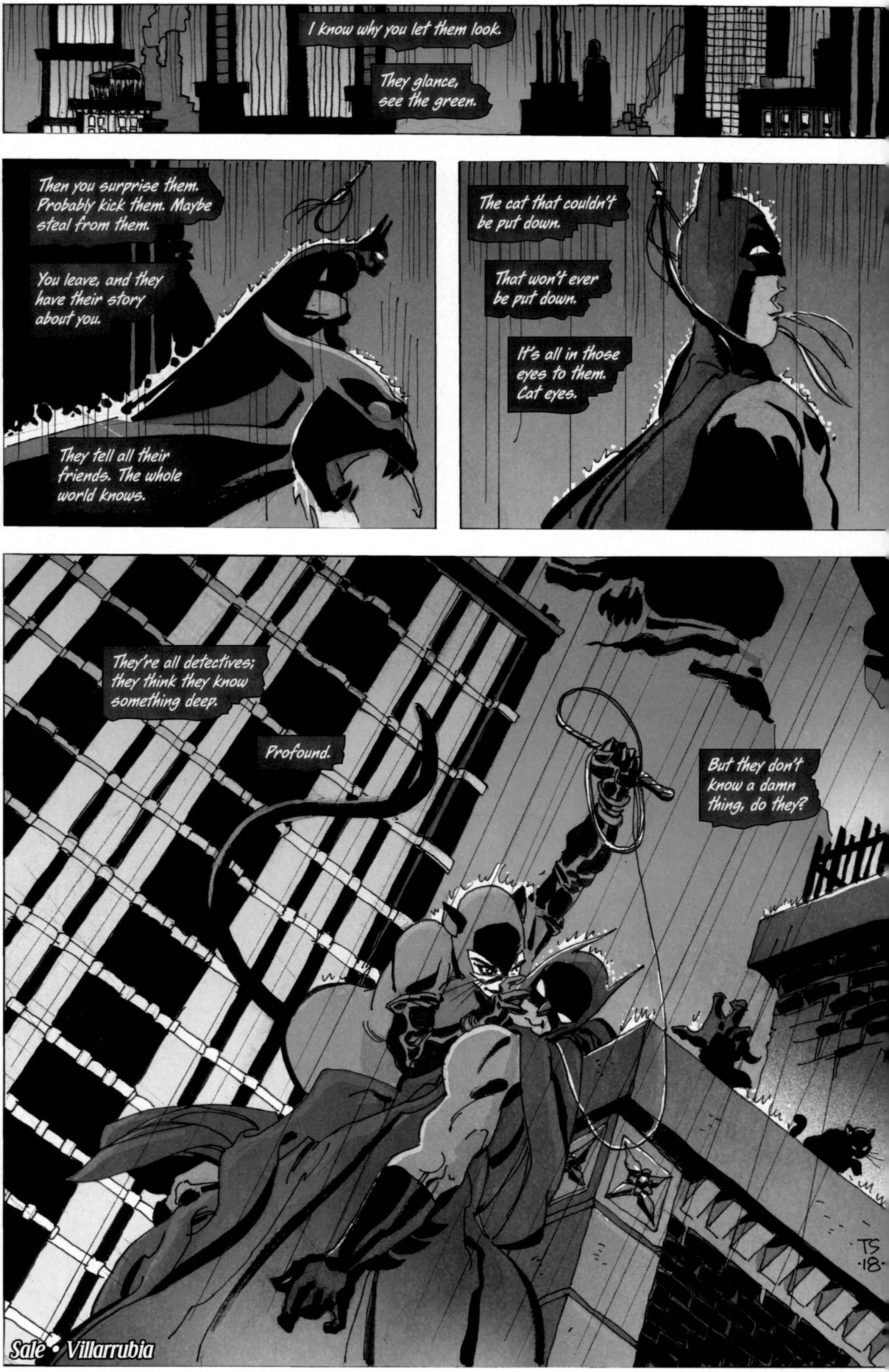
I know why you let them look.
They glance, see the green.
Then you surprise them. Probably kick them. Maybe steal from them.
You leave, and they have their story about you.
They tell all their friends. The whole world knows.
The cat that couldn't be put down.
That won't ever be put down.
It's all in those eyes to them. Cat eyes.
They're all detectives; they think they know something deep.
Profound.
But they don't know a damn thing, do they?
TS ·18·
Sale • Villarrubia

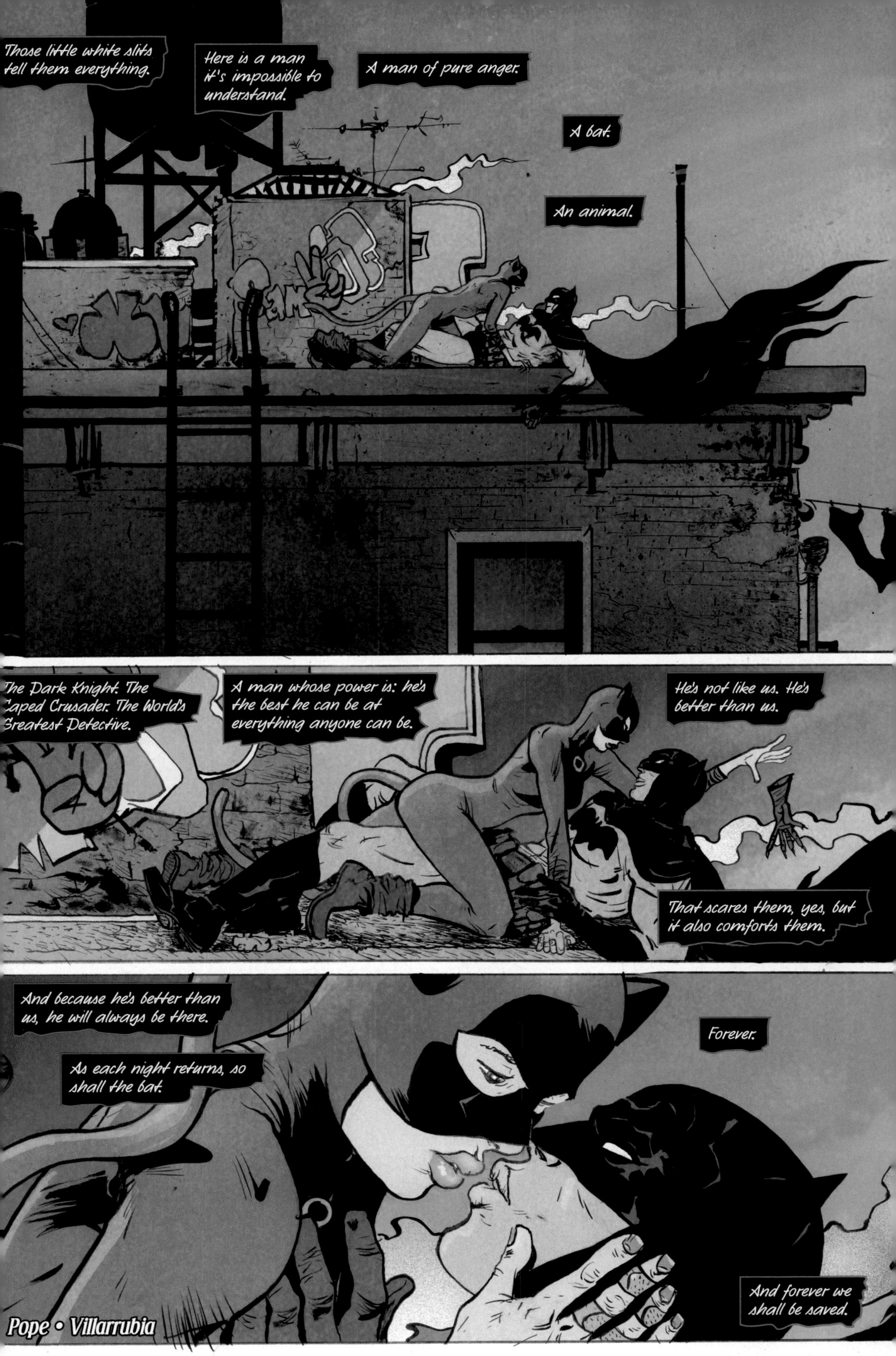
Those little white slits tell them everything.
Here is a man it's impossible to understand.
A man of pure anger.
A bat.
An animal.
The Dark Knight. The Caped Crusader. The World's Greatest Detective.
A man whose power is: he's the best he can be at everything anyone can be.
He's not like us. He's better than us.
That scares them, yes, but it also comforts them.
And because he's better than us, he will always be there.
As each night returns, so shall the bat.
Forever.
And forever we shall be saved.
Pope • Villarrubia

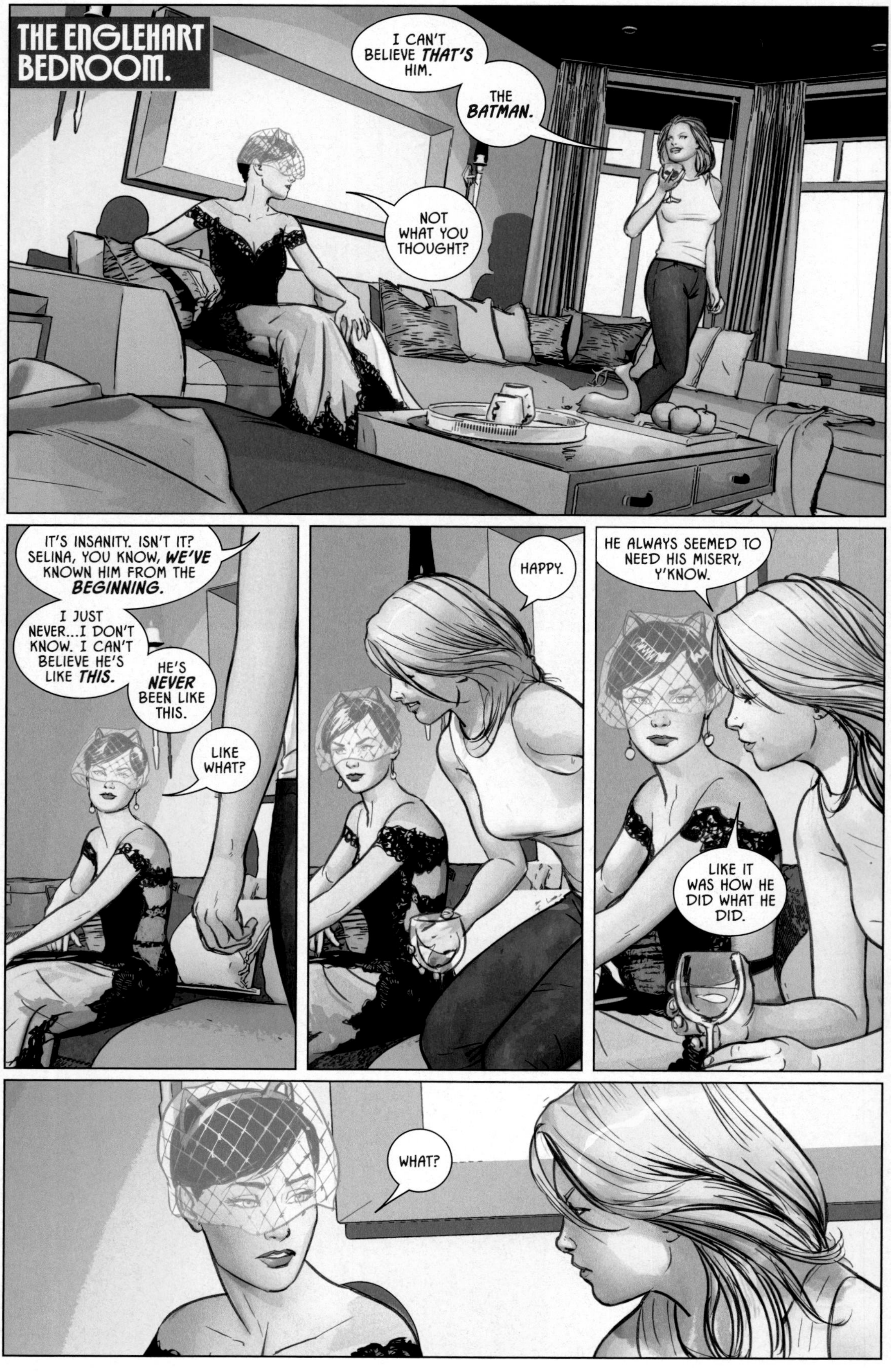
THE ENGLEHART BEDROOM.
I CAN'T BELIEVE THAT'S HIM.
THE BATMAN.
NOT WHAT YOU THOUGHT?
IT'S INSANITY. ISN'T IT? SELINA, YOU KNOW, WE'VE KNOWN HIM FROM THE BEGINNING.
I JUST NEVER...I DON'T KNOW. I CAN'T BELIEVE HE'S LIKE THIS.
HE'S NEVER BEEN LIKE THIS.
LIKE WHAT?
HAPPY.
HE ALWAYS SEEMED TO NEED HIS MISERY, Y'KNOW.
LIKE IT WAS HOW HE DID WHAT HE DID.
WHAT?

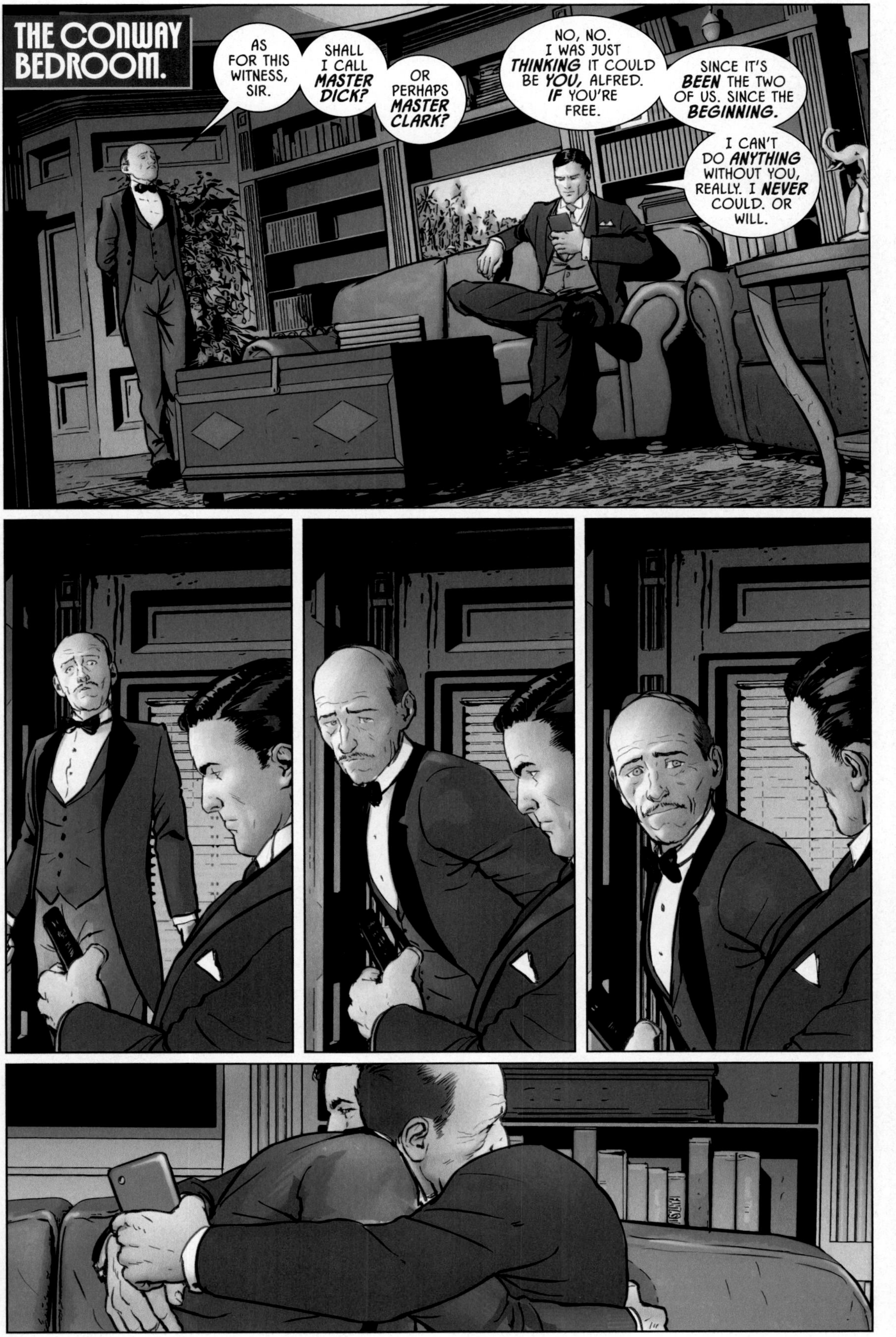
THE CONWAY BEDROOM.
AS FOR THIS WITNESS, SIR.
SHALL I CALL MASTER DICK?
OR PERHAPS MASTER CLARK?
NO, NO. I WAS JUST THINKING IT COULD BE YOU, ALFRED. IF YOU'RE FREE.
SINCE IT'S BEEN THE TWO OF US. SINCE THE BEGINNING.
I CAN'T DO ANYTHING WITHOUT YOU, REALLY. I NEVER COULD. OR WILL.

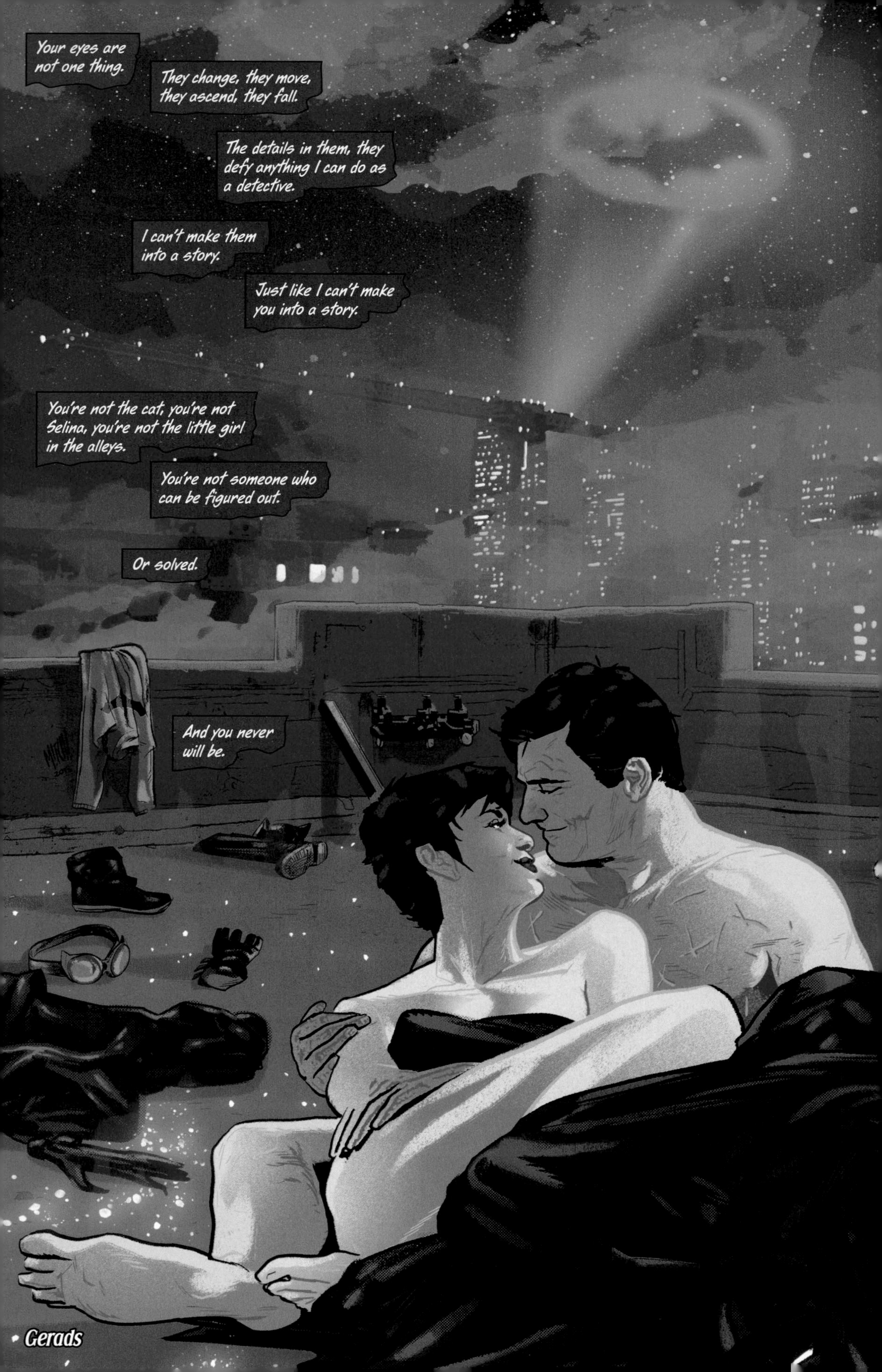
Your eyes are not one thing.
They change, they move, they ascend, they fall.
The details in them, they defy anything I can do as a detective.
I can't make them into a story.
Just like I can't make you into a story.
You're not the cat, you're not Selina, you're not the little girl in the alleys.
You're not someone who can be figured out.
Or solved.
And you never will be.
Gerads

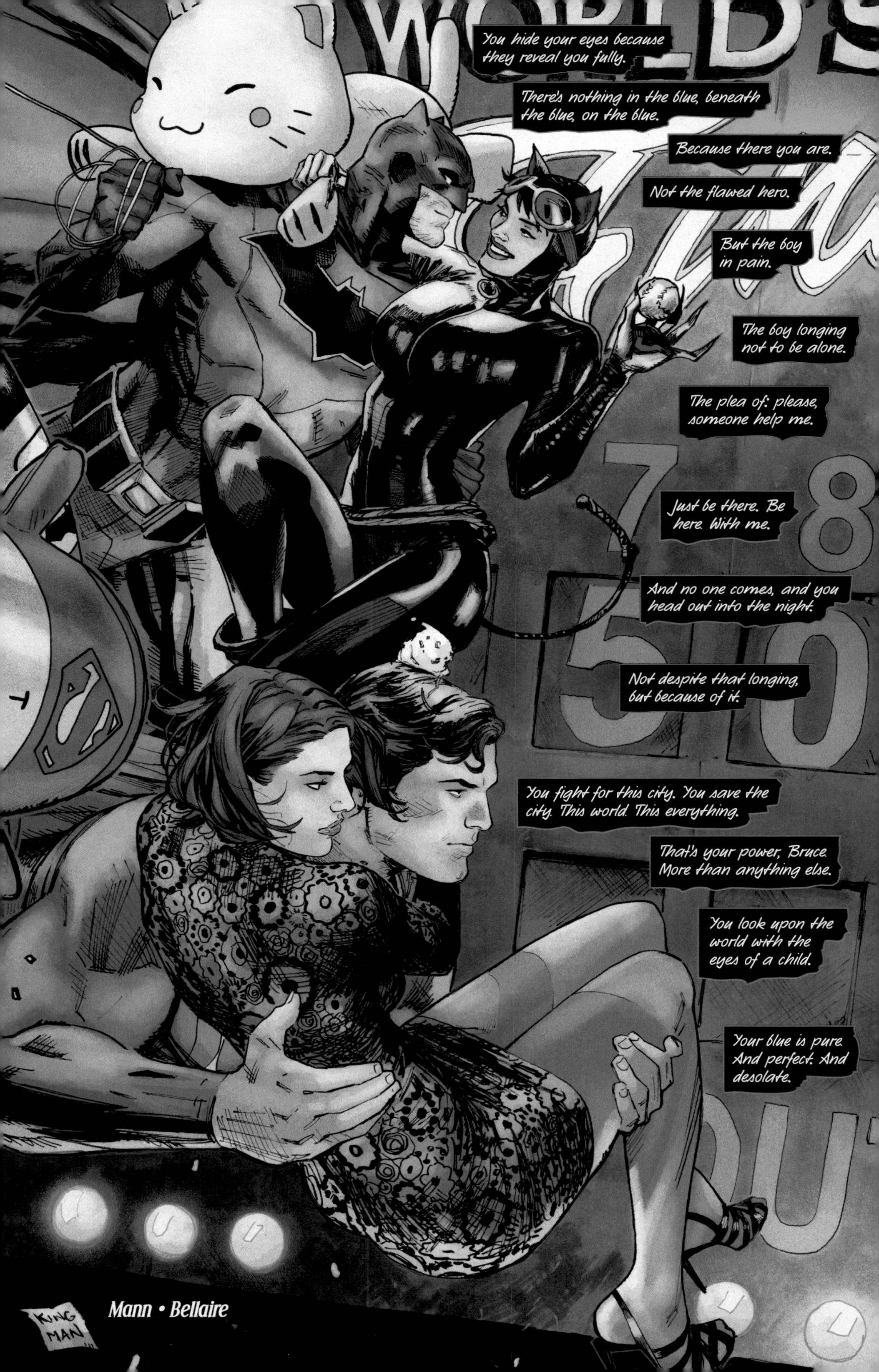
WORLD'S
You hide your eyes because they reveal you fully.
There's nothing in the blue, beneath the blue, on the blue.
Because there you are.
Not the flawed hero.
But the boy in pain.
The boy longing not to be alone.
The plea of: please, someone help me.
Just be there. Be here. With me.
And no one comes, and you head out into the night.
Not despite that longing, but because of it.
You fight for this city. You save the city. This world. This everything.
That's your power, Bruce. More than anything else.
You look upon the world with the eyes of a child.
Your blue is pure. And perfect. And desolate.
KING MAN
Mann • Bellaire

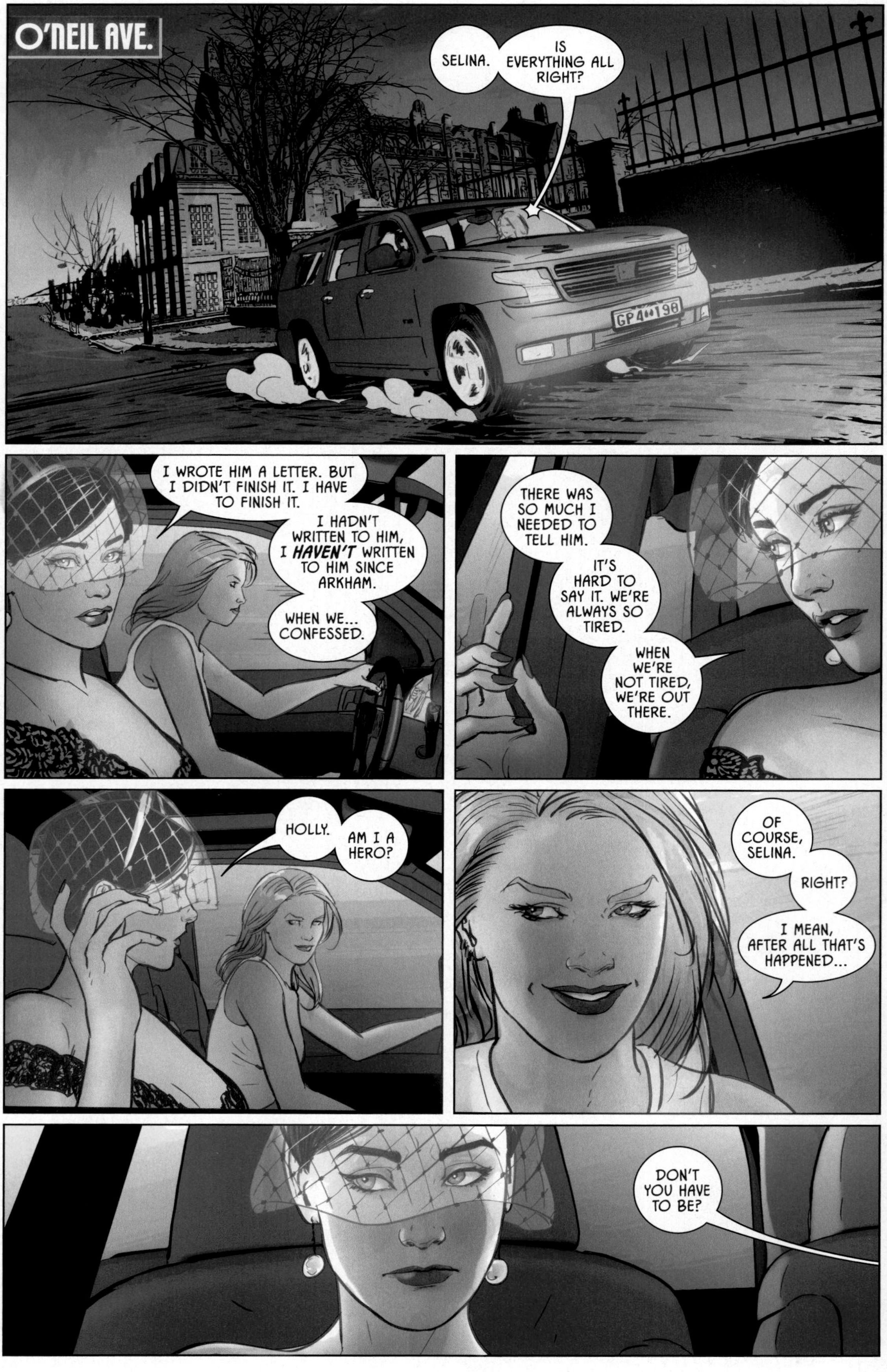
O'NEIL AVE.
SELINA.
IS EVERYTHING ALL RIGHT?
GP4 198
I WROTE HIM A LETTER. BUT I DIDN'T FINISH IT. I HAVE TO FINISH IT.
I HADN'T WRITTEN TO HIM, I HAVEN'T WRITTEN TO HIM SINCE ARKHAM.
WHEN WE... CONFESSED.
THERE WAS SO MUCH I NEEDED TO TELL HIM.
IT'S HARD TO SAY IT. WE'RE ALWAYS SO TIRED.
WHEN WE'RE NOT TIRED, WE'RE OUT THERE.
HOLLY.
AM I A HERO?
OF COURSE, SELINA.
RIGHT?
I MEAN, AFTER ALL THAT'S HAPPENED...
DON'T YOU HAVE TO BE?

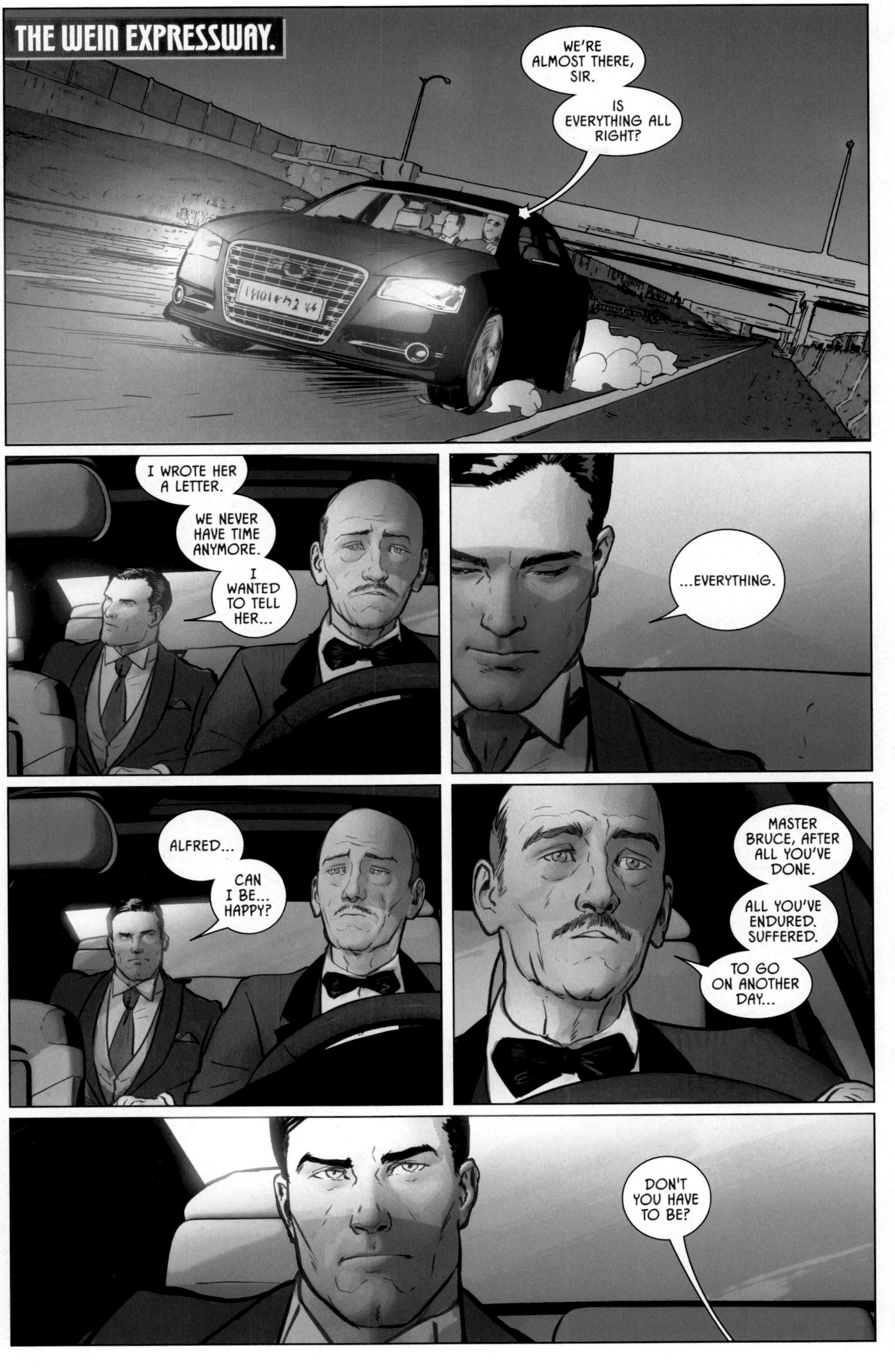
THE WEIN EXPRESSWAY.
WE'RE ALMOST THERE, SIR.
IS EVERYTHING ALL RIGHT?
I WROTE HER A LETTER.
WE NEVER HAVE TIME ANYMORE.
I WANTED TO TELL HER...
...EVERYTHING.
ALFRED...
CAN I BE... HAPPY?
MASTER BRUCE, AFTER ALL YOU'VE DONE.
ALL YOU'VE ENDURED. SUFFERED.
TO GO ON ANOTHER DAY...
DON'T YOU HAVE TO BE?

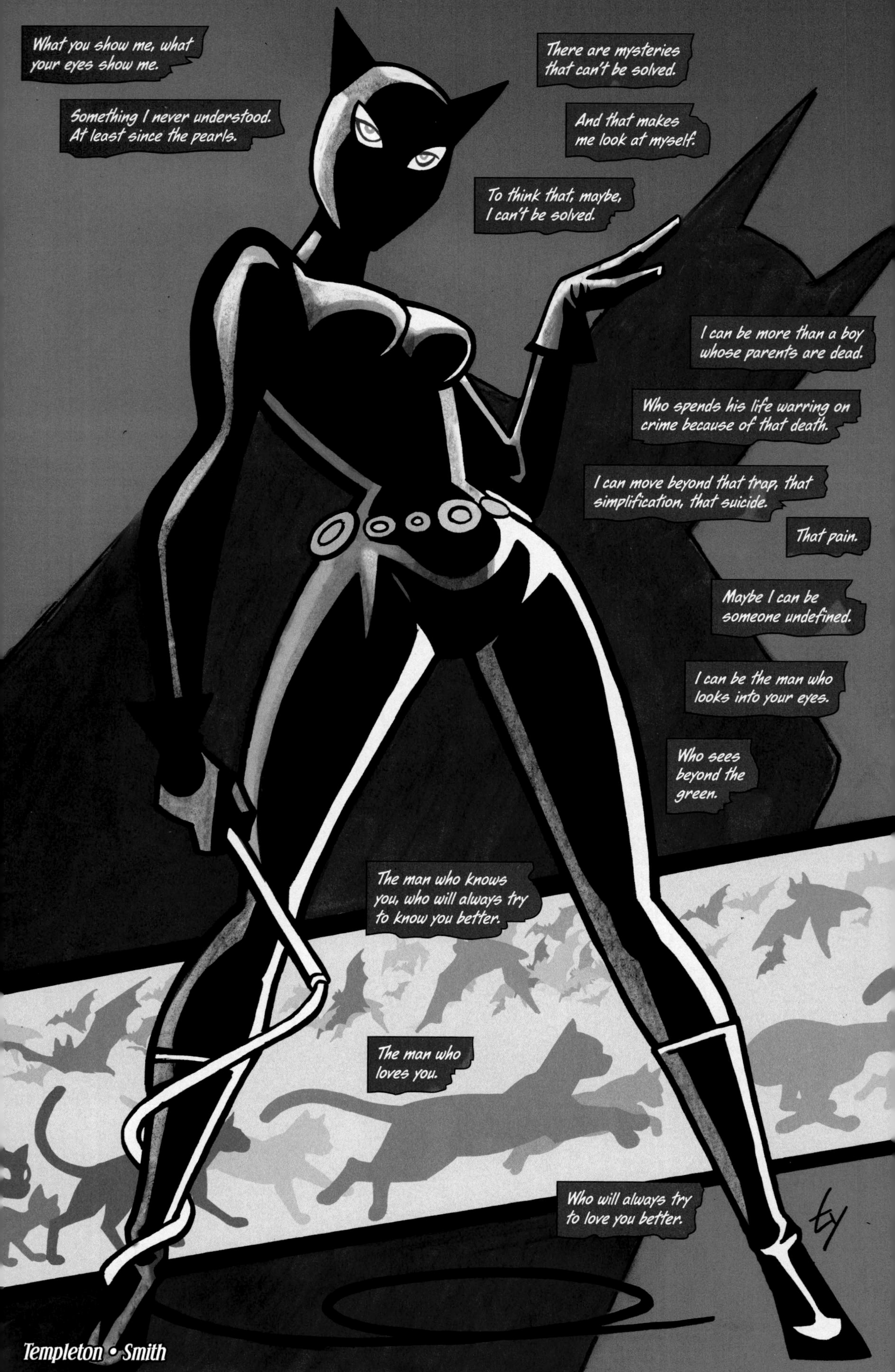

Templeton • Smith

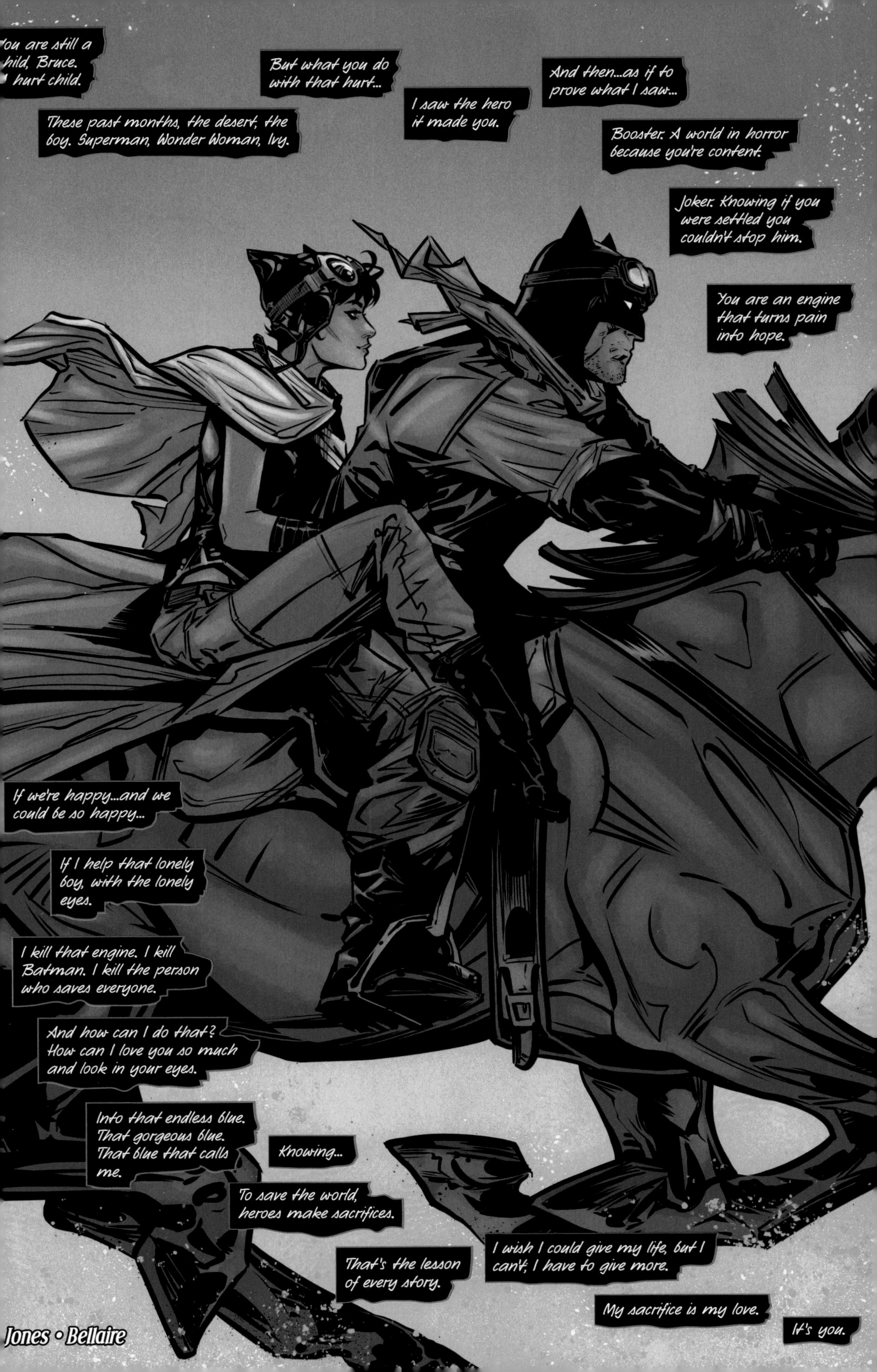

You are still a child, Bruce. A hurt child.
These past months, the desert, the boy. Superman, Wonder Woman, Ivy.
But what you do with that hurt...
I saw the hero it made you.
And then...as if to prove what I saw...
Booster. A world in horror because you're content.
Joker. Knowing if you were settled you couldn't stop him.
You are an engine that turns pain into hope.
If we're happy...and we could be so happy...
If I help that lonely boy, with the lonely eyes.
I kill that engine. I kill Batman. I kill the person who saves everyone.
And how can I do that? How can I love you so much and look in your eyes.
Into that endless blue. That gorgeous blue. That blue that calls me.
Knowing...
To save the world, heroes make sacrifices.
That's the lesson of every story.
I wish I could give my life, but I can't; I have to give more.
My sacrifice is my love.
It's you.
Jones • Bellaire

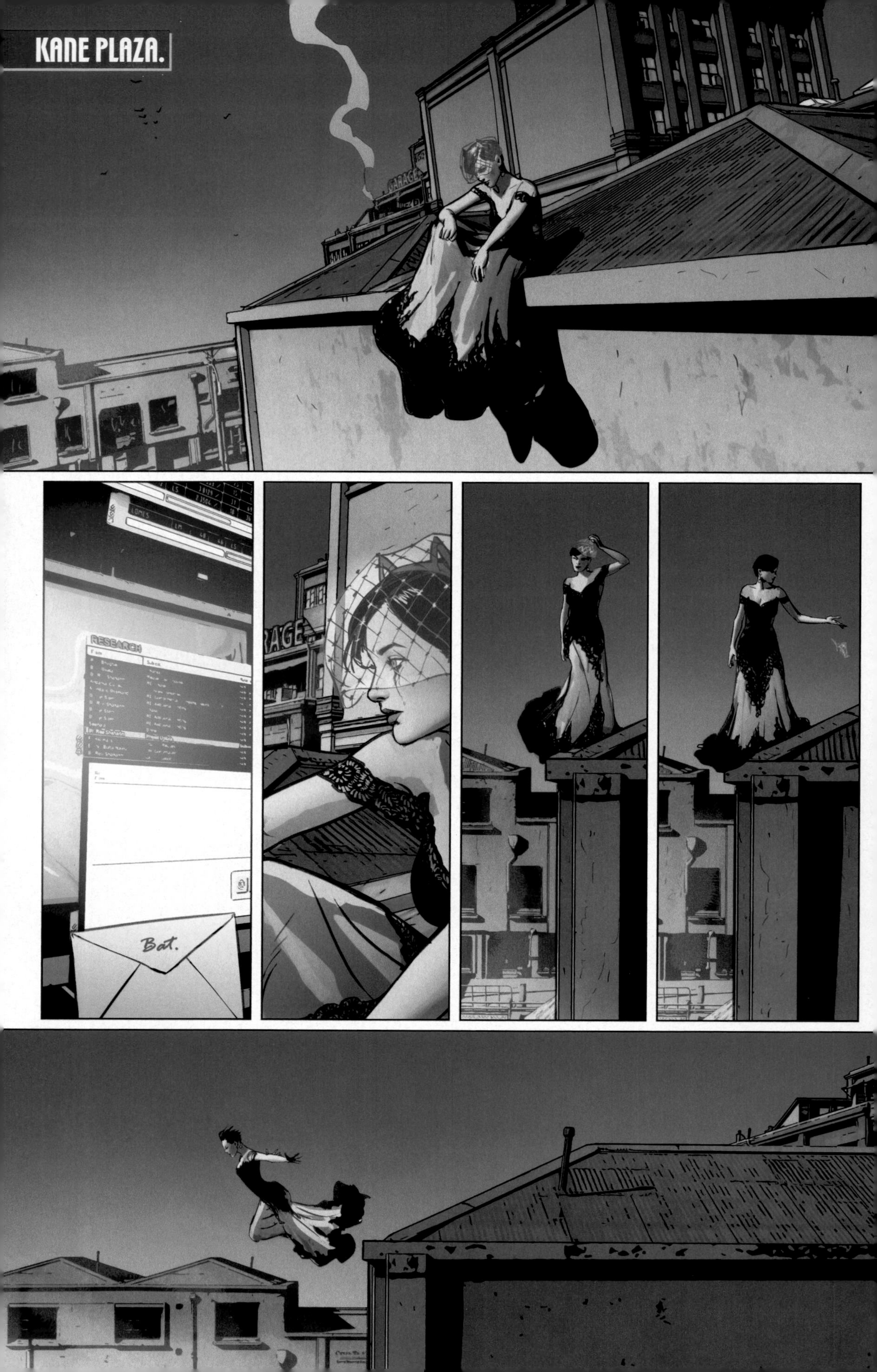
KANE PLAZA.
RESEARCH
Bat.

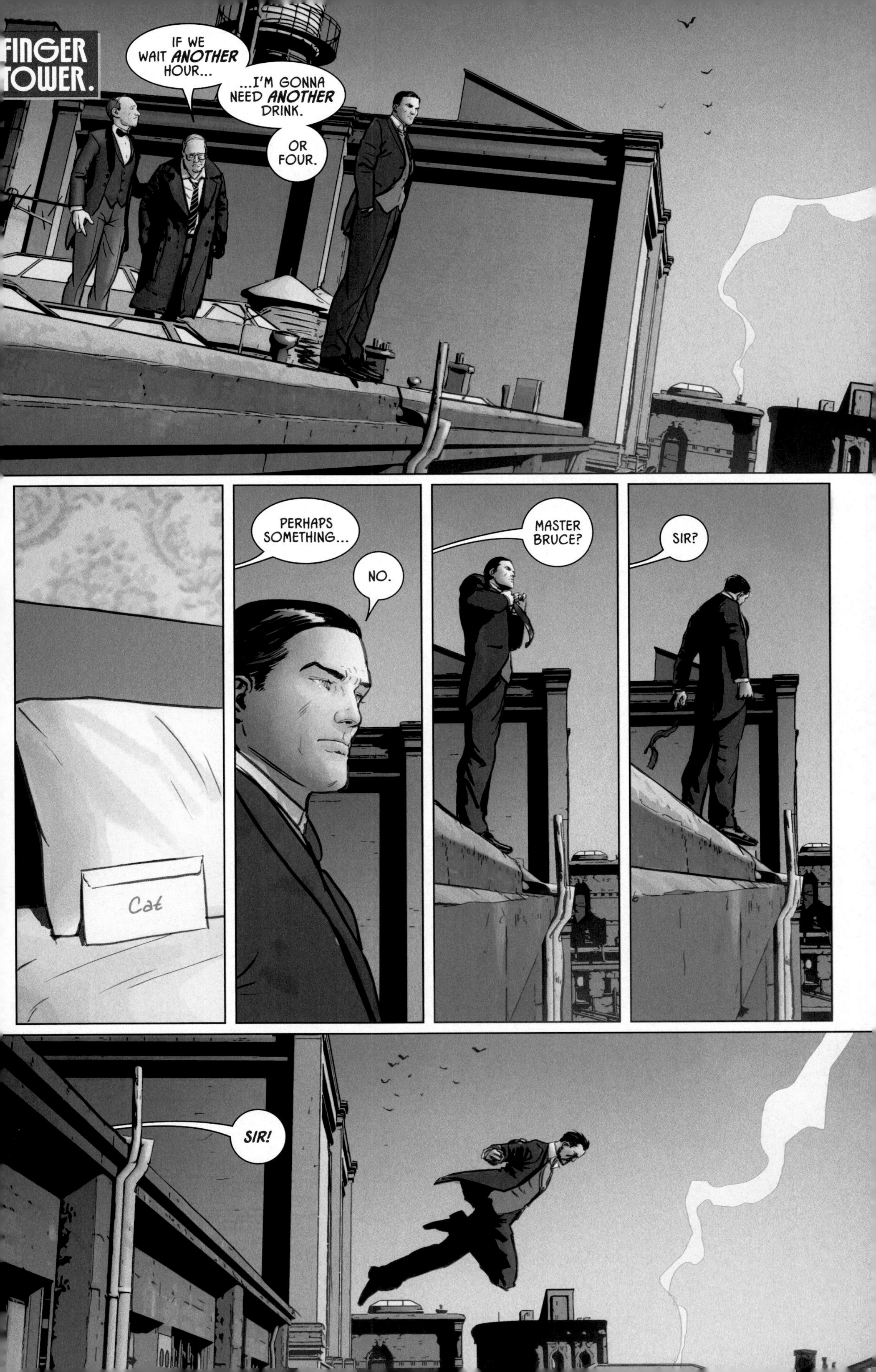
FINGER TOWER.
IF WE WAIT ANOTHER HOUR...
...I'M GONNA NEED ANOTHER DRINK.
OR FOUR.
Cat
PERHAPS SOMETHING...
NO.
MASTER BRUCE?
SIR?
SIR!

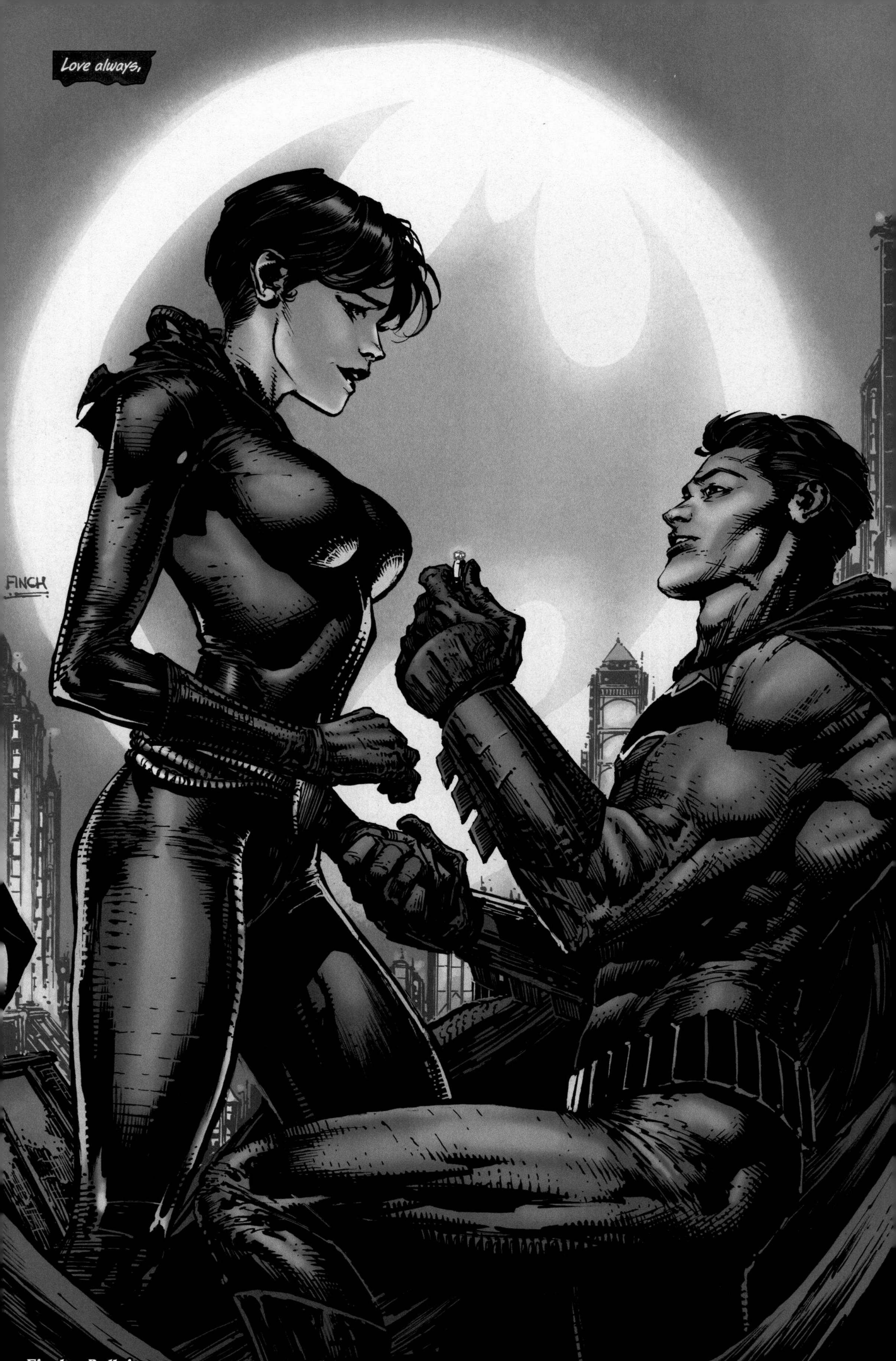
Love always,
FINCH

Finch • Bellaire

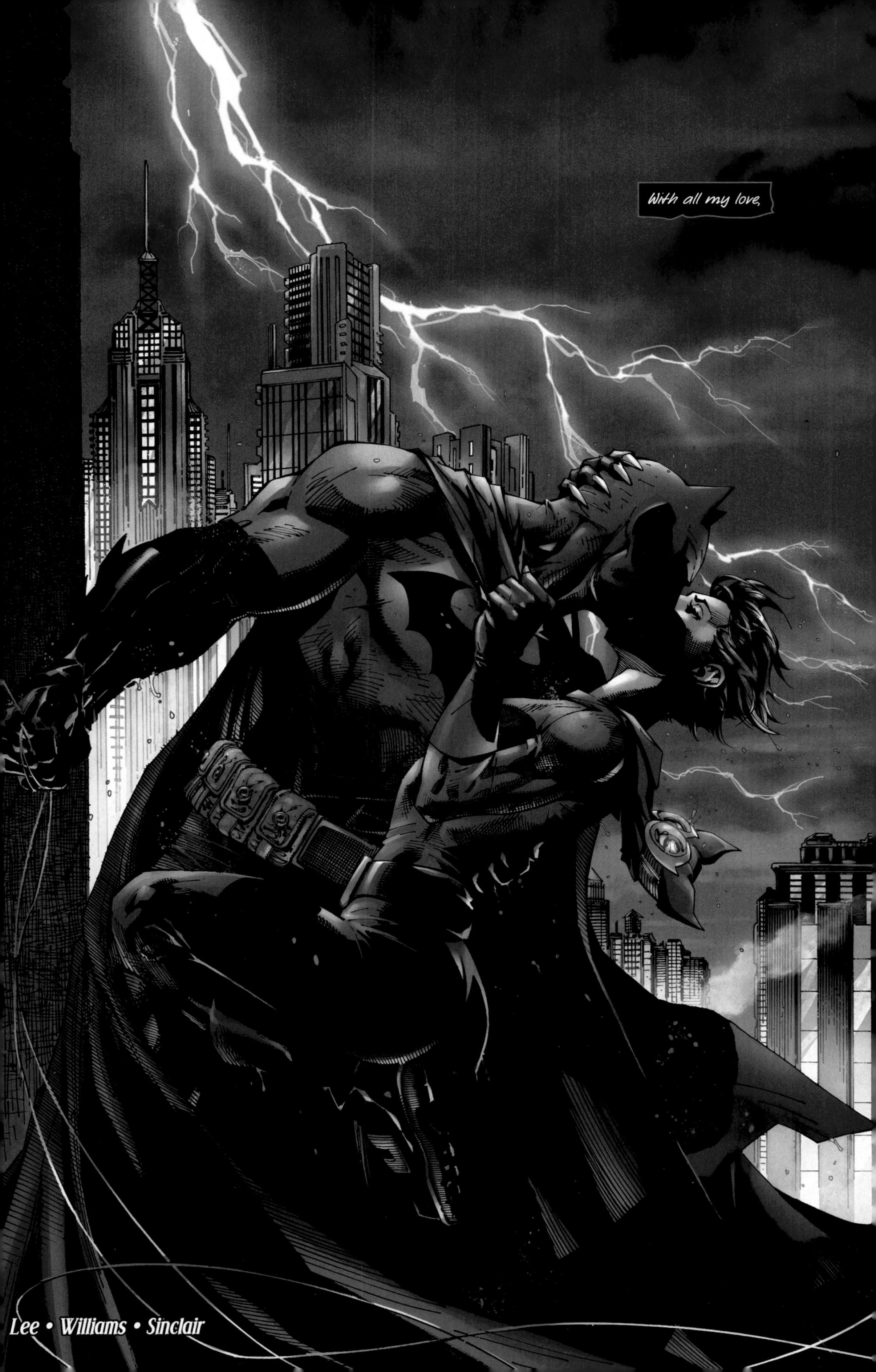
With all my love,
Lee • Williams • Sinclair

Bat

Capullo • Plascencia

CAPULLO
'13
+fco

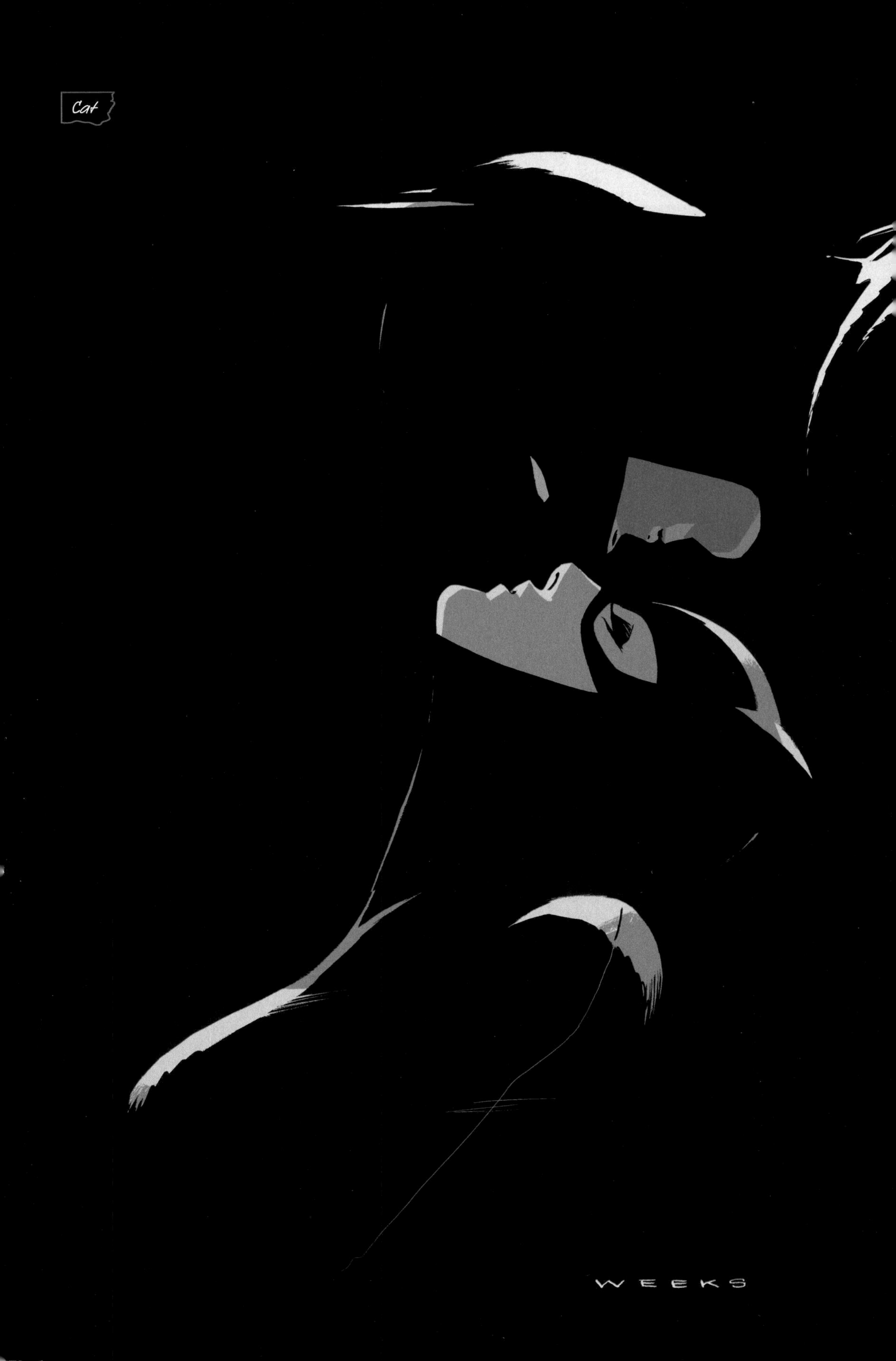
Cat
WEEKS

Weeks

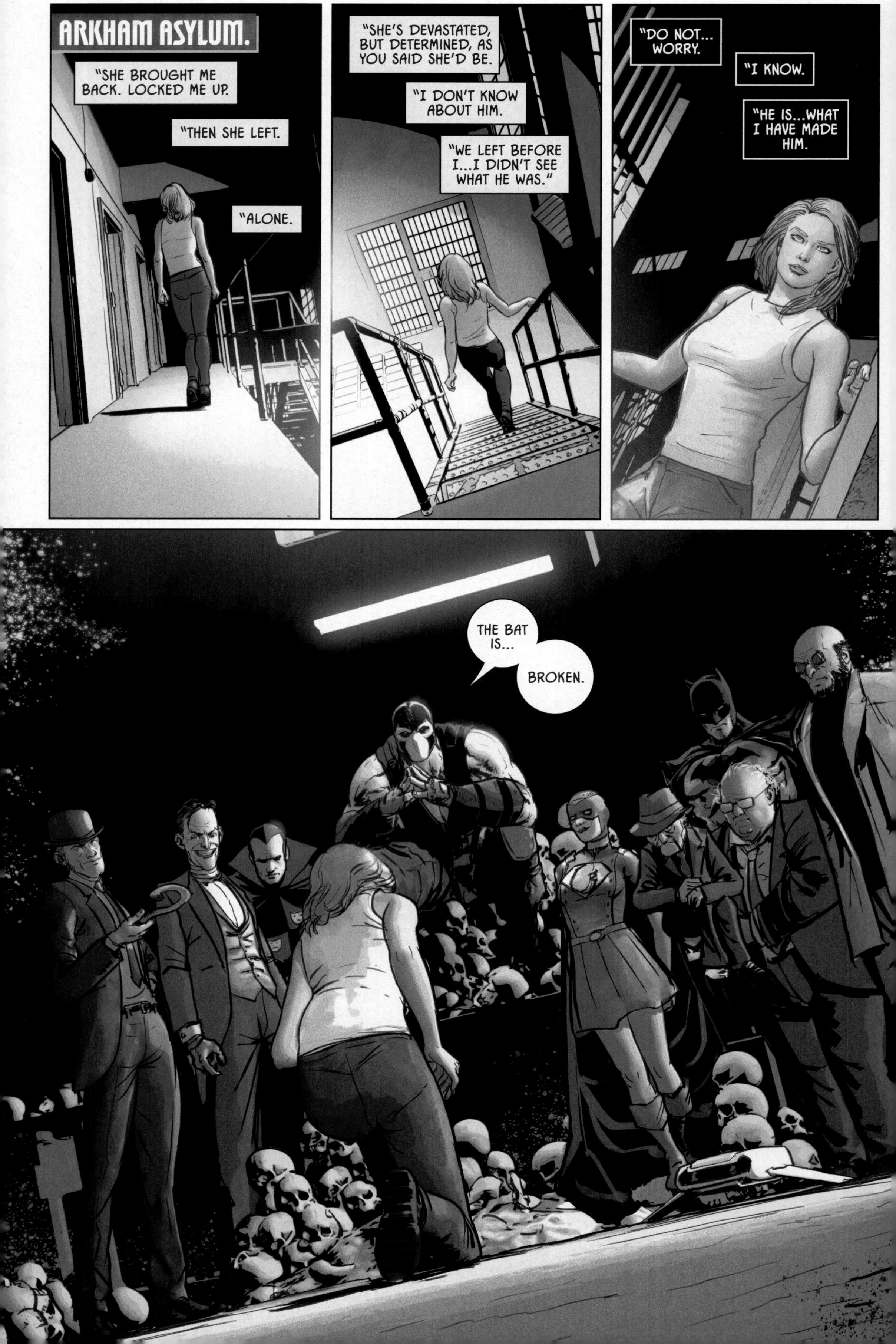
ARKHAM ASYLUM.
"SHE BROUGHT ME BACK. LOCKED ME UP.
"THEN SHE LEFT.
"ALONE.
"SHE'S DEVASTATED, BUT DETERMINED, AS YOU SAID SHE'D BE.
"I DON'T KNOW ABOUT HIM.
"WE LEFT BEFORE I...I DIDN'T SEE WHAT HE WAS."
"DO NOT... WORRY.
"I KNOW.
"HE IS...WHAT I HAVE MADE HIM.
THE BAT IS...
BROKEN.

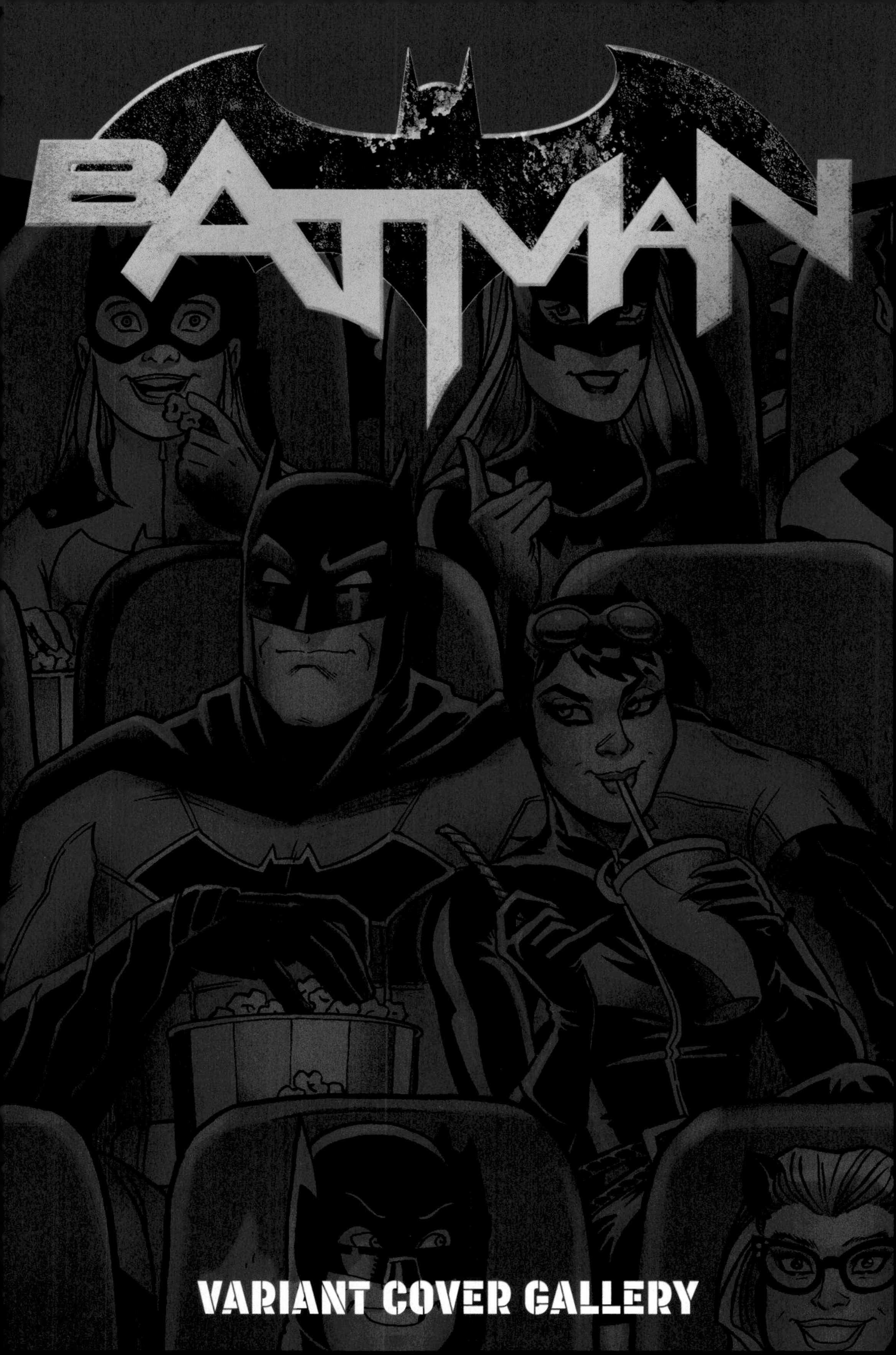
BATMAN
VARIANT COVER GALLERY

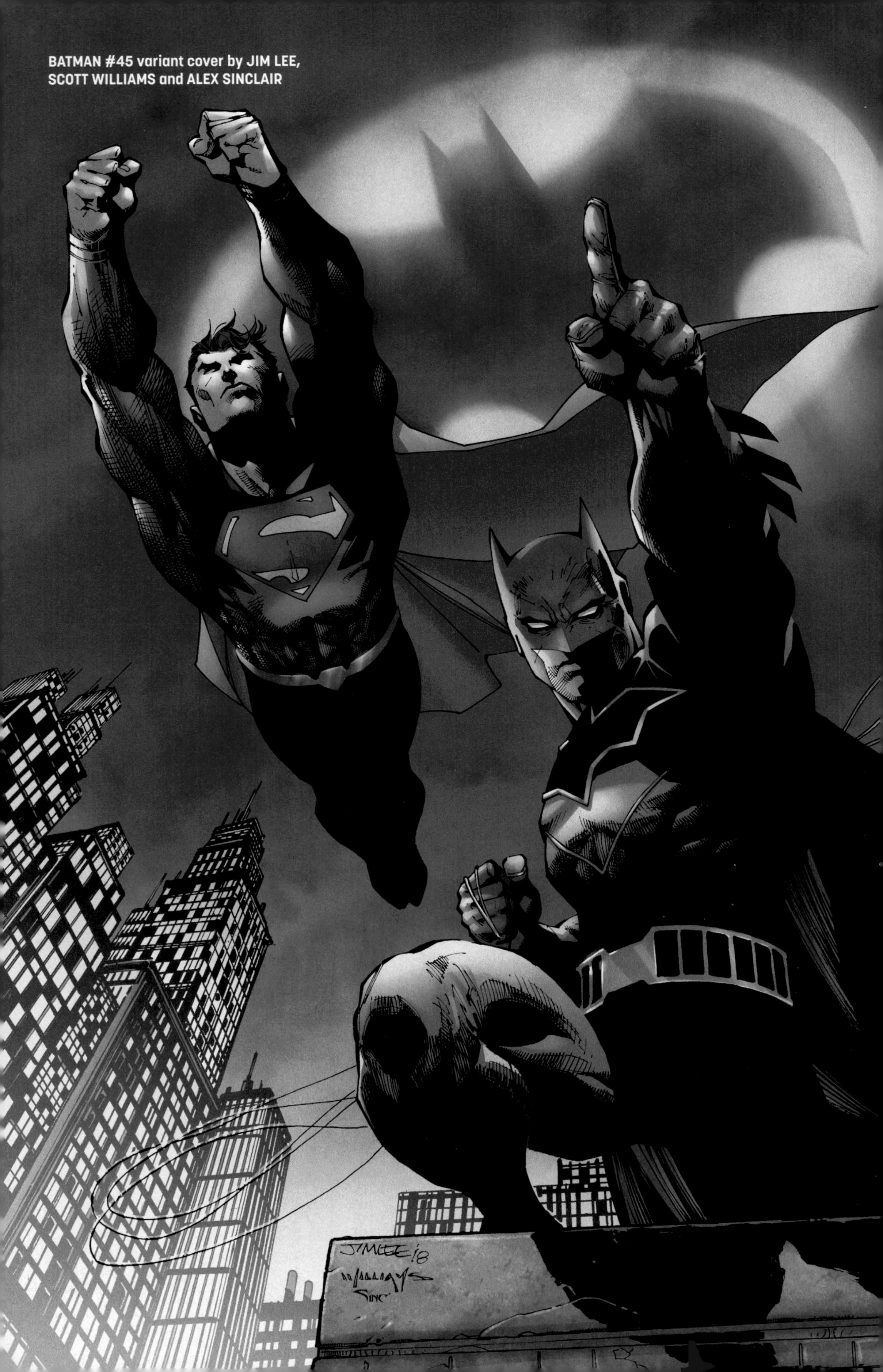

BATMAN #45 variant cover by JIM LEE,
SCOTT WILLIAMS and ALEX SINCLAIR

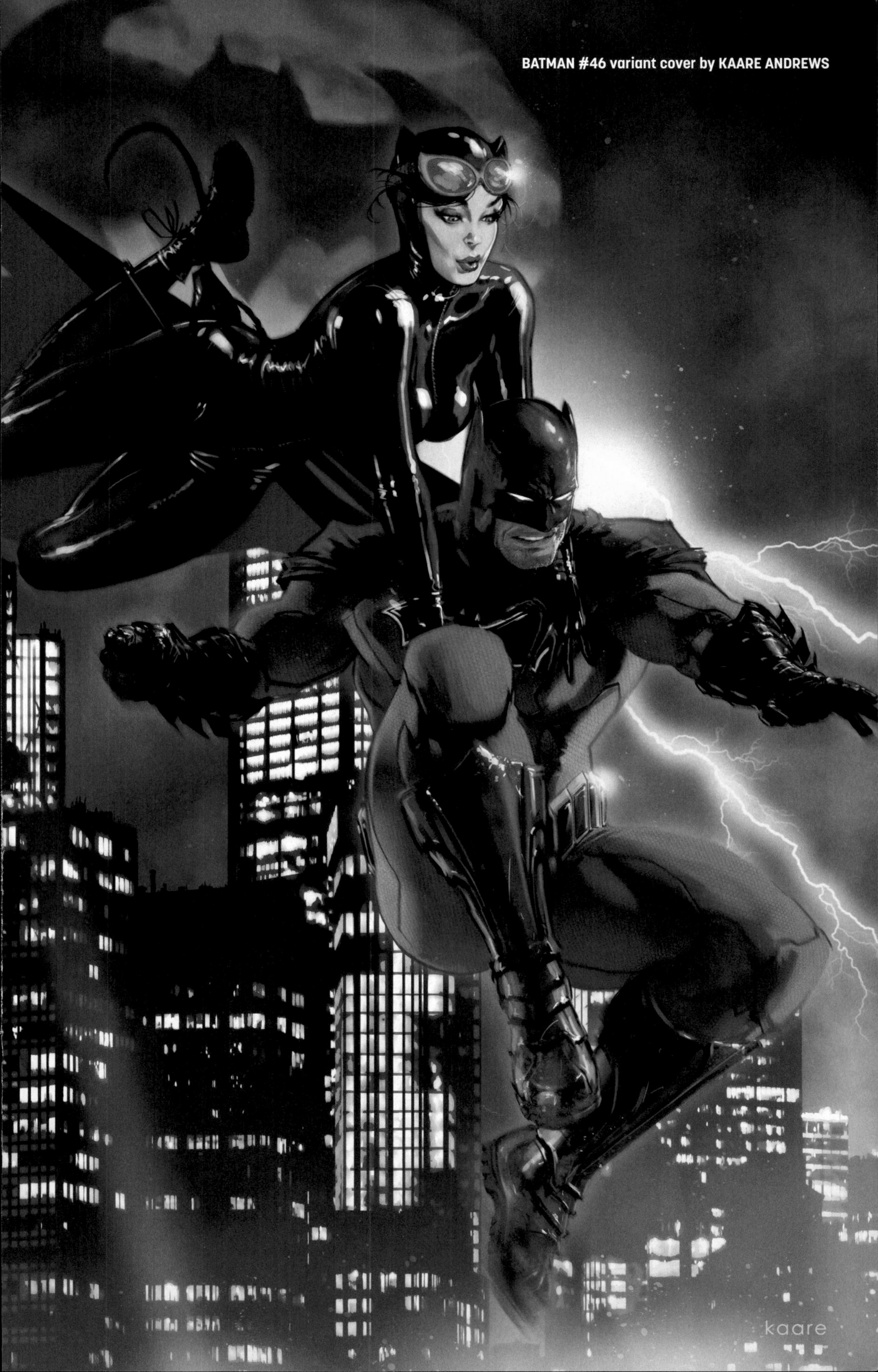
kaare

BATMAN #46 variant cover by KAARE ANDREWS

BATMAN #47 variant cover by AMANDA CONNER and PAUL MOUNTS

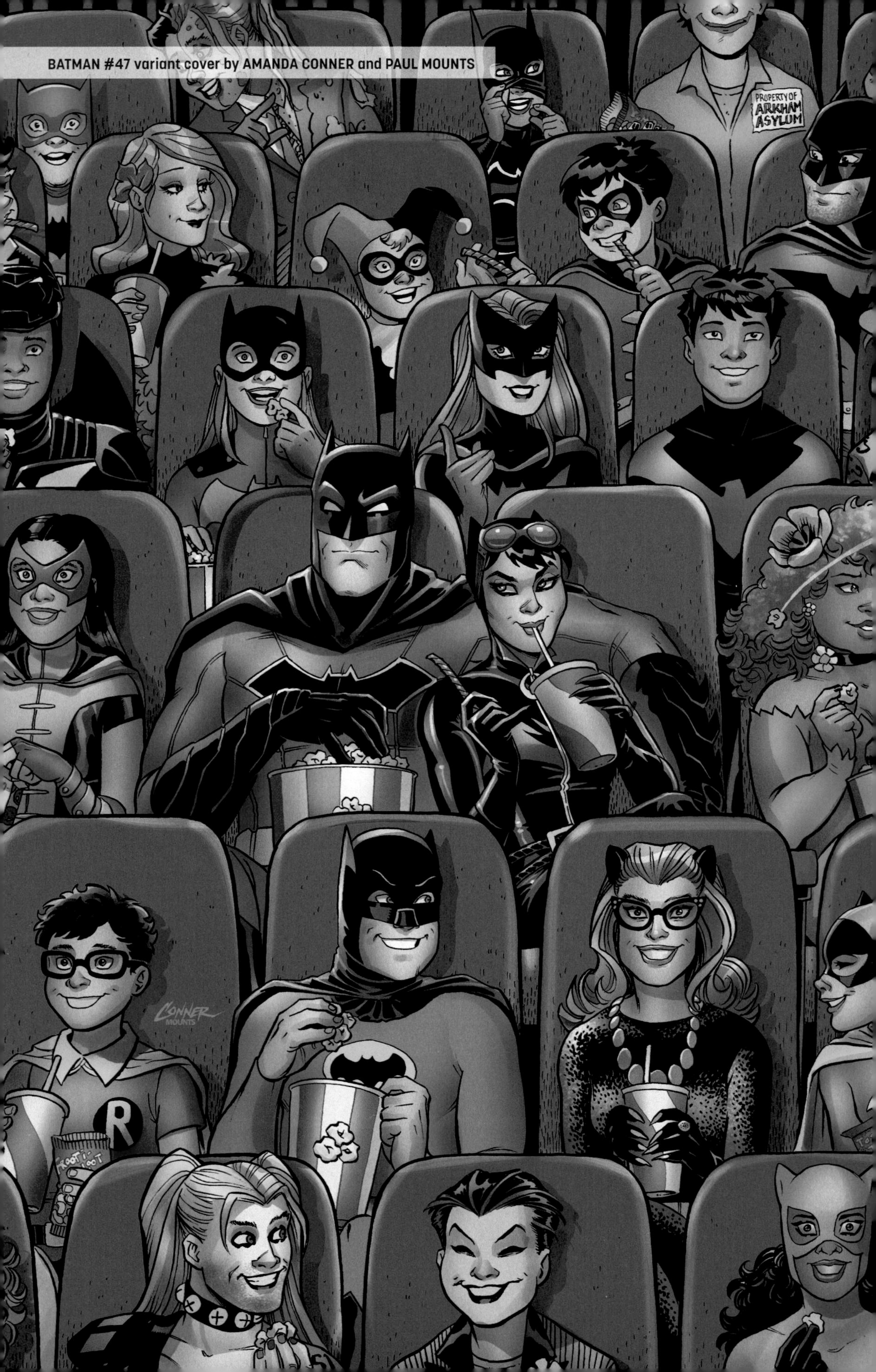
PROPERTY OF
ARKHAM
ASYLUM
CONNER
MOUNTS
R

BATMAN #48 variant cover by FRANK CHO

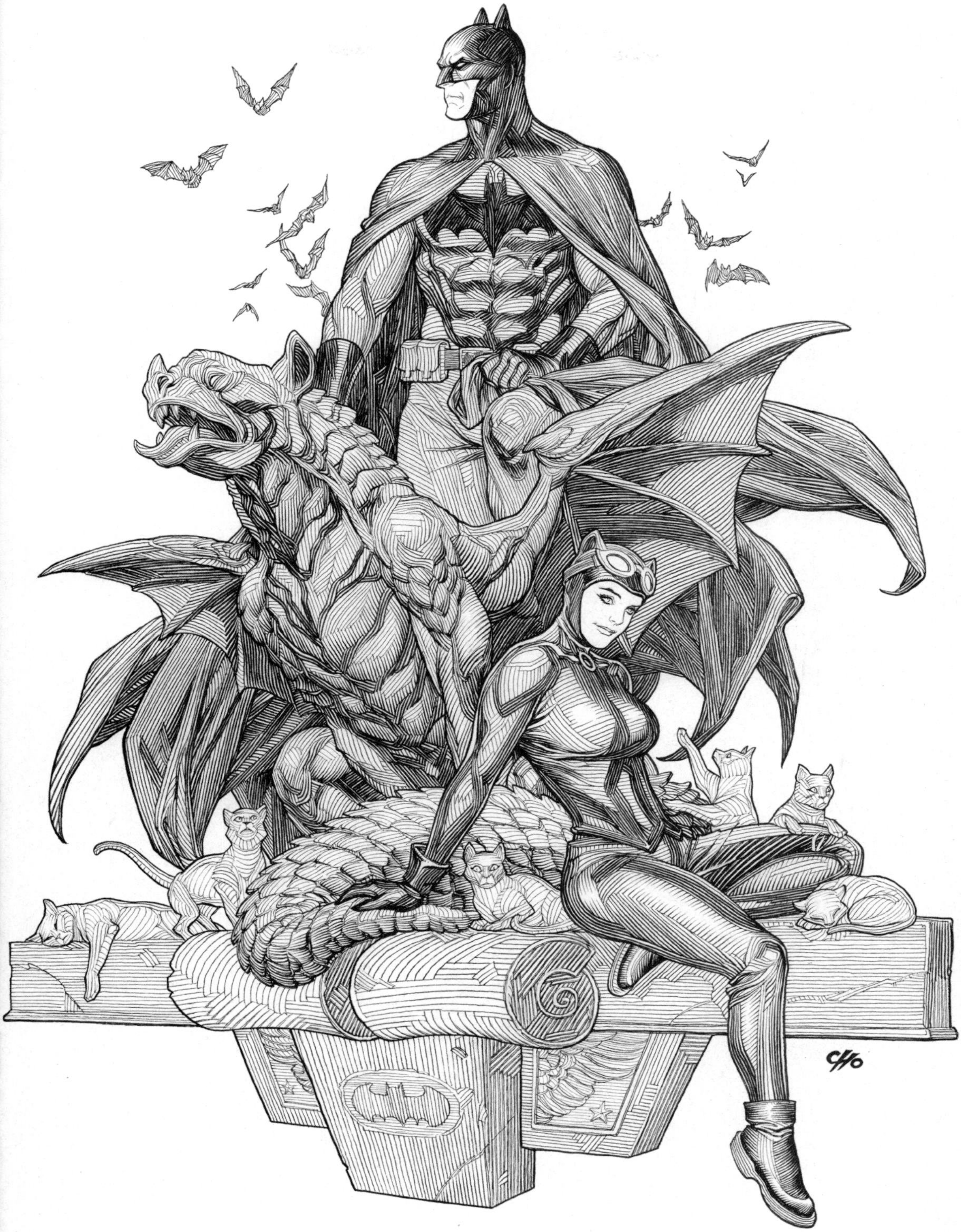
CHO

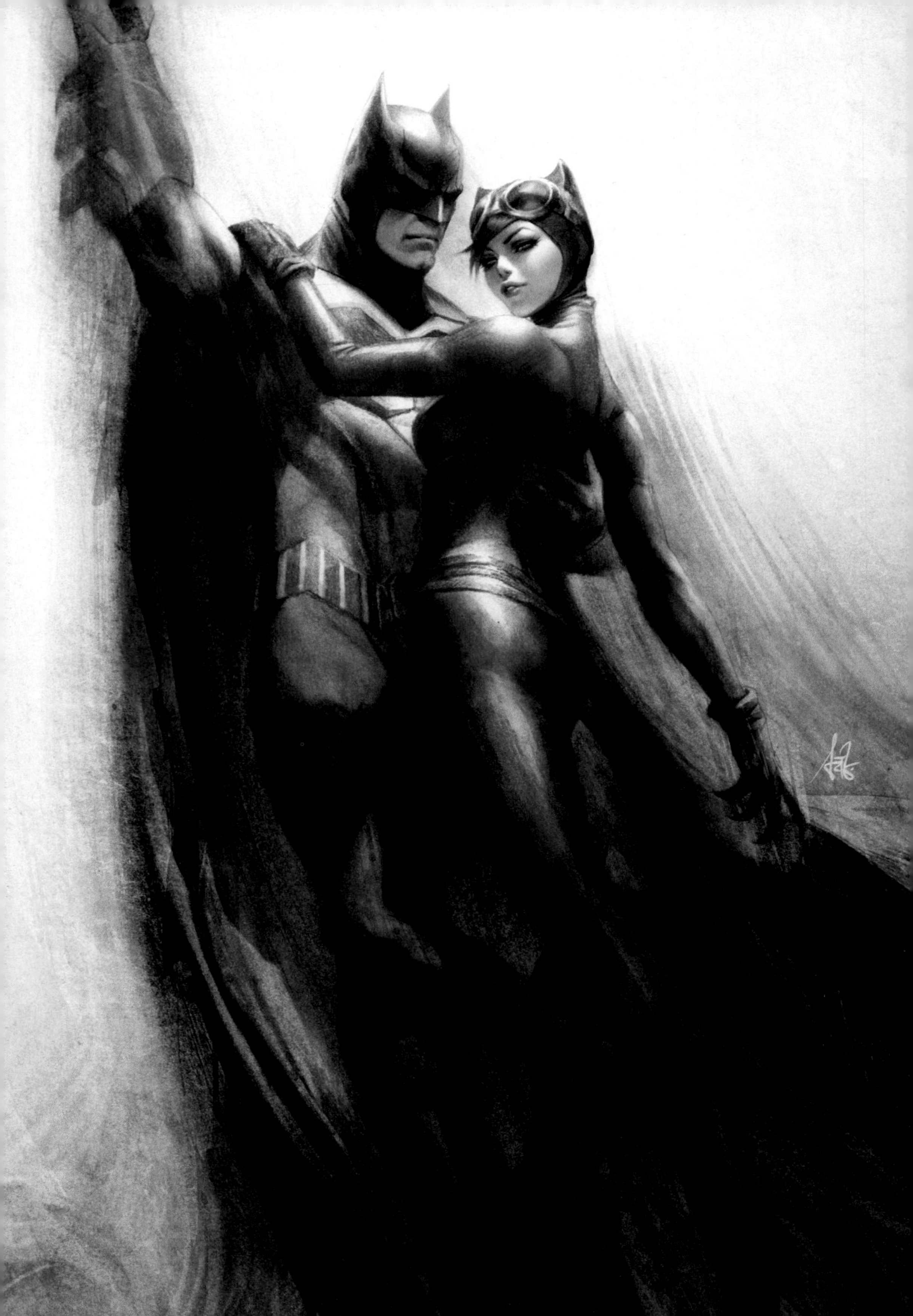

BATMAN #49 variant cover by STANLEY "ARTGERM" LAU

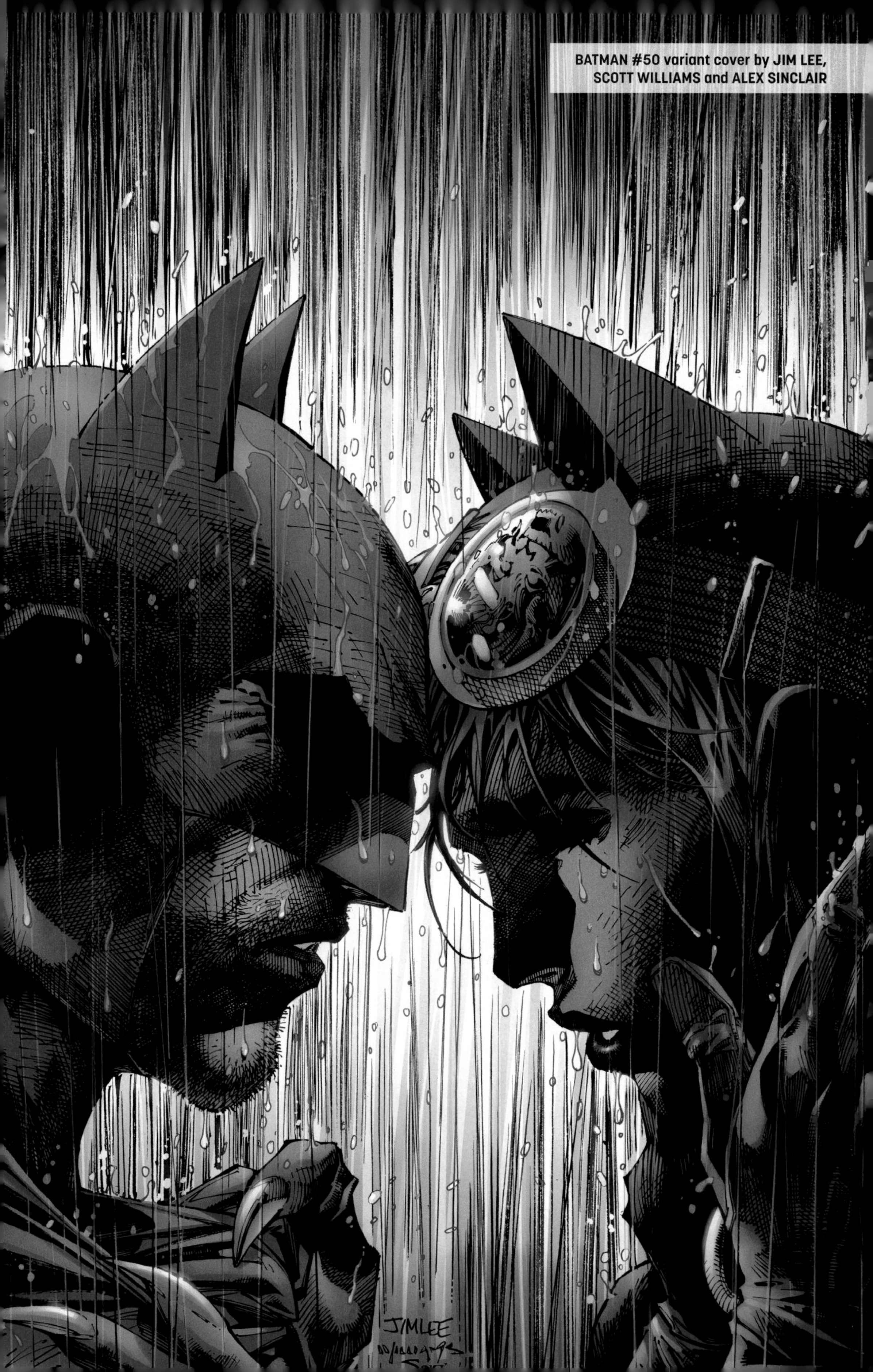
JIMLEE

BATMAN #50 variant cover by JIM LEE,
SCOTT WILLIAMS and ALEX SINCLAIR

BATMAN #50 variant cover by ARTHUR ADAMS and ALEJANDRO SANCHEZ

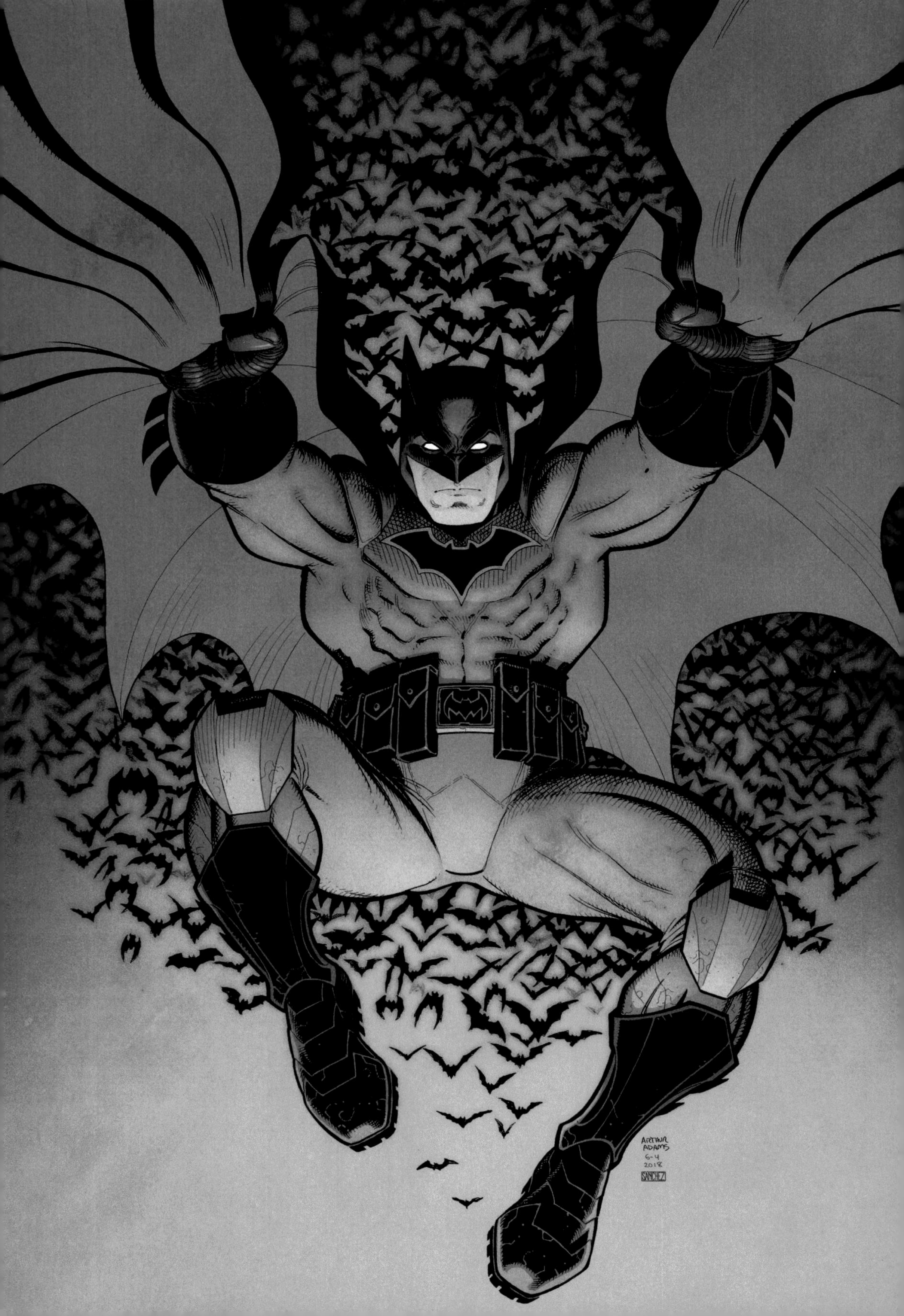
ARTHUR ADAMS
6-4
2018
SANCHEZ

DC NATION #0 variant cover by CLAY MANN
and JORDIE BELLAIRE

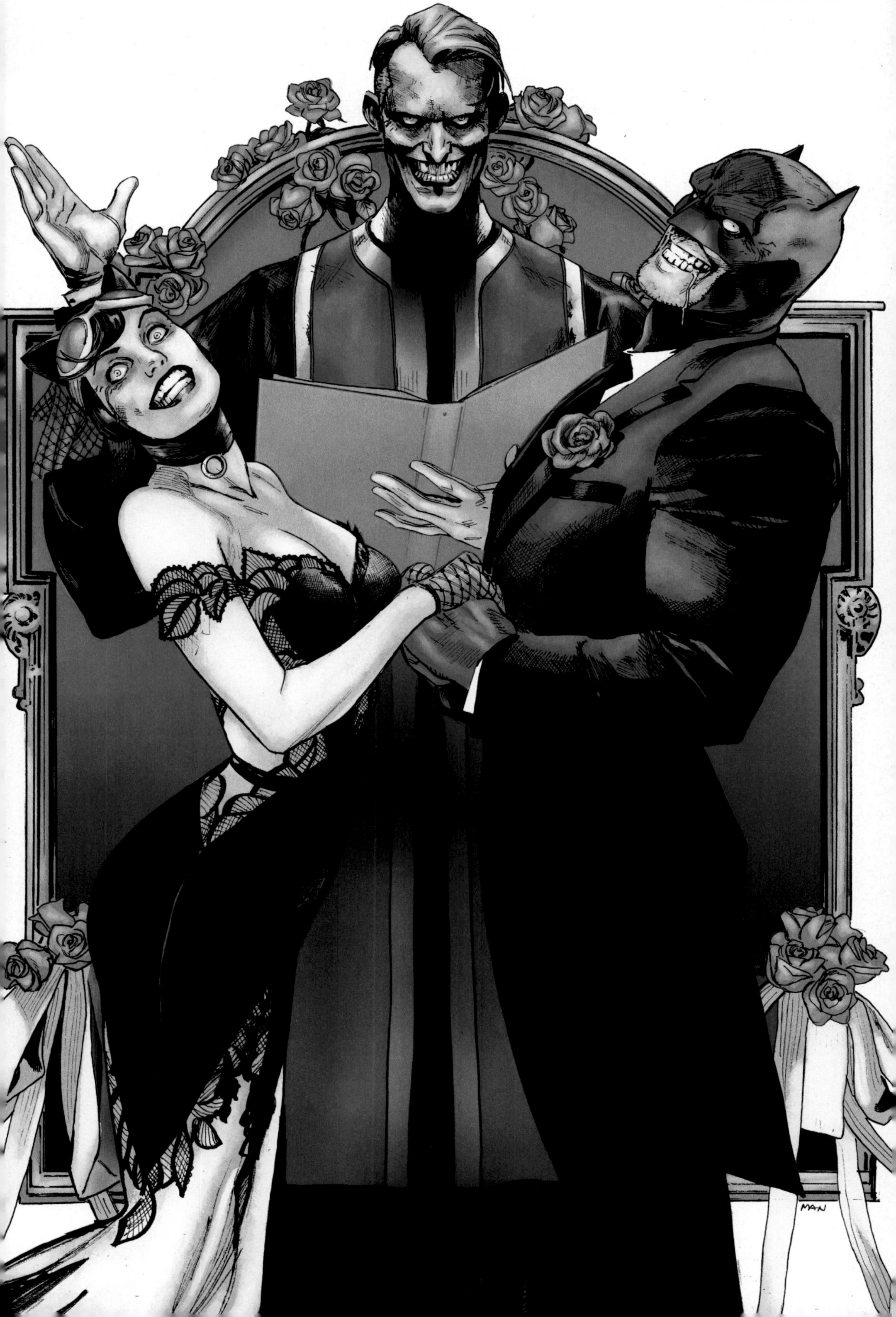
MAN

WEDDING DRESS DESIGNS
by JOËLLE JONES

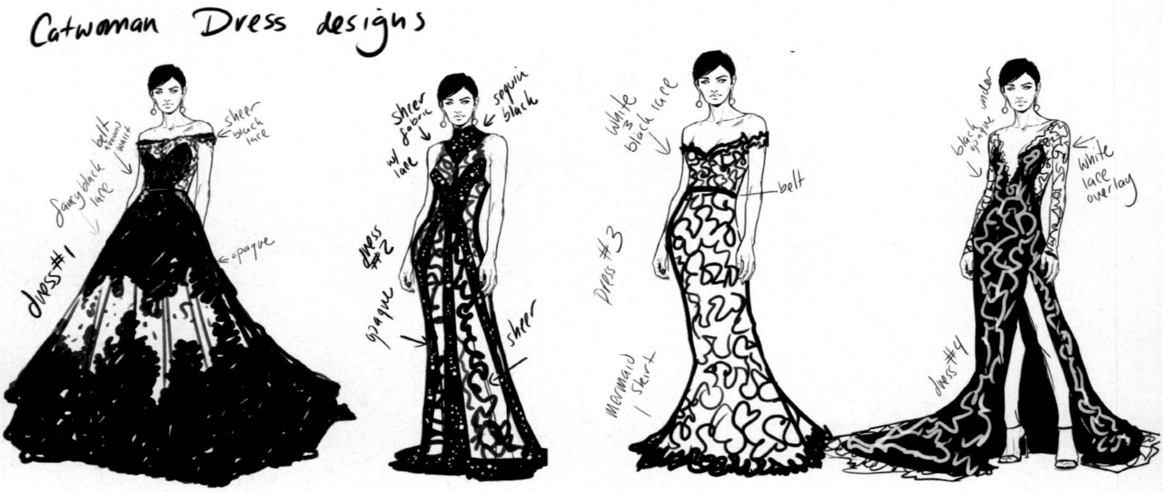
Catwoman Dress designs
belt
sheer black lace
fancy black lace
opaque
dress #1
sheer fabric w/ lace
sequin black
dress #2
opaque
sheer
White & black lace
belt
Dress #3
mermaid skirt
black under opaque
White lace overlay
dress #4

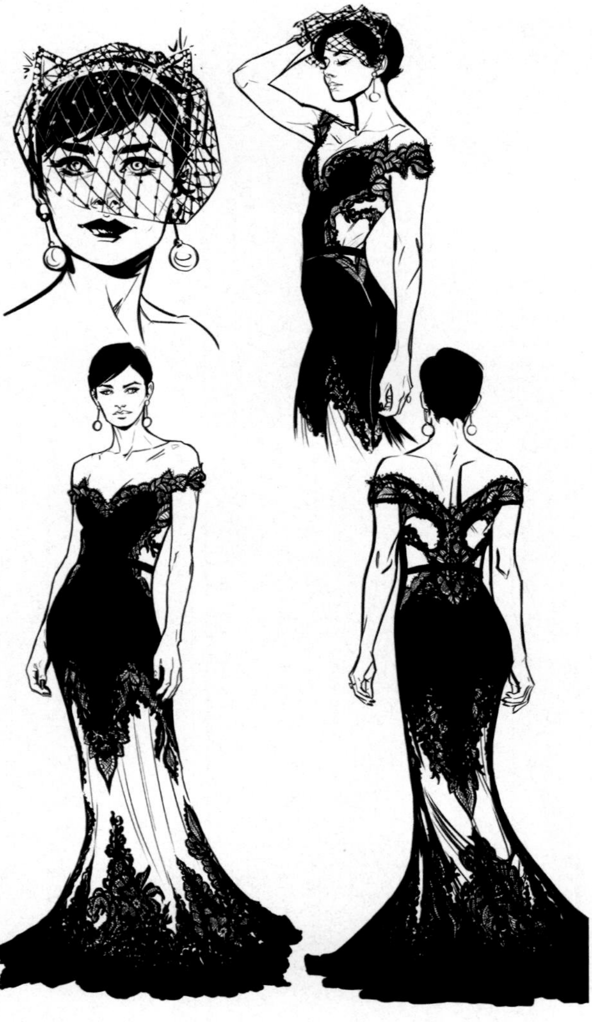

BATMAN #50 COVER SKETCHES
by MIKEL JANÍN

INTERIORS
DC
UNIVERSE
50 | $2.99
BATMAN
KING
JONES
JANIN
CHUNG
DOUBLE PAGE SPREAD: CUT AS SHOWN, ABUT PAGE EDGES, TAPE ON BACK, DO NOT OVERLAP

INTERIORS
DC
UNIVERSE
50 | $2.99
BATMAN
SUPES
ALFRED
BAT FAMILY
&
JL
KING
JONES
JANIN
CHUNG
DOUBLE PAGE SPREAD: CUT AS SHOWN, ABUT PAGE EDGES, TAPE ON BACK, DO NOT OVERLAP

INTERIORS
DC
UNIVERSE
50 | $2.99
BATMAN
You are invited.
KING
JONES
JANIN
CHUNG
DOUBLE PAGE SPREAD: CUT AS SHOWN, ABUT PAGE EDGES, TAPE ON BACK, DO NOT OVERLAP

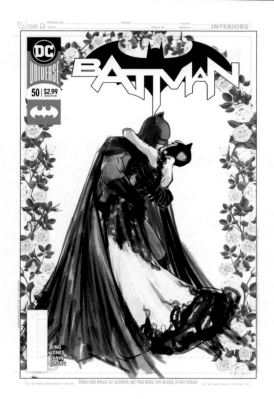

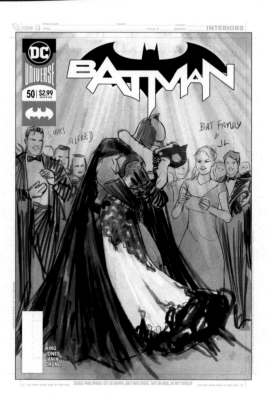

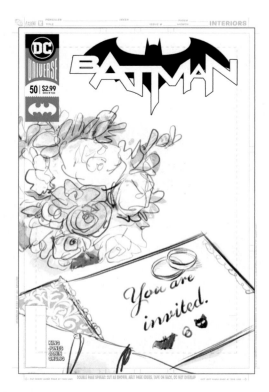

FROM THE ARTIST OF
JUSTICE LEAGUE
JIM LEE
with JEPH LOEB

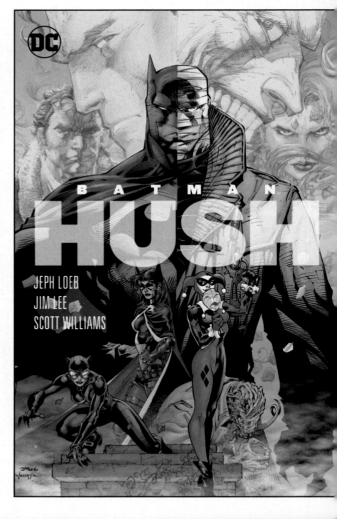

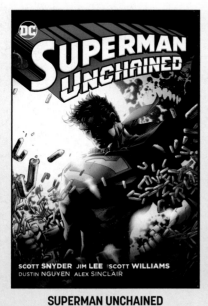

SUPERMAN UNCHAINED
with SCOTT SNYDER

**JUSTICE LEAGUE
VOL. 1: ORIGIN**
with GEOFF JOHNS

**ALL-STAR BATMAN AND ROBIN
THE BOY WONDER**
with FRANK MILLER

Get more DC graphic novels wherever comics and books are sold!

"THE LONG HALLOWEEN is more than a comic book. It's an epic tragedy."
–Christopher Nolan (director of BATMAN BEGINS, THE DARK KNIGHT and THE DARK KNIGHT RISES)

"THE LONG HALLOWEEN is the preeminent influence on both movies [BATMAN BEGINS and THE DARK KNIGHT]."
–David Goyer (screenwriter of THE DARK KNIGHT RISES)

FROM THE AWARD-WINNING TEAM BEHIND *SUPERMAN: FOR ALL SEASONS*

JEPH LOEB & TIM SALE

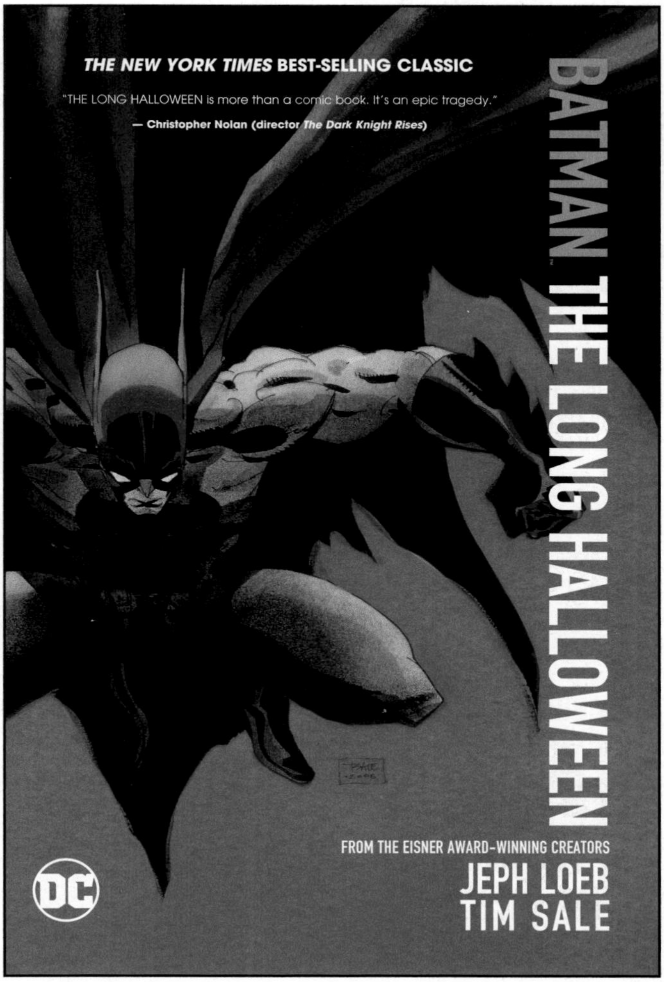
THE NEW YORK TIMES BEST-SELLING CLASSIC
"THE LONG HALLOWEEN is more than a comic book. It's an epic tragedy."
— Christopher Nolan (director The Dark Knight Rises)
BATMAN THE LONG HALLOWEEN
FROM THE EISNER AWARD-WINNING CREATORS
JEPH LOEB
TIM SALE

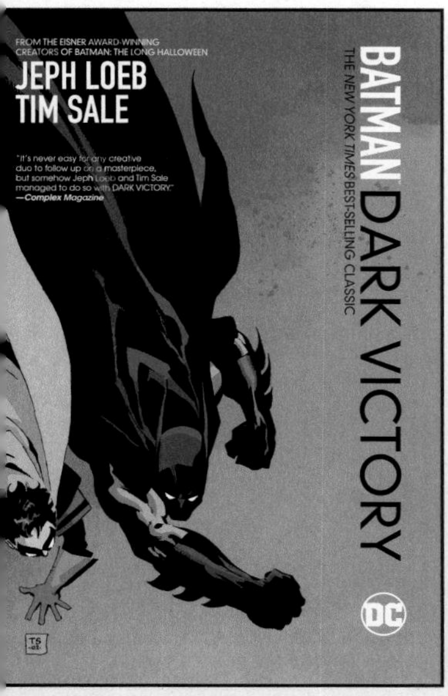
FROM THE EISNER AWARD-WINNING CREATORS OF BATMAN: THE LONG HALLOWEEN
JEPH LOEB
TIM SALE
BATMAN DARK VICTORY
THE NEW YORK TIMES BEST-SELLING CLASSIC

BATMAN: DARK VICTORY

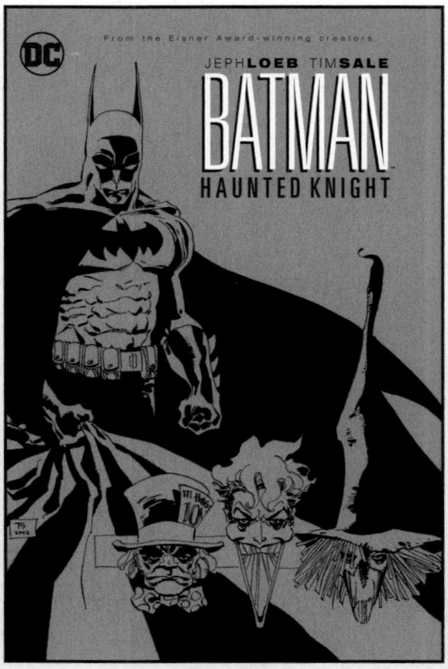
From the Eisner Award-winning creators
JEPH LOEB TIM SALE
BATMAN
HAUNTED KNIGHT

BATMAN: HAUNTED KNIGHT

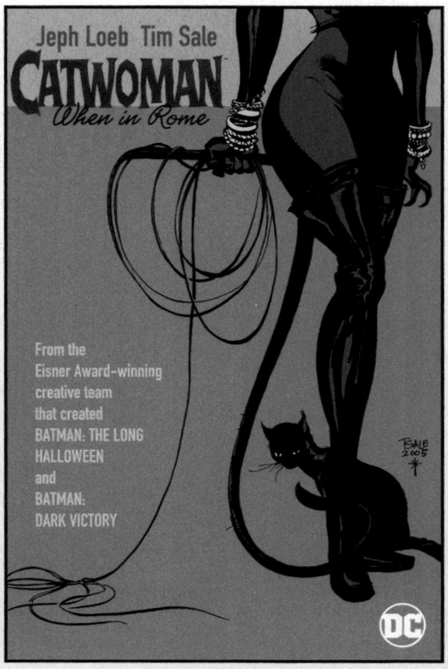
Jeph Loeb Tim Sale
CATWOMAN
When in Rome
From the Eisner Award-winning creative team that created BATMAN: THE LONG HALLOWEEN and BATMAN: DARK VICTORY

CATWOMAN: WHEN IN ROME

Get more DC graphic novels wherever comics and books are sold!

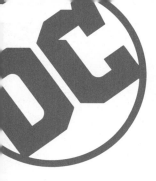

DC UNIVERSE REBIRTH
BATMAN
VOL. 1: I AM GOTHAM
TOM KING
with DAVID FINCH

DC UNIVERSE REBIRTH

BATMAN

VOL.1 **I AM GOTHAM**
TOM KING · DAVID FINCH

VOL.1 MY OWN WORST ENEMY
SCOTT SNYDER · JOHN ROMITA JR. · DECLAN SHALVEY · DANNY MIKI

**ALL-STAR BATMAN VOL. 1:
MY OWN WORST ENEMY**

VOL.1 BETTER THAN BATMAN
TIM SEELEY · JAVIER FERNÁNDEZ · CHRIS SOTOMAYOR

**NIGHTWING VOL. 1:
BETTER THAN BATMAN**

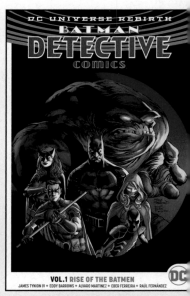

VOL.1 RISE OF THE BATMEN
JAMES TYNION IV · EDDY BARROWS · ALVARO MARTINEZ · EBER FERREIRA · RAÚL FERNÁNDEZ

**DETECTIVE COMICS VOL. 1:
RISE OF THE BATMEN**